Aristocracy and the Modern World

By the same author

Whig Renaissance: Lord Althorp and the Whig Party, 1782–1845 (1987)
Born to Rule: British Political Elites (2000)

ARISTOCRACY AND THE MODERN WORLD

Ellis Wasson

First published 2006 by
PALGRAVE MACMILLAN
Houndmills, Basingstoke, Hampshire RG21 6XS and
175 Fifth Avenue, New York, N.Y. 10010
Companies and representatives throughout the world

PALGRAVE MACMILLAN is the global academic imprint of the
Palgrave Macmillan division of St. Martin's Press, LLC and of
Palgrave Macmillan Ltd. Macmillan® is a registered trademark in
the United States, United Kingdom and other countries. Palgrave
is a registered trademark in the European Union and other
countries.

ISBN-13: 978–1–4039–4072–8 hardback
ISBN-10: 1–4039–4072–X hardback
ISBN-13: 978–1–4039–4073–5 paperback
ISBN-10: 1–4039–4073–8 paperback

This book is printed on paper suitable for recycling and made
from fully managed and sustained forest sources.

A catalogue record for this book is available from the British
Library.

A catalog record for this book is available from the Library of
Congress.

10   9   8   7   6   5   4   3   2   1
15 14 13 12 11 10 09 08 07 06

Printed in China

In memory of
David Spring
who first surveyed the field

CONTENTS

ACKNOWLEDGMENTS

Aside from the debts to scholars acknowledged in the Introduction, I owe special thanks to the Tower Hill School for granting me a sabbatical, and to Wolfson College, Cambridge, whose offer of hospitality as a visiting fellow in 2004 allowed me to complete the research necessary to write this volume. I am also grateful to Carole Haber of the University of Delaware, who made it possible for me to teach a seminar on modern European aristocracies, and to the students in those classes who asked excellent questions and helped me gain new perspectives. Gordon Mork first encouraged me to speak on the topic at a meeting in Moscow at the Academy of Sciences during an exciting period when Russian and East European scholars were beginning to feel free to talk and write about the subject objectively. George Munro further fostered the cultivation of the theme by inviting me to join in a session he organized at an American Historical Association annual meeting. Michael McCahill has been a regular sounding board, collaborator, and friend. David Stedman several times pointed me in interesting directions and read the final manuscript with sensitive and informed care. My overlords Tim Golding and Harry Baetjer have been generous and understanding.

For suggestions on readings thanks go to David Spring, Jonathan Parry, Michael McCahill, Deirdre McMahon, and Peter Mandler. I am also grateful to Count Nikolai Tolstoy for his comments on the Russian aristocracy, even if we had to agree to disagree on at least one point.

I was singularly fortunate to study as an undergraduate under Robert Forster and David Spring. They charted new territory and all of the rest of us have followed in their wake. David, who first surveyed the field, remained an incomparable advisor, kind critic, and mentor.

What I owe to my family and to Joey is greater than ever.

E.A.W.
Wilmington

INTRODUCTION

In this country it is so much to be a lord.

Anthony Trollope, in *Anthony Trollope* by James Pope-Hennessy,
p. 295

In 2003 Aleksandr Sokurov produced a film, *The Russian Ark*, about the Winter Palace in St. Petersburg – home of the Tsars and the imperial court. Sokurov believes the Westernized elite with its theaters, paintings, music, poetry, and architecture was a crucial bearer of European culture in a still immature nation. The last scene of the film follows the aristocracy as they descend the magnificent Jordan staircase for the final time after a ball on the eve of obliteration. The image echoes Sergei Eisenstein's vision of the Bolsheviks surging up the same flight of stairs in his celebrated film *October* (1928), bent on destroying Russia's fledgling democracy during the communist revolution of 1917.[1]

The majestic conclusion of the *Ark* restores dignity and importance to the aristocracy in modern Russia. Sokurov pays the elite a civilized farewell that was not granted by history. After the catastrophe of exile, dispossession, and the gulags came contempt, ridicule, and silence. Both in Russia and the West aristocracies in the twentieth century came to be seen as at best obsolete or silly and at worst parasitical, dissolute, oppressive, selfish, and philistine. Aristocratic self-confidence and assumption of privilege rooted in lineage make their world seem alien to the modern mind. In his film, however, Sokurov moves beyond romanticizing or demonizing. *The Russian Ark* is complicated and full of more questions than answers, but it is neither caricature nor polemic. The director understands that all of those medals and feathers, tailcoats and tiaras, had significance, and we owe to the past more than merely imposing our own values and interests on a world that is lost.

1

Russia was, of course, not the only country with an aristocracy. Throughout Eastern Europe, history before 1918 and in some areas even after that date is the story of dominance by the nobility. Even in the West no great event in modern times until the Cold War can be understood without including landed elites in the analysis. They were at the heart of the German and Italian unifications. Many patricians were deeply implicated in the outbreak of World War I as well as in its calamitous conclusion. In the postwar period aristocrats played a significant role both in the rise of Hitler and in his defeat. Their attitudes and leadership influenced art, culture, literature, science, education, sports, business, and agriculture. The present layout of great cities and the appearance of the rural landscape are their legacies fixed in stone, brick, water, trees, and fields. Forms and styles of government and social life still bear their deep imprint. Even the iconic phrase "the Cold War" was coined in the "Iron Curtain" speech made by Winston Churchill, grandson of a duke.

Aristocracies existed in many other parts of the world. From China to the American south they exerted considerable authority. It was the European elite, however, that formed the dominant ruling class of the modern world. When the Japanese transformed their social and political structure in the 1860s it was to France, Germany, and Britain that they turned for terms such as "marquis" and "count" to designate a new power elite. European dukes and barons governed most of the globe in the nineteenth century from Cabinet rooms and governors' palaces. David Cannadine has offered a persuasive argument for the mutual recognition and affinity between Western and non-European elites during the era of imperialism. He emphasizes the centrality of status, rank, and hierarchy that trumped cultural difference in the assertion of Western power.[2] The present crisis in the Middle East, upon which so much of the world's attention is focused, was spun into its present configuration by European aristocrats. The Lord Balfour of the eponymous Declaration and Mark Sykes of the Sykes–Picot Agreement of 1916 were both members of great landowning families. Winston Churchill authorized the modern boundaries of Iraq as Colonial Secretary in 1921. Count Folke Bernadotte and Lord Moyne were assassinated during their missions to Israel and Egypt at the end of the World War II. Anthony Eden, from a titled landed family, precipitated the Suez Crisis of 1956.

Textbooks recount the significance of noblemen such as Lafayette, Byron, Metternich, Tocqueville, Bismarck, Cavour, and Tolstoy, but once the French Revolution is over they rarely address the continuing story of the modern aristocracy beyond the activities of a few individuals. By the twentieth century the old elite gets little mention at all. Yet Lord Irwin and the Marquis of Linlithgow were supreme rulers of India during the inter-war years, and in Hungarian and Finnish history Count Bethlen and Baron Mannerheim were pivotal figures as late as 1944. The 14th Earl of Home was British prime minister in the 1960s. Even a century after Anthony Trollope wrote his novels about aristocratic politics, being a lord still mattered. In 2005 Prince Simeon of Saxe-Coburg headed the government of Bulgaria.

A systemic problem with the analysis of modern aristocracies is that their history is written in terms of decline. The elite was assumed to be "on the defense" against the forces of modernity.[3] The story of aristocracy since the French Revolution has been largely presented as one of disintegration, decadence, and decay. The landed elite in the 1870s, for example, is described by a noted historian as shrouded by "the shades of the prison house closing in."[4] Most analysts have focused on the rise of the state, business, industry, the bourgeoisie, and the working class. A pall of inevitability colors everything that is written about the titled nobility. We are thus deflected from focusing on continuity and durability.

It may come as a surprise to readers to learn that the current thrust of research relating to nineteenth- and early twentieth-century nobilities emphasizes the resilience, adaptability, and adroitness with which they adjusted to the challenges of modernity. Heinz Reif, a leader among historians of the German elite, goes so far as to list the ability to accommodate to changing circumstances as one of the qualities that defines an aristocracy.[5] Even when their political power was on the wane it is not an open-and-shut case that landed elites ceased to be arbiters in the social sphere, makers and shapers of culture, and successful capitalists.[6] Traditional authority can be reconstituted over time in different forms as outdated mechanisms for sustaining status erode. Lost ground can be recovered.[7] It is commonly assumed, for example, that aristocratic wealth shrank when the elite began to sell land during the later nineteenth and early twentieth century. What has gone largely unnoticed is that other noblemen were still to be found buying the estates of colleagues who fell by the wayside while those who did divest were not necessarily retreating but rather diversifying their investments as profitable new opportunities in the stock and financial markets became available.

David Cannadine, a historian of the British landed elite, which until recently has received more attention than its peer groups on the Continent, reminds us that: "In their declining years, as in their heyday, they were very interesting, very important, very complex. . . . There was . . . much vigor and resolution, much resourceful resistance, much outright defiance, much adroit adaptation."[8] Other historians make the same case for other aristocracies. Fritz Stern argues: "the relations of the older elite to the new elites of the nineteenth century touch on every aspect of Germany's political, economic, social, and cultural history of the period. . . . [The Junkers] continued to 1914 – and beyond – to have a profound impact on the shaping of German society and politics, on the administration of the state and the army, on the ethos of an entire people."[9] Undoubtedly, after 1918 landed elites ceased to exert great influence as a class, but individual aristocrats, especially those prompted by strong warrior impulses, such as Churchill, Mannerheim, and Count Claus von Stauffenberg, continued to provide Europe with leaders who stood for hereditary values and traditions. Like the filmmaker Sokurov, we must take the aristocracy seriously, even in the twentieth century. This book is an attempt to examine and explain that crowd on the Jordan staircase.

* * *

It would have been impossible to write this account had not many innovative and distinguished historians laid the groundwork. Soon after World War II the Canadian David Spring and Englishman Michael Thompson began to publish accounts of the modern British elite that exploited newly opened archives and took seriously the aristocratic class as a dynamic economic, cultural, and political force. They saw the nobility not just as antique has-beens but as leaders of political and economic modernization.[10] The work of Spring and Thompson gradually awakened the next generation of British historians to a new way of seeing the nineteenth century, but it took longer for Continental scholars to get past the mental barrier of 1789, the demonization of Junkerdom, and assumptions about the marginalization and irrelevance of landed elites in the era of bourgeois industrialization.

Arno Mayer's *The Persistence of the Old Regime* (1981) came like a thunderclap. He argued that historians had "vastly overdrawn the decline of land, noble, and peasant."[11] However, many of his colleagues resisted the story of resilience and tenacity because Mayer tied his conclusions so closely to a dubious interpretation of the origins of World War I. Nonetheless, greater attention began to be paid to the continuing importance of agriculture, and the complexity of the interaction between the nobility and middle classes began to be acknowledged. It was only with Dominic Lieven's brilliant comparative study of aristocracy in England, Germany, and Russia between 1815 and 1914, not published until 1992, that we gained a deeply learned, synthetic vision of the old elite as a dynamic and important force in modern Europe.[12] Scholars such as Shelley Baranowski, Seymour Becker, J. V. Beckett, David Cannadine, Anthony L. Cardoza, Francis L. Carsten, Palle Ove Christiannsen, Ralph Gibson, Mark Girouard, William D. Godsey, Jr., David Higgs, Gregory W. Pedlow, Priscilla Roosevelt, Wojciech Roszkowski, W. D. Rubinstein, and Heide W. Whelan have begun to make accessible in English the fruits of work by native historians and added their own perspectives and analysis. The Germans have produced a vast amount of new research in the last few decades, led by Heinz Reif, Hans-Ulrich Wehler, Armgard von Reden-Dohna, Stephan Malinowski and others. French, Italian, and Spanish scholars have been hampered by the concept of "Notables" – as opposed to separate categories of nobles, the upper professions, and *haute bourgeoisie* – and it is thus harder to follow the story of aristocracy in those countries. The collapse of the Soviet empire has encouraged Polish and Hungarian historians to look objectively at their own nobilities, but only a limited amount of work has yet emerged written by Russian, Czech, or Baltic scholars.

My hope is to build on the achievements of the historians mentioned above, and to bring to a wider audience a sense of the current vibrant energy in the field. However, I am deeply conscious of the problems inherent in this task. Many nuances and exceptions to general rules have had to be skimmed over. Elites from different countries and in different periods were often quite distinctive in their wealth, status, and relationship to the state. It is only via a broad survey, however, that we can follow the story of aristocracies in modern society. I do not mean to imply that Europe had a single, unified elite. In the space allotted me I have tried to highlight common characteristics and when possible point to differences and distinctions. What I hope to avoid, indeed to extirpate, are the caricatures and stereotypes that even professional historians are apt to lapse into based on lack of detailed knowledge, ideology, or casual assumptions. I also hope to prod authors of general textbooks on European and world history to reshape accounts of the nineteenth century in the light of our current knowledge of the economic, cultural, and political dominance of landed aristocracies.

In the belief that most readers of this book will either not have mastered many of the languages in which research is being published nor have access to much of that material, I have mainly cited in endnotes the sources available in English. Much recent work has been undertaken in a number of countries such as Hungary, Sweden, Romania, Italy, Portugal, and Poland, in languages with which I have no facility. However, I have tried to gain some sense of what is being done through abstracts, reviews, and translations of this material.[13]

This book is intended to be accessible to students, helpful to professional historians, and yet of interest to a wider audience of general readers. Experts in the history of particular countries and periods will find errors and misunderstandings. I have tried to avoid overly ambitious generalizations for these can resemble smashing into bits a delicate porcelain tea service just so it will fit snuggly into a small box. However, the benefits of an overview outweigh the problems. Where I generalize glibly, at least there should often be a footnote that will lead the conscientious reader on to more expert analysis.

*   *   *

The following themes will be central to the argument of this volume. I will highlight the broad similarities and differences between aristocracies in different countries and contrast the wealth, authority, and adaptability of the top elite with the struggles and failures of the lesser nobility. Merger with the middle classes was often slower and less seamless than is usually assumed. The great threats to aristocratic leadership were expanding conceptions of equality, nationalism, and democracy. These eroded the foundation on which inherited privilege rested and undermined aristocratic self-confidence. Here decline began early in the nineteenth century, accelerated after 1848, and wreaked mortal damage by 1900, although this process did not proceed uniformly across the Continent. After 1918 individual aristocrats with vital memories of lineage and service continued to play commanding roles on the national stage, and the elite's influence in rural communities ebbed much more slowly than at the national level.

NOTE: After centuries of Turkish rule, neither indigenous nobilities nor large landed estates existed in some Balkan countries. Therefore Greece, Serbia, Montenegro, Macedonia, Bulgaria, and Albania, will not figure significantly in this book.[14] Iceland and Norway also did not possess modern native aristocracies.[15] Some cantons in Switzerland are inhabited by old families of considerable wealth, but comparatively little research has been conducted about them.[16]

1

Defining Aristocracy

In no other era, not even when the most aristocratic institutions flourished, has there been so much talk of genealogies and noble titles as in our century of democracy. . . . The loss of privileges has not arrested the stream of titles and honors sought for adornment by the sons and grandsons of the men who made the revolution.

Alberto di Montenuovo, Italy 1903[1]

I cannot define the word "aristocracy" perfectly. Like a flickering holograph, the image is hard to capture. Moreover, the definition has changed over time. In fact, perhaps only at the beginning of our period, after the wars of the French Revolution, did the word "aristocracy" take on its modern meaning, the meaning used in this book.[2] During the course of the nineteenth century the term may have further evolved in a variety of ways in particular countries.[3] Sociologists, economists, philosophers, political scientists, and historians use the term in the context of their separate disciplines, often carelessly, sometimes simply as a substitute for other words such as "upper class" or "oligarchy" to avoid repetition. Ideological combat has further confused the meaning of the word "aristocracy."

Today people often confuse monarchs and their families with the landed elite. In fact, rulers and nobles formed distinct species, often with different interests and ambitions. This book is not about royalty; I am interested in the courtiers, ministers, generals, and magnates who surrounded, guided, and occasionally deposed kings and emperors.

Marx, Pareto, Mosca, Weber, Mannheim, Schumpeter, and Mills, among others, have given us conflicting models of elites that leave a pragmatic historian like myself doubtful. Their work has stimulated much thought, but I am unconvinced theory helps much in placing landed elites in their context during the nineteenth century. Indeed, as we shall see, much violence has been done by doctrinaires to accurate understanding of the role of landed elites in the modern world.

Class is a clumsy conceptual framework, yet a necessary simplification used by everyone because there is no suitable alternative. In reality it is a term that is recognized to have both economic and cultural parameters, though no universally accepted definition exists. Societies are so diverse, complex, and multi-layered that individuals cannot be assigned to a single class.[4] Trying to decide how to incorporate *status* into the discussion of class compounds the difficulties, for the power to elicit respect is not an economic category, and the two can exist independently in the modern world. When did "orders" become "classes"? Everyone has a different idea about that. Historians duck and weave, using broad categories in the plural form or weasel words to escape being pinned down. Yet to retreat to terms such as "upper classes," "elites," "patricians," or "notables" is to fall into a descriptive miasma. "As a methodological tool," notes J. M. Bourne, "this is useful only for papering over cracks."[5] The term "aristocracy" was used and understood by contemporaries. It is indispensable.

For the purposes of this study the following criteria will serve as our guide. Aristocrats were nobles. Monarchs conferred elevated rank on individuals that passed on to further generations.[6] This did not necessarily entail a title, though in most countries aside from Britain, Ireland, Poland, and Russia nobles bore some indicator connected with their name, such as the particles "von" or "de" of Germany and France.[7] In Britain and Ireland the peerage was confined to small groups of titled families, although even there a ramshackle but official system of heraldic lore was used to encompass a larger elite. Coats of arms became an essential prerequisite for nobles by our period, even in Russia, where they were something of a novelty. So long as nobility conferred prestige it remained the premier prize in social advancement.

Most aristocrats were landed proprietors. In earlier eras urban patriciates functioned very much like aristocracies and even gained titles without owning much acreage. Over time, however, land was usually purchased or inherited by all titled families. A grand residence, supported at least partly by landed wealth, either in the city or countryside, was a *sine qua non*. Mere purchase of land, however, did not itself gain admission to the elite. Living "nobly" was generally seen as an essential aspect of aristocracy. This involved lavish hospitality, education, rural recreations, carriages, dress, and culture.

Power is inextricably associated with aristocracy. It could come in many forms. In some countries automatic entry into the legislature was granted. In others aristocrats had to compete for national office, but virtually all of them performed, either directly or through intermediaries, functions as local governors. Service to the state was a powerful ingredient in the aristocratic character, more evident, perhaps, in Russia and Prussia than Spain or Denmark but existing nearly everywhere. Until the twentieth century the vast majority of aristocrats invested considerable time and energy carrying out duties attached to elective and appointive offices. Access to the monarch was usually automatic. Agriculture did not set the timetable of aristocratic social life; functions at court and the meeting of parliament were of premier importance, followed by hunting seasons and the religious calendar.

Finally, it is generally conceded that a collective set of values were shared by aristocrats: a sense of exclusivity, peculiar notions of honor, of being the sole bearers of high culture and civilization, of being the guardians of the general interest. A British statesman of the early twentieth century, Marquis Curzon, declared, "All civilization has been the work of aristocracies."[8] Even the relatively enlightened Sicilian landowner and Prime Minister of Italy in the 1890s, the Marquis di Rudinì, spoke of the lower classes as "complete savages."[9] A Prussian Junker summed up his sense of mission in the early nineteenth century when he wrote that lordship over peasants by nobles "planted in the hearts of the lowest class the idea of a higher law and a more noble custom, and the respect for a more educated life."[10]

Some of these conceptions, such as a strong sense of honor, could be found in other groups in society. However, aristocrats associated this characteristic with a powerfully developed attachment to family and lineage. Of course, for new entrants, this took time to develop, but it was not unusual for a landed proprietor to plant trees in his park that would not mature for more than a century. He was laying down pleasure for the eye and money in the bank for his great-great-grandson. Longitudinal sinews ran through aristocracies preserved in family memories that directly shaped the way aristocrats conducted themselves, and it is what distinguished them from plutocracies, military juntas, and meritocracies.[11]

Common misconceptions about aristocracies include the assumption that landowners needed serfs and legal privileges to sustain their importance. This was not the case. The British aristocracy got on very well for many centuries with neither. Nor is it useful to assume aristocrats were philistine, decadent, amateur, and "backward."[12] Certain individuals possessed those characteristics, as did members of other social groups. These epithets, however, do not identify aristocrats in a collective way. W. E. Mosse's contemptuous dismissal of the court nobility in Russia as a "residual *noblesse d'eppée*" not worthy of consideration is a classic example of misplaced presentism.[13] It is a serious anachronism to assume that men or women with titles and high social rank are incapable of understanding the complexity of modern government or unable to manipulate it to their own advantage. Finally the "new entrant" fallacy must be avoided. Historians of the nineteenth century often assume that recently ennobled *nouveaux riches* were an innovation that somehow diluted or altered aristocracy in modern times. Nothing could be further from the truth. European titled elites had been absorbing newcomers, often very rough diamonds indeed, for many centuries. Without them aristocracies would have rapidly become extinct. Absorption of newcomers was the single most traditional characteristic of landed society.

The edges of my description of aristocracy in the modern age are still rather ragged. Like rules of grammar, historical definitions are always subject to exceptions. Only by looking at a combination of qualities and characteristics is one able to bring the outline into view. It is not useful to think in terms of mechanistic descriptors. For example, the Marxist definition of upper classes as the owners of the means of production has long been shown to be incorrect. Possession of land in predominantly agricultural societies gave estate owners great leverage, but as Raymond Aron once pointed out, distribution of power changed radically in Germany between the Kaiser's Reich, the Weimar Republic, and the Third Reich even though the owners of the means of production remained in their places.[14]

Noble status, substantial landed wealth, political power, high social position, living nobly, and "noble" values form a mixture of qualities and characteristics that enable us to identify aristocrats in the nine-teenth century. However, within nobilities who displayed these ele-ments various layers could be discerned. There was no *lumpen* elite. In this case the modern eye can easily miss the significance of what was of vital importance to contemporaries.

It would be nice, as Dominic Lieven did in his book, to include the "provincial gentry," the largest layer of the landed elite, in this study as well as the aristocracy.[15] That is not possible, however, due to limi-tations of space. Lieven is right to argue that the lesser nobility played a vitally important role in modern European history, but they were often at odds with the aristocracy, and their story deserves its own historian. "The seething ant heap of poor and impoverished nobles," as Robert Frost calls them, did not usually have the wealth or interest to participate in the top levels of government.[16] Alexis de Tocqueville, the son of a count of ancient lineage, spoke dismissively of the petty squire "squatting in his den in the country."[17] In Germany the East Elbian lower nobility were so deeply divided from the vastly wealthier southern upper elite that they lived in almost totally different mental and social worlds.[18] Modest gentry families in England had horizons that often ended at the boundaries of their parish or at best their county. Lesser nobles tended to be intensely conservative politically, unlike the aristocrats who were often divided across the ideological spectrum. Under the old regime in France, Spain, Hungary, Poland, and Russia governments moved by financial considerations under-mined the status and even existence of lesser nobles. The Habsburgs ruthlessly liquidated the native Czech nobility for religious and politi-cal reasons in the 1620s and 1630s and created a new, tiny magnate class. Across Europe the revolutionary era of the later eighteenth century reduced the size and significance of the lower echelons.[19] Great nobles consolidated ownership of land at the expense of the lesser breed.[20] One Baltic noblewoman contemptuously called the survivors among the impoverished families, "peasants in frock coats with a genealogical tree."[21] In the later eighteenth century 60 percent of the nobles in Poland-Lithuania did not own any land at all.[22] In the aftermath of serf emancipation that unfolded between the mid-eighteenth and mid-nineteenth centuries magnates had the financial resources to recover and prosper while owners of small estates went under. The agricultural depression of the 1870s and 1880s knocked out most of those who were left.[23] Peasant revolts often targeted smaller landowners, not the magnates, who could afford to be more generous landlords.[24] With the loss of legal privileges titles became more and more important in establishing the social hierarchy. In the twentieth century most of the untitled *petit noblesse* were impoverished and bitter. In France they wore black ties on the anniversary of Louis XVI's execution and stuck postage stamps with Republican symbols upside down on their letters.[25] In the eighteenth and nineteenth centuries large numbers of military officers and government bureaucrats were ennobled. They owned no land nor possessed much wealth. Many were no better than petty clerks. They rarely gained promotion into the aristocracy.[26]

From time to time this book will include discussions of elites that would in major countries have been considered gentry, notably the hereditary knights of Hesse–Cassel, some of the German landowners in the Russian Baltic provinces, and the Prussian Junkers. These were "lesser" nobles who enjoyed political power in spite of comparatively modest resources. The levels within the East Elbian elite cannot be drawn using a dividing line between simple "vons" and those who held the title baron or count. However, not all Junkers can be included in the aristocracy. Count Yorck von Wartenburg, father of the famous anti-Nazi resister, owned over 7000 acres and a large country house. He thought the local lesser nobility "were raised like simple cattle," preoccupied with hunting and socially antiquated customs that were of less importance to the richer and more cultivated families like his own.[27] "Aristocratic" Junkers were those who aspired to become captains of the army or the state. The leading families of Hesse-Cassel and the Baltic provinces with their special "corporations" formed the equivalent of the aristocracy elsewhere.[28]

I will be obliged occasionally to use data collected about *all* nobles because some researchers draw no distinctions between tiers within landed society. In these cases I will make it plain that I am referring to the broad category and not aristocrats alone.

Within all aristocracies a small group of famous families stood at the apex, what Lawrence Stone called the "durable and extremely tenacious core."[29] Each nation had at least a handful if not a dozen or two dynasties whose rank and continuity in office made them household names. In Vienna they were known as the "Twelve Apostles," who, mixing metaphors, were also called, "Olympus."[30] In France *gratin* and in Russia *znat'* designated membership of the inner elite.[31] Among the great names at or near the pinnacle in Bohemia stood Liechtenstein and Schwarzenberg, in England Percy and

Howard, in Austria Starhemberg and Schönborn, in Hungary Széchenyi and Esterházy, in Scotland Hamilton and Buccleuch, in Russia Galitzine and Dolgorouky, in Prussia Dönhoff and Pless, in Germany Hohenlohe and Stolberg, in Ireland Leinster and Abercorn, in the Baltics Benckendorff and Lieven, in Sweden Douglas and Oxenstierna, in Poland Radziwill and Zamoyski, in Italy Colonna and Borghese, in France Polignac and Rochefoucauld, in Spain Alba and Medinaceli, in Belgium Ligne and Merode, in Denmark Moltke and Reventlow, in Portugal Pombal and Palmella, and in Romania Stirbey and Ghika. Many of these families were princes or dukes, the highest ranks of honor in Europe outside royal families.

In France it was not enough simply to be titled. The *crème de la crème* were "*Duc et Pair*" while to the south the designation was "*Grande*" of Spain. In Germany and Austria the princes and counts deposed from their mini-thrones in the Holy Roman Empire by Napoleon and Metternich were denominated "mediatized" and retained their right to intermarry with reigning royalty. Monarchs also reserved certain orders of knighthood, such as the celebrated Golden Fleece of the Habsburgs, for their own kin and members of exceptional families upon whom it was conferred generation after generation as reaffirmation of stupendous status. English dukes wore the star of the Order of the Garter even on their dressing gowns. Some of these families had risen by meritorious service to the state, but most were simply enormously rich. As late as 1874 the Grosvenor family in England were made Dukes of Westminster and in Hungary in 1913 the Festetics were raised to the rank of prince due solely, to use a British prime minister's phrase when offering a title to a man with no pretensions of merit, "in recognition of your great position."[32]

Below the heady summit stood families who also bore lesser titles. As terms of status rather than class, titles reflect a peculiar system of social hierarchy that could be remote from the reality of power, but titles gave access to power.[33] Titles performed a kind of alchemy, employing flesh instead of lead.[34] Titular aristocrats were a race apart, a barrier that neither education nor merit could overcome.[35] In places such as the Baltic provinces or Hesse–Cassel even quite prominent families were not titled, although they thought of themselves collectively as "barons."[36] In other countries, such as Poland, where save for a few princely dynasties all nobles formerly had been equal and the use of titles banned, ranks were instituted by the partitioning powers in the 1780s and by the middle of the nineteenth century most large landowners were elevated into a distinct aristoc-racy. Similarly, after a hiatus of several republican centuries, the creation of counts and barons resumed in the Netherlands when Holland became a kingdom in 1813. In Prussia, where thousands of new ennoblements were seen to be devaluing the precious "von," old families sought promotion in rank to differentiate themselves from the mob of newcomers.[37] On the other hand, in Piedmont, where titles were more common, the monarchy monitored distribution of rank with greater rigor in order to increase the value of being a count or marquis.[38] In Naples and Sicily, where the Habsburg practice of selling hereditary rank had produced a plethora of titled nobles, almost all the best families became princes. In Russia titled families were thin on the ground compared to the vast nobility, but honorifics carried magic. The tsars surrounded themselves with princes and counts at court, and aristocrats placed high value on titles, lineage, and ownership of landed estates.[39]

Along with consolidation of estates in the hands of larger landown-ers, the other prominent trend in nineteenth-century aristocratic life across the Continent was the gathering in of untitled families and promotions in rank within titular hierarchies.[40] With only a handful of exceptions every untitled family who owned great estates in England was brought into the peerage before World War I. Among the last, the Leghs of Lyme, who had been superbly indifferent to membership in the House of Lords for centuries, succumbed in 1892.

Titles were not a perfect indicator of membership in the aristoc-racy. In the Austro-Hungarian Empire, some counts and numerous barons were not admitted by their colleagues as true members of the top elite. The Habsburgs distributed lesser ranks with considerable abandon to Jewish bankers and armament manufacturers of uncer-tain pedigree during the nineteenth century. They were lumped with the ennobled bureaucrats in what was called the "second society." However, a surprising number of these ersatz barons purchased landed estates, married the daughters of old families, and produced polished sons and daughters who were being admitted to aristocratic society without many ripples just as darkness fell on the Viennese court for ever.[41]

For our purposes, painting with a broad brush across two centuries and more than a dozen countries, titles are the single most effective means of separating aristocrats from the lesser nobility. As Princess

Fugger von Babenhausen wrote in her recollections of aristocratic Vienna *circa* 1900: "No matter how old or distinguished a family might be – if it had no title, it was not considered to be of noble rank. The one and only criterion was the Gotha Almanac within whose pages the family must be listed."[42] Launched in 1763 and gathering momentum in subsequent years, the publishing house of Justus Perthes in the Thuringian duchy of Saxe-Gotha issued almanacs that catalogued the European aristocracy.[43] Different-colored volumes gathered different ranks into their appropriate categories. Teutonic mania for organization and classification had something to do with the enterprise, but compendiums arose in every country to record blue-blooded species with Darwinian delicacy. After the *Gotha* the most famous register was Britain's *Burke's Peerage and Baronetage,* which began publication in 1826.[44] The editors of these volumes were so devoted to the idol of hierarchy that they eventually assigned a number to every person in the titular elite so that hostesses did not have to worry about ensuring the rules of precedence were followed when seating guests at the dinner table. The *Mémorial historique de la noblesse* appeared in France in 1839.[45]

Titles were not the only thing unique about the aristocracy. The structure of their wealth was also distinctive. Unlike the lesser nobility, most enjoyed income streams that ranged from official salaries to mineral royalties. Aristocrats were much more likely to mechanize their agricultural operations and engage in manufacturing and mining because of the extent of their properties and also because they possessed or had access to capital on a large scale. As the nineteenth century progressed many invested heavily in stocks and shares. The greater landowners were intimately connected with the business elite; the smaller landowners were not. In the later part of the century a third of all English dukes were directors of business corporations, while few members of the gentry served in that capacity.[46] Lesser nobles tended to be exclusively agriculturalists with little extra cash to play the market and often unable to adjust and adapt to changing conditions. Aristocrats spent money buying more land as smaller proprietors around them failed.[47] In Burke's register of untitled gentry in Britain only about one-quarter of the families owned estates of over 3000 acres while virtually all aristocratic families owned more than that.[48] In Russia in 1905 only 3 percent of all nobles owned three-quarters of all land belonging to those who held that rank. In late nineteenth-century Italy the top 15 percent of the nobility controlled 65 percent of noble wealth.[49] Heiresses were always on the lookout for impoverished dukes and counts to marry, and the latter reciprocated. Across Europe great wealth and titles became more and more congruent.[50] A study of French nobles in the 1840s showed that those with a title paid a mean land tax of 2050 francs. Those with only a particle in their name paid 871 francs.[51]

Aristocrats lived grandly, and they were able to project their status and power by regularly enlarging their country seats and constructing palatial dwellings in capital cities.[52] In Poland no false modesty restrained the magnates from calling their houses "palaces" while the lesser nobles lived in "manors."[53] Regular residence near the court gave aristocrats access to information about fashion, culture, foreign visitors, and politics that set them apart from their noble brethren immured in the countryside 12 months a year. Rich families could afford well-qualified tutors and tuition for years spent at boarding schools and universities. In Russia, at the two premier boys' academies, only the sons of titled families and nobles who had held that rank for over 100 years were admitted. The service nobility, however high their office, were excluded.[54] In Romania only the aristocracy could afford to go regularly to France, which they considered a second home.

The aristocracy was multi-lingual, often raised by foreign nannies and governesses. They were owners of estates straddling national and ethnic boundaries. In Russia the first language of many aristocrats was French while in Bohemia, Latvia, and Wales they often did not speak the native language at all. Aristocrats in Russia routinely employed the familiar *thou* when conversing with lesser nobles, a form of address also used for children and servants, not the *you* customary among social equals.[55] A patrician American who married an earl's daughter described a dinner party with some untitled English neighbors: "a ghastly house smelling of gentry – china in cabinets, higgledy-piggledy, water-colours in gilt frames on the walls. Horror."[56] Only the cream of the nobility served in the famous guards regiments with which all sovereigns surrounded themselves. Even in Russia, where there were some great families without titles, Baron Nicholas Wrangel noted that only four out of a group of 15 young officers with whom he joined the army in the 1870s were not princes, counts, or barons.[57] Throughout Europe titled officers were promoted more rapidly than untitled ones. In Russia princes and counts reached the rank of general three to five years sooner on average than barons, and barons were promoted to top posts almost four years earlier than untitled officers.[58]

Access to royal courts offered titled parents a natural opportunity to restrict the range of marriage partners for their offspring. The higher up the scale, the more likely endogamy was to be found. Even in countries with diverse styles of aristocratic life, such as Italy, marriages in which both partners were titled were a characteristic of all the highest echelons whether in Milan or Naples.[59] This could be taken to extremes. Of 177 marriages that can be identified among an aristocratic Prussian family, the Counts von Dohna, between 1700 and 1860, 34 were intra-family matches and most of the rest were made within a circle of only 18 other dynasties of comparable rank.[60] Aristocrats were more likely than mere nobles to practice genealogical solidarity, primogeniture, and entail their estates, so that female children of the head of house were passed over to ensure that the title and property remained united even if this meant the family fortune went to a distant male heir.[61] In Britain the daughters of peers had lower mortality rates giving birth than untitled women. It was by no means a misfortune to be a great lady.[62]

In the nineteenth century, aristocrats held high office out of all proportion to their numbers. They often dominated the top ranks of the army, church, court, and cabinet. The families who were governors of provinces and members of the Privy Council in Russia in the seventeenth century continued to hold those posts until 1917: Galitzine, Scheremeteff, Lvov, Urusov, Gagarin, Apraksin, Tolstoy, Dolgorouky, Trubetskoy.[63] The diplomatic corps was a particular reserve. Every Austrian ambassador to London between 1748 and 1938 was titled, all but one a count or higher in rank.[64] The prime ministers of Hungary were regularly counts until 1940.

Aristocrats were groomed for high office in diets and parliaments, which they often entered at an early age. In some countries they were guaranteed places in upper chambers, which gave the titled elites political strength and special identity. In a number of cases aristocrats were actually granted an enhanced place in legislative systems during the course of the nineteenth century as new constitutions were written. The Hungarian elite expelled non-magnates from their upper chamber. Aristocrats also entered the electoral lists to win seats in lower houses. In 1883, 82 percent of dukes were elected to the British House of Commons before inheriting their titles (or succeeded before the age of 21), 55 percent of earls, and 41 percent of baronets, while only 29 percent of heads of untitled families owning substantial landed estates gained a seat in the lower house.[65] Titled elites also voted in legislatures and associated in parties in ways that were distinctive from lesser nobles.[66] Regular attendance and mentoring by experienced members helped even improbable candidates to learn the rudiments of parliamentary debate and achieve a basic competence for government service. With such advantages the able ones rocketed to the top.

No definition of aristocracy is perfect. Our focus will be on the titled elites who owned substantial amounts of land, recognizing that some barons were not part of the aristocracy and that some important nobles were never raised to titular rank. Above all we are concerned with substantial landed families who upheld a unique set of aristocratic values relating to family and honor and who perceived it their duty to rule. Cosmopolitan perspectives rendered aristocrats more flexible and adaptable to the torrent of change that came with the French and Industrial Revolutions than the rest of the agricultural community. They were exceptionally tenacious in holding on to their wealth and power. Hereditary titles strengthened the sinews of lineage. The need to sustain a dukedom or barony seems to have been decisive in stiffening parental resolve to reduce the inheritance passed on to younger children. Democracies had difficulty dismissing titled elites; revolutionary states found that the aristocratic tail still had a sting. Hitler discovered this almost too late. Lenin and Stalin were obliged to scorch the earth. Many patrician values were ill adapted to the modern world and led to crippling dissonance and malfunction. However, when the circumstances and hour was suited to their best qualities, especially in the conduct of war, there was still a place for aristocrats in the twentieth century, and they seized it.

2

THE *ANCIEN RÉGIME*

In the nineteenth century, what does caste matter?

Ivan Turgenev, *Fathers and Sons*, p. 224

In 1610 an English sea captain sailed north from Virginia and entered what the Dutch called "South River." He renamed it Delaware Bay in honor of the newly appointed governor of the Jamestown colony, the 12th Lord Delaware. Thus what became an American state gained its name from an English peer, part of a process that aristocized topographical nomenclature around the world between the fifteenth and twentieth centuries.

The De La Warrs, as they finally came to spell their name, began as French occupiers of Norman England and gained a peerage in 1299. They fought in the Hundred Years' War, went on a crusade, and helped capture the French king on the battlefield at Poitiers in 1356. In the early fifteenth century the family suffered a genealogical derailment when the male line became extinct, but, as was often the case in medieval Britain, the title continued through the female line of the West family. Unfortunately, the Tudor holders of the title managed to bankrupt the family and bring the barony to a halt in disgrace in the midst of a murder gone wrong.

The momentum of great names, however, is hard to halt. A well-timed bit of treason and some military exploits restored the title though not the finances, hence the 12th Baron's dangerous expedition to the back of beyond. He needed the salary. Two strategic marriages recovered the family fortunes. The first, to an heiress, gained an earldom and the second, a brilliant match with the sister of the last Duke of Dorset (Sackville family), restored the family to the magnate class. The 7th Earl gilded the lily by drowning in a yachting accident weeks after having taken out a large insurance policy.

Many members of the family served as generals, courtiers, and diplomats. They held high office in North America in three successive centuries, the last as Minister to Washington in the 1880s. In the twentieth century the family produced a poet and novelist of distinction, V. Sackville-West, and a Cabinet minister. The 9th Earl, overcome by boyish enthusiasm, served in the Labour government under Ramsay MacDonald, and then, more true to type, in the Conservative ministries of the 1950s where he helped establish commercial television. John Major appointed his grandson, Tom Sackville, a junior minister in 1997.

The De La Warrs were not typical of the British peerage in the modern era. Few families have stood in the front rank of national life for so long. However, looking only at the date of creation of a title in modern lists of aristocrats can easily fool one. Often wealth, arms, estates, castles, names, and position have been passed from generation to generation with recreations of titles concealing the bloodlines and rank that stretch back literally into the mists of time. Researchers rarely bother to master the intricacies of the enormously elaborate system of heraldry and hierarchy surrounding aristocratic life in the last few centuries. Their ignorance leads them not only to commit technical solecisms, but also to miss the spirit that infused the filling in of dance cards, the making of ministries, and heroism on the battlefield.[1] Continuity is as important a part of our story as change. The study of aristocracy requires us to begin by understanding the world in which families such as the De La Warrs lived.

* * * *

A Polish visitor in Edinburgh during the 1820s who attended many parties noted: "The footman standing in the doorway is well trained and knows what to do on all occasions; the greater the title, the louder he pronounces it. One could make a special scale of the rising tones of his voice which increases in volume crescendo: whispering 'Mr.', speaking 'Sir', announcing 'Lord', exclaiming 'Count' or 'Marquis' and shouting 'Prince' or 'Duke'."[2] Central to the ladder of social ascendancy were titles. The baroque subtlety of the system of honors that evolved over five or six hundred years of European history mirrored the complexity of society as a whole.

The small change in hereditary distinctions was knighthoods that could be passed down through the generations. France, Italy, Holland, Austria, Bavaria, and Britain granted such honors. The British "baronets," however, were always a rather mixed lot and had no access to the House of Lords. The lowest rung on the full-fledged titular ladder, baron, was also somewhat indiscriminately conferred. The rank was universal among European aristocracies. It could be a mark of ancient lineage, or it could be tossed out to newcomers like door prizes at a party.

European titles of honor

> Prince
> Duke
> Marquis
> Count (Earl)
> Viscount
> Baron
> Hereditary Knight
> (Baronet, Chevalier, Jonkheer, Ritter)

Viscounts were the rarest of the major aristocratic denominations, except, for some reason, in Portugal where the title was the most popular single rank. Only a handful of countries bestowed it. However, the next step up, count (earl in Britain and Ireland), was widely used and in the Scandinavian countries stood at the top of the noble hierarchy.[3] Marquis was fairly widely distributed in Italy, Spain, and France. Napoleon, unlike the Bourbon kings, did not confer it. Hence in France the title retained a special place among loyal royalists.[4]

The most important and the most complex set of titles were duke and prince. This is partly because they frequently overlapped with honors used within royal families, although sovereigns slapped prefixes such as "arch," "grand," or "hereditary" in front of duke in order that no mistakes were made. Even so, identifying what type of top aristocrat one had encountered required considerable care. Most dukedoms were held by only one man (or woman in countries where direct female succession was permitted) at a time and passed by primogeniture, that is, to the eldest male heir. The title of prince could also descend that way. This was most common among German "*Fürsts*," one of two words for the rank in the Holy Roman Empire. In Russia, Italy, Belgium, Poland, and elsewhere all male heirs and the unmarried daughters of princes enjoyed the use of the title. In Britain, Portugal, and Scandinavia no non-royal princes existed. Even these distinctions do not tell the whole story. In Russia over a quarter of the princely titles were borne by Georgians, a huge proportion for such a small territory that had been absorbed into the empire only in the late eighteenth century. Although their lineages were ancient, they were usually no matches for the grand Lithuanian and Russian dynasties that claimed descent from the Viking founder of Russia, Rurik. These immemorial and once sovereign titles did not owe their origins to creation by the Tsar or Holy Roman Emperor (to whom Russian monarchs turned for help until they took on the right to produce princes themselves).

The trouble with titles that passed to all male descendants was that estates were rarely large enough and extinctions of junior lines not frequent enough to prevent even dukes from sinking downwards in wealth. Stories are told of Russian musicians and servants who were princes.[5] This may have been the case, but three things made hordes of impoverished cadets unlikely. First, titles attracted heiresses, and many a prince found salvation in marrying money. Second, jobs that offered opportunities for aggrandizement were more likely to come a prince's way than to others. Third, really destitute nobles of high rank tended simply to disappear. If many princely servants ever existed, they ceased to use their titles or had no children. The title of prince usually was born either by men of great wealth and distinction or by cadets who had found employment in respectable positions in government or the military, and this was generally true for noblemen of all ranks in countries that permitted widespread descent of honors. The poor ones got good jobs, married well, or did not marry at all.

Many titles were limited in various complicated ways to help avoid the possibility of indigent patricians. In Denmark, the Netherlands, and France, "*decrescendo*" allowed secondary members of the family to make a show while reserving the highest title for the head of house. Generally the son of a marquis was a count and other junior members used lesser titles. Another clue to precedence was whether the Christian name of the titled person came before or after the rank.[6] In

Britain peerages were reserved for the heads of houses alone. Eldest sons and eldest grandsons might hold "courtesy" titles of junior status, but they remained commoners in law. The rest of the children got lesser marks of distinction such as being designated "Lady" or "the Honourable."

In Russia, despite their rarity (or perhaps because of it), titles did not possess quite the luster that attached to them elsewhere. The Narishkin family, on the strength of Peter the Great's mother being born one, never condescended to accept a title in later years.[7] The demi-royal status of the mediatized princes and counts of the Holy Roman Empire was mentioned earlier. Forced to give up rule of their statelets, they tended to hold themselves aloof above the rest of the German and Austrian nobility, which produced a tradition of endogamy second to none among European aristocracies.[8] In Ireland and Scotland clan chiefs of ancient lineage and sometimes vast estates bore exotic names such as the Knight of Kerry, O'Conor Don, Mackintosh of Mackintosh, or Lochiel. Finally, Papal titles fell into two categories: the Roman aristocracy, including relatives of many holders of the triple tiara, and individuals who were created counts or marquises by popes across Catholic Europe.

Salic Law blocked female succession to titles in France and the Holy Roman Empire. However, in Hungary, Scotland, Sicily, Naples, Milan, Portugal, and Spain, women could inherit high rank if there were no male heirs. Medieval baronies and titles specially designated could also pass by female succession in England. In Spain families with several titles can distribute them among their children with the king's permission.

*   *   *   *

Historians fumble around when it comes to calculating the size of nobilities. Experts have examined the evidence for pre-revolutionary France with a fine-toothed comb and their estimates range from 110,000 to 400,000, which gives one some idea of the problem.[9] Within this massive array were a smaller number, perhaps 4000 or 4500, who owned a substantial château and lived nobly.[10] In the years after 1815 there were fewer nobles, but estimates still vary from 30,000 to 200,000.[11] In Eastern Europe the size of nobilities could be vast. Russia had over 600,000 in 1858.[12] Even much smaller Hungary was said to have half a million.[13] Britain in the nineteenth century counted between 10,000 and 15,000 "landed" families.[14] Thus we have only a rough idea of the proportion of all nobles to the rest of the population. In the nineteenth century this ranged from approximately 0.1 to 0.2 percent in Bohemia and Finland, less than 1 percent in most of the German states and France, 1 to 2 percent in Russia, 4 percent in Spain, between 4 and 9 percent in Hungary, and 8 to 15 percent in Poland.[15]

Elite families were in constant stages of transition. Old ones died out, estates merged through marriage, and, except in the countries that ceased to confer titles, constant additions were being made. In Finland the number of titles tripled during the nineteenth century; in Spain they doubled.[16] Nonetheless, we can make rough estimates of the size of aristocracies based on the criteria listed in Chapter 1. The smallest were to be found in Finland and Croatia where they numbered around 50 to 100 families in each during the mid- to late nineteenth century. The next step up, 100 to 200, included many of the smaller countries or regions of Europe such as Austria proper, the Baltic provinces of Russia, Bavaria, Belgium, Bohemia, central Italy, Denmark, the Netherlands, Scotland, and Sweden. Between 200 and 300 families dominated Hungary, Ireland, Portugal, Romania, and the Kingdom of the Two Sicilies.[17] Somewhere around 500 families formed the aristocracies of England and Wales, Northern Italy, Prussia, and Spain. Perhaps as many as 1000 such families existed in France and Russia, though these estimates may be high.[18] The case of Poland is very complicated. It is best until the twentieth century to include the Polish elite in the court circles of Berlin, St. Petersburg, and Vienna.[19]

A striking aspect of many European aristocracies was their mongrel nature. Luigi Barzini referred to the elite of the newly united Italy in 1861 as "an *antipasto* of nobles."[20] In nations that had been cobbled together or divided up nobilities were merged or tossed like salad. Deep divides lurked beneath the surface. The Piedmontese Marquis d'Azeglio looked down on the "black" Roman aristocracy with contempt: "daughter and servant of the Papacy for the most part, what can one expect from that? . . . Sloth, abasement, and ruin!"[21] Even in the early twentieth century Prince Hubertus Löwenstein noted that southern German aristocrats looked at the Prussian Junkers as "very different people."[22] Some historians argue that the English, Welsh, Scottish, and Irish aristocracies were merged into a supra-national elite during the late eighteenth and early nineteenth centuries, but considerable evidence suggests the melding was not seamless.[23]

Mediatized German princes such as the various branches of the Hohenlohes, whose core estates lay in Württemberg, became courtiers, soldiers, and statesmen with equal facility in Vienna and Berlin. The Fuggers from Bavaria might serve in the Austrian or Prussian armies. Transylvanian aristocrats lorded it over a Romanian peasantry, while "colonial" elites ruled ethnically distinct populations in Ireland, Estonia, Latvia, Finland, Ukraine, and Bohemia.

Italy was only a geographic expression until the 1860s. Not only were there separate jurisdictions ruled by independent governments, from the Grand Duke of Tuscany to the King of Sardinia, but also dynasties and dominions changed over time, depositing geological layers of noble titles. In the north various cities and provinces, once free, fell under the rule of the Holy Roman Emperor. Later, parts became Spanish and then Austrian. The Sicilian and Neapolitan nobilities were quite distinct even though they shared a king.[24] The Bonapartes also created Italian titles. Finally, the Kingdom of Italy after 1861 added a crust on top.

In Germany a similarly wide variety of arrangements existed. After 1815 the ruling families consisted of real kings in places like Prussia and Bavaria comparable to monarchs elsewhere in Europe. Pipsqueak states, however, such as Reuss or Saxe-Meiningen, though technically sovereign, were ruled by princes less affluent and grand than English dukes or Hungarian magnates. In Spain, older titles had been created by the kings of Castile and Navarre. The Baltic Germans bore Swedish and Russian titles. The Russian Tsar, the Habsburg Emperor, and Ottoman rulers ennobled Romanians.[25]

The Habsburg elite was not only Austrian, Czech, Polish, Hungarian, and Croat, but also it was made up of émigrés from other parts of Europe. Exiled Irish "wild geese" ended up gaining titles in Austria (and in France, Spain, and Italy), where some became quite prominent. The Dutch Bentincks followed William III to England and a dukedom. Russia encompassed the most cosmopolitan elite. Directly incorporated into the aristocracy were Lithuanians, Georgians, Tartars, Baltic and other Germans, Italians, Poles, Turks, Englishmen, and Frenchmen. In addition nobles from Portugal, Holland, Sweden, and Moldovia attended the St. Petersburg court. The Scottish Barclay de Tollys became Baltic German nobles and then Russian princes.[26] The Bohemian aristocracy had its origins in German,

Austrian, Czech, Spanish, Italian, French, and Irish families. The Rothschilds of Frankfurt were ennobled in Austria, Germany, France, and Britain. In Prussia in the eighteenth century the new military and administrative structure created by the Hohenzollerns was staffed by Junkers, Polish and Austrian nobles from Silesia, French Huguenots, and nobles from other German principalities, Denmark, Ireland, Scotland, Italy, and Sweden.[27] The Irish Ascendancy was composed of a combination of native Celts, Normans, English, Welsh, Scots, and Huguenots.

*   *   *   *

Aristocracies faced a variety of challenges to their status, economic well-being, and power during the seventeenth and eighteenth centuries. Monarchs were their rivals, although each needed the other to prosper. A trend toward centralization of government and absolutism is often seen as damaging to the culture and independence of nobilities. Following the argument of the sociologist Norbert Elias, textbooks on early modern history still present royal courts as places where a once independent landed elite was defanged and domesticated by "rising" absolutists. Real power, so the argument runs, was transferred from the old nobility to newly emergent bureaucracies beholden to the ruler.[28] We imagine them all standing around arguing about who should have the privilege of taking off the king's nightshirt.

Recently, however, scholars have become skeptical about attempts to represent court history in terms of the enfeeblement of the aristocracy. In fact the court was designed to meet the interests of the elite more fully than its traditional image as the stronghold of absolutism has allowed. Great families almost always held the most prestigious offices and were virtually irremovable. The main source of more "civilized" behavior was the spread of education, which was required in order to perform successfully in the administration of complex modern government that aristocrats still largely headed. If anything, this upgrade in nobles' abilities strengthened their position. Aristocrats went to court seeking opportunities to gain more wealth and power, and many were successful in this pursuit. It was also the principal aristocratic marriage market and a school of manners and conduct for young men and women of quality. Aristocrats also reasserted their cultural hegemony that was being

challenged by new non-noble elites.[29] As titles proliferated and corporate privileges were eliminated, the non-courtly lesser nobility
tended to lose status at an accelerating pace.[30]

Kings found asserting discipline over nobles akin to herding cats.
None of the weapons at the monarchs' disposal were adequate to
ensure noble subservience. The Habsburgs gradually lost their grip
over the princes and counts of the Holy Roman Empire. The Hungarians were always recalcitrant. Even in Bohemia, where the aristocracy
was remade in the mid-seventeenth century, a sizeable group
endorsed the overthrow of the Empress by the Elector of Bavaria in
1740 after he invaded Prague during the succession crisis.[31] The
Polish elite never fully reconciled themselves to Tsarist rule. Various
aristocratic conspiracies across Europe murdered monarchs, or dis-
placed the line of succession. Russian princes were still throttling
and poisoning royal favorites in 1916.

Territorial expansion, increase in population, involvement in
European power politics, expansion in military establishments that
advanced technology made too expensive for individual nobles to
sustain, concomitant taxation, large bureaucracies needed to collect
and spend the money, and the entrance of the state into new sectors
of activity all generated an ever-growing demand for aristocratic
governors. Monarchs needed the cooperation of a powerful aristocracy to rule effectively. There was no contradiction between a strong
monarchical state and strong nobility. "Their power grew in
tandem."[32]

Another force once believed to have weakened the aristocracy and
eventually rendered it redundant was the ending of serfdom. Jerome
Blum argued that the process of peasant emancipation marked the
dividing line between the *ancien régime* and the modern world.[33] Most
students of aristocracies in the eighteenth and nineteenth centuries
would now question that assumption. Monarchs and their advisors
often spearheaded the abolition of serfdom. The Baltic and Hungarian aristocracies took the initiative to end the practice. Seigneurial
fees had become an accounting headache or were simply uncollect-
able. In Hesse-Cassel dues splintered among heirs over time so that
an obligation might mean paying an eighth of a chicken or fractions
of an egg a year.[34] Many aristocrats became capitalist entrepreneurs
impatient with decaying remnants of older economic practices.[35]
Generally reforms of feudal tenures worked to the advantage of the
aristocracy, and even enhanced the dependence of the peasantry on

the landlords.[36] Investments purchased with cash paid by peasants to gain possession of farms could produce four times the income received from the old labor rental. In Russia the former serfs gained less than 30 percent of the agricultural land and nearly half got none at all. In Hungary only a fifth of the arable land went to the peasants. The Baltic barons managed to leave the former serfs virtually landless. The clan chiefs of Scotland swept the poor crofters away in a series of notorious "clearances." The division of common lands almost always favored the lords. Aristocrats used compensation for seigneurial rights to buy more acreage.[37] Distribution of some land to wealthy peasants buttressed the traditional order, and, as we shall see in Chapter 7, the nobility continued to exercise strong control over the countryside across Europe into the twentieth century.[38]

The radon in aristocratic basements emitting deadly rays turned out to be the Enlightenment. This movement was corrosive and dangerous to the aristocracy and was followed by the wrenching upheaval of revolution in France. Much of what was written by the *philosophes* was stately and profound, but a venomous stream of satire and ridicule that included portrayal of the aristocracy as parasites and morally corrupt accompanied their critique. Attacks were made on the Church and secularization encouraged. Privilege, especially that based on birth, was denounced. Merit became the criterion of advancement. New emphasis was placed on intimate family life in contrast to the strutting, public existence of the aristocracy. Institutions were to be judged by reason and utility, not by their antiquity. Rationalism, humanism, individualism, social utility, patriotism, and science were held to secure human dignity and encourage progress. In 1791 Edmund Burke warned his patron, the English magnate Earl Fitzwilliam, that the real object of the French Revolution was not the destruction of absolute monarchy "but totally to root out that thing called an *Aristocrate* or Nobleman and Gentleman."[39]

Eventually even the aristocracy challenged the fundamental assumptions and practices of the *ancien régime*. It was they who patronized writers and filled the salons of capital cities with critics of existing society.[40] The Marquis di Beccaria attacked torture and the death penalty, and Baron de Montesquieu authored the *Spirit of Laws*. Nearly half the purchasers of the *Encyclopédie* were noble; many read Adam Smith. When the *philosophes* praised constitutional government and urged that French politics become more like the English, most nobles found themselves in vigorous agreement. The Prince de

Ligne, a grandee from the Low Countries, habitué of Versailles and
Austrian Field Marshal, wrote in the early 1770s: "One good thing
that [the Enlightenment] has brought with it, in almost all countries,
is a complete contempt for *les grands seigneurs*."[41] Aristocrats enjoyed
the mockery aimed at narrow-minded provincial gentry. They
accepted that high rank ought to rest on ability and property as well
as birth.[42] They supported educational reforms to promote literacy.
Aristocrats were in the forefront of fostering agricultural innovation.[43] Some English aristocrats greeted the French Revolution with
open delight. Lord Holland's son, Charles James Fox, called it "the
noblest cause that ever was in the hand of Man." His aunt, the
Duchess of Leinster, wrote of her son, Lord Edward Fitzgerald, on
his return from Paris in 1792: "He is mad about French affairs – the
leveling principle . . . One must not say mob before him, but the
people."[44] Countess Louise Stolberg in Denmark burnt her family
tree in the drawing room fireplace, while Count Moltke replaced the
three birds in his coat of arms with Jacobin caps of liberty.[45]

In Paris the early leadership of the Revolution was hardly bourgeois at all. The most influential body that took upon itself the task
of educating the nation in its rights was the Society of Thirty. Of the
55 identifiable members, 50 were nobles, many of them from the
most ancient and illustrious families in the aristocracy. The Declaration of the Rights of Man and Citizen closely followed drafts composed by the Marquis de Lafayette. Donald Sutherland argues that
the renunciation of feudal rights on the night of August 4 sprung
not from the Great Fear but from a concerted campaign by "Patriot"
aristocrats to achieve a goal they had adopted before the Revolution
began.[46] Many nobles participated in the legislative bodies between
1789 and 1791. A sizeable minority of nobles remained at the cutting
edge of radicalism through both the Terror and the Directory.[47]

*   *   *   *

The ideas of the Enlightenment were toxic for aristocracy. However,
the immediate aftermath of the French Revolution was far less damaging than might have been expected. Most of the émigrés got their
estates back and Napoleon's conquests rarely led to confiscation of
property.[48] The decline in deference to the elite in the countryside
appears to have been modest. The Revolution and Napoleon purged
the ranks of the idle and non-functional elements within the old elite

and revamped the institutional framework. The younger generation of nobles born between 1770 and 1790 looked on the world with fresh eyes and met the new order with a renewed readiness to assume responsibility.[49]

Successful resistance to the Revolutionary armies and Napoleon invigorated European aristocrats as military leaders, patriots, and servants of the state. The British had long used titles to encourage success in battle and state service, and to this practice they now added substantial financial endowments to be paid for three or four generations.[50] At the same time "Old Corruption," a system of sine-cures and outdoor relief for the idle members of the elite, was ended.[51] Tsarist nobles marched across Europe to crush Napoleon. The Piedmontese and Spanish gained the opportunity to purchase expropriated church property and profited from new investment opportunities.[52] The Prussian state was reformed.

Of course, not all aristocrats embraced the Enlightenment with enthusiasm or survived the Revolution unscathed. Some noble families suffered grievous losses both of life and property, especially among the poorer *noblesse*.[53] Thus the Enlightenment and the Revolution undermined the basis of aristocratic privilege, enervated the self-confidence that was necessary to live as aristocrats, and ultimately the laws and institutions, including the Church, which upheld the *ancien régime*. The new economic thinking also promoted bourgeois prosperity and challenged the system of inheritance of property and family solidarity that had ensured dynastic continuity and strength. Robert Forster noted that the French Revolution accelerated a change in attitudes among nobles as well as non-nobles, irrevocably dislocating the hierarchical society of the old regime.[54] The revolutionary war and the Napoleonic occupation disrupted the Piedmontese nobility's collective confidence and sense of security. Military defeat, loss of their monarchy, economic deprivation, petty humiliations, and in some cases exile, were devastating blows. The French occupiers introduced egalitarian legal reforms that undermined privilege. In the words of de Tocqueville, the Revolution taught aristocracies "to tremble before the people."[55] Many observers believe the nobility limped into the nineteenth century severely weakened, "a pale shadow of its former self."[56] Over the next six chapters we will examine the extent to which this proposition is true.

*   *   *   *

Finally, mention must be made of two other sources of danger for
the aristocracy moving inexorably forward during the modern era.
One was a relative decline in numbers. In some countries titles
ceased to be granted. Natural attrition wore away at the stock of old
families. Lower birth rates followed a decline in infant mortality and
abolition of entails, which made the margin of error in ensuring
continuation of a lineage less easy to judge.

Second and even more dangerous was the decline absolutely and
proportionally in the population living and working in the countryside. Agriculture ceased to be the predominant occupation of an
increasing segment of the European population at the same time as
demographic growth exploded upwards due to better nutrition,
reduction in disease, and a variety of other factors. In addition, commercial fortunes were being made in such large numbers and sizes
that not all of them could be absorbed into the nobility as they had
been in the past. The changing structure and dynamism of the
economy held unprecedented danger for landed elites. The bourgeoisie and industrial proletariat became new threats.

Of course, aristocracies had always been very small as a proportion
of the entire population, and a few counts and princes less here or
there was probably not a big problem. Moreover, aristocrats were
more likely than the lesser nobles to participate in and benefit from
an expanding economy. Rural tranquility was restored as a result of
the liberal reforms of the first half of the nineteenth century. Factories sucked up surplus population that might have become restive in
an agricultural setting. Across much of central and eastern Europe
the overwhelming majority of peasants remained in the countryside
well into the twentieth century.

On balance, it is clear that at the outset of the nineteenth century
aristocrats faced great challenges to their continued power, self-confidence, and sources of income. However, their habit of authority and
mastery over government offices gave them considerable ability to influence the course of state building, foreign policy, and domestic control.
They also continued to make themselves rich. They tossed overboard
excess baggage to keep the ship afloat. Their titles marked them out
as special even when other privileges were removed. Acquisition of a
hereditary honorific remained the apogee of success for most ambitious
Europeans throughout the nineteenth century. That tells us much
about the continuing importance and resilience of the aristocracy.

3

WEALTH

> Work assiduously to introduce on our estates, wherever it is possible, manufacturing, trade, traffic and commerce, including skilled artisans, weavers of cloth and stockings, dyers, tanners, locksmiths, hatters and the like.

> Prince Anton Florian von Liechtenstein, 1717, quoted by J. V. H. Melton in "The Nobility in the Bohemian and Austrian Lands," p. 136

The Liechtensteins emerged in the mid-twelfth century and took their name from a castle near Vienna. They were granted fiefs in what is today Slovakia in 1249, although they did not acquire the little nation they now rule until 1699. In 1606 the family agreed to a system of primogeniture that preserved its vast holdings intact, and they were soon afterwards created princes. More land was acquired in the wake of the Battle of White Mountain at which the Protestant nobility of Bohemia was crushed and afterwards dispossessed. This bonanza quintupled the size of the family holdings. Liechtensteins served the Habsburgs as field marshals and statesmen for three centuries and stood at the apex of great landed families in the Austro-Hungarian Empire. Their property amounted to almost 474,000 acres in 1914.

Initially, the twentieth century was not kind to the family. Nearly three-quarters of their income came from their Czech estates, half of which were confiscated in the 1920s. They lost the rest when the communists took over after World War II. However, the Liechtensteins still had holdings in Austria and owned a private mini-country bordering on Switzerland to which the Prince withdrew with his art collection in 1944. The Principality of Liechtenstein had survived the cull of tiny states at the Congress of Vienna in 1815 and still exists as an independent entity, issuing postage stamps, competing in the Olympics, and with a membership in the United Nations.

Economic setbacks periodically visited the Liechtensteins but the family's grip on land was never shaken loose. They could retreat to their mountain fastness and ride out virtually any storm. Their fortunes have so far recovered that at the turn of the twenty-first century a democratic referendum of the citizens, counter to every trend in modern history, granted the reigning prince additional political powers. Hans-Adam II recently spent $28 million refurbishing one of his two remaining palaces in Vienna in order to return it to its nineteenth-century function as a museum for the family art collection. It is open to the public but not expected to make a profit. The Prince has resumed collecting to add to the show. He recently purchased for $37 million a handsome chest of drawers, sold by the English Duke of Beaufort a few years earlier, to decorate the Vienna palace.[1]

The durability of landed wealth sustained the Liechtensteins through nearly a millennium of high status and authority. Lali Horstmann, a wealthy bourgeois owner of a small Prussian estate, wrote in 1945: "By giving a basic security to man's essential needs for food and fuel, [land] offers a chance for a family's survival in hard times, provides an unchanging background, against which tradition, beliefs and habits can develop, to be handed down without interruption from generation to generation."[2] She found that "hard times" had not disappeared even in the mid-twentieth century. Her summary of the advantages of landed property touched on the essence of acreage. A warrior class understood that when worse comes to worst you can eat beef and corn but not coins and shares. Landed estates with parks and houses, fields and streams, stables and spinneys, villages and servants halls rooted families in the soil and formed memories and human relationships that fostered continuity, self-confidence, a deep connection between generations, and the stature to command. Land also gave to aristocrats not so much an escape from the ignoble task of earning a wage but time to devote to education for and conduct of government and war. It also conferred independence from having fully to rely on favors from either the people or the king. The organization of the estate gave structure to aristocratic lives and integrated their social and political status with their wealth. No wonder that noblemen looked after their estates, the novelist Count Tolstoy observed, "like ancient vestals" tending a sacred fire.[3] Among old families the name of the estate was often the family name, and later cadet branches of large clans would add estate names to their surname. Land and family became ineradicably combined. Country seats also contained family portraits that might hang in the same spot where the original sitters had placed them four centuries earlier. Heirlooms and archives were housed in musty muniment rooms that were shrines to dynastic glory.

Commoners were banned from owning land in many European countries from Russia to Denmark until reforms were enacted during the nineteenth century. Even the Venetian elite, though protected by their lagoon, gradually reached out to the mainland, attracted by the magnetic force of landed estates. By the sixteenth century they were building some of the most beautiful country houses in Europe. Every effort was made to avoid selling land, especially the core estate around the family seat. Elaborate legal devices were constructed to preserve inheritances intact.

The majority of Europeans remained engaged in agriculture during the nineteenth century. In the east this stayed true well into the twentieth. In France in 1850 three-quarters of the population resided in rural areas, while in England, the birthplace of industrialization, more than half the people still lived and worked on farms. Industrialization only "took off" in northern Italy just before World War I. During the 1930s nearly one-third of the German population still depended on agriculture for their livelihoods.[4] Thus, even where industry burgeoned the leadership of aristocrats was critical to modern economic development.

*   *   *

Accounts of the size of aristocratic estates stagger the imagination. In the modern world one only thinks in these terms when considering sheep ranches in Australia. Within the intensely populated and cultivated confines of quite small countries such as England and Hungary, single individuals owned gigantic tracts of real estate. This was true virtually everywhere except Scandinavia, the Low Countries, and France. In some regions only a handful of families were giants while in other areas magnates were relatively commonplace.

A few caveats should be noted. First, detailed and accurate evidence on landholding collected on a regular basis does not exist for any country over the last two centuries. Second, not all large landowners were nobles. In Apulia in the nineteenth and twentieth centuries typical landowners, even among those who possessed great *latifundia*, were absentee bourgeois speculators.[5] Third, a number of elites were largely composed of small estate owners. Most of the Baltic barons, Piedmontese marcheses, and Prussian Junkers were not able to live on the scale even of prosperous Parisian nobles, who were themselves often modestly endowed. On their home turf, however, they remained formidable.[6]

In the eighteenth century Prince Karol Radziwill was said to have owned a piece of Poland the size of Belgium. Estimates from that period also calculated that about one-third of Spain was in the hands of four great families. About 90 dynasties controlled two million peasants in Naples *c*.1800.[7] In the first half of the nineteenth century 15 to 20 families presided over one-third of Wallachia and Moldovia. In 1896 the Prince of Liechtenstein owned 5 percent of the entire province of Moravia. Two hundred and fifty magnates possessed more than 30,000 acres each in the United Kingdom. In the late nineteenth century at least two dozen families owned more than 250,000 acres apiece in the Dual Monarchy, while in Russia 43 persons held like amounts.[8]

Counting land area alone can be misleading. A vast estate in County Galway full of moors and bogs or many square miles of mountainous Scotland were far less valuable than relatively small and compact estates in the English Midlands. The value of land varied immensely all over the Continent and within countries. A small estate in Piedmont could bring a comparable income to that of a property seven times as large in the south.[9] Total income is a better measure of rank in the pecking order of aristocracies, but a really big estate, even if not hugely profitable, conferred grandeur on the owner, especially if it had long been in the family. A list of some notable examples appears in Table 3.1.

Great magnates owned large portions of all the land in Austria, Bohemia, Hungary, and Scotland during the nineteenth century.[10] Half the area of the latter country was owned by 118 people, the most concentrated pattern in Europe. Perhaps three-quarters of Sicily belonged to a small group of great landowners, while in southern Spain they owned nearly two-thirds of all property. In Ireland pos-

Table 3.1 Examples of great landowners, 1870–1930.[11] (Dates vary and acreages are approximate.)

Owner	Acres
Count Stroganoff (Russia)	3,955,440
Prince Thurn und Taxis (Germany and Austria-Hungary)	3,057,279
Duke of Sutherland (Scotland and England)	1,358,545
Count A. D. Scheremeteff (Russia)	610,200
Prince Esterházy (Hungary)	558,403
Prince Schwarzenberg (Bohemia and Austria)	511,290
Count M. Zamoyski (Poland)	469,300
Prince K. Radziwill (Poland)	383,689
Duke of Palmella (Portugal)	250,000
Duke of Devonshire (England and Ireland)	198,572
Duke of Medinaceli (Spain)	195,493*
Duke of Northumberland (England)	186,397
Prince of Pless (Prussia and Poland)	173,243
Prince Festetics (Hungary)	169,534
Count J. Colloredo-Mansfeld (Bohemia)	153,900
Duke of Peñaranda (Spain)	126,009*
Marquis of Bute (Scotland and Wales)	116,668
Count Pejácsevich-Viroviticki (Croatia)	99,575
Count Hoyos (Austria)	80,517
Duke of Leinster (Ireland)	73,100
Prince Borghese (Papal States)	56,810
Prince zu Putbus (Prussia)	45,030
Prince D. Sturdza (Romania)	41,357
Count Mayneaud de Pancemont (France)	15,561
Barons von Dörnberg (Hesse-Cassel)	12,844
Prince d'Esling (France)	12,103
Marquis Falletti di Barolo (Piedmont)	10,398

*Does not include forest and pasture, which might, if included, double these amounts.

sessors of estates larger than 5000 acres held more than half the acreage.[12]

In the later nineteenth century in Britain, Austria, Bohemia, the Baltic provinces, Poland, Romania, and Prussia 30 to 40 percent of the land was owned by the nobility, while in France, Holland, Belgium, Hungary, Denmark, Sweden, southern Germany, northern Italy, and Finland 15 to 33 percent. Russia had one of the lowest proportions at around 14 percent (west of the Urals). Of course, that country was

filled with vast tracts of northern wastes and marshland. At the low
end of our assessment the Hessian nobility owned only 7 percent of
arable land and 15 percent of the forests in the electorate.[13]

The typical holding among the higher nobility in the southern
areas of Spain was probably around 6000 or 7000 acres. For a Junker
1000 to 1600 acres was common, although it is a myth to say that
there were hardly any large estates in Prussia. One hundred and
forty-eight people owned over 12,300 acres each in Prussia in 1880,
and estates over 20,000 acres could be found in every province.[14] The
Baltic manors were larger than in East Elbia. However, much of the
land was unsuitable for agriculture. Only three families in Estonia
were considered rich by the standards of the St. Petersburg court.[15]
In Romania in 1907 66 people held 12,000 or more acres each.
Mediatized princes tended to enjoy much larger estates than the
non-royal local nobility of Westphalia and Franconia. Piedmontese
properties were relatively small, while the princely Roman and Neapolitan families held larger blocks.[16] No leviathans existed in France;
big estates stood at between 2500 and 5000 acres.[17]

In some countries the proportion of land owned by the nobility
declined during the nineteenth century. The Swedish elite dropped
from owning perhaps one-third c.1680 to one-fifth in 1845; in
Bologna down from 77 percent in 1789 to 51 percent in 1835; in
Denmark 60 percent c.1775 to about 33 percent c.1865; in Russia less
than half the land held in 1861 before serf emancipation was still
owned by the nobles in 1914. In other countries such as France and
England the proportion held steady. In Umbria the old nobility actually increased their holdings mainly due to marriage and inheritance
strategies. The Land Law of 1889 in Romania authorized the sale of
state land amounting to almost 3,000,000 acres, and the bulk of it
passed into the elite's hands.[18]

*　　*　　*

Modern economists have seen inefficiency as inherent in aristocratic
agriculture. Indolence and mulish traditionalism among the landowners are assumed to be natural. Recent research has shown,
however, that the prevailing conception of "modernization" is based
on false assumptions about the role of the nobility in economic
development. For centuries aristocrats had been innovative managers. Even in the most benighted empires of the east or "backward"

Spain the elite had long grasped the importance and accepted the legitimacy of markets.[19] They also understood, however, that extracting the maximum amount of rent from one's tenants was not good for aristocratic influence and that part of the rent was paid in "respect, regard, and duty."[20] Ruthless management with an eye only for profit would have quickly endangered rule by the nobility. Undoubtedly, stupid or desperate landlords rack-rented their tenants. The absolute power masters enjoyed over their serfs in Russia corrupted even sensible men, but, by and large, aristocrats practiced agriculture with an eye to a combination of income and power.

Interest in and advocacy of agricultural innovation during the eighteenth and nineteenth centuries came largely from the aristocracy. Had the great landowners of Europe eschewed expanding the food supply it is difficult to see how the population could have grown or industrialization taken place. From Moravia to Andalusia and Argyllshire to Mecklenburg aristocrats became well-attuned participants in a continent-wide market economy, creatively operating their estates to make a profit from the early modern period onwards.[21]

The huge estates accumulated by late medieval and early modern grandees cried out for sophisticated management. Hungarian magnates authorized more and more complex layers of supervision in the eighteenth century with an eye to developing all commercial possibilities.[22] Big landowners in Britain hired professional agents, often lawyers operating out of London estate offices, who had the education and skills to manage what were really large corporations. Below them were teams of accountants, bailiffs, and stewards. The relationship with the owner was rather like the present-day arrangements between chairmen and CEOs. The landowners were essentially businesslike and not mere passive receivers of rents. Serious mismanagement and bankruptcies were rare.[23]

In the nineteenth century magnates gave the lead in founding agricultural and forestry training schools to recruit and educate managers for their estates. In England innovative grandees founded the Royal Agricultural Society in 1838 and helped to establish an agricultural college. Noblemen endowed chairs in agronomy at universities. Counts Istvan Széchenyi of Hungary and Andrzej Zamoyski of Poland advocated agricultural reform, mechanization, food-processing factories, expansion of railways, and innovation in agricultural techniques.[24]

Aristocrats holding government office, such as Count P. D. Kiselev in Russia in the 1840s, promoted the introduction of new crops, organized model farms for the purpose of instruction and demonstration, and established training institutes.[25] Others lobbied for government investment in canals, roads, bridges, and railroads. The English elite used their legislative power to promote efficient agriculture and higher profits through parliamentary enclosure. On the Continent aristocrats persuaded governments to accept tariff protection, distilling monopolies, subsidized transport and land reclamation, cheap credit, and tax rebates.

Historians debate the level of success with which the Russian nobility met the challenge of losing land and control over their labor force in 1861. Jerome Blum was scathing about absenteeism, incompetence, prodigality, and inability to cope with changing conditions. Seymour Becker, on the other hand, has sought to revise the interpretation of the post-emancipation period as one of decline. He concedes that the majority of nobles sold their estates and moved into other areas of employment. However, the remaining landowners adapted well.[26] Similarly, a number of historians challenged the traditional view that during the nineteenth century northern Italian proprietors were idle absentees. In fact the nobility proved precociously capitalist in economic management.[27] Landlordism in post-Famine Ireland emerged stronger and healthier than was once believed. The weak and indebted went to the wall. Those who were not overburdened by debt and were optimistic about the future bought up land from those who had failed and increased their incomes. They took rational and effective steps to make estate management more efficient and modern.[28]

High-yield agriculture spread widely through Europe during the nineteenth century, and aristocrats led the way. Nobles introduced innovative machinery and farming practices on their estates: new ploughs, harrows, threshing machines, steam presses, chemical fertilizers, and haymaking and seeding machines. Wheat-growing fields were turned over to pastureland for livestock, sugar beets, and forestry.[29]

The rise of sugar beet production constituted a virtual revolution in its own right. It began with aristocratic leadership in the Habsburg monarchy. In 1800 the Bohemian Count Wrbna started manufacturing beet sugar raised on his estate, and by 1810 a substantial industry was established. Technical improvements took place in the 1820s and early 1830s. The initial impetus came from Count Franz Potocki in Galicia, Prince Anselm Thurn und Taxis and Prince Friedrich Oettingen-Wallerstein in Bohemia, and Baron von Dahlberg in Moravia. The business spread across Europe and was particularly important in Prussia. Intensification of production after 1850 required vast investments in fertilizer, machinery, and energy.[30]

In France, Bohemia, and Hungary aristocrats drained marshes. Count Franz Zichy was reputed to have recovered over 400,000 acres from swamplands. In the eighteenth century landowners in Lombardy developed large-scale plantations for rice culture. It required big capital outlay to undertake the necessary irrigation, and only the greatest landlords could do this. Investment in canal building projects and irrigation reservoirs continued in the nineteenth century. The work dramatically raised yields and sometimes doubled or tripled incomes.[31]

Forestry became an increasingly important element in the exploitation of estates. The great mediatized families of the south and central regions in Germany drew much of their income from wood products. The vastly increased construction of wooden ships and houses, and from the 1840s demand for railway sleepers and pit props, made them rich. More scientific methods of forestry were implemented, and some nobles studied the subject academically to become experts in the field. In order to finance these changes smaller pieces of land were sold to raise capital. The Barons von Dörnberg quadrupled their forest income by this means in the first 50 years of the century, and then doubled it again in the next decade. During the nineteenth century aristocrats in central and eastern Europe rapidly expanded plants on their estates to process commodities such as tar, potash, bricks, barrels, and the like.[32]

Aristocratic agriculture was never confined to simple staples. Landowners aimed at making full use of the land, water, rock, and anything else that they could find on or under their estates. They also sought to achieve diversification in sources of income so that poor harvests or unfavorable markets for one product would not affect other sources of production and income. Salt mining on a grand scale had long been practiced in Transylvania, where one noble sold 100,000 salt blocks in 1699 alone. Estates all over eastern and central Europe operated stud farms to supply ever-expanding armies with cavalry and draft horses. Spanish ranches were devoted to raising bulls for the ring. The Sykes baronets of Yorkshire carried a large agricultural estate through the severe depression of the 1880s and 1890s with profits from a successful racing stable. The Counts Benckendorff in post-emancipation Russia owned a stud, fishponds, starch factory, and distillery. Aristocrats raised pigs, sheep, cattle, and potatoes. Innovation increased the productivity of already existing subsidiary rural enterprises such as breweries, saw mills, and flour mills. The sale on the St. Petersburg, Hamburg, and London markets of oxen raised on distilleries' draff brought the Baltic barons additional income. So did exploitation of deposits of limestone and dolomite and cement factories for export to Sweden and Finland. They were even in the business of leasing inns and taverns. Count Larisch-Mönnich and Duke Albert of Saxe-Teschen pioneered use of steam engines to build large-scale distilleries in the Habsburg Empire. For some owners liquor production became a chief source of revenue. [33]

Not all innovations were successful. Increasing sheep production in the Baltic provinces, for example, turned out to be risky. Epidemics struck down animals and competition emerged from Australia. Innovation and good management were not universal. Some aristocracies were highly resistant to any form of change and uninterested in investment. Perhaps the most notorious of these was the old landed elite of Sicily. They were noted for absenteeism and oppression of the peasantry.[34] The Romanian landowners were very remote from the management of their estates and the suffering of the peasantry. But these were the exceptions, not the rule.

When aristocrats failed to invest heavily in innovation and capital improvements this was not always irrational or backward-looking. Ambiguities of formal property rights and scattered inheritances caused difficulty.[35] Irrigation projects or drainage could provide too little return on investment. When prices dropped in the 1880s, landowners who borrowed too heavily in the years of high farming to finance improvements found themselves in dire straits.[36]

*　*　*

If aristocrats had relied solely on agriculture and related activities to sustain their position as the nineteenth century progressed, serious economic decline would have set in far before it actually did. In fact many of them managed to maintain their position or even get richer. This was only possible if they were willing to look beyond the field and the plow to commerce and industry. Many historians believe aristocrats were either unsuited for this world or by entering it lost caste.[37] Indeed, members of the landed elite often said that they saw business as ignoble and demeaning. These assertions have led historians to assume commercially minded nobles were deviants or transients who shunned direct involvement. In Tolstoy's novel *Anna Karenina* Prince Oblonsky condemns being careful in business dealings. To the nobleman, a descendent of an ancient line, it was unaristocratic to lower oneself before others to gain wealth. Yet, the Prince chooses to do exactly this and enters into the world of business rather than service to the state in order to increase his income.[38] The unromantic realism of Tolstoy's observant eye teaches us to look at what aristocrats do and not at what they say.

In fact many aristocrats saw manufacturing as a beneficent activity that provided employment to the poor and prosperity for the nation, which accorded with their paternalistic ethos. They also developed a sophisticated awareness of the effect of interest on rents and the value of land, and understood their prosperity was intimately linked with the world of bankers and lenders. A "feudal" outlook as defined by Marxist terminology and so often assumed to have been the prevailing value system of the elite never really existed. Wealth created aristocracies and to live nobly over generations and to enhance a family's rank required substantial and increasing financial resources. This could be gained by marriage and the favor of sovereigns, but it was also earned the old-fashioned way by innovative exploitation of resources. Aristocratic entrepreneurship in metallurgy, colonial commerce, glassmaking, tax farming, mining, earthenware manufacturing, and dozens of other activities in the early modern period continued without a break into the twentieth century. Aristocrats suffered far less embarrassment and dissonance in their dual roles as bluebloods and capitalists than bourgeois historians have projected on to them.[39]

Commercial activity among the elite was not uniform. Within Germany, for example, it was the nobility of the southern and western regions who were most inclined to view trade and industry as unaristocratic. In the Rhine–Ruhr–Westphalian area landed proprietors played a modest role. However, some old princely families such as the Stolberg-Wernigerodes and Castell-Rüdenhausens profited from mines or invested in industry. So too did some of the Hessian knights, although most purchased land or bought government bonds with the redemption payments for feudal dues. In the south nobles who remained involved with iron and other industries did not do well. On the other hand, in Silesia the magnates operated profitably on a big scale and actively managed their businesses well into the twentieth century.[40]

Aristocratic involvement in business and industry took the form of exploitation of resources on individual estates and urban property, investment in larger enterprises, managing banking and commercial services, joining boards of directors, and promoting business interests as government ministers and military leaders. Bohemia was a particularly noted region for aristocratic involvement in commercial exploitation of estates and industrial development, but similar activities could be found in Transylvania, Russia, Italy, Spain, France, Sweden, Britain, and Prussia.[41] Famous names from Wallenstein and Rochefoucauld to Cavendish led the way. Prince Bismarck built lumber mills on his Varzin estate, established distilleries, gunpowder mills, and paper factories. He also bottled mineral water.[42]

Mining became a central preoccupation of hundreds of aristocrats across the Continent. Tuscan nobles could be found working deposits of iron, mercury, pyrites, lignite, and marble. The Russian Prince Demidov San-Donato received over ten million roubles profit from his mines between 1895 and 1901. In Silesia the Prince of Pless employed 8000 coal miners. Some members of the French elite managed mines directly while others such as Viscount de Hocquart and the Duke d'Aremberg served as company directors. D'Aremberg was one of the administrators of the Anzin coal company, which employed 4500 workers in 1830. The Marquis de Louvois constructed blast furnaces to produce high-quality iron in his château park.[43]

English law put fewer obstacles in the way of landowners developing subsoil wealth than was the case on the Continent.[44] The most dedicated entrepreneurial landowner in Lancashire in the nineteenth century was the 6th Earl of Balcarres. For 45 years he committed himself to a huge range of industrial and entrepreneurial enterprises, from coal and canals in Wigan and Wales to sugar in Jamaica. He wrote his son in 1822, "the basis of our fortune is our coal . . . we are and colliers we must ever remain."[45] The 3rd Marquis of Londonderry not only actively managed his coalfields that employed 2000 pitmen but also organized and built the harbor at Seaham in the 1820s and 1830s. His biographer noted that he "brought a passion for industrial activity into the affairs of his estates."[46] Other peers such as the Earls of Dudley, Dartmouth, and Bradford were equally active.

Large numbers of Swedish nobles continued their involvement in the iron-making business in the nineteenth century. Half or more of the country's ironworks were in the possession of landowner nobles. Iron production trebled between 1830 and 1870 and no less than four-fifths of the output in the late 1860s was exported, so they were accustomed to the need for salesmanship and efficiency in a competitive market.[47]

The Marquis de Louvois was also known for his keen interest in transportation technology. French nobles enthusiastically participated in the railway revolution both at home and abroad. Magyar aristocrats helped encourage the building of the railway network in Hungary that reached a density greater than that of Germany, Holland, or France. The investment of the 3rd Marquis of Stafford was critical to the opening of the first passenger line between Manchester and Liverpool in 1830. British peers of distinguished ancestry became the active managers of railroad companies.[48]

In Romania princely families such as the Bibescos came to rely mainly on revenues from a large cement factory for their income while the Ghika-Comanestri Prince in 1900 was becoming rich through possession of the Ploesti oil fields. The Youssoupoffs in Russia also had oil holdings on the Caspian Sea. In Spain even the Dukes of Alba and Sevillano and other grandees associated themselves with foreign capital to build railways and shipyards and to produce armaments.[49]

Aristocrats were particularly active all over the Continent in real estate development. Rising urban property values benefited the elite, who usually lived in the most desirable parts of large cities. Often no more than renting out storefronts at the street level of multi-story palaces was involved. By the 1890s commercial rentals could make up as much as half a Piedmontese aristocrat's income, twice or more the return on capital provided by rural estates. Some began to purchase additional commercial properties. Grand Russian families in St. Petersburg built apartment blocks in which they reserved a floor as their own residence and rented out the rest. Others such as Prince Beloselsky-Belozersky and Count Scheremeteff became real estate developers.[50]

The Dukes of Norfolk in Sheffield and the Lords Calthorpe in Birmingham became huge beneficiaries of urban rentals in provincial cities. Almost half of the Earl of Derby's titanic income in 1900 derived from rentals in and around Liverpool and Manchester. The Dukes of Medinaceli in Spain sold estates in Córdoba in the later nineteenth century in order to transfer wealth to urban properties and industry. The "black" papal aristocracy of Rome such the Princes Borghese held much of the land around the old city and successfully exploited the speculative opportunities in the capital's rapid expansion after 1870.[51]

Prince Clary developed his country seat at Teplitz in Bohemia into a popular spa during the later eighteenth century with hotels, bathhouses, and a theater, and the family continued to manage the enterprise into the twentieth century. Several Russian princes built resort hotels and subdivided plots on the Black Sea coast of the Crimea. The Dukes of Devonshire developed Eastbourne in the nineteenth century and the Earls De La Warr did the same for Bexhill-on-Sea in the twentieth. Lord Mostyn and his family played a key role as land speculators and developers of resort towns on the North Wales coast.[52]

Aristocrats not only pursued conventional industrial development in mines and forges but also contributed to entirely new sectors of development such as steamboats and gas lighting.[53] They were much taken with the advent of the automobile. Both in Turin and Paris ancient names became shareholders and directors of companies. Charles Rolls, younger son of Lord Llangattock, owned one of the first autos in Cambridge, became a car dealer in London in 1902, and raced as well. He formed a partnership with the engineer Royce in 1904, and then moved on to making airplanes before being killed in a flying competition. In 1899 Count Emanuele Cacherano di Bricherasio first proposed to his partner, Giovanni Agnelli, the idea of building a modern industrial complex to produce motorcars that became Fiat. The organizational meeting was held in the count's Turin palazzo, and he provided the land. Count Roberto Biscaretti di Ruffia was also a founding partner.[54]

In 1801 Count Hugo Salm-Reifferscheidt traveled to England and smuggled out a number of blueprints of spinning machinery obtained by bribery in order to establish a large textile-manufacturing firm in conjunction with some titled colleagues.[55] Prince Guido Henckel von Donnersmarck played an exceptionally active and enterprising role, expanding into a number of new spheres of industrial activity such as the manufacture of cellulose, wire, chrome, and paper, and he developed multi-national interests in Russia, Austria, France, and Italy.[56] A number of aristocrats were important inventors who went on to exploit the commercial possibilities of their ideas. Count Ferdinand Zeppelin created the first viable airships in his works on Lake Constance in southern Germany and in 1909 founded the first airline, which eventually established a trans-Atlantic service after the War. Charles Parsons, younger son of the Irish Earl of Rosse, invented and manufactured the steam turbine in 1884. The Count de Chardonnet developed a process to manufacture artificial silk, the precursor to modern rayon, and made a fortune. The Marquis de Dion built innovative automobiles.

Service on boards of directors of businesses became a common activity for aristocrats during the nineteenth century. In France men such as the Dukes de Gallièra, de Noailles, de Valence, and d'Albufera, along with many other titled nobles, served on a number of boards of large companies. By 1900 a substantial proportion of all boards of directors of railroads, steel, and banking firms were princes and counts from Vienna to Moscow. By 1910 half the English peerage were company directors.[57]

Some businesses paid for the use of aristocratic names to add respectability to their firms, and some poor noblemen leaped at the chance of adding to their income without effort. Others, however, were active businessmen. We have already noted that grandees were the managing directors of railway companies and coal mines. In the decade before 1914 the Baltic Baron Nicholas Wrangel was chairman of the large Siemens works in Russia. The Roman Prince Colonna headed the board of a large chemical company. The Genoese patrician Marquis Giacomo Durazzo Pallavicini presided over the boards of five industrial and real estate companies. In England one-quarter of landowners with landed incomes over £50,000 in the 1880s served as company directors. These were not men who needed fees to sustain their style of life. Far fewer board members were recruited among lesser landowners who could have used the money. Nearly a quarter (23 percent) of all British great landowner directors were chairmen or vice-chairmen of one or more companies.[58]

A unique feature of the Austrian credit system in the first half of the nineteenth century allowed members of the court aristocracy to sell partial amounts of their financial obligations to the public, just as the government did with public bonds. These "partial obligations" were backed by the state, and the system basically granted aristocrats the privilege of printing fixed amounts of currency.[59] Grandees were also not averse to joining as partners in important banks. The Princes of Fürstenberg, Schwarzenberg, and Auersperg and Count Choteck became founders of the great Viennese finance house of the Credit-Anstalt in 1855. Count Miroslav Kulmer founded a series of banks and served as President of the First Croatia Savings Bank. He became one of the most influential businessmen in the region in the early twentieth century. Dukes and marquises were among the leading figures in setting up French insurance companies.[60]

As industrialization progressed, opportunities to increase income tempted many aristocrats to invest windfalls from redemption of feudal dues and services and divert other resources to the stock market. Risks taken there were more manageable than sinking huge sums into one industrial project on a private estate, and diversification meant more reliable income protected from the price fluctuations affected by the vagaries of weather and availability of labor. Thus, progressively across the century and the continent the titled nobility became shareholders on a large scale. This process began earliest in Britain and Sweden and by the 1880s even the Baltic barons were shifting investments from land to urban industry and property. In Russia, where the value of agricultural land rose by over 600 percent in the 50 years after emancipation, many landowners sold off some or all of their land to pay off mortgages and to invest in other, more productive, sources. Great Roman landowners such as Prince Paolo Borghese and Prince Prospero Colonna also expanded their activities in the business world, to the extent that the bulk of their incomes came from non-landed sources by 1900.[61]

There were exceptions to this process. Piedmontese aristocrats owned relatively little besides property. Of the 59 greatest noble estates that passed through probate between 1862 and 1885, 44 contained no stock portfolio at all. Only after the agricultural depression at the end of the century did more families invest in stocks and bonds. Elsewhere in Italy, however, aristocrats began diversifying earlier. Prince Ommaso Corsini became heavily involved in railroad development, insurance, and high finance. This became the main source of family wealth after the Unification. By his death in the late 1870s the Florentine Baron Bettino Ricasoli left a third of his estate in stocks and bonds.[62]

Before 1800 much industry was rural and owned by nobles who were entrepreneurs and investors of capital. The Industrial Revolution changed this, making landowners only one element in a multi-faceted process of development. But we must guard against common assumptions such as aristocratic involvement being finicky and amateur. It is true that by the end of the nineteenth century, with notable exceptions, most coal owners and urban landlords no longer directly exploited their mines or developed their real estate.[63] The employment of leases and aversion to making the huge investments to capitalize modern mining operations does not, however, necessarily reflect diminishment in aristocratic enthusiasm for making money or being involved in commerce. They demonstrated shrewd business acumen in spreading risks and relying on the advice of experienced professional agents.[64]

The elite continued to pursue active management in other, innovative ways. In the first decade of the twentieth century Prince Lajos Windisch-Graetz, eldest son of a great Hungarian magnate, completed an engineering diploma in machine construction, and his father also arranged for him to work as a volunteer apprentice at the great Krupp works at Essen to learn about manufacturing first hand. He took a job for a time as a stoker and engine driver on the Austrian State Railways as part of his civil engineering course. The industrial activities near Penza, personally supervised by the Obolensky princes, at the turn of twentieth century employed about 2000 people. They made a huge variety of wares for customers as diverse as Fabergé and the Persian export market, as well as items for mass consumption in Russia. Just before the Great War Count Benckendorff was part owner of a platinum mine that produced half of the metal mined in the world. Prince Christian zu Hohenlohe-Oehringen stood among the largest titled industrial magnates in the German Empire. The Hohenlohe fortune was estimated at 150 million marks, with four-fifths invested in industry and only one-fifth in land. Fifty million marks were in the Hohenlohe-Werke AG, a coal and zinc complex founded by Prince Christian in 1905. A joint stock company formed by Count Stenbock in Reval in 1899 financed expanded cement production in the Baltics.[65]

Aristocrats also played a critical role in getting bills passed in parliament to facilitate exploitation of natural resources, building railways, and imperial expansion at a time when governments were still dominated by titled nobles. Aristocrats were also heavily involved in promoting manufacturing through the organization of events such as the Great Exhibition in London in 1851.[66] Swedish nobles such as Baron De Geer, who headed the government for many of the years between 1858 and 1880, and Baron Gripenstedt, Finance Minister from 1856 to 1866, strongly supported a free trade policy. Count Cavour in Piedmont was involved in railways and other business ventures and used his position as prime minister to further economic development both to modernize his country and strengthen the aristocracy.

Even after big projects became vastly expensive, some British grandees invested huge sums, often greatly enhancing the industrial infrastructure of the nation. Docks and harbors were built by the Dukes of Devonshire and Buccleuch and most famously in Cardiff by the Marquis of Bute. These ventures could be risky. The 3rd Marquis of Londonderry, who invested titanic sums, said that on one project he had "staked his life on a throw."[67] When it proved difficult to find the income grandees expected via royalties, families sometimes resumed direct management of mines and iron works, or they worked the thick seams and left others to develop the thinner deposits.[68] In Bohemia in the nineteenth century the great coal mines belonging to men such as Count Larisch and Baron Wilczek stayed in family hands. Three-quarters of the distilleries, two-thirds of the sugar refineries, and nearly 60 percent of breweries belonged to magnates in the late nineteenth-century. More than 400,000 Czechs worked for the Bohemian nobility.[69]

Many aristocratic enterprises remained small in scale and often became unprofitable.[70] The co-founder of Fiat, Count Bricherasio, was something of a dilettante who saw the car industry as an extension of his equestrian interests. By 1908 the aristocratic names on the board of directors of the Italian car company had disappeared.[71] Over time more and more non-nobles became leaders of the commercial and industrial world, while most active aristocrats either withdrew to more passive management or confined their activities to the development of resources and infrastructure rather than actual production.

It is well to remember, however, that many bourgeois businesses were small in scale and often went bankrupt. Many successful "new men" sold out when the going was good and withdrew to *rentier* status after becoming millionaires. The richest people in England, Austria, and Germany in the later nineteenth century were still the Duke of Westminster, the Prince of Liechtenstein, and the Prince of Pless, leaders of society from ancient families who captained giant business organizations. No one for a moment could mistake them for anything but quintessential aristocrats. They and their numerous cohorts cannot be bundled into some sort of "embourgoised" mish-mash. Indeed, income from business and industrial investments and royalties sustained the wealth and power of the grandees into the twentieth century at a level that enabled them to continue to live in grandeur.[72] What disappeared was their political influence, not their economic strength.

*   *   *

Aristocrats were fortunate to find new ways to increase their wealth during the nineteenth century because a variety of new threats to their economic well-being arose. Some historians have seen unmanageable indebtedness, for example, as becoming an ever-increasing danger. The requirement to spend lavishly was part of being noble. Even the fabulously rich Prince Esterházy got into serious financial difficulties in the 1860s due to excessive expenditure. He had to sell the family art collection to the National Museum to recoup. Spectacular bankruptcies took place where even the gold braid on the lackeys' liveries went on the block.[73] However, across Europe it was the gentry who found it difficult to sustain their positions and who became more sharply divided from the aristocracy. Hundreds of thousands of the lesser nobles in Eastern Europe, France, and Spain disappeared into destitution, urban professions, or extinction.[74]

State-funded credit institutions came to the rescue of the indebted elite; heavy borrowing could become a spur to regenerate economic practices. Many aristocratic families proved highly adaptable. Nor was spending heavily necessarily irrational or foolish. If rents were rising, if more land could be acquired by successful marriages, and if sustaining a splendid style of life helped gain access to the monarch and personal favors of offices and more land, it was a shrewd investment. Noble indebtedness seems to have been chronic throughout modern European history, and although individual families went under, the elite as a whole seems to have kept afloat rather well.[75]

Taxation also became a new and threatening burden on aristocratic estates that developed during the nineteenth century. Many countries had previously exempted nobles from some impositions. The value of land was often ignored entirely or subject to lower rates than other owners had to pay. It is a myth that nobles escaped from taxes altogether, but only in England did the elite pay higher percentages of taxation than their fellow countrymen. Rising poor rates and a new income tax began to make substantial inroads into landed incomes there after 1800. Expansion of the state and larger military budgets forced aristocrats into accepting higher taxes nearly everywhere. The movement towards social democracy was also costly to the elite. In countries where few people owned land, expansion of the electorate made estate taxes appear particularly attractive to many politicians. British death duties, levies on estates as they passed to the next generation, were introduced in 1894 and rose inexorably. World War I led to massive increases in taxation across the Continent. In 1870 the Scottish Marquis of Aberdeen paid £800 in annual estate taxes; in 1920 his bill was £19,000.[76]

Most serious of all threats to aristocratic finances arose from an unprecedented fall in world agricultural prices that took place between 1873 and 1896. Landowners whose income came mainly from cereal production were placed in serious jeopardy. Both contemporary observers and subsequent scholarly opinion have tended to view the Great Agricultural Depression as a watershed in the history of Europe's landed elites. From the grain regions of England to the Russian steppes, the structure of agricultural society was shaken, and the power and prestige of landowners undermined. The importation of cheap grains from overseas and improved rail connections that brought Canadian, American, and Russian wheat to ports led to an unprecedented and prolonged decline in farm prices. The bottom was reached in the 1890s, leaving many lesser nobles stricken. Heavily indebted grandees also suffered seriously, but they were few in number. The aristocracies in Europe did not sustain a fatal blow.

Some elites suffered more than others. In Ireland few landowners had much urban, industrial, or mineral wealth. Those who had survived the earlier disruptions to their income were now extremely vulnerable, facing a hostile London government and an embittered peasantry. The French nobility confronted not only the agricultural depression, but also the devastating spread of a disease of the vines, the great phylloxera infestation.

In Piedmont the crisis was serious but not catastrophic. Ownership of urban property helped a substantial portion of the elite weather the storm. Big landowners were initially protected from the effects of the price drops by their relatively long-term rental agreements. However, as leases expired, tenants dropped out and rates began to decline. The new agricultural tariffs imposed in 1887 protected cereal crops, sugar beets, and hemp largely at the expense of southern crops such as olive oil, wines, and citrus fruits. Duties on wheat quadrupled. Property taxes were reduced significantly, freeing capital for investments and improvements in the farms of the northern plains. The situation was initially extremely bad in the Baltic provinces, but the crisis encouraged more innovation and investment in cattle breeding, dairy, and timber for which expanding markets existed both at home and abroad. By 1900 half the manor income in Kurland came from forestry. Denmark shifted the weight of agricultural production from grain to dairy products in the 1880s. Livestock holdings quadrupled between 1860 and 1914.[77]

Those families that had followed a policy of diversification of assets found their incomes slightly down or unchanged. Only one-quarter to one-third of the great landowners of England derived most of their rents from the worst-hit grain-producing areas. Many converted arable land to grazing. Protective tariffs in France and Germany seem to have helped. The general fall in prices from the mid-1870s to the end of the century meant that even when rents went down they did not do so very much in real terms. Also by reducing estate expenditures large landowners could minimize the effect of falls in rents on their net incomes.[78] One estimate suggests that in England about 40 percent of the great landowners' income came from non-agricultural sources in the 1880s and 1890s. Urban rents, dividends, mineral royalties, and business investments kept most of the elite reasonably buoyant. The Duke of Bedford had an income of £234,856 in 1873 and £264,257 in 1895; by 1909 it was £313,369.[79] In Prussia sugar beet and spirits production greatly reduced the pressure on loss of income. In Spain, after the initial drop in agricultural prices, olive groves and vines replaced wheat over large areas. These required significant capital investment in production for national and international markets, and the aristocracy was in the forefront of this change.[80]

Aristocrats also owned libraries of rare manuscripts, jewels, tapestries, armor, silver, or other saleable assets such as art collections. These could be disposed of in a rising market. American collectors were beginning to haunt the salerooms and auction houses with near limitless credit. The great Spencer library of early printed books, collected by the 2nd Earl, was sold by the 5th for £210,000 to pay off debts and expand equities holdings. Aristocratic Roman families sold their archives to the Vatican.[81]

Land, however, was the principal asset of those in the deepest trouble, and they had to sell. In the Po Valley, nobles disposed of land to new commercial farmers. French estates were gobbled up by peasants with insatiable appetites to own land.[82] Irish Land Acts from the 1880s onwards precipitated large sales. On the eve of the setting up of the Irish Free State, over three-quarters of the acreage had been transferred from landlords to tenants. The Welsh elite also sold out.[83]

In England it was not until after Lloyd George's attacks on landed society between 1909 and 1911 that large numbers of estates were put on the market. The sellers included grandees who were not bankrupt by any means, such as the Dukes of Bedford and Sutherland. They were distrustful of the future, and some bought property overseas in Africa, Australia, Canada, and the United States. Not all sales of land to tenants were a sign of weakness. Some aristocrats consciously pursued a policy of divestment to build up a larger body of owners ready to defend rural values and property. Sales were also prompted by stability in the value of rents after 1910 at a time when prices were rising rapidly. In real terms by the end of the War rents may have been worth only half as much as they had been a decade earlier.[84] Dramatically better returns on capital tempted the elite to switch to bonds and shares.

Sales in Scotland gathered pace between 1910 and 1914. It is claimed that one-fifth of the country changed hands between 1918 and 1921.[85] However, in Scotland, like elsewhere, relatively few traditional estates were broken up completely. Moreover, in Sicily, the Dual Monarchy, Russia, and Hesse-Cassel, among others, aristocrats were often the purchasers as well as the sellers.[86] Much of the land given up by the lesser nobility fell into magnate hands. In Hungary the amount of acreage held by the aristocracy more than doubled in size between 1885 and 1914, while the gentry holdings declined by a third during the same period. Put another way, the magnates added territory the size of Connecticut and Massachusetts combined in a country the size of Nevada in less than three decades.[87] Extension of rights over common lands and purchase of forfeited land due to non-payment of taxes allowed very wealthy Sicilian landowners to increase and consolidate their holdings during the second half of the nineteenth century.[88]

An expert on the Piedmontese aristocracy believes that for a majority of the elite landed property remained its most important asset prior to World War I. In Russia the aristocracy was still largely composed of magnates with estates of many thousands of acres. Even after the abolition of primogeniture and entail the French and Spanish aristocracies remained rich. Few Hessian estates declined in size during the nineteenth century.[89] In Britain many aristocrats were far richer in 1914 than they had been in 1815.

On the other hand, the increasing commercialization of agriculture in the nineteenth century undermined the old forms of land tenure, transformed relations between landlord and peasant, and introduced a host of new stresses and strains into rural society. Changed agricultural practice could force the aristocracy to abandon paternalism. Rice cultivation in the Po valley, for example, required large-scale commercialized operations and replaced sharecroppers with landless day laborers on consolidated farms. The antagonistic labor structure was an ideal recruiting ground for radical organizers. Seasonal unemployment and pauperism spread, threatening revolution and even anarchy.[90] Similar flashpoints arose in Scotland and southern Spain. Boiling discontent was sometimes only restrained by the force of the state.[91]

All over France the increased mobility created by railways and urban growth upset traditional economic arrangements. The massive emigration from Sicily to North and South America began to give peasants an advantage on that island. When a strike was organized in 1901, they used the rallying cry: "Fair contracts or all to America!" The Prussian Junkers also saw their work force drain away; 1,904,000 people, mainly agricultural laborers, left the provinces east of the Elbe between 1885 and 1905, but the landowners were able to import massive numbers of Polish migrants to replace them.[92]

* * *

A call has gone out to revise our thinking on what constitutes "bourgeois capitalism" in the nineteenth century. Too much evidence now exists across time periods and countries to continue to see industrialization and modernization as a "middle class" phenomenon. Recent historians of the aristocracy argue that in Germany and elsewhere the landed elite made an early transition to the market economy and "nobles collectively exploited the opportunities offered by capitalism, but did so in a way that allowed them to protect and even promote their values and interests."[93] This was a specifically noble form of capitalism that sustained noble priorities.[94] The Prussian aristocracy was thoroughly committed to modernization and commercial agriculture and thus endured no serious economic crisis in the late nineteenth century.[95] We must find a new way to analyze the development of modernity.

Whatever was said, especially by decaying and desperate lesser nobles, aristocrats suffered no social penalties from engagement in business activities. Take, for example, Count George Hoyos, an Austro-Hungarian naval officer in the 1860s and scion of one of the great Viennese court families. He made friends with Robert Whitehead, the inventor of the first modern torpedo, married his daughter, and resigned from the service to become a partner in the Whitehead firm. His daughters married Count Plessen and Prince Herbert Bismarck, the Chancellor's son.[96] Such men and their families were neither "feudal" nor backward-looking. The painstaking study of estate archives begun in Britain by men such as David Spring and Michael Thompson more than half a century ago, and now being undertaken across the Continent, continues to reveal the subtle interplay of aristocratic values and entrepreneurship within the context of landed society. This work has yet fully to be integrated into the general understanding of modern European history.

This chapter has tried to show that the nineteenth-century European aristocracies were by no means unable to adjust to new economic circumstances, that they benefited financially from industrialization, and often led the way as entrepreneurs. They were adaptable and prudent. This was not a departure from previous practice but a long tradition among the top wealth holders. Even though some trends in the early twentieth century were flowing against them, they were by no means on their backs. Indeed most elites emerged from the Great Agricultural Depression at the end of the century in fighting trim. The changing economic position of landowners cannot be adequately described in terms either of decline or survival but rather of adaptation. We must look elsewhere for an explanation for decline.

4

FAMILY AND HONOR

[My father] would have shed his blood to spare his family grief, but rather than betray honour or duty he would have let us perish before his very eyes.

Marquis d'Azeglio 1868, in Marchese Massimo d'Azeglio,
Things I Remember, p. 5

The Dönhoffs originated in Westphalia during the thirteenth century and moved east with an order of Teutonic knights to Latvia in 1330. They lived in the region for 18 generations, establishing lines in Poland and East Prussia where the latter resided on their 15,000-acre estate at Friedrichstein until the house was destroyed by the Russians in 1945. One of the Poles became a cardinal and advisor to the Pope. Another was elevated to the rank of prince. Various members of the Prussian line served as ambassadors, generals, and ministers. One represented Prussia at the Peace of Utrecht. Another was a liberal Prussian delegate to the Frankfurt Assembly in 1848. His son was a diplomat in Vienna, London, and Washington. That count's eldest son was killed in World War II. His daughter, Marion, was an architect of postwar German journalism and became editor of the liberal weekly *Die Zeit,* among the country's most influential newspapers. She died in 2002, one of the last surviving associates of the "July 20th" plotters against Hitler.

Portraits and archives accumulated at Friedrichstein like coral on a reef, but it was not until 1859 that a family entailment was established. Count August Dönhoff wrote in the preamble:

I hope that the future proprietors will look on this endowment as
an abiding challenge and a debt of honor . . . and that they . . . will
pay serious heed to the preservation, improvement, and expansion
of the estate, to the suitable support of its widows and descendants, and to the accumulation of reserves to help out in times of
war and other calamities. I call upon the future trustees to remember that they, being relieved of the worry of supporting themselves, have a duty, if they are suited for it, to represent higher
interests, particularly the public concerns of the country.[1]

Family was at the heart of aristocratic life. The noble derived much
of his/her identity and immortality from lineage. The grander the
family, the more kin connections were acknowledged and supported;
the tighter cohesion remained. The dead, the living, and the yet
unborn constituted a "house." "Pride in race" or "family spirit" was
based on the living capital of kin and the belief that an honorable
past made the family distinctive and great.[2] This led to a constant
battle between the personal inclinations of individuals to live as they
pleased and the solidarity of the dynasty. Heads of families often had
control of most of the wealth but were expected to act as trustees for
the house. Aristocratic children were taught to reverence their ancestors and the historical myths that hired genealogists and family
hagiographers churned out in privately printed tomes. Nobles lived
in the sight of their forebears, and the portraits hanging on country
house walls testified that the country's history was *their* history.
"Already when I was eight or ten years old, I thirsted for news of our
ancestors," wrote the Piedmontese Marquis Mario della Rocchetta.[3]
He was building up vital memories that would sustain and govern
his whole life. Count Péter Esterházy, Hungary's most prominent
living novelist, repeatedly uses the term "my father" to describe his
ancestors over many centuries in a recent account of the great dynasty
from which he descends. Even in Soviet-dominated Hungary he grew
up aware of the significance and intricate connections of his family
tree.[4]

Vitally connected to family were notions of honor. The Baltic
baron, August von Kotzebue, instructed his descendants in 1850 as
follows: "My dear sons, explain to your children that no sacrifice is
too much to preserve the nobility of their mind and birth . . . Do not
taint the name of Kotzebue. . . . [My judgment in this] rests on a deep
feeling of lofty pride."[5] Aristocrats conceived themselves to be above

the rest of society because they were held to a higher concept of conduct. Only they had both the independence conferred by a landed property and the training and education to act unfalteringly on the battlefield or dueling ground. They fought, above all else, to preserve the honor of their family.

Signet rings, engraved silver, personal flags, livery for servants, coaches painted in a special hue with a coat of arms on the doors, and the family crest imprinted on tooled leather binders to hold family papers in muniment rooms formed both a material and cultural inheritance. These surroundings served as incubators for noble children that shaped them more powerfully than any tutor could do. Genealogical trees, family pews, family chapels, priests, and kin all promoted the cult of the lineage. Sometimes special characteristics such as an unorthodox religion or special party affiliation acted to supercharge already exclusive habits.[6] In Estonia, for example, virtually no marriages occurred between families with different allegiances in the Diet.[7] Being Montagus and Capulets added spice to aristocratic life.

* * *

Some courts, most famously that of the Habsburgs, required genealogical proof of noble descent on both sides of the family tree over numerous generations. In Portugal in the early nineteenth century noblemen of the longest and most unbroken descent were known as "the Pure" and did not intermarry with others.[8] The supreme duty of aristocrats was either to marry into a bloodline of comparable or of even greater distinction than their own or to make an alliance with a wealthy family that would further enhance the stability and power of the dynasty. Even in lineage-obsessed Vienna princesses carried around special memorandum books in which the incomes of prospective partners were listed.[9] The question landed ladies with daughters always asked in Jane Austen's novels was about income not acreage.

Marriage was a means of rapid social ascent. Modest gentry or lesser nobles who gained money or power through commerce or office could swing instantaneously to high places through one spectacular marriage or a series of well-plotted ones. Nothing allowed for more rapid blending into the established elite. Old families were consistently ready to marry beneath them for financial advantage.

Marriage for love was more likely to take place at the top of the hierarchy, while those still ascending guided their children's marital strategies.

During the early modern period virtually all noble marriages were either arranged or at least approved by the parents. Ideas of romance could cause tension between the family and the individual. The occasional daughter ran off with a footman or son with an actress, but these elopements usually ended in tears and even tragedy. Many partners were probably self-selected and marriages companionate from an early period.[10] In Prussia the father's absolute control over his children's marriages was only abolished in 1869, but by the nineteenth century parents were likely to retain only a right of veto on unsuitable relationships.[11] In 1829, when a Hessian noble father took steps to block his son's marriage to a bourgeois woman with no fortune, the youth retorted: "We love each other too deeply to ever consider breaking our vow. We would both be extremely unhappy, especially because my fiancée is expecting a baby in five months." The court ruled against the father.[12] Tradition and the threat of disinheritance, however, remained powerful weapons of coercion. Among the Baltic Germans legal provisions to cut a son out of the will also existed in cases of sexual relations with a stepmother or for joining a circus.[13]

Several spectacular royal misalliances led to sobering lessons for young aristocrats. Crown Prince Rudolf of Austria's love for a baroness ended in a murder-suicide at Mayerling in 1889, and his successor Archduke Franz Ferdinand's inappropriate infatuation with a mere countess was punished harshly by the Emperor. In some countries marrying within the magic circle of nobility was found most frequently among families with old pedigrees such as the leading Prussian Junkers, mediatized princes, and the provincial *noblesse* in France and Italy, who kept strictly to themselves until at least the latter part of the nineteenth century if not later.[14] Endogamy remained strong among the British peerage through the nineteenth century, actually rising slightly in the last decades among heirs to titles. On the other hand, old families in Russia were happy to marry commercial heiresses. In the eighteenth century French dukes and peers seem to have been more likely than lesser nobles to marry the daughters of great financiers.[15] In Sweden the rate of marriage among nobles to commoners rose in nineteenth century.[16]

* * *

Aristocratic women exercised power in a variety of spheres. They were often the arbiters of fashion and social acceptability, key aspects of aristocratic existence. Their role in the religious life of the family also gave them considerable leverage, and their lineage and wealth could make them as much sought-after by men as their intelligence or beauty. They also exercised patronage and supervised huge households. They were by no means hidebound and often were in advance of their husbands on issues such as smallpox inoculation, breast-feeding, and adopting liberal ideas of education.

The need to guarantee sons was the crucial mission for aristocratic women because of the laws governing the inheritance of titles and great properties, and because for so many families military service was a *sine qua non*. Women were also members of great dynasties, part of a team, with political and cultural traditions that were espoused by all members of the family. Public and private life for great families was interwoven in ways that make it very difficult to identify where one stopped and the other began. Women were active in both spheres.[17]

Quite sharp distinctions could be made between the interest of the family, understood in economic terms, and the interests of widows, whose expensive jointures were sometimes regarded as competition against necessary funding of the incumbent titleholder and the lineage.[18] In England in the eighteenth and nineteenth centuries a substantial portion of all estates among the elite passed via female inheritance: as high as nearly a third between 1760 and 1779 and never below a sixth until after 1840. When this happened, the family line was regarded as unbroken. If the woman married a man of lesser acreage he usually adopted her name, perhaps most famously in the case of the Smithson-Percy Dukes of Northumberland. Sometimes accumulations of estates and heiresses led to dizzying concoctions such as the Temple-Nugent-Grenville-Chandos-Lyttelton family. Re-creations of titles were common in England but also occurred in the Habsburg Empire and elsewhere. In Russia Prince Felix Youssoupoff's grandfather, Felix Elston, married Countess Soumarokoff, the last of her line, and the Tsar allowed him to take his wife's name and title. Their child, Count Soumarokoff, did a repeat performance with Felix's mother, Princess Youssoupoff, again switching names and

acquiring one of the great fortunes of Europe in the process.[19]
In Scotland, Spain, Sicily, and England, where medieval baronies,
special remainders, and other legal devices allowed direct female
succession to titles, entailed estates could pass directly to daughters.
In Spain women kept their patronymic and passed it on to their
children. Grandchildren had an equal claim to inheritance from
both parents. In Transylvania estates frequently passed through
female lines, which led to a high turnover of names. It was common
for daughters to inherit the father's property in Prussia if he was
without sons.[20] In Poland four women in succession owned the great
baroque country house at Wilanów during the eighteenth century.

Some aspects of the Enlightenment encouraged a greater appreciation of women's intellect and value as individuals in their own
right. The French Revolution left many women in charge of estates
while their husbands fled as émigrés. Reforms later gradually began
to improve the position of females with regard to property and
divorce. In Piedmont they clearly benefited from the new inheritance
laws modeled on those of the Napoleonic Code that guaranteed
that all legitimate heirs, including women, receive a share in the
legacy.[21]

In their second marriages, aristocratic women were often free to
espouse pretty much anybody they liked. Their jointures gave them
financial independence and sometimes they controlled their own
estates or those of their husbands when there was a minority. The
Duchess of Leinster ran into some social turbulence when she
married her children's tutor, but sailed through to family acceptance,
and similar other cases took place. Divorcées or those with outré reputations could also hold their own as famous hostesses and keepers of
salons, as the career of Lady Holland demonstrated. In Lutheran
areas divorce was not uncommon, although it aroused condemna-
tion.[22] The French Countess de Caraman-Chimay married Prince
Paul de Bauffremont in the 1860s and then fell in love with the
Romanian Prince George Bibesco. She moved to Germany, where
she was able to get a divorce, and headed for Bucharest with her new
partner whom she married in 1875. The French elite ostracized her
and her name was dropped from the Almanach de Gotha, but she held
sway successfully in her adopted country.[23]

As the nineteenth century progressed, noblewomen demanded
more respect, marital harmony, and some degree of independence
framed in the contemporary language of femininity, which meant

no expectation for marital equality.[24] Aristocratic women also began to publish their memoirs, which not only revealed their participation in politics (to be discussed in Chapter 8), but also presented them as active and intelligent commentators on their times. The British elite produced a long line of spirited and adventurous women exploring uncharted territory at home and abroad, stretching from Lady Mary Wortley Montagu and Lady Hester Stanhope to Daisy, Countess of Warwick. The wives of Russian "Decembrists," such as Princess Volkonsky, made the voluntary choice to follow their husbands to Siberia. Princess Pauline de Broglie scared off suitors with her scientific interests and "talking about dinosaurs."[25] A widowed Baltic baroness could not be forced, even by her adult children, to proceed to the partition of her husband's property until she chose to do so.[26]

The most frequent job imposed on aristocratic women was to oversee households. These could include a great town palace, where political entertaining of the first importance took place, and the management of at least one and sometimes a number of country houses, often located hundreds of miles apart. The complexity of this task could well form the basis of a modern MBA program. They employed hundreds of people, both men and women, to say nothing of looking after thousands of dependent villagers. They also supervised the annual purchase or manufacture and consumption of resources that on large estates would be now be valued in millions of dollars.[27]

In Russia there was no common property. Spouses were not likely to inherit from one another since both men and women tended to leave the bulk of their property, real and personal, to their children. Husbands often took over the management of their wives' estates, but their property and their incomes remained entirely separate.[28] In Naples widows had full control over dowry management and were a formidable force in the world of Neapolitan finance.[29] Women also achieved leadership in philanthropic activities and supervised the education of their children. The upbringing of sons who were destined for national leadership was of concern to the larger "house" and even the government.

Of course, there were plenty of flibbertigibbets in the aristocracy, among both men and women. Undoubtedly, many parents ill-prepared their daughters for large responsibilities. The education of noblewomen was almost always confined to the home and conducted by governesses of varying quality. Unlike middle-class women, however, among the aristocracy this education almost always involved the mastery of one or more foreign languages, and opportunities of being included in stimulating company and enjoying foreign travel gave even poorly educated women a chance to expand their horizons. The young Countess Marion Dönhoff was irked by her mother's contention that scholarly books were too difficult for women to understand. "The fact that some of our female visitors were unable to decipher railroad timetables filled me with shame."[30] However, she went on herself after the Great War to complete a PhD, as did Princess Pauline de Broglie. The Mitford sisters, daughters of Lord Redesdale, were largely educated at home during the 1920s, yet three of them went on to celebrated careers as writers of fiction, history, and journalism.

Families considered it essential to ensure the legitimacy of the firstborn son and preferably the second as well. This required female virginity upon marriage. After the "heir and spare," liaisons outside marriage were increasingly acceptable. Men, of course, were always free to engage in extramarital affairs with both women of their own level and courtesans. The French Count de Greffulhe lavished his attentions on a bevy of beauties, a veritable harem, which he visited daily. His horses stopped of their own accord on the Paris streets where his ladies awaited him.[31] During the eighteenth century fertility among aristocratic women began to decline while at the same time maternal mortality dropped significantly. By 1900, they had fully gained control over their fertility and also over their fortunes. The decline in the number of children was probably due in part to economic changes, and to anxiety over an unknown future in which parents hoped to offer better opportunities to fewer children. In countries where only males could inherit estates, this trend led to more and more extinctions of titles. Piedmont suffered a demographic crisis at the end of the nineteenth and beginning of the twentieth century.[32] Everywhere old families declined more rapidly in numbers than ever before, and replacements came at varying rates depending on royal beneficence.

*   *   *

Historians have argued that from the mid-eighteenth century onwards attitudes towards children changed. They were less likely to be treated as miniature adults. Parents became more indulgent and sentimental, and more respectful of the individual. The influence of Rousseau was considerable. The Duchess of Leinster, mother of 19, went so far as to try to hire the *philosophe* as a tutor for her children in 1766.[33] In Russia by the second quarter of the nineteenth century a more "modern" and "Western" conception of the family – humane, more indulgent, and less authoritarian – was on the horizon.[34] The extent to which these changes were as significant as some believe them to have been is open to debate. In nineteenth-century France nobles retained a very formal structure to the family. Little of the supposed intimacy and informality penetrated Piedmontese or Prussian titled families either. Children were treated with strict discipline and austerity, and their lives remained dominated by deference, patriarchy, and fear.[35]

Many aristocrats received much of their early education from servants and estate workers, who were often remarkable and devoted people. Boys hammered and sawed with carpenters in the workshop, girls made soup in the kitchens, both loved the stables. Marion Dönhoff remembered: "Our sense of responsibility grew out of our sense of community. The village children were our playmates; besides the workmen didn't treat us with kid gloves and had no compunction about blaming us for broken windowpanes or missing tools."[36] The chauffeur showed her how to take a carburetor apart. They were often mounted at an early age on large and temperamental horses that required courage and mastery to control and subjected the children repeatedly to violent and painful falls from which they were expected to pick themselves up and remount. Aristocratic children were also taught to carry and fire guns from an early age. Rough games led to broken limbs. For boys, brutal boarding schools and military academies took them away from home as early as age seven or eight.

Spartan conditions usually prevailed in the upper floors of country houses. Temperatures could be cool and the food frightful. Stories of gothic horror that could include starvation and beatings are prevalent in the literature of aristocratic childhoods. However, memoirs also mention protective and nurturing servants. Members of the elite often remained devoted to their nannies. Winston Churchill's nurse was one of the most deeply loved persons in his life.[37] The fact that most aristocrats did not grow up in luxurious circumstances, were often starved of parental love, and roamed country estates like feral animals, left a mark. Their frequent contact with servants and villag-

ers gave them insights into the lives of ordinary people that few
children from prosperous families today receive.

One of the distinguishing features of the English aristocracy as
opposed to Continental ones was "ease of exit." Younger sons and
their descendants simply drifted off and disappeared unless they had
the wit or luck to gain landed property of their own.[38] In the century
before 1850 the Church and the army remained the principal career
choice for the younger sons of peers and baronets, although some
went into the law and even business. The expansion in size of armies
eventually provided many opportunities for younger sons, and a
wider range of career choices gradually became open to them.

Downwardly mobile cadets also existed in other parts of Europe. In
the Baltic provinces and Germany. Itinerant noble cousins without
means moved from house to house providing amusement and good
stories in return for hospitality. Obscure kin and hangers-on collected
like barnacles in Russian country houses. The supervision of large
estates in Poland and Hungary often fell to junior kin. In Russia and
Prussia the civil service and military were usually the only options for
younger sons other than estate management. Fifty members of Estonia's
prolific Wrangell family (almost 100 percent of its male members)
served as officers under Tsars Alexander I and Nicholas I.[39] Similar
numbers accrued among the Junkers in Prussia. Clerical careers were
rare on the Continent unless boys were fast-tracked for bishoprics or
the Papal curia. In Lutheran and Orthodox countries it was also
extremely unusual for younger sons to enter the Church. Among
princely families everywhere career options were very limited. Prince
Hubertus Löwenstein was told by his father: "A gentleman is either a
diplomatist or an army officer, or merely himself."[40] In France nobles
were increasingly drawn into government administration. Aristocrats
also went off to the colonies, and medical practice eventually became
respectable.[41]

The problem for younger children was caused by the systems of
inheritance devised by European aristocracies. The eldest son usually
won the jackpot, leaving his siblings out in the cold. The vagaries of
life guaranteed genealogical conundrums, made more complex by
the labyrinthine systems by which titles descended. Love for daughters was pitted against honor. Parents wanted to provide generously
for their children even if they had no son, yet the estates might have
to pass to a remote kinsman because he was the successor to the
family name. If each generation took away an equal piece of the land,

even the greatest patrimonies could be reduced to modest holdings. As in so many other respects, the radical steps taken to ensure continuity and protection of status were easier for aristocrats to take than gentry or lesser nobles because they had greater resources, both to pay legal fees and to distribute wealth among their children. This meant that titled families became virtually indestructible, given sufficient time to generate cadet lines and the connivance of the crown. On the other hand, impoverishment of the lesser nobility in countries such as Poland and Hungary, where only the magnates used entails, was largely due to sons dividing up the patrimony and the custom that a quarter of the estate was given to daughters.[42]

The ethos of "family" characterized by emotion and sentiment threatened the previously dominant role of dynastic interests. The Milanese nobility, for example, was unable to sustain the practice of celibacy for younger sons into the modern era. In the late seventeenth century the rate was 56 percent whereas in the late nineteenth century it stood at 11.5 percent. In Piedmont *c*.1900 dynastic interests were increasingly sacrificed to individual rights.[43] The future health of the aristocracy appeared to be endangered by a loss of will.

* * *

Two solutions to protect patrimonies had arisen over time: primogeniture and entail.[44] The first meant that the eldest son inherited the bulk or all of the estates, and the second that he became a life tenant, unable to sell the property even if he accumulated large debts through incompetence in the management of his property or incontinence with money. The laws governing inheritance varied from region to region. Pre-revolutionary France had seven different systems within its own borders, ranging from strict primogeniture to equal inheritance. In Romania entailment was unknown while in other countries entailment was practiced but not primogeniture. Even within the small world of the Baltic provinces serious differences arose between Estland, Livland, and Kurland relating to laws of inheritance.[45] Important distinctions arose across Europe that tell us a great deal about the importance and survival of "pride in race" and vital memories.

Several devices softened the harsh practice of primogeniture. The dowry and marriage contract gave parents the opportunity to settle some wealth on daughters and ensure their position if widowed. Even where her property became the husband's on marriage, provisions were often made to guarantee income controlled specifically by her.[46] Younger sons were usually given the best education available to fit them for a career. Capital sums derived from savings or mortgages on parts of the estate kept out of entail were also settled on them. For the most part children cast out of the inner circle of aristocracy were raised to understand why only their eldest brother could continue to live lavishly. As late as 1920, when this happened to Marion Dönhoff, it is clear she had taken her ancestor Count August's dictat to heart: "It would not have occurred to any of us [six siblings] to criticize or even in our minds fault the arrangement that discriminated against the younger descendants. We were proud to call [Friedrichstein] our home, and we knew that it could never have been preserved had the heirs been free to divide it."[47] When families had not been granted entails by the monarch or where primogeniture was not legally sanctioned, which became prevalent after 1815, aristocrats still strived to mitigate the effects of partible inheritance and favor the title-bearer. Subsequent modifications in the Napoleonic-style codes adopted in many countries permitted one heir to be favored.

Entail, the second mechanism designed to preserve aristocratic estates, arose in the Mediterranean region during the later Middle Ages. It spread raggedly across the Continent until almost every country practiced some form of it. In Poland only a few magnates adopted the device until the nineteenth century. In Westphalia, the Baltic provinces, Prussia, Hungary, and Scotland a spurt of legal settlements of estates took place during and after the French Revolution.[48] France and Russia instituted new systems exclusively reserved for the high aristocracy.[49] The English "strict settlement" was unusual. It was not perpetual but only involved three generations vesting property in trustees. A new settlement had to be reached periodically. Provisions for younger children were also made even if their number and gender was as yet unknown. However, the system worked to reduce greatly the chances of female inheritance.[50]

Because in many cases only large landowners tended to employ entail, the proportion of land in a given country held under such restrictions could be relatively modest. The figures in the second half of the nineteenth century or early twentieth century ranged from up to or more than half the land in Scotland and Tuscany, a bit less than that in Hungary and Bohemia, a third in Galicia, one-tenth or so in

Austria, the Baltic, and Denmark, and about 7 percent in Prussia (although in Junker provinces such as Pomerania it could be as high as 15 percent). If only the land owned by magnates is considered, the British had the most extensive system of entailment by the mid-century, followed closely by the Poles and Hungarians, where the rate stood as high as 80 percent.[51]

Some historians and contemporaries assume that by tying up estates in entails landowners lost the flexibility to change agricultural practices to keep up with the times.[52] It is true that perpetual settlements made it more difficult to sell land to raise capital for improvements, such as irrigation projects, drainage, and purchase of machinery. Owners could appeal to monarchs, however, to disentail a portion of the estate if capital was needed for useful purposes. Blocs of land were also often kept out of entail in order to invest in agricultural innovation or business ventures. The argument that the system somehow discouraged innovation does not accord with the record of agricultural practice on great estates in the nineteenth century discussed in the previous chapter. Moreover, primogeniture and entail along with astute marriage alliances could double or triple a family's landed possessions over several centuries.[53] On the other hand, failure to embrace them could result in disaster. The death of the French dowager Duchess de Choiseul-Praslin in 1861 led to the division of a great patrimony among 16 heirs. The celebrated château of Vaux-le-Vicomte had to be sold.[54]

Gradually entails were abolished or severely modified as the egalitarian and progressive ideals of the Enlightenment and French Revolution spread after 1815. Spain and Portugal began the process in the 1830s. Other countries such as France, Denmark, and Italy followed.[55] The aristocracy, however, had success in overcoming the problem of fragmentation. The law allowed the favoring of one child, who, in a family of four, might receive three-quarters of the estates.[56] The group that benefited the most from land that came on the market due to disentailments in Spain was the old landowning elite. Also Spanish aristocrats augmented their patrimony through buying Church lands that were forcibly sold at the same time as entails were ended. *Grande* estates were inheritable in the female line, which led to the gargantuan growth in size of the great lineages. In the mid-nineteenth century the Duke of Osuna (who had absorbed the estates and titles of the Dukes of Lerma, Estremera, Infantado and numerous others) received 22 percent of all noble revenues in Spain. In

1902 the 10th Duke of Berwick, who was also the 17th Duke of Alba and 13th Count-Duke of Olivares, was a title-bearer of Spain 13 times over. The removal of entail thanks to the liberal revolution made most of the *grandes* richer and encouraged slow but steady growth in the agricultural sector during the nineteenth century through to 1931, although at the cost of great suffering among the peasants.[57]

The revolutionary decade of the 1790s witnessed at least some examples of the breakdown of family solidarity when new inheritance laws allowed previously debarred individuals from claiming shares. After entails were abolished continued concentration of estates in the hands of title-holders required an unparalleled degree of self-sacrifice and voluntary obedience to the family spirit.[58] On the whole, traditional kinship loyalties appear to have worked fairly effectively as substitutes for legal devices. However, it also helped to have a small number of male children. The formalism of French and Piedmontese aristocratic life gave backbone to dynastic economic strategies. However, as the nineteenth century progressed signs of decay appeared, especially among the Napoleonic nobility.[59] Younger sons and daughters were less inclined than their predecessors to renounce the pleasures of domestic life for the sake of the lineage. In the late nineteenth and early twentieth century a serious drift away from primogeniture began. In Britain the Settled Land Act of 1882, which for the first time made it possible for the life tenant of a landed estate to dispose of land like other forms of capital, marked a major symbolic turning point in the transformation of landownership into simply another form of business enterprise, though family solidarity remained intense among the members of the great aristocratic houses.[60] France finally ended the last vestiges of entail in 1905 and Germany in 1938.[61]

* * *

The celebrated Danish writer Baroness Blixen (Isak Dinesen) saw aristocrats as untamed, spontaneous, generous, virile, courageous, and honorable.[62] These characteristics of the warrior derived from the Middle Ages, the aggression of the soldier moderated by the cult of chivalry. In modern times predefined models of behavior are considered restrictions on the expression of individuality. In aristocratic societies strict codes of honor were the normal practice and considered necessary to maintain social equilibrium.[63] Burke and

Tocqueville among others believed that aristocrats embraced a code of behavior that guaranteed civilization. The system that encompassed religion and respect for education controlled excess and preserved learning and taste.[64] Service, fidelity, and honor were at the heart of the aristocratic ethos, and honor was supreme among those qualities. A prewar Austrian nobleman, wrote the novelist Joseph Roth, "would have been less shaken by the news of a sudden death of his only child than by the news of even a seemingly dishonorable action of that only child."[65] On his deathbed a nineteenth-century Marquis de Villeneuve-Trans urged his son "to have always in his mind the memory of his ancestors, great by faith and by their chivalrous devotion to France, to always carry in a worthy way a name illustrated by so many generations."[66] Aristocrats conceived themselves capable of being better governors than people from other walks of life because of their conception of honor.[67]

Aristocratic life in the Middle Ages involved constant risk of death while engaging not only in war but also tournaments and the hunt for large and dangerous wild animals. War and dueling, the modern equivalents of jousts, lingered long after plate armor became decorative. Distinctive customs and rituals enhanced the stature of the nobility and separated it from the rest of society. Elaborate coming-of-age celebrations, participation in coronations, wearing of uniforms and gala dress, grand funerals, and chivalric orders characterized aristocratic life. The last of these were greatly reverenced. Every court had at least one: the improbable Elephant of Denmark, the St. Andrew of Russia, the Thistle of Scotland. The Order of St. George in Russia and of Maria Theresa in Austria conferred automatic ennoblement on those who received it. Some ribbands became debased because of too frequent conferral. Victor Emmanuel II of Italy liked to say that there were two things he never refused: a good cigar and the Order of St. Maurice.[68] The top orders were old and prestigious. Hermann Göring lusted after the Italian Order of the Assumption with the same ferocity with which he looted Rembrandts; the Garter was Britain's reward to Winston Churchill for winning World War II.

To appear as if not to care what things cost and to be unstintingly hospitable were ways to assert honor. In fact, careful calculation was often secretly indulged in this process, but even misers unbelted with gusto at critical moments. Accounts of such liberality make our toes curl, but to assume aristocratic actions were irrational and imprudent is anachronistic. As a landowner notes in *Anna Karenina*: "To live with largesse is a nobleman's business, which only noblemen know how to do."[69] To own a country house with more rooms than one could count was part of the show. The Prince of Lampedusa described the great house at Donnafugata as "the perennial expressed in stone and water, time congealed."[70] The austere grandeur of Holkham, the serene beauty of Friedrichstein, and the bold thrust across the river at Chenonceaux were majestic assertions of the aspiration for honor and the family's devotion to the ideal. The long enfilades of state rooms were aisles for the rituals of deference and condescension. Nobles tended to preserve older aspects of châteaux when rebuilding because medieval towers and moats emphasized connections with the past. When a family with two seats encountered economic difficulties, abandonment to decay of one of the houses was more common than sale.[71]

Houses and the associated activities of entertaining, hunting, and adding wings could consume lots of money in a flamboyant way, but nothing provided that combination of danger, expense, and living by a code of honor better than gambling. Today we see such behavior as a disease like alcoholism, for which counseling and medical treatment should be prescribed. Nobles, on the other hand, exulted in the opportunity to demonstrate nonchalance, self-control, and coolness under fire. The novelist Count Miklós Bánffy captured the essence of aristocratic gambling in this passage describing the values upheld in a Budapest nobleman's club at the turn of the twentieth century:

> in that world the gambler was the true master, the hero whom everyone respected. And how should it be otherwise? The man who can say the little word *banco* and thereby risk thousands of crowns . . . what gesture can be more lordly than that? *Banco!* Everything was in this one word – superiority, will power, calmness, the capacity to make quick decisions, courage and, of course, contempt for the vileness of mere money. And more than that this little word could be uttered with indifferent abandon, with carelessness and style, the more the speaker was obviously a superior being.[72]

The most conspicuous way to revel in the cult of honor was by fighting a duel. Hunting and steeplechase races provided thrills and public affirmation of disregard for death, but for nineteenth-century aristocrats the duel was a badge of honor, an assertion of unique pre-eminence. It required both skill and courage and was a powerful incitement to action "as eager as hunger or lust."[73] The participant risked not just ruin but death.

The vicissitudes of the duel illustrate the wide variations in aristocratic life that could be found across the Continent. In France and Germany the practice became so common that even ordinary tradesmen and socialist politicians were slashing and shooting at each other by the 1830s. This can be attributed to aspiring bourgeois laying claim to social recognition, new conceptions of masculinity, and perhaps efforts to reconcile the mixed heritage of the *ancien régime* and the French Revolution.[74] Ironically, it was the British aristocracy's desire to appear more respectable to a widening electorate that led to the decline of dueling in England and Ireland. The last important clash took place in 1829 between the Earl of Winchelsea and the Duke of Wellington, while the latter was serving as prime minister. The practice disappeared altogether by the 1840s. In France, on the other hand, General Boulanger and Prime Minister Floquet fought a duel with swords in 1888.[75]

Much dueling bore no resemblance to a life-and-death struggle. University fraternities provided members with little scars like "school ties that could never be taken off."[76] The Germans regarded dueling in the Third Republic as something of a joke because of its low fatality rate, while the number of actual deaths in Italy was also small.[77] Transylvanian noblemen fought with swords washed in antiseptic by doctors who applied protective bandages before the fight. The sight of a drop of blood finished the affair.[78] This was the harmless butting of sea elephants without the grunting.

German officers, however, shot at each other using pistols with much higher rates of mortality. A tiff at lawn tennis at The Hague in 1892 led to a duel with pistols between the secretary of the German Embassy, Baron von Gärtner-Griebenow, and the secretary of the Spanish legation, the Marquis de Vallarda. The Spaniard fired into the air, while the German aimed at and wounded the Marquis. Most duels in the early twentieth century were fought between military officers, egged on by the German, Russian, and Austrian emperors. Those who refused to fight were hounded out of their regiments.[79] In 1908 Prince Nicholas Youssoupoff, the heir to one of the greatest fortunes in Russia, was killed in a duel with pistols at 20 paces by

Baron von Manteufel, a Lieutenant in the Horse Guards. The Hungarian Minister, President Count Tisza, was a frequent duelist. In the spring of 1914, when political tempers were fraying fast, he received an almost endless series of challenges. He even fought the former Speaker of the House.[80]

Serious dueling went on among aristocrats until the blood bath of World War I made the practice seem meaningless. But as late as 1937 a Prussian nobleman regretted the 1918 ban on dueling: "there has come about a complete bolshevisation of all standards of honour, and . . . a man's good name has become free game."[81] Hitler and Mussolini encouraged dueling, but most noblemen did not regard the "honor" of fascist elites worth fighting over. Only Hungary, still dominated by aristocrats after the war, legalized the practice again in 1930.[82]

*   *   *

It was no accident that dueling survived longest among military officers. Only in the armed services has self-sacrifice and the disdain for mere wealth remained potent in modern societies. War, in a sense, was a duel between kings. Honor was tested and displayed most fully on the battlefield. Other than landownership, the most common attribute of aristocrats was participation in war: making plans in the Cabinet Room and offering their bodies to danger. Nowhere did the new egalitarian and democratic spirit arising in the eighteenth century seem more greatly to endanger the traditional aristocracy than in their role as soldiers.[83] The scale of modern armies required far more officers than aristocracies could supply. The declining use of horses and the advent of barbed wire, machine guns, and poison gas seemed to render irrelevant the importance of individual acts of heroism.[84] Some aristocrats simply could not adapt to the requirements of modern warfare. In 1914 the Russian General Prince Dolgorouky insisted that his regiment not conceal themselves under fire, yelling: "The Chevalier Guards do not lie down!"[85]

However, Michael Geyer argues: "we cannot assume that military professionalism and aristocratic privilege were antithetical."[86] In the two centuries before 1789 many changes had taken place in the conduct of military operations. Rather than threatening the role of the aristocracy, they probably enhanced it. After 1815 more sophisticated command structures created new career hierarchies. As in so many areas in the early modern period, aristocrats demonstrated the ability to adapt in order to retain their disproportionate pre-eminence in society.[87]

Aristocrats were often raised in an intensely military environment. The leader of the militant nationalists in Austria in the 1930s, Prince Starhemberg, recollected that the only adults he came into contact with as a child were, "my father's brother-officers and relations, who held the same views as my father." He went on:

> In the old castle where we lived . . . a long vaulted passage led to our nurseries. It was hung from one end to the other with scenes depicting the military history of Austria, past and present. There were paintings and engravings of old-time battles, portraits of Austrian generals and of military leaders in the days of the Holy Roman Empire, including numerous Starhembergs. Rows of colored plates showed the uniforms. Facings and badges of the different imperial regiments from earliest days to the present time. Best of all was a series of gaily colored pictures, called "The Golden Book of the Army," illustrating notable exploits of Austrian officers, N.C.O.s and men in wars of bygone days, with notes designed to impress these events upon the memory and inspire enthusiasm in Austrian boys. We knew these texts by heart before we could read or write. . . . Often we would slip into the armoury with its collections of old family armour and weapons of all ages. . . . When I was given a toy railway, I used it solely for the transport of my tin soldiers.[88]

Some military academies, founded in many countries during the seventeenth and eighteenth centuries, were exclusively reserved for boys of noble descent. Blue bloods dominated the intake of most. The Corps de Pages in St. Petersburg only admitted the grandest families while in England the Whigs abolished scholarships at Sandhurst in 1838 on the grounds that it was unwise to have officers without independent means.[89] The Schwerins of Pomerania had 280 officers in their genealogy. Among the von der Goltz family between 1800 and 1925, 44 percent of the male members were active officers, including 43 generals.[90]

Not every aristocracy had a military tradition. The Sicilian nobility was notably averse.[91] Much of the old Austro-Hungarian aristocracy withdrew from active army careers during the eighteenth century.

The use of *Du*, an intimate form of address, rather than the more formal *Sie*, came into general use among officers after 1849. Thus even a Jewish reserve lieutenant (in private life a shopkeeper) was on an equal footing with a prince or count. This contrasted strongly with Prussian practice. During World War I, the custom resulted in so many painful incidents between allies that officers from the Dual Monarchy had to be forbidden to introduce themselves to their German colleagues when they shared the same railroad compartment.[92] In Spain also, the *grande* families largely withdrew from active military command during the second half of the nineteenth century.[93]

As the size of military establishments expanded and then exploded during the second half of the nineteenth century the presence of aristocrats diminished. However, the nobility retained great influence if not dominance over both the values and the command of armies until 1914. This was because they served in hugely disproportionate numbers in the elite regiments closely associated with the court and monarch, were promoted to staff positions and high ranks in very large numbers, especially as generals of divisions and field marshals, and because their ethos and conception of honor was hardwired into the military structure of education and training. The great armies of Europe trundled into World War I with royalty and aristocrats in key positions of command. Some of this was for show. Crown Prince Rupprecht of Bavaria had a very able staff that made most of the decisions as his army pushed into Lorraine in September 1914. However, the strategic plan had been devised by Count von Schlieffen and was under the overall command of Count von Moltke, working generals. At the outbreak of war in 1914 all commanders of the 18 Prussian and German army corps came from the ranks of the nobility.[94] Grand Duke Nicholas was fully in charge of the Russian army. Count von Spee commanded the German High Seas Fleet; the British First Sea Lord (the operational head of the Royal Navy) in 1914 was Prince Louis of Battenberg.[95] Such men were members of the last generation that fully embodied the conceptions of honor that we have discussed in this chapter, and they expected that most of those who were close to them and led their divisions and battle squadrons should as much as possible be people like themselves.

Data from various countries are hard to compare concerning the proportion of army officers who were aristocrats. Most studies include all nobles in the count. Using that broad category, we can say that after 1850 no army was led by an officer corps that was mainly composed of nobles. Prussia had been early in the nineteenth century, but less than a third of officers were still drawn from the patriciate in 1914. On the other hand, the French military leadership was only one-quarter noble in 1825, and one in ten on the eve of the Great War. Only the British army, because it remained small, was dominated throughout the century by "landed" officers, many of whom, however, were from modest gentry backgrounds.[96]

Among the higher ranks, colonels and generals, nobles formed a much larger share of officers across the Continent. These figures could reach 80 to 90 percent in the most elevated categories, although in Russia and Austria automatic ennoblement came as one neared the top.[97] Even in Republican France a sizeable proportion of generals remained noble as 1914 approached.[98] During the Franco-Prussian War of 1870 the young Marquis de Castellane, who had no military training, joined up and was immediately given seniority because of his status.[99] The Marquis de Chasseloup-Laubat headed the commission to reorganize the army the following year, after the disastrous defeat by Prussia. In many countries, however, such as Spain, Britain, Sweden, and Italy, much lower proportions of nobles became members of the military elite.[100] In every country aristocrats maintained a visible and influential position even in mass armies by clustering in special cadet corps and "guards" and cavalry regiments, elite units closely associated with the monarch and carefully tended by grandee colonels and generals.[101] When a detachment of the British Household Cavalry reached Egypt in 1882, every officer was a peer, or a peer's son.[102] Other nobles took to the air instead of staying grounded in guards units. Among the famous aces of the First World War were Baron von Richthofen and Count Leopold Fugger von Babenhausen while Prince Heinrich von Sayn-Wittgenstein shot down 83 Allied planes in the Second.[103]

*　*　*

The traditional conception of honor became seriously dislocated in the eighteenth and nineteenth centuries. Forces antithetical to it – nationalism, evangelical religion, and above all the spirit of egalitarianism – corroded or challenged the aristocratic ethos. Napoleon redefined honor for his officers as a "reasoned bravery achieving outstanding feats for the sake of the community."[104] Honor could not

remain the principal shibboleth of a single class pitted against powerful new forces. Napoleon's conception of service to the community
blended potently with the rise of a new nationalism. Aristocrats
either endorsed this spirit and thus lost their identity in the mass of
their fellow countrymen or resisted submersion only to be swept aside
by the flood.

The Enlightenment helped reshape the matrix of qualities that
formed the aristocrat's self-image. In the 1840s the Baltic Baron von
Foelkersahm wrote: "Worth comes not from the rights that a person
exercises, but from the duties he imposes on himself."[105] The egalitarian emphasis on measurement by merit could and was successfully
embraced by many aristocrats, but it undermined their sense of
special status. Strict religious values revived among the elite both
before and after the shock of the French Revolution. Evangelical
emphasis on respectability militated against extravagance, promiscu-
ity, dueling, and gambling: no fun and no honor![106]

Titles had always been used to reward meritorious service, but
during the *ancien régime* most honorifics had been conferred purely
to recognize landed wealth and power. The comparatively small
number of such awards kept aristocracies exclusive. In the nineteenth century a double attack was launched. First, more and more
titles were granted solely on the grounds of service. In 1902 King
Edward VII of Britain even instituted the extremely prestigious
Order of Merit that carried no title at all. Second, expanding state
bureaucracies and armies created a wave of new nobles that flooded
the upper levels of society.[107] Further danger to the value of honors
came from the rising number of *faux* nobles with dubious or fraudu-
lent claims. Usurpations mushroomed in France and Italy.[108]

The Piedmontese prime minister in the 1850s, the Marquis
d'Azeglio quoted in the epigraph, was the last of his line. He contem-
plated his lack of an heir with equanimity. D'Azeglio was pessimistic
about the future character of his countrymen, and of his own lineage.
Therefore, for him it was better "to see [my house] finish honourably
now, than later with inept – and quite likely worse than inept –
successors."[109] The achievements of his predecessors and his own
conduct had brought the family to a high point of honor, which was
unlikely to be sustained. Increasingly, older aristocrats worried about
the changes they saw in the conduct of the younger generation. The
materialism, lack of vital memories about the lineage, and the disappearance of a distinctive sense of honor among his grandchildren

occupied the thoughts of Giuseppe Lampedusa's fictional Prince of Salina as he lay dying near the end of the nineteenth century.[110] Was this fear merely the routine crotchets of the old lamenting the deficiencies of the young? Or had something changed, had at its core the aristocracy begun to fade into an upper class in which the bourgeois and landed elements were becoming indistinguishable? In France in 1826, when the Count de Villèle proposed changing the law so that fathers could favor their eldest sons in inheritance of the family estates, the Duke de Broglie attacked the attempt to tamper with the Napoleonic legacy. He accused de Villèle of proposing "a manifesto against the present state of society. The right of primogeniture is the foundation of an inequality of conditions, it is pure privilege, . . . It is a social and political revolution, a revolution against the Revolution accomplished in France forty years ago."[111] A landed aristocracy could not long survive if Broglie's views became widespread among its members.

What protects an ascendancy? What thoughts, habits, and culture lend a ruling class cohesion and nourish its inner life? The bedrock is economic power, but in order to appear impressive to itself and the world it must have an ideology and self-imposed standards of behavior.[112] Psychologically many aristocrats were still sound in 1914. Many families could summon up the will to block the pursuit of individual claims to a part of the dynastic inheritance. Many were still willing to gamble, duel, and above all face death in battle. Economically most titled aristocrats were rich enough to put up a good show, even if limousines were replacing their stately coaches and more of their wealth was invested in the stock market than in acreage. The military hero maintained a special place in national life even in democracies. Reminiscing in the 1980s about her parents' generation in East Prussia in the years before 1914, Countess Dönhoff remembered: "back then honor played the role money plays today as the most highly prized possession."[113]

5

THE BEAU MONDE: CULTURE AND SOCIETY

> The old Hungarian count . . . was heard to mutter as he lay
> dying, "And then the Lord will say, 'Count, what have you
> done with your life?' and I shall have to say, 'Lord, I have
> shot a great many animals.' Oh, dear! Oh, dear! It doesn't
> seem enough!"
>
> Rebecca West, *Black Lamb, Grey Falcon*, vol. I, p. 73[1]

The Bánffy family emerged in Transylvania in the fifteenth century
and became among the foremost dynasties of the country. They owned
the grandest palace in the capital city of Koloszvár and one of the
province's largest castles at Bonczhida. One branch was raised to a
barony in the 1660s, while another became counts in 1855. The barons
produced a nineteenth-century prime minister of Hungary. The
counts held important offices at court. Among the latter was Count
Miklós, born in 1873. He was elected a Member of Parliament in 1901
and became Director of the Hungarian State Theaters from 1913 to
1918. He wrote five plays, two books of short stories, and a distinguished novel. He was both a traditionalist and a member of the avant-
garde. Overcoming fierce opposition, his intervention made it possible
for Bartok's works to have their first performance in Budapest.

Bánffy became Foreign Minister of Hungary in his cousin Count
István Bethlen's government of 1921. Although he detested the
politics of the Regent, Admiral Horthy, he worked to modify the
harsh boundary revisions imposed at Versailles by which much of
Transylvania had been handed over to Romania. Little progress was
made, and he retired from office. His trilogy, *A Transylvanian Tale*,

also called *The Writing on the Wall*, was published between 1934 and 1940. He portrayed prewar Hungary as a nation in decline, failed by a shortsighted aristocracy.[2] Though not in the same league as Tolstoy and Lampedusa as a novelist, Bánffy was a gifted writer whose sprawling work powerfully evokes a lost world.

Bonczhida was burned and looted in 1945 by the retreating German army in revenge for Bánffy's visit to Bucharest to persuade Romania, together with Hungary, to desert the Axis and sue for a separate peace. Hungary and Transylvania were soon after invaded by the Soviets, bringing an end to the Count's world. His wife and daughter fled to Budapest while Bánffy stayed on in Romania hoping to salvage something from the wreckage of his estates. Soon the frontier was closed. The family remained separated until 1949 when he was able to get to Budapest, where he died in the following year. A mellowing communist regime permitted the reissue of *A Transylvanian Tale* in 1982, and it was translated into English for the first time in 1999. The Castle of Bonzchida is now being restored as a cultural center. An apartment is being prepared for the use of the Count's family.[3]

* * *

Along with monarchs and the Church, aristocrats for centuries had been the chief patrons of European art, architecture, literature, music, and learning. Although the relationships between lords and artists changed, the former possessed money and taste that remained indispensable to the latter. Alternative sources of financial support began to emerge in modern times, but wealthy aristocrats continued as patrons of importance. Because of advantages of education and leisure they also were creators of knowledge and culture. Any list of scientists or novelists over the last two centuries will include among the greatest practitioners a number of aristocrats. Many non-noble artists and writers continued to focus much of their attention on the aristocratic world. From Proust to Waugh, Sargent to Visconti, and Tolstoy to Jean Renoir the arts in the nineteenth and twentieth centuries remained a well-roamed territory by the landed elites. Aristocratic influence pervaded fashion, sport, entertainment, and even modes of speech. The landed elite popularized scientific agriculture, new types of crops, new breeding techniques, sponsored scientific lectures and institutions, museums, libraries, schools, concert halls, churches, and shaped city planning.[4] A number of historians see the tenacious perseverance of traditional styles in the arts as a mechanism that sustained aristocratic hegemony.[5] Elite cultural values helped transfer patterns of behavior to the rest of society. By these means the aristocracy continued to define their identity and legitimize their ascendancy.

*   *   *

Aristocrats were educated in one of three ways: home tutoring, at military academies, or in secular and religious schools. The first option was normal for all girls and the sons of magnate families. The alternative systems were practiced variably according to family traditions and resources. During the course of the nineteenth century more and more noble boys, even from grand families, began to attend schools and universities. This was due to the increased complexity of fighting wars, which required a higher standard of professional training for successful military careers, the need to pass qualification examinations to gain entrance to government office, and a wider range of career options open to younger sons. Schooling for boys, however, tended to be much more thorough and purposeful than that open to their sisters.

Military educations were Spartan, even brutal. Violence was often a part of the routine. The "battles" between classes in the Austrian academy at Wiener Neustadt involved setting furniture on fire and sent participants to the hospital. In 1862 the entire cadet corps at Sandhurst mutinied over living conditions.[6] Ironically, curricula at military academies was often more "modern" than at schools attended by civilians.

Something like two-thirds of the English peerage was educated at Eton between the 1870s and the 1950s, yet no more than one-third of the fathers of Eton boys were landowners at any point in the nineteenth century. Elsewhere the sons of the aristocracy were distributed among a larger number of schools where they also mixed with a wide range of students.[7] Many noblemen had at least encountered boys from outside the magic circle before they became men, though the degree of social interaction between the groups in schools is hard to measure. The study of Classical civilization remained the core subject at most schools attended by aristocrats, although more modern subjects were gradually introduced.[8] The relentless tedium of Greek and Latin grammar was off-putting, and many gained only an imperfect grasp of the material. Yet few better foundations could have been devised for a ruling class than to study Aristotle, Plato, Thucydides, Plutarch, and the chronicles of the Roman Republic and the Caesars. The shape of Latin sentences, the examples of statesmanship, and an endless supply of quotations and tags helped train politicians for public life.

Modern languages were also an important part of many aristocratic educations. French, English, German, and Italian were all spoken by the elite on the Continent. It was not uncommon for a Viennese grandee and his wife to speak all of them: German as a matter of course, English learned from nannies, and French and Italian taught by tutors. A Hungarian magnate would also speak Magyar. The Russian aristocracy spoke French, although it was increasingly common for them to know and use their native tongue. Many Romanians, on the other hand, seemed to value French culture and language more highly than their native inheritance.[9]

Only certain universities were acceptable to the elite, or, in the case of England, only a few of the colleges at Oxford and Cambridge. Preparation for careers in political administration was both lengthy and expensive. In Germany sons of the elite were required to qualify through the *Arbitur* examination after high school, attend the law faculty of a university, pass a series of state service examinations, and spend years of unpaid service as an apprentice in various offices before they could start earning an income.[10]

Education at institutions open to the broader society held the danger of insinuating middle-class values into the elite. Even the most seemingly innocent sources could reach aristocratic children with ideas their parents might not want them to hear. Little princes were amazed to read in the beautiful French children's books they received as presents stories of *republican* heroism.[11] In Russia growing awareness of Western European thought was accompanied by the diffusion of liberal, democratic, and revolutionary ideas among the faculty and students at universities. The exposure of young and impressionable nobles to these currents aroused concern.[12] However, many nobles associated only with their own kind and frittered away their time in the pursuit of pleasure. The Grand Tour had largely vanished by 1815, but it was not unusual for young men to spend some time in a distant university. Czartoryski princes studied at Edinburgh and Széchenyis in the Netherlands. Trains and steam

ships made travel much easier after 1850 and many young men took
advantage of the change to see the wider world.[13]

* * *

Aristocrats were attracted to cities by the court, parliament, culture,
fashion, and ease of living. Provincial capitals across Europe, where
the elite had town houses, filled in the winter, and weekly balls were
held. Lithuanian nobles were still building grand urban palaces in
Vilnius in the 1860s, although in England the practice of town houses
in the provinces died out.[14] Powerful groups of great families in
Russia and Sicily remained loyal to Moscow and Palermo. The Moscow
elite considered court society in St. Petersburg too cosmopolitan; the
latter found the former a backwater.[15] When Transylvanian aristocrats moved to the Hungarian capital, even though ethnically Magyar,
they often were looked down upon by resident society and were
treated almost like foreigners. One reported: "the Budapest dowagers, if they spoke to [us] at all, did so condescendingly with a patron-
izing air they did nothing to hide." Sly and spiteful allusions to
Transylvanian birth were made: "Lots of bears where you come from,
aren't there?"[16] As with mountain climbers, one reaches one peak
only to discover that there is another, even higher, behind it. After
gaining acceptance in Budapest society, the next step was the court
in Vienna. Even aristocrats had from time to time to attach crampons
to their boots.

Unlike the lesser nobility, magnates had the means and the influence to take maximum advantage of urban life, although the smoke
of thousands of coal fires, street noise, and the heat of the summer
were powerful incentives to retreat back to Arcadia, or at least to
suburban villas. David Spring noted that the English aristocracy lived
happily in both the urban and rural worlds and was more successfully
"amphibious" than any other landed elite. Nevertheless, English
landowners were at heart land animals. It was to the country that
they moved their libraries and principal art collections that had once
been housed in London, and there, Spring noted, "they laid out their
gardens and parks, those visible symbols of the secret life of their
imagination."[17] It was in the country that they indulged their obsession with killing game, riding horses, and playing with dogs. They
also spent a good deal of time on management of their estates and
local government. No other landed elite, with the exception of the

Prussian (and the Legitimist French during their periodic bouts of political hibernation), was as much resident upon its estates. The Spanish and Sicilians were once country dwellers but in the nineteenth century had become mostly absentee landlords living in cities or suburban villas, especially in Madrid and Palermo. Northern Italian nobles also preferred their town palazzos to their country houses, unlike the Austrian nobility, who maintained residences in Vienna but stayed mostly in the country. The boyars of Moldovia tended to live quietly on their estates while those in Wallachia were drawn to Bucharest.[18] Stereotypes of Russian nobles spending little more than vacation time in country houses that they bought and sold with regularity, and the Portuguese never leaving Lisbon, have some validity. However, there is evidence that a number of great families cherished their estates, sought to become active agricultural managers, and lived for generations in the same place.[19] The coming of railways made it easier for the Russian elite to move back and forth from the countryside to the capital. Eventually some great families visited the country throughout the year. It is true many Legitimist families retreated to the countryside in France after the Bourbons were overthrown in 1830, but the aristocracy was largely metropolitan, except for the summer months.[20]

Aristocratic estates tended to be found most frequently in areas that were either convenient to the capital or in the regions with the richest soils. Swedish nobles were thick on the ground in the provinces around Stockholm while the French favored the Ile de France and the rich farmlands to the northwest. Russian noble estates concentrated in the west and south with little to the north or beyond the Urals. This lack of even distribution around the country left some areas weakly patrolled by landowners or else under the suzerainty of a few grandees.

Country houses were the administrative centers of estates. Building campaigns allowed aristocrats to compete with rivals and offer hospitality. Great parklands could stretch to thousands of acres. During the eighteenth and nineteenth centuries country houses were more and more cut off from the surrounding inhabitants. Gardens and parks separated the residence from the farm buildings. In England villages were moved elsewhere and newer houses were built in more isolated locations. However, this process did not necessarily imply that the aristocracy was fleeing contact with the rural inhabitants but was part of a movement to celebrate and appreciate nature.[21]

Many houses in England were built between 1780 and 1880, accelerating in number after 1840. The French elite continued to build châteaux at a good pace from the 1820s to 1880s and at a lesser rate up to 1914.[22] The Austrian Countess Wydenbruck noted in 1912 that English country houses seemed "luxurious to continental eyes." "Country life in Germany and Austria is, on the whole, much simpler; there is still a touch of the Middle Ages about our stone-built, thick-walled castles."[23] As the nineteenth century advanced large stone manor houses in classical or pseudo-Gothic style increasingly replaced simpler wooden houses of earlier periods in the Baltic provinces. The Russian country house was typically neo-classical surrounded by a spacious natural garden. The magnates had great parks built comparable to English ones with pavilions, grottoes, and lakes. In Ireland the peak building period concluded in 1850. The Great Famine brought the boom to an end, although remodeling continued during the second half of the century.[24]

*   *   *

Before World War I in the more rural parts of central and eastern Europe it was still the fashion for peasants to kneel before a lord and kiss the hem of his coat.[25] Nowhere did deference of this kind linger longer than within the circles of servants that supported life in the great houses. Armies of lackeys, many wearing livery in the family colors, sustained grandeur and authority. In the last years before World War I the Roman Count Greppi reproved the petulant Princess Rospigliosi for complaining about her footmen: "Try to tolerate it," he said. "When there are no more servants, there can be no more Society."[26] Elaborate systems of hierarchy below stairs reproduced the world above. At the Dönhoffs' in the early twentieth century the cook would never have sat down to eat with the kitchen maids, nor the housekeeper with house maids. The three assistant coachmen were obliged to eat in isolation in a passageway.[27]

At Friedrichstein in the years just before World War I there were six housemaids, a lady's maid, valet, cook, three kitchen maids, housekeeper, butler, four footmen, and four coachmen. In addition, there were numerous grooms and gardeners. Earl Fitzwilliam's Wentworth Woodhouse in Yorkshire had a façade 600 feet in length and covered three acres of ground with over 100 bedrooms and stables for 100 horses. In 1850 the indoor staff numbered 80 and the outdoor 200 including six who tended a private zoo.[28] Management of an estate and demesne also required squads of stewards, agents, accountants, and inspectors as well as ornamental hermits lurking in garden bowers and oarsmen rowing boats on the lake to create a decorative effect.

In France households were much smaller than the English equivalents. Even among the grandest old nobility, employing more than 20 servants was unusual in the late nineteenth century. Prince Emanuele Dal Pozzo della Cisterna in Piedmont left legacies to 33 servants in 1864. Before 1861 Russian country houses were crammed with maids and lackeys of every description. Prince Kurakin had 800 house servants at Kurakino in 1820, including singers, musicians, and artists. The Polish Countess Potocki still kept liveried dwarfs to run messages in the 1880s.[29] Crews of shipwrecked women served as nannies and governesses – French, Swiss, English, Scots – in alien lands, driven by poverty and family disaster or an adventurous spirit to live among often merciless children and people whose language they did not speak.

Fewer males were employed as servants as time went on, and total numbers fell when the coming of the railway age enabled aristocrats to take their retainers with them from place to place. When Prince Felix Youssoupoff traveled from Russia to Oxford in 1908 to study as an undergraduate he took along with him a chef, chauffeur, valet, housekeeper, groom, polo ponies, a bulldog, and a macaw.[30] Further shifts in outdoor staff took place as carriages and horses gave way to automobiles. Chauffeurs were hired along with mechanics to operate electricity plants. Lifts, telephones, refrigerators, and modern ovens also made life easier for servants but did not necessarily lead to reductions in numbers. Hunting establishments continued to require regiments of servants.

The cocoon of lackeys tended to disassociate the elite from the concerns of ordinary people. Every whim could be satisfied. Constant cries of complaint arose prompted by peas under mattresses. Vladimir Nabokov remembered: "there was always something amiss – a spell of hay fever, the death of a peacock, a lost borzoi."[31] The Earl of Glasgow threw a waiter out the window of an inn with the cry, "Put him down on the bill."[32] Yet, a mutual dependence was recognized. Servants were often allowed considerable space for self-expression and even defiance. One Spanish grandee's butler had his own ideas about protocol. Oblivious of disapproving frowns he would place guests at the dinner table where he thought best and not by official precedence. When expostulated with afterwards, he would stand in stony silence. " 'Why don't you answer?' 'I don't want to perturb the peace of my soul.' "[33] The Prince of Salina in Lampedusa's novel had an extraordinarily close relationship with his huntsman, yet at the same time he felt free to lock him up in a cellar.[34]

The Enlightenment's emphasis on domesticity, good manners, and family values led to greater efforts to exclude servants from intimate contact. Back stairs were built and bell pulls installed. Kitchens were put in basements; tunnels were excavated to bring supplies into houses discreetly. By Edwardian times English lower servants were sometimes required to turn to the wall and try to become invisible when family members walked by.

* * *

When not at their country seats, visiting friends and relations, or attending court, aristocrats could most frequently be found taking the waters at a popular spa or resort where they went to the races, concerts, gambled, and dieted. Baden Baden became the equivalent of Mustique or Aspen today with the added excitement of casinos. Other destinations included: Spa in the Ardennes, Marienbad, Carlsbad, and Vichy.[35] Health spas also opened in the Caucasus from the 1840s to serve the needs of the Russian elite. Lord Brougham made the Riviera fashionable in the 1840s. The Russians established a direct train service from St. Petersburg to Nice. Abbazia on the Adriatic coast became a favorite winter retreat for the Hungarian aristocracy. The Romanovs had estates in the Crimea from the 1830s. The British discovered Corfu during their occupation of the island, and cricket is still played there. In France, Dieppe became fashionable as a temporary residence in the summer, thanks to repeated visits of the Duchess of Berry. Deauville, Le Touquet, and Dinard were the beau monde's refuge from the Parisian summer. Biarritz owed its popularity in the 1860s to the Empress Eugénie's fondness for the resort.[36] Spanish grandees favored Santander.

Trains were a mixed blessing. The rich could travel quickly and comfortably to distant destinations, but they had to junket in the company of the *hoi polloi*. Lady Palmerston reported to her husband in 1849: "My journey yesterday was very safe but not agreeable. . . . I had to get into a Carriage with four Shopkeepers, who had got excursion tickets to return Monday – but they were not acquainted with each other and none of us spoke."[37] Except on ceremonial occasions noblemen no longer traveled about the country with outriders and trumpeters. Nor would they any longer dress in bright colors, wearing swords and high wigs. Although a trend towards more sober dress had begun in the later eighteenth century, the soot and bustle of the railway age made simpler and more easily cleaned clothing popular. Swords did not fit easily through compartment doors. The pageantry surrounding aristocratic life began to wane. Great landowners, however, had special clauses inserted in contracts for the sale of property to railway companies that provided for private stations where even express trains could be obliged to halt to suit a lord's schedule. An English peer, as late as the 1920s, when traveling to Scotland for the summer holiday, took with him on the train a cowman and cow so that his children could be nourished en route without having to drink strange milk.[38]

On the other hand, railways and steam ships made the world accessible in a safe and more comfortable way. Younger sons went off to ranch in the Wild West of Canada and the United States.[39] Big game hunting in Africa became the rage. Two of Viscount Grey of Fallodon's brothers were killed by a lion and wild buffalo, respectively. Prince Lajos Windisch-Graetz took his new wife Countess Széchenyi on their honeymoon in 1907 to Egypt and the Sudan, where a crocodile bit her maid.[40] A number of female aristocrats were intrepid travelers. Baroness de Meyendorff and her husband, a Russian naval officer and diplomat, explored deep into South America, and she was the first woman to reach the peak of Cerro Tolosa (5730 m) in the Andes.[41]

Most aristocrats had considerable amounts of leisure time, the resources, and the inclination to play games and indulge their competitive urges. The range and variety of sports that became fashionable among the European elite during the nineteenth century is astonishing. Many of the activities, such as croquet, billiards, and lawn tennis, began in England and then spread to France, Germany, Italy, Austria, and Russia. Polo was brought back from India to London, but exclusive clubs in Paris, Budapest, and St. Petersburg were established. Yachting had existed in the seventeenth century but became a craze in the nineteenth. Great noblemen began to sail to exotic places such as Iceland. Steam yachts allowed cruises around the Mediterranean and then the globe. Cowes Week, and to a lesser degree the races at Kiel in Germany, became important events in the social calendar. Racing autos and airplanes caught on quickly in the prewar years.[42]

The aristocracies of Europe played a principal role in spreading the knowledge and practice of modern sport broadly across society.[43] These included not only traditionally elitist and expensive activities but also many modern games popular with wide audiences, notably track and field sports and organized team games. The British nobility patronized modern boxing in the early nineteenth century and later the Marquis of Queensberry established systematic rules. Badminton began at the Duke of Beaufort's seat. In Russia the founder and first chair of the Athletic Society in the 1890s was Count Riboper.[44] The greatest example of aristocratic patronage still in existence today is the Olympic movement founded by Baron Pierre de Coubertin.[45] The organizing committee was filled with titled members from the beginning and remains an important relic of aristocratic leadership.

De Coubertin was not only responsible for the revival of the ancient games, but he also took the initiative to add new events to the track and field competition. In addition, he fostered sports such as cycling, sharp shooting, tennis, crew, weightlifting, fencing, and swimming. One historian writes: "No modern institution of comparable significance owes so much to a single man."[46] His key companions at the outset were Counts de Sauvigny, Mercati, and Baillet-Latour and many dukes, counts, and lords founded national committees.

Above all else aristocrats loved to kill animals. Shooting became more and more important in the nineteenth century, with the development of accurate rifles for stalking and efficient shotguns for driven birds. Tracking down large animals remained a solitary sport, fishing on the move, but organized slaughter of winged prey changed from a few men and dogs walking through fields into massive massacres involving a dozen or more guns and hundreds of beaters. Animals were artificially reared to provide the huge numbers necessary for a *battue*. Lodges were built from Ireland to Romania to house shooting parties. In Britain grouse, pheasants, and woodcock were the favored targets. On the Continent everything from the prized capercailzies to snipe were obliterated. In every country rabbits were in danger. In France, Denmark, Germany, and Austria-Hungary rigid rituals grew up around the process that became highly formalized with a private vocabulary, uniforms, and music. Many Russians found all this rather silly and continued to shoot in a more informal manner.[47]

Shoots reached their zenith in size and grandeur between 1880 and World War II, long enough to be captured on film in Jean Renoir's famous sequence in *The Rules of the Game* (1939). Aristocratic memoirs of men who grew up in those years grow lyrical on the subject. Baron Guy de Rothschild's description of an interwar shoot at his Château at Ferrières captures the drama and exhilaration. As the drive reached its climax:

> Hundreds of pheasants in ordered ranks took flight in a flurry of feathers. The guns didn't know where to shoot first: the loaders could hardly reload fast enough; the gun barrels burned our fingers; the stricken birds seemed to explode in sprays of feathers, tracing strange trajectories before falling all around us with dull thuds. The air seemed to tremble and echo like the thunder of war, with barrages of explosions filling the sky.[48]

David Cannadine has called the grandiose expansion of shooting "plutocratic."[49] The leading figures, however, in the largest late nineteenth-century *battues*, were men such as Archduke Franz Ferdinand, the Duke of York (later King George V), Prince Schwarzenberg, Prince Esterházy, and the Marquis of Ripon. These were no more plutocrats than Stalin was a refined courtier. Lavish excess was an aristocratic trait. The sport grew as technology changed, and aristocrats adapted to changed conditions.

More energy was required to stalk deer across the highlands of Scotland, hunt elk in Poland, shoot wild boar in France, and chase wolves, bison, lynx, moose, and bears in Russia. These sports were risky and difficult. In Russia coursing with borzois was competitive among the dog owners. Elk hunts were conducted on skis and could last for days. The most elaborate and dramatic of all hunting with dogs and horses was practiced in England. As with Continental shooting, the rituals, the colorful uniforms, and ceremony surrounding foxhunting became increasingly elaborate. The post of Master was one of the most important positions in the hierarchy of county life. Immortalized in poetry and painting, the sport developed a unique mystique associated with aristocratic life.

All over Europe aristocrats used their influence to enact legislation to protect the right of the landowners to hunt and shoot game. However, by the second half of the nineteenth century French, Russian, and German peasants no longer tolerated noble huntsmen trampling crops, and they had the law on their side.[50] Legislation either revoking special privileges or rearrangements of laws governing tenancy and property also made it harder for aristocrats to keep control of hunting even on their own domains. In Germany nobles fought a rearguard action to preserve their rights, but these were mostly eliminated after 1848. In Britain relationships were carefully cultivated with local farmers and compensation paid for damaged crops and fences.

Women were by no means excluded from the world of shooting and hunting. Empress Elizabeth of Austria became a celebrated hunter of foxes and pursued the chase all over Europe. Many women, from Ireland to Hungary, followed her example, fully equal to men in what was a grueling and dangerous activity, and they did so riding sidesaddle.[51] Women began to participate in shooting and fishing as well.

The Marquis of Ripon between 1867 and 1923 killed over half a million head of game.[52] Even in sports where the numbers were less awesome, modern sensibilities are offended by this slaughter. We are shocked by a lust for blood that seems almost irrational. It is well to remember, however, that there was little waste in the process. Unlike trophy shooting in Africa, everything killed was destructive vermin or ended up on the dinner table. The aristocracy remained a warrior class, and the young men introduced to sports that required accuracy with a rifle, horsemanship, technical mastery of intricate processes, physical fitness, leadership, and courage could have found few better training grounds for their life's work. Leading a cantankerous field of farmers and lords using horse whips indiscriminately on their mounts and on fellow hunters, settling disputes over damaged property, raising the funds necessary to finance the operation, and having the courage to sustain repeated injuries was also an excellent preparation for life in local government and national politics. Hunting rituals reinforced hierarchy, but in country communities the love of nature and the chase was also a genuinely shared interest that bonded men across class lines.

An outgrowth of foxhunting was steeplechase races with horses, an occupation even more reckless and risky than ordinary hunting. It became popular, especially among military personnel, even in southern Europe.[53] However, it was flat racing that became the avatar of aristocracy and at the same time the first modern mass spectator sport. The Derby, founded in 1780, became a red-letter day for nearly every Englishman and many French noblemen as well. In France serious racing began during the Restoration under the patronage of Louis XVIII, who had lived in England during part of his exile. The great Count Széchenyi established horse racing in Budapest in the 1830s. The Russian elite adopted the sport, and from 1861 the court attended races near Peterhof every summer. The Swedes, Spaniards, and Italians did not take to it seriously until just before World War I and never with the same enthusiasm.

Jockey clubs popped up all over Europe and become bastions of social exclusivity well into twentieth century. Big races began to mark the beginning and conclusion of social seasons in capitals. Courses such as Ascot, Longchamps, and Punchestown became sites of social interaction as important as court balls. For some members of the French elite who had abandoned political life, racing filled literally every waking hour seven days a week as they moved hither and yon among the ring of courses surrounding Paris.[54] The sport remained an aristocratic stronghold until the 1890s when *nouveau riche* owners and breeders appeared on the scene. Then, after 1918, American millionaires, Indian maharajas, and Argentine ranchers proliferated.

* * *

The British elite, whose dress, manners, and habits were copied with increasing regularity, profoundly influenced the style and type of activities pursued by European aristocracies in the nineteenth century. Two Transylvanian counts in Bánffy's novel discussed their favorite topic: "Both worshipped England and all things English, the country itself, English gentlemen, English horses, English sports, English clothes and footwear, English girls, English bandages for horses' tendons, English guns and cartridges, English razors, English gardens and English dances."[55] Hungarian fox hunts employed hunting vocabulary that consisted mostly of English words: "a meet," the "master," "run," "check," "whipper-in," etc. Stables were arranged on English models. St. Petersburg luxury shops were crammed with English goods. Fashionable Russians even sent their laundry to London.[56]

Aristocratic Anglomania affected almost every aspect of life. English parks were constructed around country houses even in such improbable locations as Finland and Transylvania. Oxford and Cam-

bridge welcomed a steady stream of Russian and Hungarian aristocrats before World War I including, daringly, Princess Viazemsky. It
was the English who set the style of dining in white ties and black
tailcoats. Sir Walter Scott's novels precipitated a rash of neo-Gothic
castles.[57] Austrian and Hungarian aristocrats felt that in England "lay
the central shrine" of the horse kingdom, "of speed and huge fences
and broken necks, and their eyes would cloud over at the memory of
antediluvian seasons in the shires."[58] English breakfasts were served
from a sideboard. Tolstoy's aristocrats do things *"Tout-à-fait à
l'anglaise,"* quite in the English style.[59] French Anglomaniacs founded
clubs, took up horseracing, and even cricket. Their enthusiasm was
heightened after 1871 because of the elite's antagonism towards the
republic.[60] Spanish *grandes* went shooting in Scotland, played polo,
and yachted at Cowes. The English nanny became ubiquitous. Even
Junkers lusted after English style, but could rarely afford it. However,
the Silesian magnates embraced it, and even married English wives.
Uniforms for servants were supplied by London tailors, the guns by
Holland and Holland and Purdy, and the fishing tackle from Hardy's
of St. James's. Transylvanian ladies wore English tea-gowns, played
English gramophones, and sliced their sandwiches thin in the manner
of London hostesses. In the wilds of Bukovina and Sicily noblemen
ordered hair lotion and shaving soap from London. Princesses were
given English names. Even the Tsar gave "English" balls to which
invitations were much sought after.[61]

Considering that England during the nineteenth century was one
of the most democratic societies in Europe, the Continental elite's
admiration might seem puzzling. In the previous century many aristocrats had considered England a remote and dowdy place not worthy
of much consideration.[62] The British triumph over Napoleon, the
continued wealth and stature of the elite, and the immense empire
transformed the island's reputation. English novels came to be widely
read and served to disseminate information about how the elite
lived.[63]

Not all English habits were copied. Port never caught on, and
women leaving the men after the meal was less practiced on the
Continent than in Britain. Some items passed the other way. Sir
Charles Isham, 10th Baronet, imported the first garden gnomes into
Britain from Germany and transplanted them into a giant rockery
at his estate in Northamptonshire, armed them with spades and
picks, and placed them as if mining the area.[64]

* * *

The lapse in taste displayed by Sir Charles and the vacuity of the Hungarian count's life portrayed by Rebecca West testify to an image of philistine and boorish behavior often attributed to nineteenth-century aristocrats. Manners even in the mid-nineteenth century could be gross. A young English lady was horrified to discover that at dinner parties in Scottish castles in the 1850s it was the custom of the men to drink themselves under the dining room table and be carried out one by one and dumped into their respective carriages, after which wives were summoned from the drawing room to join them for the homeward trip.[65] Yet, if one looks through books of photographs of Baltic country houses built between 1850 and 1914 or follows in the footsteps of a traveler such as Patrick Leigh Fermor, who mingled with the Magyar aristocracy in the 1930s, one is struck by the cultivation and discernment common among the elite.[66] Of course, there was ignorance and vulgarity to be found among modern aristocracies, but it would be hard to demonstrate that the rate was lower in eighteenth-century Estonia or Transylvania than a hundred years later. The nineteenth-century elite continued to act as patrons of the arts and transmitters of intellectual advances in a traditional manner as well as taking on new roles as curators and preservers of Western culture.

The English landed elite was still turning to gifted architects such as Edwin Lutyens in the early twentieth century. Most of his practice was devoted to building country houses, for the old as well as the new rich, in the same manner that Adam, Soane, and Salvin had done before him. His largest project was an ensemble of buildings to house the British Raj in New Dehli. They figure among the greatest works of twentieth-century architecture.[67] With only a couple of exceptions, the Viceregal Palace was occupied right to the end in 1947 by landed grandees. The standard of culture remained very high in English aristocratic circles late into the nineteenth century among families such as the Russells and Cecils or in Hungarian families like the Bánffys and Andrássys. In early twentieth-century Württemberg the young Counts von Stauffenberg were deeply imbued with love and respect for literature. London's innovative Crystal Palace of 1851 was designed by the Duke of Devonshire's gardener and commissioned by a blue-blooded committee chaired by Prince Albert. Prince Trubetskoy's brutally honest equestrian memorial in

St. Petersburg to Tsar Alexander III was literally a stunning achievement. Salvador Dali was able to paint freely in the 1930s thanks to the financial assistance of a group of noble patrons organized by a French prince.

A good example of a cultural initiative made by aristocrats was the *Penny Magazine*, launched by a group of English Whigs in 1832. Their enterprise demonstrated alertness to technological innovation and a flair for marketing. The secret to attracting a really broad audience of poorly educated people with little leisure time was to use pictures. Multi-cylinder stereotype steam printing had become available in 1827, and within five years a group of grandees had exploited its potential to reach beyond the traditional literate classes, and in so doing created the first genuinely mass-market publication in history. The *Magazine* was purchased 10 million times in 1833. Although these numbers were not sustained once competitors emerged, at a minimum the journal was seen by 1 million readers an issue and perhaps by nearly everyone in Britain, since even children and the illiterate could enjoy the illustrations. The *Penny Magazine* published a magpie collection of articles on the dexterity of goats, mice in Iceland, and the singular intelligence of cats. It contained, however, serious and informative stories and reviews. The didactic nature of the magazine led to moralizing to the working classes about frugality, temperance, industriousness, obedience, and forbearance. Embedded throughout were articles endorsing the agenda advocated by the Whigs: praise for technological innovation, Classical economics, and the march of the intellect. Moral lessons could turn into social critiques about the insensitivity of the rich towards the poor and the evils of an irresponsible aristocracy. The British elite was neither out of step with the times nor afraid to innovate.[68]

In the age of mass politics the importance of aristocratic salons diminished. Nonetheless, Parisian countesses and duchesses continued into the early twentieth century commanding literary, musical, and artistic meeting places where the titled and the talented interacted.[69] Aristocrats sponsored academies, chorale societies, orchestras, as well as a plethora of charities including hospitals, zoos, and botanical gardens.[70] The elite continued to shape and modify the physical appearance of cities with an eye to the display of their power, just as they had in the eighteenth century. Russia produced a remarkable array of writers and musicians from the ranks of the nobility.

The English aristocratic coterie known as "The Souls" pursued serious intellectual interests with formidable attentiveness.[71]

The Duchess of Alba was a great patron of Goya while the Earl of Egremont was the friend of Turner and Constable. Aristocrats continued to commission family portraits in large numbers. Among the greatest practitioners during the nineteenth and early twentieth century were Winterhalter, Sargent, and de László. Winterhalter is now conceded to have been a master and Sargent is coming to be regarded as a great artist. László, who in his heyday could command £2000 for a picture, only recently has begun to achieve the recognition he deserves.[72] Their reputations had suffered from the stigma of being "society" painters, which tells us more about the social prejudices of twentieth-century art critics than the substance of the artists' work.

Grandees continued to build great collections of old masters and good contemporary painting and sculpture throughout the nineteenth century. Some of these assemblages of art were donated to public institutions. The Irish Viscount Fitzwilliam left his superb collection to Cambridge University along with funds to construct what remains one of the finest small museums in Europe. The Marquis of Hertford's house and acquisitions were established by his son in the shape of the Wallace Collection. The great Liechtenstein assemblage of art, still among the finest ever formed by a single family, was largely the product of the connoisseurship of the nineteenth-century Prince Johannes II. During the reign of Emperor Franz Joseph Counts Karl Lanckoronski, senior and junior, served as gifted curators of the imperial collections and amassed superb assemblages of paintings in their own right.[73] The Czartoryski house in Cracow, with its great Leonardo, was open to the public. The gallery at Bridgwater House in London was accessible in the mid-nineteenth century and at one point was viewed by 5000 people a week.[74] Unfortunately, we have no records of the collections formed by the Russian aristocracy in the nineteenth century so they cannot be documented. After 1917 many of the paintings were either destroyed or moved to museums and the records lost.[75] The French Prince of Wagram was one of the greatest collectors of the Impressionists. He purchased hundreds of Renoirs, Cézannes, and Van Goghs before he was killed in the war in 1918.[76]

The importance, vibrancy, and genius of nineteenth-century aristocrats can best be appreciated in the field of literature. Imagine the absence of Lord Byron and Count Tolstoy. Tennyson and Trollope

came from baronet families. Where would we be if the landed elite
was erased from Jane Austen and Marcel Proust? Theodore Fontane
wrote extensively about the Prussian Junkers. In nineteenth-century
France authors such as Stendhal, Barbey d'Aurevilly, Balzac, Sandeau,
and Cousin gave an aesthetic evocation of nobles in their novels and
biographies. The "Big House" enjoyed a central place in Irish literature from the time of Maria Edgeworth in the eighteenth century,
through Trollope, Lever, Yeats, and Somerville and Ross in the nineteenth, to Molly Keane and Elizabeth Bowen in the twentieth.[77] Polish
literature was full of noble life. The 3rd Earl Spencer was a patron
of the troubled poet, John Clare. Countess Zichy and Countess
Nádasdy Lipótné supported Hungarian writers financially as well as
holding literary salons, and Prince Pál Esterházy spent large sums
adding works in Magyar to his great library. In Paris in the 1870s and
1880s the Duchess de Maillé and the Countess d'Agoult held salons
that attracted all the major literary figures. The latter also enjoyed
a fling with the musician Liszt.[78]

Victor Hugo was created a viscount as a gesture to the arts under
the July Monarchy while Macaulay and Tennyson became barons.
Those who already held titles were also active in the world of literature. Count Robert de Montesquiou wrote complicated symbolist
poetry. The Count de Vogüé was a novelist and critic. Countess de
Noailles (born a Romanian Princess of Brancovan) became a considerable poet. Winston Churchill won the Nobel Prize for Literature. The Romanian writers Princesses Elena Vacaresco and Martha
Bibesco were lionized in Paris and won prizes from the French
Academy. [79] Count Tolstoy's novels were incomparable. No one has
ever written a better book on America than Tocqueville.

An occasional aristocrat walked on the wild side. The Prussian
Countess Franziska zu Reventlow left her husband in 1895 to enter
a Bohemian circle of artists in Munich and became a writer in her
own right, although her articles on women's liberation condemned
females who wanted to compete professionally with males and
depicted the movement as the enemy of the erotic culture of the new
heathens she had joined.[80] George Sand, married to Baron Casimir
Dudevant, outraged convention on a regular basis.

Italian opera was a place where composers could synthesize popular
and elite values. In Piedmont aristocratic status was measured by
proximity to the royal box. Each fall the king and his Grand Chamberlain personally oversaw the assignment of keys.[81] Even provincial

capitals such as Kolozsvár had opera houses and the aristocracy held the same places there for generations. Vienna had been a Mecca for music in the eighteenth century and aristocratic patronage continued in the nineteenth. When more venues and larger audiences for public performances of music threatened to erode aristocratic leadership, they continued to support artists in salons, after-dinner music, employing musicians as teachers, and commissioning secular and religious pieces. They became more knowledgeable connoisseurs, although they failed to sustain complete hegemony. The popularity of musical salons and patronage in Paris and St. Petersburg seems to have grown during the nineteenth century.[82]

Count Constantine Benckendorff grew up in the top echelon of St. Petersburg society and served as an army officer, but also he learned to play the flute and participated in an amateur orchestra under the auspices of Count Scheremeteff. After the revolution he played in a professional orchestra until he was able to escape to the West.[83] Private theaters became the rage in Russia in the eighteenth century, and serf actors continued to perform until the time of emancipation. Prince Alois Josef of Liechtenstein maintained a permanent troop of actors in the first half of the nineteenth century, their heavy costs defrayed by letting them give public performances. Aristocrats all over Europe built many private theaters and frequently mounted amateur theatricals in their country houses. This began under the old regime and continued into the twentieth century.[84] Lady Gregory in Dublin was the key figure in the revival of Irish theater.

We have already seen that aristocrats took the lead in founding agricultural societies that disseminated the latest scientific information to farmers. Individuals experimented with different crops and breeding techniques and published the results of their researches.[85] In earlier centuries noblemen had often made important contributions to science, from Brahe to Boyle. During the nineteenth century the 3rd Lord Rayleigh continued this tradition as a professor at Cambridge and won the Noble Prize for Physics in 1904 for his discovery of argon. Prince Louis-Victor de Broglie won the same prize in 1929, while his cousin, Edmond de Polignac was a distinguished mathematician. Numerous German, Russian, and British aristocrats constructed laboratories in their country houses and made significant contributions to science.[86]

Count Karl Harrach, though from an ancient and rich family, became an obstetrician with a practice in the poorer sections of early nineteenth-century Vienna where he did not charge his patients.[87] Following in the footsteps of his father who had written a book on spectroscopy, the 12th Duke de Gramont became an eminent physician and founded the Institute Optique in Paris in 1916. As a result France became the leading nation in optical research for many years. Count Erwein Schönborn, master of the great Wiesentheid estate, became a leading surgeon in the early twentieth century, while Prince Alfred Auersperg became a successful neurologist.

Robert Fitzroy, grandson of the 3rd Duke of Grafton, was the captain of the HMS *Beagle* that carried Darwin on his long voyage. Later Fitzroy studied meteorology, and collected data by telegraph, assembled and analyzed it in London, and in 1861 issued the first storm warnings for shipping published in newspapers. He brought the term "forecast" into the meteorological vocabulary.[88] The 3rd Earl of Rosse erected one of the largest telescopes in the world at Birr Castle with which he made important discoveries. The Prince of Salina in *The Leopard* was also an astronomer of distinction (modeled on a real Sicilian nobleman). Annabella, Lady Byron, who married the poet in 1815, was referred to by him as "the Princess of Parallelograms." Their daughter, Ada, Lady Lovelace, published papers on mathematical topics.[89] In the 1870s the progressive 7th Duke of Devonshire laid the foundations for the most celebrated single center of science in the modern world with his gift of the Cavendish Laboratory to Cambridge.

* * *

It would be misleading to suggest that most aristocrats were bent over Bunsen burners or writing great novels. Much more effort and enthusiasm was devoted to socializing, a tradition at which aristocrats excelled. The most celebrated social calendar unfolded in London. First came the pre-Easter period, from the opening of Parliament to April with political receptions, dinners, small dances, and political evening parties. From Easter to the end of July was the high season, time for the big society events, state balls, concerts at the palace, parties in the great town houses, and outdoor occasions such as Derby Day and Ascot.

The Viceregal Court in Dublin was held in February and March before those who participated in the London season set off across the Irish Sea. Although the Union of 1801 ended the parliamentary sessions and cut back on the importance of the Irish season, it was still an important aspect of Dublin life. Its end in 1922 was an irreparable loss to the surviving members of the Ascendancy.[90] The Paris season began in January and ended with the Grand Prix de Paris run at Longchamps. Winter before Lent was when the great court balls took place in Vienna, but the aristocracy stayed on into the spring. When the dust and heat became bothersome they moved to the country. A cycle of great court ceremonies connected with religious festivals was conducted throughout the year, most majestically in Passion Week. Budapest had no court, although an archduke was usually in residence as the sovereigns' representative. The height of the Season took place during Carnival in the two hectic weeks before Lent. After that there were no public balls and society remained in their town houses and amused themselves with luncheons and small informal evening parties. The social season was at its peak in May with horse races, balls, and a new session of Parliament. "Everyone felt it their duty to be there." Count Bánffy noted. The Derby followed in Vienna when "nobody" would be left in Hungary.[91]

In the provincial capital at Kolozsvár, where aristocrats maintained palaces and houses even after World War I, the high season was the autumn because that was the time for hunting and steeplechases. Balls and post-opera dinners were held, and there was an after-Christmas carnival season as well. The Bohemian grandees passed the winter social season in baroque palaces in Prague and the remaining months of the year when not in Vienna at their castles in the countryside. A smaller social season took place in the Austrian part of Poland centered on the "court" of the governor at Lemberg.

In Rome society gathered for Christmas and the season ended in the celebration of Mardi Gras. The winter "season" in St. Petersburg was held from late September to Lent, but most people stayed on till after Easter and the 1st of May Review of the Guards on the Field of Mars. Summer and autumn were spent in the country, and towards the end of October those who had palaces or villas in the south headed for the Crimea.

As courts diminished in importance during the nineteenth century the aristocracy was able better to control access to social prestige purely on its own terms. Stephen Kale argues that a trend in society that measured entrance to the elite by cultural sophistication rather than purely by birth may have prolonged rather than weakened the dominance of aristocratic society.[92] Boxes at the opera, guest lists set by important hostesses, and clubs also allowed powerful women and committees of both genders to sustain exclusivity. A small number of British peeresses were still recognized in 1900 as leaders of Society: the Duchesses of Buccleuch and Devonshire and Ladies Londonderry, Cadogan, Ilchester, and Ellesmere. It was said that one was not a member of "Society" unless one had been invited to dinner at Devonshire House. The Season became more open to the merely affluent and less connected in its calendar with the meeting of Parliament. The crown was more anxious to be the leader of national society, not just court society, and access to presentation at court became more fluid. That meant the decisions made by private hostesses were more critical in terms of admission to the inner circle. In Britain and elsewhere the tone of the politico/social world at the top continued to be set by the old high aristocracy at least until 1914.[93]

The Faubourg Saint-Germain was the Parisian district where many of the nobles lived in the nineteenth century and for long it remained strictly Legitimist and reactionary. The Marquis de Castellane admitted it was "a little haughty, but exquisitely well-mannered."[94] Under the Second Empire the great hostesses included the Marquise de Chasseloup Laubat and the Countess Tascher de la Pagerie. In the 1870s the nobility gathered around the Duchesses Pozzo di Borgo, d'Avaray, and de Gallièra. The Duchess de Noailles said: "We are people who have recovered our health after all the doctors had given us up." Later the Duchesses de Rohan and de Maillé became important. In the years before World War I great hostesses included the Countess de Trédern and the Duchess de Gramont.[95]

Men increasingly gathered in organized clubs filled with cigar smoke, gambling, billiards, coffee drinking, libraries, dining, gossip, and political discussions. As usual, the English invented the institution during the eighteenth century. By the mid-nineteenth century all major urban centers in Italy had them. They served both as a place of pleasure and stimulation and also as a means to protect exclusivity.[96] In Paris upper-class clubs emerged in the late 1820s. The Nobles and Guards Clubs were founded in Berlin, the Kildare Street in Dublin, the Kaszino in Budapest, Jockey Clubs in Vienna and Bucharest, and the Cercle de Chase in Warsaw.

* * *

In 1840 Lady Charlotte Fox deplored the arrival of the cheap and democratic penny post. "It goes to my heart to see disappear all the little privileges, the *prestige* that we enjoyed – but low Vulgar penny wise and pound foolish ideas are the order of the day."[97] Aristocrats, like everyone else in the nineteenth century, had to adjust to cultural modernization, universal education, rapid changes in technology, and a broadening of conceptions of social equality. In 1851 an English aristocratic officer was sent to hard labor in prison for striking a policeman. Pierre Simoni's innovative study of aristocratic obituaries in Provence suggests that the nobility retained cultural importance and social power. However, as time went on, the "oldness" of a subject's family was mentioned less frequently and more emphasis was placed on achievements and being productive. Admiration was directed at those who had moved up in society and been go-getters.[98] The social, economic, and political challenge of the middle classes was at hand.

6

SWALLOWING THE TOAD: THE ARISTOCRACY AND THE MIDDLE CLASSES

Most people [in Budapest] had already switched to automobiles but the Princess Kollonich was so proud of her carriage and beautifully matched pairs of horses that she did not want to part with them. Their perfection had been a labour of love only achieved after many years' study and careful preparation and, after all, anyone with enough money could own an expensive motor. A perfect *équipage* was only for those who understood such matters and to whom tradition and style were more important than the latest fashion.

Count Miklós Bánffy, *c.*1906, in *The Writing on the Wall*,
vol. I, p. 318

The fabled Rothschild banking family began their spectacular ascent in Frankfurt during the 1760s. Sons of the house fanned out across Europe to establish branches of the business in Vienna, Naples, Paris, and London. The British, French, and Austrian lines all became barons within a generation or two and began to live as noblemen. They also acquired great landed estates and built famous country houses where they received personal visits from Queen Victoria and Emperor Napoleon III. Ferrières, near Paris, where the park alone extended to over 1000 acres, was acquired in 1829 and remained a principal seat until Baron Guy de Rothschild donated it to a university in 1975. The English Rothschilds purchased vast expanses of Buckinghamshire, where some of them still live. Perhaps most remarkably, the barons in Vienna gained entrée to the exclusive soirées of the court aristocracy and became intimate with Habsburg grandees.[1] Three Rothschild women married French princes, while in Britain daughters of the house made equally spectacular matches. One became the wife of a prime minister, the 5th Earl of Rosebery. Rothschilds were mad about foxhunting, commanded great racing stables, joined cavalry regiments, and continued to go to the office. No other "new" family of the nineteenth century ever became quite so rich and quite so aristocratic, but many made the running.

The simple fact is that aristocracies require constant replenishment. Two centuries of republican rule in the Netherlands thinned out the Dutch nobility to such an extent that by the end of the eighteenth century a crisis was imminent. Only the restoration of the monarchy in 1813 allowed William I massively to revive an order rapidly fading towards extinction.[2] Failure of male lines was not the only danger. Mismanagement and bad luck put many families on a downward track. The assumption that aristocracies are "old" is a serious misconception. Some historians of the nineteenth century have been misled by the lamentations of established families decrying the rapid acceptance of "new" men into the elite. In fact movement of commoners into the nobility was always frequent.[3] The process continued uninterrupted into modern times. At the end of the sixteenth century, in most French provinces two-thirds of all noblemen belonged to families that had not been part of the nobility a century earlier.[4] The haughty Piedmontese aristocracy of the nineteenth century had few medieval families in it. The bulk of the elite owed their rank to men who rose through business and government service relatively recently. Many of the Russian magnate families of the nineteenth century had only entered the top level in the eighteenth. In Sweden the aristocracy was anything but a closed caste. Manufacturers, merchants, and financiers were ennobled in the seventeenth and eighteenth centuries. The Prussian Junkers lost many families to war and reckless land speculation. A steady stream of arrivistes who bought up estates and accepted the noble ethos replaced them. The Habsburgs sold noble patents like fish cakes in Milan and Naples. Merchants in Riga, which Austria did not even control, could buy advancement in rank from a dynasty always on the lookout for extra revenue. Even in the supposedly exclusive circle of the "court" aristocracy in Vienna, where official edicts required elaborate documentation of many generations of noble ancestry for admission to the sovereign's presence, the rules were frequently bent or ignored by the emperor. Ernst Biron, perhaps the grandson of a

groom in the stable of the Duke of Courland and the son of a low
official in the duchy's forestry administration, was created a Count
of the Holy Roman Empire by Charles VI in 1730. Within seven years
he was the reigning duke.[5]

Much misinformation exists about the social backgrounds of newly
minted aristocrats. Perhaps the most serious source of error to creep
into the literature derives from the work of the distinguished historian, Lawrence Stone, who challenged the prevailing orthodoxy
about the openness of the English elite. It had long been assumed
that Continental aristocracies were more exclusive than the English,
and that the island society was constantly reinvigorated by the admission of new men from commerce and finance. This paradigm of
businessmen enjoying rapid absorption into the elite has been used
to explain the productivity of English agriculture, the primacy of
England in the race to industrialize, the creation of a stable yet flexible political system, and Britain's economic decline over the last
hundred years. Stone argued that most of the recruits came from
traditional genteel backgrounds connected with land, law, and office.
They were not truly "new men." Only after 1880 did businessmen and
bankers begin to compose a majority of the intake.[6] Unfortunately,
he based these assumptions on a study of country house ownership
now known to be seriously flawed.[7] In Britain and elsewhere, significant numbers of businessmen were ennobled throughout the eighteenth and nineteenth centuries.[8] Great rivers of money made in
trade, finance, and industry flowed into European aristocracies via
marriage, inheritance, and newly created titles throughout the
modern period.

* * *

Even though aristocracies had always been open to and readily
accepting of newcomers from commercial backgrounds, there were
several factors at work unique to the nineteenth century. One was an
increase in the rate of elevations to the nobility already noted earlier.
The second was the massive size of the fortunes industry made possible. After c.1875 the scale of this new wealth began to exceed that
of all but the greatest landed proprietors in the Western industrialized states. "The nineteenth century was characterized by the rise of
the middle classes on the one hand and on the other by its surrender
to the nobility," is the oft-repeated refrain.[9] What impact did this

development have? Did the landed Delilah seduce the businessman Samson in an "aristocratic embrace."[10] In England, it is argued that such a process led to loss of economic dynamism.[11] Did the burgeoning middle classes dilute the aristocracy by overwhelming it with numbers, leaving it "bourgeoisified"? Did a merged elite of "notables" develop, each element still retaining some distinctive features but for all practical purposes fused into a single class? Or did the members of the new business classes who either failed to gain acceptance into the aristocracy or chose not to aspire to titles constitute a rival source of power and wealth that overwhelmed the traditional leadership? On a more sinister note, did bourgeois willingness to defer to the old families lead Germany on a militaristic path with disastrous consequences both for the homeland and much of the rest of the world? These questions touch on some of the most important themes that modern historians seek to address.

A number of difficulties surround simple explanatory stereotypes. In parts of Italy we can find middle-class behavior determined by "traditional" values and interests, whereas "modern" attitudes were evident in the behavior of the aristocracy.[12] How could a thrusting, entrepreneurial English nobility enervate the aptitude for innovation of the businessmen it assimilated? It is a cardinal error to believe that business values were exclusively middle class.[13] Historians bandy about terms such as "feudalized" and "embourgeoisment" too casually. Serfdom was largely dead long before 1789 in England and France, and in Russia the system was always far from traditional conceptions of that system. How can Junkers who were cost-conscious agronomists and greedy speculators be characterized as "feudal"?[14] They could be harsh managers but so, too, were factory owners. Even primogeniture was never a "feudal" practice. In most of Europe medieval barons divided their estates among all their sons, and only in comparatively recent times had aristocracies embraced the idea of the whole inheritance going to the eldest son. Similarly, "bourgeois" is a term so loaded and fugitive in its meaning that the wise tend to fall back on the plural "middle classes." The word "notables" is the worst of the lot. It may superficially cover a multitude of cases; no doubt in many communities the worlds of business, the professions, and the *noblesse* overlapped, but each group retained vital distinctions that are lost to view when a portmanteau word is applied. Can one speak of the marquis and the agrarian entrepreneur, both of whom could be found owning large estates in Italy during the nineteenth century, as members of a single class, when the former resisted lockouts and excessive exploitation of workers while the latter sought to destroy the traditional structures of rural communities?

Undoubtedly, increased interaction between the aristocracy and the middle classes took place during the nineteenth century. The Parisian habituée, Princess Radziwill, commented soon after 1900: "American and Jewish elements have entirely invaded French society and imported into it not only their easy ways but also an independence of speech and action which would have horrified dowagers of olden times."[15] More marriages between commercial and landed wealth took place than had been the case in the past. The Prince of Salina in Lampedusa's novel *The Leopard* acts as the go-between for his favored nephew, the Prince of Falconeri, in marriage negotiations for the hand of the daughter of a peasant woman and an egregious businessman prepared to re-endow a decayed fortune so that the young nobleman can build a career in politics and diplomacy. The Prince likens the task to swallowing a toad. The rapacious father of the bride was a crook and probably a murderer. Yet the grandee is ready to masticate all the bits of the reptile down to the last claw in order to open up his nephew's path to power.[16] Throughout Europe during the nineteenth century similar compromises were made by thousands of aristocratic families. Sometimes the new money was garnered to support younger sons. Such was the case of Lord Randolph Churchill, the father of Sir Winston. Randolph's eldest brother, the 8th Duke of Marlborough, also married an American heiress in order to revive the financial underpinnings that supported Blenheim Palace and a great landed estate.

But this was nothing new. Aristocrats had been making astute marriage alliances for centuries. Great families in every country of Europe could count misalliances made for money in their genealogies from medieval times to the present.[17] The matches with Jews and Americans were new. Reference has already been made to the success of the Rothschilds among the highest reaches of the European aristocracy. In hidebound Piedmont the Marquis Della Chiesa della Cinzano married the daughter of Baron Ignazio Weil-Weiss, a newly ennobled Jew. In Paris four rich Jewish sisters married a marquis, a viscount, and two counts. The Prince de Lucinge married Mle. Ephrussi. The Prince de Polignac espoused the daughter of the railway speculator, Jules Issac Mirès. In Hungary even the great Batthyány dynasty married into the Jewish nobility. Similar examples can be found in Prussia, Poland, Italy, and Belgium. Only in Russia, Spain, and among the mediatized families of southern Germany did anti-Semitism – and in the latter case devout devotion to endogamy – virtually rule out such attachments.

American brides were not unknown among the British elite early in the nineteenth century, but the trend became broadly accepted only after the Civil War when North American fortunes began to outstrip European commercial wealth.[18] After all, if one was going to dirty one's hands, why do it by halves? By 1915 at least 42 Americans had become European princesses, 17 duchesses, 33 marquises, 136 countesses, 19 viscountesses, and 64 baronesses; numerous others married hereditary knights and lesser nobles.[19] The number of American-born British peeresses rose from four in 1880 to more than 50 by 1914.[20] Many of the great names of France were among the beneficiaries of American cash. Moth-eaten escutcheons were reupholstered with wads of dollars.[21] Italians, mainly from the Roman aristocracy, followed suit. "Cotton, oil, and sausage queens" from New York and the Midwest married into the cream of the Hungarian aristocracy.[22] A few Americans married Russian and Romanian princes.

In the provinces of northern Italy, France, and Britain in the first few decades of the nineteenth century, aristocrats and *haute bourgeoisie* created closely intertwined networks within the world of banking, commerce, industry and agriculture, shared directorships and investments, and social interactions.[23] Undoubtedly, changes in business practices and technology and a proliferation of upwardly mobile sons of the bourgeoisie created new challenges for the landed elite in competing for jobs in government and the officer corps. Innovations in agricultural science and practice were embraced and promoted by the landed elite that made them ever more businesslike in the management of their estates. However, aristocrats had always vied with each other in war and politics. They had long striven to outshine each other in conspicuous consumption. No sudden "embourgeoisment" overtook them because they had to compete or to make money or prove their fitness to rule.

The high nobility continued to set the criteria for elite status by judging who could or could not gain admission to balls and clubs. Late nineteenth-century professors complained of a "social-aristocratic" spirit in the German universities created by the exclusive dueling fraternities.[24] Aristocratic women remained the principal holders of salons where they and their husbands decided what habits, morals, and values should prevail. Active and alert aristocrats had always sought to meet and be entertained by people of great intellectual or artistic ability, irrespective of birth, and to get to know merchants and bankers with rich daughters. They continued to show scant interest, however, in hobnobbing with anyone outside their circle who was not either on the cutting edge of fashionable ideas or magnates in the making. The great hostess Princess Lieven's advice regarding the acceptance of invitations was: "No little people! If in doubt, one gains everything by abstaining."[25] When the Crown Prince of Italy came to Palermo in 1874 to unveil the statue of a businessman the Sicilian princes did not like, the aristocracy boycotted the occasion despite the presence of their future king.[26] Baron Fernand de Christiani gave the President of France a hefty blow to the head with his cane when the chief executive unwisely went to the races during the Dreyfus Affair.[27] More decorously, the Governor of a Russian province pulled a paper rouble from his pocket and put it in the outstretched hand of a *nouveau riche* merchant who had failed to wait for the prince to extend his first.[28]

In Turin the old families remained in their central palazzos when the merely rich moved to new suburban villas.[29] A Polish tutor of young Czartoryski princes noticed that at social affairs, "if one mixes with the industrialists and the middle classes, one can more easily indulge in some neglect of the adopted ways, but if one has to do with the upper classes this would be an unpardonable sin."[30] The Prussian system of educating military cadets was specifically designed to prevent the bourgeoisification of the officer corps.[31] Style remained a critical and subtle divider, as Count Bánffy observed in the epigraph to this chapter. All the signs are that aristocrats remained robustly confident about their social superiority. They preserved an elegant mode of life and traditional set of values.[32] High rank, distinctive ideologies such as Whiggism or supranational loyalty to the Habsburgs and conceptions of lineage set them apart from the middle classes.[33] Rich men purchased landed estates, though they were rarely either very large or held for more than a generation by those without ambition for a title. Aristocrats had an entirely different orientation toward long-term development of property. They thought in terms of centuries and were anxious to maintain workable relationships with tenant families that may have lived on their estates for a dozen generations and might do so for hundreds of years to come. Throughout the nineteenth century one finds aristocrats reluctant to create a "battle zone" between masters and men. In 1892 Count Giuseppe Grabinski, a great landowner in the Po Valley, worried that "the abuses of capital . . . too often lead to physical and moral sufferings for the people." This feeling represented a widespread anxiety among his peers. In the early twentieth century the aristocrats broke ranks with large-scale commercial farmers in signing agreements with labor organizations in order to preserve rural peace.[34] The Duke of Buckingham and Chandos, Governor of Madras in the 1870s, struggled unsuccessfully against the central administration of India to provide adequate relief during a horrific famine that took millions of lives. He felt that humanity should trump Classical economic theory.[35] The ruthless exclusion of younger children from the bulk of the family fortune, still practiced by the British, Hungarian, and Prussian elites until World War II and by great families in England until recently, was profoundly, unambiguously unbourgeois.

In England two-thirds of the marriages of sons of peers were with members of the aristocracy or gentry until World War I.[36] Landed society remained the single largest source of new peers until 1911, while truly self-made men remained no more than a quarter of creations.[37] Fortunes directly derived from industry were not rewarded with peerages until 1873, and for a time infrequently thereafter.

The aristocracy stayed rich. Many elites across Europe proved themselves adaptable and prudent. The wealth of French aristocrats did not significantly diminish between 1815 and 1914. In the mid-nineteenth century two-thirds of those whose incomes on the electoral rolls were listed in the top category were noble. Their wealth increased at a faster rate than society as a whole from the late 1790s to the 1840s while at the same time the aristocracy declined in absolute numbers. Many stayed rich into the twentieth century.[38] On the whole the nobility remained a decidedly affluent and privileged segment of Italian society up to the Great War, while in certain provinces in the south a shrinking group of titled families actually increased their share of the wealth.[39] Rising land values continued to make owners of large estates in Prussia richer and richer. In the teeth of the agricultural depression the sale prices of estates continued to rise. A Pomeranian property worth 70,000 thalers in 1800 sold for 92,700 in 1838, 246,000 in 1871, and was valued at 320,000 in 1894.[40] Mineral deposits, industrial investments, and urban property sustained the upper reaches of the British peerage at the top of the wealth tables into the twentieth century. The Duke of Sutherland was the richest man to die in Britain before 1840. Half the richest men there in the 1880s were great landowners. The Duke of Westminster was wealthier than the richest American, W. H. Vanderbilt, as late as 1885. The great expert on millionaires, William Rubinstein, estimates that probably until the 1920s Britain's half-dozen wealthiest men included among them more than three aristocrats.[41] As Arno Mayer noted, down to 1914 "industrial capitalism never generated sufficient material and social strength to challenge successfully and enduringly the *ancien régime* in favor of a liberal bourgeois order."[42]

It is true that aristocratic incomes declined relatively in position to the middle classes. Aristocratic estates produced smaller returns on capital than other sources of income.[43] In Belgium it is estimated that in 1846 60 percent of the national fortune was represented by land. This had dropped to one-fifth in 1913.[44] In Britain between 1855 and 1913 profits from agriculture dropped from £57 million to £46 million while industry surged from £123 million to £517 million.[45] In 1911 in Paris few of the fortunes valued at over 1 million francs belonged to nobles.[46] In Prussia in 1912, only seven out of the top 30 millionaires belonged to the aristocracy.[47] Even in late imperial Russia the incomes of non-aristocratic capitalists were reaching and exceeding those of landowners.[48] The data are tricky to interpret, however. For example, often only the acreage owned by aristocrats is counted in calculating their wealth, when we know they also owned urban property, industrial enterprises, shares in banks, and portfolios of stocks and bonds from Britain to Bohemia.[49]

* * *

To what degree did the new families adopt the manners and prejudices of the old patriciate? Was there a social and cultural symbiosis between land and business that allowed the old elite to perpetuate their political hegemony through and beyond the great transformations of the Industrial Revolution and the advent of democracy? The French sociologist Pierre Bourdieu argues somewhat opaquely: " 'Parvenus' who presume to join the group of legitimate, i.e., hereditary, possessors of the legitimate manner, without being the product of the same social conditions, are trapped, whatever they do, in a choice between anxious hyper-identification and the negativity which admits

its defeat in its very revolt."[50] Fritz Stern spoke more simply of the bourgeoisie's "furtive glance upwards."[51] Gordon Craig believed the wealthy sons of Prussian bourgeois families who flocked to the colors "aped and exaggerated the modes of thought, the manners, and even the vices of their aristocratic brothers in arms."[52] Whether their motive was desire for inclusion within the magic circle, the offer of a *quid quo pro* in exchange for the state support of industrial development, or an alliance in the defense of property against the oppressed masses, many historians conclude that no serious challenge against the authority of the aristocracy came from the bourgeoisie during the nineteenth century. Many see craven and sniveling deference to an outmoded order.[53] There was something slightly absurd and demeaning about the English middle class calling their offspring Stanley, Percy, Cecil, and Neville, names to conjure with in the world of aristocracy. On the face of it this practice was an open-and-shut case of social groveling or not-so-secret aspiration. Could it be, however, that they were merely associating themselves with the national story just as they might by using names such as William, Nelson, or Arthur?

There is no doubt that titles remained a much sought-after mark of success by industrialists, merchants, and financiers, even among previously spurned unconverted Jews.[54] The founder of Zionism, Theodore Herzl, confided to his diary: "If I wanted to be anything, it would be a Russian noble."[55] In Austria-Hungary the bourgeois demand for "vons" and baronies, even though they did not bring entry into court society, has been called "insatiable."[56] The avalanche of faux counts and pseudo "de's" and "di's" was another indicator of the desirability of titles.[57] Many new families went on to purchase substantial estates, take up horse racing, and cast aside their bourgeois connections. They intermarried with old families, and became authentic aristocrats.[58] Even in Spain, the new wealthy demanded titles. The number of grandees almost doubled between 1787 and 1896, many of them with business or industrial connections.[59] In Italy almost a third of new ennoblements in the decades before World War I were conferred on industrialists and financiers.[60]

The trouble is, we do not know the percentage of businessmen who bought land before 1800, so the rate in 1850 or 1900 does not help us identify whether a significant shift in ownership was taking place. A particularly impassioned debate among historians about what proportion of men from business backgrounds purchased estates in

Britain swirls back and forth. Irreconcilable discrepancies emerge.[61] Most observers would acknowledge that substantial buying was going on, but the extent is unclear. However, whatever was happening, the "aristocratic embrace" or "embourgeoisment" operated below the level of the magnates.

Desire to purchase land did not necessarily mean that successful members of the middle class wanted to join the aristocracy. Atavistic peasant impulses could be at work. One of the richest businessmen in Poland remembered that: "all Polish industrialists aimed at buying a piece of land at the first possible moment. . . . They bought land not to invest – they had better investment opportunities . . . they were simply land hungry."[62] By 1900 the Faltz-Fein family owned 641,000 acres in the Russian empire. However, they were purely businessmen experimenting with raising kangaroos in the Ukraine, ostriches in Kenya, and rapaciously exploiting their forests in Poland.[63] Many business families who sought admission to the titled elite had purely utilitarian reasons for doing so that were not related to rosy romanticism or "selling out." It helped them gain access to exclusive clubs and social circles where business could be done and connections made. "Networking" allowed end runs around obstructive bureaucrats. It added prestige to their firms and attracted new business. Bankers were particularly reliant on government contracts and needed to convey stability and respectability.[64] In the Po Valley and Apulia entrepreneurs assembled large blocks of land in order to achieve economies of scale in agri-business operations. Land purchase could simply be a way of diversifying assets or asserting success, not a capitulation to landed values.[65] The newly wealthy may have emulated aristocratic lifestyles in terms of consumption simply because they could afford luxury. Junkers may have embraced a frugal lifestyle out of necessity or religious feelings not because they had adopted middle-class habits of thrift.[66] It is true that a small element of the rising middle classes aspired to enter the inner circle and had the wherewithal to do so. The rest either lacked the means to get to the top or were content to focus on other ambitions.

* * *

Perhaps the most celebrated debate related to the interaction of the middle classes and the aristocracy surrounds the so-called "Sonderweg" (special path) thesis. What went wrong on the German way to modernity? Many tributaries lead to this great river of interpretation and many subtexts emerge from it. The gist of the argument is that Germany experienced an industrial revolution while retaining a "feudal" social tradition and militaristic ethos. Commentators from Marx to Barrington Moore have asserted that the failure of the bourgeoisie to seize control of the burgeoning German colossus in 1848 allowed for the machinations of Bismarck and subsequent Junker manipulations of the political system. This in turn led to the failure of liberal democracy, the world wars, and the rise of Hitler.[67]

Many flaws infest the "Sonderweg" thesis. It assumes a peasantry compliant and servile to the wishes of the East Elbian elite that careful study in the localities does not substantiate. It assumes either a bumpkinesque or a supremely media-savvy Junker class, neither of which is realistic.[68] The problems connected with the Junker obsession with protective agricultural tariffs, which supposedly twisted the German political system into knots and discouraged modernization, have been shown to be much exaggerated.[69] It is now clear that the Prussian nobility had long been thoroughly committed to modernization and commercial agriculture and endured no serious economic crisis in the later nineteenth century.[70] German conservatism was by no means an aristocratic preserve. Embracing conservatism was a perfectly rational act on the part of capitalists, irrespective of aristocratic allure. Radical nationalists, Catholics, peasant groups, workers, and women all challenged social and political institutions, not just the Junkers.[71] The army, especially the general staff, was by no means incapable of grasping the advantages of industrialization and modernization.[72] A fully "modern" parliamentary political structure developed in Germany between the 1890s and the 1920s. Just as in other developed countries, the proportion of aristocrats gaining election to Parliament diminished as this process unfolded.[73] The submission of the German middle classes to a narrowly defined East Elbian aristocratic ethos has become an untenable thesis.[74]

A Spanish "Sonderweg" proposes that the ascendant bourgeoisie seized power between 1812 and 1843, reformed law and society to serve their own interests, and promoted capitalist development. This conglomeration of new landowners, merchants, and bureaucrats became increasingly more conservative until they merged with the traditional landed aristocracy, which then impeded industrialization and democracy. That a "bourgeois revolution" took place in the first half of the nineteenth century has become a central pillar of Spanish historiography.[75]

Based on careful statistical analysis, Jesus Cruz has argued convincingly that although important – even revolutionary – changes took place in the Spanish polity, these were not enacted by a "new" class, but one that was largely composed of men from lesser noble families who rose by traditional routes to success, assisted by traditional methods of patronage, family, and kinship. They came from the same social ranks as the elite of the old regime. Spanish social history in the nineteenth century was not a struggle between a new ascendant bourgeoisie and an old "feudal" dominant class to control power because they were one and the same thing.[76] The Spanish elite remained dominated by the titular aristocracy who were the wealthiest segment of society into the twentieth century.

The notion of a conflated amorphous class of "notables" amalgamated from both *haute bourgeois* and aristocratic backgrounds has come to dominate French historiography. André-Jean Tudesq elevated the term to historical orthodoxy in the 1960s. The argument rests on common sources of investment, participation in business, and practice of politics tied together by social conservatism and willingness to make reforms that worked to the various elements' mutual advantage. For example, bourgeois republicans from the professional classes, who clearly rejected the Legitimism of the nobility, were nonetheless products of a "backward" and rural France.[77]

A number of historians have questioned Tudesq's arguments. P. M. Jones has demonstrated the pre-eminence of the nobility in the Massif Central in the nineteenth century, where he studied local communities closely. Ralph Gibson's regional studies confirm that it is not possible to say that the aristocracy simply dissolved itself in the world of the *grands notables*. The Higonnets showed that the July monarchy failed to meld the *haute bourgeoisie* and the aristocracy, and the old cleavages continued into the 1870s. The leading authority on the nineteenth-century French nobility, David Higgs, argues that the nobles remained psychologically and socially a distinct entity.[78]

A process of fusion similar to that which Tudesq perceived in France is said to have also taken place in Italy, where the word *aristocrazia* came simply to mean "good society," a hybrid elite of nobles, wealthy businessmen, some professionals, and higher government officials. The distinction, it is argued, between bourgeois and noble largely disappeared.[79] Anthony Cardoza, Paolo Macry, and others have challenged this idea of fusion. In Piedmont and Naples, it is clear, the aristocracy continued to seek to lead society, remained consciously at a distance from the merely wealthy, and separateness was valued by them at least down to 1914.[80] Similar objections can be made to the use of the term "notable" in other nineteenth-century societies.[81]

One other important theory affecting a European aristocracy requires attention. Martin Wiener has proposed an interpretation of the British experience that also posits a form of exceptionalism. He argued that the business elite was enervated by deferring to and accepting the values of landed society that allegedly embodied amateurism, anti-competitiveness, hostility to technology, and preference for rural pursuits. This is said to explain the relative economic decline that set in during the late nineteenth century.[82]

The Wiener thesis is odd in many respects. First, it posits that the most entrepreneurial and acquisitive aristocracy in Europe, noted for digging mines, constructing harbors, managing railroads, promoting resorts, and investing heavily in the stock market somehow destroyed the dynamism of industrialists. At the same time, it has been argued that the aristocracy suffered an "embourgeoisment" during the second half of the nineteenth century that brought an end to its distinctive system of values as it merged into a plutocratic elite. The paradox here is built on a chimera of impressionistic evidence.

Michael Thompson, whose pioneering studies and intimate knowledge of the British landed elite give his opinions weight, has argued that the business elite remained robustly autonomous. He and others emphasize continuity and adjustment both by the entrepreneurial class and the aristocracy in the later nineteenth and early twentieth century.[83] Pat Thane argues that we need

> to think in terms of a negotiated relationship among the major social groups, resulting in a more or less satisfactory accommodation between them based on largely shared values. Landowners played the more prominent political role, but with middle class consent and responsive to their needs. It was consent rather than subordination since the middle classes had nothing obvious to lose from the arrangement. . . ."[84]

It is generally acknowledged that the aristocratic government of eighteenth-century Britain successfully promoted the expansion of one of the largest commercial empires in history. G. R. Searle points out that "entrepreneurial values" were also incorporated into the mid-Victorian state by an aristocrat-dominated regime.[85]

Throughout Europe aristocrats remained distinguished by attachments to lineage, military service, land, endogamy, paternalism, and social exclusivity.[86] In some countries there may have been a hardening of the arteries, with fewer newcomers accepted than in the past, while in others the door may have opened very widely. To think in terms of a single upper class, distinguished only by wealth, however, is a serious mistake before 1918.

Many middle-class and aristocratic values were compatible. The religious seriousness of the bourgeoisie was matched by strong Pietist and Evangelical streaks among the Junkers and the British Victorian elite, while a Catholic revival affected southern German and French nobles and commoners. Both the middle classes and the landed elite valued education and high culture. They shared interests as property owners especially when confronting the threat of socialism. The desire to sustain political stability was a powerful mutual interest. Many aristocrats became nationalists and imperialists, as did the middle classes. Aristocratic regimes of the nineteenth century showed little sign of hostility to industrial or commercial interests. If anything, the ending of legal privileges engineered by governments still dominated by the titled elite suggests the opposite. Arno Mayer and Joseph Schumpeter were right to argue that the aristocracies, at least in most countries, lived in peace with the middle classes during the later part of the nineteenth century but wrong to assume that "feudal" landowners only at that late hour showed a friendly interest in rational economic management.[87]

Much continued to sustain a distinction between the aristocracy and the *haute bourgeoisie*. The devotion to lineage and primogeniture were alien to the middle classes. Members of the latter who lost their fortunes slipped out of their class. Titled aristocrats, however hard up – unless their foibles became dangerous or criminal – were not excluded from society. Bourgeois aspirants seeking to enter aristocratic salons had to bring something exceptional to the table while doltish dukes could attend as a matter of course.

The interrelationship between the landed elite and the bourgeoisie during the nineteenth century was subtle and complex. This was a story of accommodation rather than absorption or decline. Aristocrats proved willing to swallow the occasional toad, while most members of the middle classes never had in the past nor ever could in the future gain access to the inner sanctum of court society. They went on doing what they had always done, socializing amongst themselves and accepting that the most prestigious posts in society and government should be held by blue bloods. The middle classes vastly expanded in numbers in industrializing countries, but for a long time this had relatively little effect on existing arrangements. The obvious persistence of the aristocracy calls into question the value of traditional models of "bourgeois" society. Instead of labeling "surviving" nobles exceptions or mere "remnants," we need to think again about the presently accepted conception of a "bourgeois" nineteenth century.[88]

Princess Radziwill's complaint mentioned earlier was made at the end of the *belle époque*, couched in terms often echoed in aristocratic lamentations of the past. Entry into "Society" was merely becoming a matter of money. The Countess of Cardigan fondly remembered that in the 1840s Cowes during the yachting season "was full of lighthearted gaiety, over which the shadow of the American millionaire and knighted plutocrat had not yet fallen."[89] Such suspirations are almost always misleading. The cry of "wolf" was premature.

7

THE HABIT OF AUTHORITY: LOCAL POWER

> To the peasant, the State was something as distant and alien as the sense of belonging to a great nation. His thoughts and sensibilities were limited to the authority of his immediate lord.
>
> Hans Kudich, Austrian peasant leader, describing the situation in Lower Austria in 1848 in his autobiography published in 1873[1]

Giesegaard lies south of Copenhagen. The estate was acquired by Anne Sophie Schack, widow of General Schack of Schackenborg, when she called in a loan made to the owner in 1736. She was descended from the old noble dynasty of Rantzau and had great ambitions for her husband's family. She built a new house and acquired further large estates in Jutland. These passed to her step-grandson, Count Frederik Schack, in 1787. From 1775 the estate was entailed on his descendants. In the mid-nineteenth century the family held 27,000 acres at Giesegaard along with the additional estates on the mainland.

In 1821 Giesegaard passed to the Brockenhuus family by marriage. They took the additional name Schack. Uneventfully, the counts lived out their lives on the estate, managing their properties and enjoying their hunting. Changes in Danish law enabled many of the workers on the estate to purchase their land and the entail was annulled in 1922 after a law ended the practice. The present owner still retains 7700 acres and the splendid house and park.[2] Periodic bouts with debt and a strain of endearing eccentricity provided the only major excitement in the family history. Count Knud (d. 1823) used to invite peasants to dinner along with neighboring landowners, and Count Frederik (d. 1977) set out decorative pink turkeys that noisily flew up from the courtyard when cars arrived at the front of the house.

The state began to intervene and regulate the powers Danish landowners exercised over their peasants as early as 1787. The imposition of corporal punishment upon most estate workers was banned in 1791. Then the lord's right to select military recruits, a powerful instrument of control, was abolished. Further reforms were enacted that gave farmers land and independence at the expense of the aristocracy. As the privileges melted away, the moral authority of the counts also began to wane. Peasants demonstrated in front of the house in 1848 and had to be calmed by the police. In 1883 the Count was not re-elected as chairman of the Parish Council, being replaced by a radical peasant farmer. The next year most of the peasants attending a parish meeting walked out of the room in protest against estate policies when the Countess tried to take the initiative. However, in 1914 a neighboring landowner still had enough authority to order his workers to throw an intrusive labor organizer into the moat.[3]

Yet, succeeding counts continued to enlarge and expand the amenities of the house and park. The present incumbent, who previously worked as an engineer in Copenhagen, moved his family to the country upon his inheritance. The social fabric of the rural community around Giesegaard remained strong. Children continued to be taught not to do anything that could in any way offend the estate. Jobs and housing remained in the Count's gift. Self-prompted, the Giesegaard employees choose to fly the flag to mark the Count's birthday. Charitable institutions bear the family name and were funded by the lords. Life in the big house forms a frame of reference around which life in the Giesegaard area still revolves. The anthropologist Palle Ove Christiannsen, who studied the estate in the 1970s, noted: "Nearly everybody knows every step the lord and those closest to him take – including the farmers round about the estate who were emancipated from Giesegaard over 100 years ago."[4] When Count Frederik Brockenhuus-Schack died in 1977 workers from the home farm covered the funeral route with pine branches, and horses pulled the coffin to the church. The estate tractor drivers became a bit intoxicated, but their shouts of "good-bye" as the coffin passed, if a bit too informally delivered, appear to have been well meant. Those who gathered from around the district for what Christiannsen described as a "mythic" ceremony became witness to a symbolism that has its only modern analogy in funerals of heads of state. The Count's passing had to do with succession, lineage, identity, loyalty, and the "communication of differentness."[5]

Russian landlords ruled over their domains in the first half of the nineteenth century like absolute monarchs. When referring to noble owners of estates, usage of the phrase "*mon maître*" persisted among dependent sharecroppers and farm laborers in France into the later nineteenth century.[6] Counts were known to use canes to knock off the hats of those who failed to doff their headgear. Garibaldi was unsuccessful in abolishing servile hand kissing of lords by peasants during his occupation of Sicily in 1860. Rural laborers in the Baltic provinces were still obliged to dismount from their carts or horses, remove their hats, and step aside when they met nobles on the road. Even in the years just before World War I great landowners returning to their estates in rural Sicily were met with bands playing and *Te Deums* sung at the local church. The villagers lined the streets as if royalty were arriving.[7] Grandees in the countryside lived very differently than squires. They were driven in elaborate equipages or enormous limousines. They were more likely to chair county councils, and serve as lord lieutenants and governors. Their wealth had an exponential effect on their visibility, influence, and authority. Those long settled in an area could arouse a kind of patriotic attachment. If they were ruthless and mean-spirited, they were dreaded and hated. For the most part, however, the limited knowledge of the outside world on the peasants' part and the glamour and grandeur of noblemen's existence made aristocratic rule seem natural and inevitable.

Local power was at the heart of aristocratic power. Although their control over central governments decayed during the later nineteenth century, even in the states where aristocracies were not dominant at the national level, personal associations of long standing with the populace in rural areas conferred considerable influence (willing deference has not yet absolutely disappeared in some corners of Europe even today). The countryside was a complicated place. Often several layers of tenantry existed, from large and prosperous farmers to totally bedraggled paupers barely surviving on the margins of village life. Almost always, when taking a closer look at relations between landlords and peasants, things become more complicated than they appear at first glance. The stereotype of crass exploitation and dumb submission interspersed with periodic bursts of *jacquerie* was rarely to be found in the nineteenth century. In some places oppression was ascendant. The rural masses in Sicily, Romania, and Ireland, due to the unusual land tenure systems in those countries, suffered greatly. On the other hand, the peasants of Sweden and Finland were largely free from interference of any kind from above. Most of the rest of the working population in the countryside experienced variable conditions from estate to estate, region to region, and harvest to harvest. In some places the tenantry remained deferential allies. Some big farmers owned considerable amounts of land and became rivals for local authority, challenging the aristocracy on its home turf.

In Russia serfdom and police and judicial powers disappeared at the same time in 1861. However, in other countries such authority lasted in the hands of nobles long after labor service ended. Aristocrats often exercised responsibility for morals, labor, poor relief, roads, water, game, construction, fire, and security. Seigneurial powers were removed in Spain in a series of reforms between 1811 and 1836, although the urban residence of many landowners meant that agents or other substitutes had exercised these powers in the past and often continued to do so in a "boss" system that rested on corruption and brute power rather than legal intent. In Austria and Bohemia, Vienna relied heavily on nobles for civil and police administration, although the government assumed jurisdiction in all criminal matters after 1845. Within Germany, proprietors in Bavaria, Württemberg, and Hanover lost these powers in 1848 while in Saxony not until 1855, and in Mecklenburg 1877.[8] In Prussia owners of knights' estates retained full police powers until 1872, and important political and legal controls were not abolished until 1927. Corporal punishment continued in use in some countries into the twentieth century.

Countries differed widely in their systems of local government. In Britain there was little control from the center, while in France almost everything important was decided on in Paris and the concept of unpaid public service was alien.[9] At the provincial or county level governors were almost always titled magnates in Britain, Hungary, Austria, and Prussia. In Russia many of the governors and marshals of the nobility were grandees but more subject to bureaucratic control than their peers elsewhere.[10] While in Sweden and Finland many were recruited from the nobility, the proportion declined in the early twentieth century.[11] In France, Italy, and Romania prefects were often drawn from the middle classes. In Lower Saxony and Westphalia the mediatized families held aloof and had little active role in the administration of the regions, although the sovereign princely families of Anhalt, Reuss, Waldeck-Pyrmont, and the like were the actual rulers of their miniature kingdoms and retained some authority even after 1871.

Aristocratic influence was more prevalent as one moved down the ladder to the local level. In Prussia over half the administrators, called *Landräte*, were nobles in 1911. In some of the eastern provinces the rate was 90 percent.[12] Mayors in France and Italy were often local nobles while aristocrats governed many of the big cities such as Marseilles, Bordeaux, Turin, Madrid, Stockholm, and Moscow.[13] In parts of France the rate of noblemen serving as mayors increased dramatically over the course of the nineteenth century. Many British cities also more frequently turned to local magnates as mayors, but the office was largely ceremonial. However, English grandees often chaired the county quarter sessions, which managed most of the business of local government.[14] Command over military recruitment and local militias added marshal discipline to civil authority.

When particularly agitated by some issue, English noblemen called county meetings. These were extraordinary mixtures of plebian and aristocratic politics. Howling mobs of laborers, more sober tenantry, country gentlemen, and grandees came together to draw up petitions and let off steam. Magnates stood on platforms above the crowd like captains of storm-tossed ships shouting out their grievances before the gathered masses.[15] Only a violently contested parliamentary election in a large constituency could match the drama and ferocity of such a gathering. Throwing dead cats, swung above the head by the tail to gain momentum, was a traditional sign of disapproval. Most Continental nobles would have shuddered at the sight.

Elective councils became common in most countries as the nineteenth century progressed. Even Russia established a system in 1864. Those nobles who remained in the countryside after emancipation were able to build independent political power bases that laid the foundations for the political parties that emerged after 1905.[16] The Baltic, Prussian, and Habsburg elites retained dominance in local assemblies even after electoral reforms, and the English aristocracy sailed through the establishment of democratic county councils in 1888 in good order. Just before World War I over half the new assemblies were led by peers or baronets.[17] In 1840 only 17 percent of the local councils in France were composed of nobles, but in 1870 this had risen to 28 percent. In some departments noble representation rose to one-third, but a part of the increase may have been due to the proliferation of bogus titles. Radical decline set in after the Third Republic was well established.[18]

For most aristocrats informal rule was more important than legal powers in the localities. The grandeur of the house and park at the center of a great estate imposed visible authority on the landscape. Castles that sat high on crags and hills could be seen for miles, hovering over the lives of peasants like great watchtowers. Even where mansions lay invisible behind walls and forests, surrounding villages felt their presence pressing down upon them. Carriages, estate buildings, mills, and laborers' houses were painted in uniform colors taken from the family coat of arms; servants and huntsmen were dressed in the family livery.

Informal influence could be benevolent. The Marquis d'Azeglio as a child once hit a servant with a stick. "My mother," he recounted later, "forced me to go down on my knees and beg his pardon in full sight of the crowd of by-standers."[19] Earl Fitzwilliam, one of the richest and grandest of all the peers in England, forced his teenage son to turn around and ride back to a tenant farmer he had passed without raising his hat to apologize.[20] Funds flowed to the sick and old. Help was given with dowries and interfering officials. Churches and village halls were built and repaired. Feasts and celebrations provided entertainment and largesse. Reducing rents in times of woe could be literally life-saving. Patronage over local jobs, often with housing attached, both on the estate and in the state sector was distributed through magnates' managers. All of these activities encouraged loyalty and blunted antagonism. Charity was encouraged by religion, burnished the lordly image, and was an excellent way to foster dependence.[21] Aristocrats also became directors of railways and business enterprises, which continued their prestige and influence in the localities.

Shared enjoyment of rural sports and the majesty of the rituals involved helped integrate the rural community. The special language, colorful dress, hierarchy, and drama of a hunt in full array were emotive and significant. Harvest festivals emphasized deference and common bonds. In East Prussia workers processed to the manor house and formed a semi-circle around the front stairs where the lord and his family waited. The Junker was presented with a harvest crown – a bundle of rye, wheat, and oats and barley tied together with colorful ribbons – and then hymns were sung. Christmas ceremonies of gift giving by the lords, kissing hands, and singing hymns also tied paternalism to religion and community.[22] Estate workers waiting in long lines to receive a holiday gift from the hands of a duke or baronet continued in great English houses even in recent years.

Support from parish clergy and the hierarchy of the established churches often reinforced aristocratic rule. Tocqueville noted that the French Revolution "had cured [the aristocracy] of their irreligiousness; it had taught them, if not the truth, at least the social usefulness of belief."[23] In France the strong alliance between the château and the presbytery was mutually strengthening in areas where traditional values remained strong.[24] Across Europe, from the Protestant north to the Catholic south to the Orthodox east, aristocrats and clergy participated in popular rituals that encouraged consensus, deference, and social hierarchy. The family pew usually had a central or elevated position near the altar and the dynastic coat of arms was often the only decoration in the austere churches of the north. In a number of Protestant countries such as England, Sweden, the Baltic provinces, and Prussia the nobility retained control over the appointment of priests and pastors to parishes into the twentieth century.[25] However, religion could be a divisive issue, as it was between the Protestant Irish Ascendancy and their Catholic tenantry or the Orthodox nobles in Lithuania ruling over a Catholic peasantry.

Agricultural associations were also an important point of leadership in rural communities. The most successful exploitation of this source of power developed in France. In 1884 the government legalized agricultural syndicates that offered various services to farmers including bulk purchase of fertilizers and equipment, insurance, credit, loans, help in selling crops, and dissemination of technical advances, all linked to a central union in Paris. This allowed aristocrats in various parts of the country to strengthen their position in rural communities and encourage stability. Influenced by the Social Catholic philosophy of Count Albert de Mun and the Marquis René de la Tour du Pin, the aim was to draw as large a part of the peasantry as possible into non-political activities and exclude the bureaucratic arm of the state and labor organizers as intermediaries between themselves and the people. In some departments up to 80 percent of the peasantry joined syndicates headed by noblemen that retained broad support until after World War II, although in other areas they were not as successful in countering the influence of "republican" organizations.[26]

The Spanish landed elite ruled the countryside through *caciquismo*. The *cacique* stood outside the official hierarchies: a local boss, a manipulator of votes, and a dispenser of patronage. Unlike local officials in Prussia or Russia, his chief function was to circumvent the central government. This network of influence and power frustrated both bureaucratic and party agents in the localities and undermined the judiciary. The system allowed the landed elite to get its way via proxies and agents. It guaranteed low taxes for large landowners and selective enforcement of the law. In southern Italy corruption similar to the "boss" system in Spain also prevailed.[27]

In Denmark labor service was converted into paid wages after 1850. This meant there was no longer a guaranteed stable work force. Landowners tried to deal with this in a variety of ways. Estates provided "free service dwellings" for permanent hands. After the disruptions of 1848 no further strikes or riots took place for 80 years. From 1900 more and more leased land was drawn in under the demesne form of estates, where the workers lived in tied cottages. This process of increasing direct farming by the landlord and ending leases continued at Giesegaard into the 1980s. The estate became a "hungry monster," amalgamating acreage at the expense of small independent peasant farmers.[28]

In Bologna and Tuscany the link between landownership and power rested upon a system of social control called *mezzadria*. It was a sharecropping arrangement; the lord provided land on an annual lease with house, barn, well, etc. and half the seed. The peasant contributed the labor and work animals. The owner received half the product along with other contributions such as transporting the lord's share of the crop to market, producing olive oil, and even washing the landlord's linen. The system gave landlords tremendous leverage in dealings with the work force. The aristocrat exercised the right to regulate the private life of the peasant and his family, superintending his dress and religious observance, and forbade him to marry without consent or to attend cafés and gaming rooms. The sanction was eviction. The system went on pretty much unchanged until World War I.[29]

From the eighteenth century onwards in Romania rural big businessmen rented huge blocks of land from the nobles and then released it at increasing rates to the downtrodden and embittered peasantry who were locked in ever-deepening servitude worse than serfdom. Over 73 percent of the large estates were leased in this way. By 1905 the Fischer family alone rented over 380,000 acres. Land reforms in 1864 and 1889 actually strengthened the system. This monstrous regime was perhaps the most grotesquely irresponsible landlordism to be found in Europe.[30]

Crucial to the healthy power of the aristocracy in the countryside was the extent to which they lived on their estates. For example, in Navarre on the lands of the Duke of Villahermosa, where the family spent part of every year and actively interested themselves in the fortunes of their tenants, deference was deep-rooted and genuine, while on the estates of the Duke de Infantado, who seldom appeared, tenant resentment exploded in 1919–20 in the shape of a rent strike and clashes between peasants and the Civil Guard.[31] In Bologna, Tuscany, Piedmont, and elsewhere, Italian nobles sustained a face-to-face relationship with their peasants up to 1914.[32] In France country houses did not turn into mere vacation homes until after World War I. On the other hand, most aristocrats in Spain, Sicily, and Romania were absentees living in large cities or even abroad. An increasing proportion of the Russian and Irish gentry left the countryside in the second half of the century. Land sales diminished the weight and extent of their influence. In Ireland, where many estates in the South were reduced to little more than the gardens around the big house, the elite became isolated, vulnerable, and irrelevant. Social, political, and economic leverage evaporated as the acreage vanished.

Peasant revolts had not been unknown in earlier times, but the injection of nationalism and socialism added new elements to civil disturbances. The Galician uprising of 1846 owed its origins to seigneurial exactions. Unrest in the Baltic provinces in 1805, 1845–8, and in the 1850s forced the German barons to make concessions. Ethnic differences between the Estonians and Latvians, on the one hand, and the Germans, on the other, left the nobles without allies in the countryside against either the peasantry or the Tsarist regime. Despite abolition of many of the feudal services and fees in Hesse in 1832, tension was strong in the countryside, and a number of hated exactions remained. When news of the uprisings in Paris in 1848 reached the peasants, they sought to rid themselves of these burdens. Noble families were terrorized by mobs and concessions were extracted. Isolated episodes of violence broke out in parts of France, exploited and intensified by republican politics. Aristocrats were rumored to be in sympathy with the Prussians in 1870, and a peasant mob in the Dordogne lynched a local noble, burning him alive because of his alleged disloyalty. The four peasants later guillotined for this crime were regarded as martyrs.[33]

Seething anti-landlord feeling underpinned the Irish Land War of 1879 to 1882. Murders of Irish landowners had taken place before. However, it was unusual for peers to be killed. The murder of the Earl of Leitrim in 1878 opened a new chapter in the history of Irish resistance to the Ascendancy.[34] Lord Salisbury concluded as early as 1882 that nothing could be done to save the Irish landlords in the long run, and their only hope was to sell out on the best terms they could get. In Scotland anti-landlord disturbances in the Highlands required gunboats and marines to quell them. The Crofters' War was the most severe crisis in the Highlands since the heyday of Jacobitism. Fortunately for the Scottish elite, the Crofters' Act of 1886 gave the tenants fair rent and security of tenure, but left landed society intact.[35]

The uniquely exploitative Romanian system of land tenure produced a major uprising in 1888. Further eruptions occurred in 1892, 1894, and 1900. These climaxed in the Great Peasant Revolt of 1907 that broke out the estate of Prince Sturdza. The peasants seized the whole of Moldovia until an army of 120,000 troops suppressed the uprising, killing some 10,000 peasants.[36] One can see why the Romanian elite might wish to divert attention to national rivalries with neighboring states.

Russia suffered many rural disturbances throughout the nineteenth century. Village revolts increased in the years immediately following the emancipation decree, reflecting the peasants' bitter disappointment with the terms. In March and early April 1902 a massive uprising erupted in Poltava Province and spread elsewhere; 105 estates were destroyed. The governor, Prince Ivan Obolensky, ruthlessly put it down. Then came the 1905 revolution that spread throughout the country including the Baltic provinces. Many aristocrats felt helpless and afraid. One baron wrote upon his return to his estate in 1906: "I had set foot on my manor as a powerless stranger among my laborers, who went on living there undisturbed, watching me with grins on their faces."[37] In the immediate aftermath massive land sales occurred.

A general population increase that took place from the mid- to late eighteenth century became considerably more rapid and constant after 1800. Where industrial development was underway much of the demographic expansion could be absorbed into the cities, although that took men and women out from under the supervision of the aristocracy. In France and elsewhere the thinning in numbers of the rural inhabitants caused a shortage of adequate numbers of workers in the agricultural sector. In non-industrialized countries emigration reduced some of the strain but large surpluses of young people without adequate incomes or housing became increasingly dangerous to the elite's authority in the countryside.

The accelerating commercialization of agriculture in northern Italy after 1860 threatened the relationship between the aristocracy and farmers. Rising farm prices in the 1860s and 1870s encouraged landowners in the Po Valley to adapt their production to the demands of new national and international markets. Then the onset of the agricultural depression, which brought falling prices and sharpened competition, placed even greater pressures on the elite to intensify their methods of cultivation and develop specialized fodder and industrial crops. Agricultural modernization came at the expense of social stability. Growing numbers of peasant families were pushed off farms. More and more land was purchased or leased by bourgeois owners. Socialist organizers began to build a strong labor movement. Aristocrats lamented the changes, and favored a conciliatory approach. The bourgeois entrepreneurs were contemptuous of paternalism and pushed aristocratic leadership aside. In 1913 a greatly expanded suffrage put much of the political power in the hands of leftists both at the local and national level. Traditional deference politics died.[38]

Sicily was unique in Europe for the cooperation between the criminal gangs of the Mafia and the landowners. They worked together in the management of estates and in electoral politics. The Italian government abandoned the island to the bosses in return for Sicilian support of the current ministry in Rome. Aristocrats who opposed Mafia corruption were murdered. The Marquis Notarbartolo was killed in 1893 for passing on incriminating information to officials. Although reports periodically raised the possibility of land reform, nothing was achieved prior to World War I. Sicilian politicians, such as Baron Majorana, successfully used their influence to block changes. Even after the war an alliance with the fascists helped stave off effective legislative action until 1950.[39]

Frequent land sales in the later nineteenth and early twentieth century in Prussia and Russia weakened the relationship between lords and peasants. Sales of estates, even if motivated by a desire for diversification of assets and not due to debt, reduced local control, as well as undermining aristocratic influence in national life. The noble monopoly on landownership in the Baltic provinces was abolished in 1866, and indebted nobles began to sell land to urban buyers. The Irish Land Acts culminated in more than 200,000 sales.[40]

Trains, newspapers, and expanded literacy broke down the isolation of the peasantry and thus made it harder for landowners to keep out new ideas and agrarian organizers. In the 1880s agitators arranged to sabotage Count Brockenhuus-Schack's firewood auctions at Giesegaard. Instead of bidding against each other, an association arranged joint bulk purchases and then distributed the less expensive wood among the members.[41] Cooperative movements also lessened landlord influence and profits. Increasingly, governments took responsibility for what had previously been left to charity and paternalism. Delocalized national wealth replaced aristocratic influence.

Rising nationalist feeling was a danger to landlord influence in places such as the Baltic provinces, where ethnic, religious, and language differences made the barons an alien and isolated group in a sea of Estonians and Latvians more and more conscious of their own identities and exploitation.[42] The Transylvanian elite of Magyar extraction was threatened by the large Romanian underclass. The Polish aristocracy in Galicia, who ruled over rebellious and unhappy Ukrainian peasants, remained loyal to the Habsburgs on whose protection they relied. The much-despised Anglo-Irish Ascendancy has already been mentioned. The Welsh resented their landlords not so much as aliens, since many descended from old native families, but because of their distinctive religion and manner of life. Most members of the elite could no longer speak the language.

* * *

The resilience of the landed elite should not be underestimated. Local studies by historians have repeatedly found extensive aristocratic influence at least until 1914. In the depths of rural France deference and great influence still remained in the hands of nobles. Many of the estates over 2500 acres were owned by dukes and princes throughout the nineteenth century.[43] In Spain the landowners did not face a mortal threat to their rule until 1930s, with the collapse of the monarchical state. Throughout the second half of the nineteenth century the Bolognese nobility continued to rule supreme over the political, economic, and social life of the province. In Poland in 1922 most large landowners were still titled aristocrats.[44]

The English elite never became isolated from the community in which they lived. Church, cricket, and foxhunting allowed landowners to "bond" with rural communities and sustain the illusion if not the reality of shared interests across class lines. Mutual trust between landlord and tenant generally prevailed and the former took farmers' needs and interests into account if for no other reason than that good tenants were hard to find. Radical efforts to exploit possible resentment against the aristocracy failed. The Industrial Revolution brought far fewer conflicts between landed and bourgeois forms of wealth than was once thought. The Ground Game Act of 1881 removed one of the few persistent national irritants in relations between landlords and tenants by allowing the latter to destroy rabbits and hares on their farms without first asking the landowner's permission. The Agricultural Holdings Act of 1883 ensured that landowners compensated tenants for improvements made to their land.[45] Studies have shown that even in the 1930s old-line families could "mobilize a large and spontaneous deference vote" in local elections in predominantly rural counties.[46]

The core of the East Elbian agrarian elite, even in the 1920s, consisted of the nobility despite infiltration by commercial wealth. Moreover, the larger the estate, the more likely it was to belong to a noble family.[47] Liberals and radicals were not allowed to canvass on estates. Until 1914 the only ballot paper a laborer was likely to see was the Conservative one, handed to him by his foreman outside the polling booth. Open-air rural meetings were illegal and the Junkers controlled the village halls. Rural hostility to city liberals could be exploited. So too could class divisions within the rural population. Substantial peasants shared with nobles a desire to suppress any indiscipline by their landless laborers and keep wages low.[48]

In rural Piedmont the leadership of old-line families proved to be particularly resistant to erosion, especially in those localities where country houses and estates were located. Strong presence of the aristocracy on the land helped to preserve vertical ties and local loyalties and bolster traditional notions of "natural" leadership. When socialist labor organizers tried to penetrate the Piedmontese countryside, they encountered strong resistance in the fields and at the ballot box from a coalition of anti-socialist forces commanded by titled nobles.[49]

Huge estates existed in Scotland, Poland, Hungary, Russia, England, Spain, Bohemia, and Germany. In Denmark, Sweden, Italy, France, Austria, and elsewhere, aristocratic properties remained widespread even if individual holdings were not massive. At least until 1914 landed influence in the countryside across Europe was immense, and it continued beyond the war. However, the declining proportion of the population living in rural areas, the surge in the industrial contribution to the economy, and radical political ideologies made sustained aristocratic authority at the national level far more problematic.

8

EAGLES AND PEACOCKS: NATIONAL POWER

> It seems to me that the upper classes have a duty of involving themselves in public life in order to prevent society from falling into the hands of the worst elements. . . . You have an illustrious name and I must invoke *noblesse oblige* to induce you to accept an office that will require authority and decorum from your name.
>
> Count Giovanni Codronchi to Count Nerio Malvezzi,
> 1884, in Cardoza (1991), pp. 183–4

Few Scottish families have produced more soldiers or statesmen than the Ramsays. Their seat for two dozen generations at 'Dalwolsie' Castle in Midlothian was granted to them by King David I in the twelfth century. The first prominent chief was a member of the Council of the Magnates of the Realm in 1255. Notable early Ramsays included Sir William, who was a friend of Robert Bruce and signed a letter to the Pope asserting the independence of Scotland in 1320. Another was one of the principal commanders of the Scottish forces that defeated the English at Boroughmuir near Edinburgh in 1335. He perished of hunger in a dungeon at Hermitage Castle, where he was dragged in chains by his enemy, William Douglas. Another Ramsay was killed at Flodden in 1513.

Two Ramsay brothers helped to save King James VI's life during the still mysterious Gowrie Plot at Perth in 1600. The elder of the two was made Lord Ramsay in 1618. The 1st Earl of Dalhousie was a colonel in the Scottish armies that invaded England in 1640 and 1644. General George Ramsay, a fiery, brave soldier, led a division at the battle of Killecrankie and was Commander-in-Chief of the forces in Scotland under William and Mary.

The 5th Earl, a brigadier general, fought with the Scots Guards during the War of the Spanish Succession. The 9th commanded a division under Wellington in the Peninsular War and was promoted to full general by the time of his service at Waterloo. Later he governed Canada and was appointed Commander-in-Chief of the forces in India. The 1st Marquis of Dalhousie was the youngest man ever appointed Viceroy of India and emerged as the imperial ruler most admired by the Victorians. He charted the great Indian railway system, promoted education, introduced the telegraph, and launched vast irrigation projects. His successor, the 11th Earl, was a modestly successful politician, who served in Liberal cabinets. The 13th Earl was one of a small number of great aristocrats to stay loyal to the Liberal Party when Gladstone declared for Home Rule in Ireland, and was made Scottish Secretary.

The 16th Earl served with the Black Watch in World War II. During the invasion of Sicily he earned a Military Cross for leading an attack on an enemy machine-gun position. After the war, he won the parliamentary seat for Forfarshire as a Conservative in the teeth of the Labour landslide of 1945. Harold Macmillan appointed him Governor General of Rhodesia and Nyasaland in 1957, where for six years he dealt skillfully with the tense and deteriorating relations between British settlers and the native population. Forced to sell some land to pay death duties, he continued to preside over an estate of nearly 50,000 acres and played the role of a traditional grandee, courtier, and elder statesman until his death in 1999.

Like so many aristocratic families, the Ramsays not only surmounted the challenge of the revolutions and wars between 1789 and 1815 but also emerged resurgent, ready for another century and a half of leadership. Even the French nobility absorbed the lessons of defeat and faced the new order with more confidence and optimism than is often supposed.[1] The victories at Leipzig and Waterloo and the diplomatic triumph at Vienna were masterpieces of their kind, and marked the restoration of aristocratic generalship and statecraft in Europe. Moreover, a new "conservative" ideology shaped by Edmund Burke, Viscount de Chateaubriand, and others arose in conscious contrast to the Enlightenment, and the Catholic revival in the second half of the nineteenth century also helped to erect formidable ramparts to staunch the flow of democracy.[2] On the other hand, many aristocrats led liberal and nationalist movements that also helped to sustain their dominance.

Judicious concessions and pragmatic compromise dampened working-class militancy and fended off middle-class ascendancy.[3] Social Darwinism supported the notion of a "natural" aristocracy that gave pseudo-scientific backing to the notion that breeding and "blood" justified privilege. Vertical unifiers such as religion, patriotism, and sustaining the health of agriculture helped moderate the sharpening horizontal divisions of class. Aristocrats were still prepared to act ruthlessly to get their way and produced leaders of outstanding quality throughout the nineteenth century, from Wellington and Metternich to Bismarck, Cavour, and Salisbury.

Although aristocrats exuded grandeur and self-confidence, only some of them soared like eagles. Others displayed the plumage of peacocks, whose rasping shriek was no substitute for talons and wings that could sustain mastery. Historians are not always in agreement about which aristocracies were still hunting prey and which merely provided pageantry and playboys. Some argue, for example, that the Russian high nobility, despite storied wealth and ancient lineage, had virtually no capacity to thwart the will of the autocrat or set a course for the nation.[4] C. A. Macartney believes that in Austria and Bohemia by 1890, "the direct power of the aristocracy was a shadow of what it had been in 1848.... [They] spent their time gambling, horseracing, exchanging scandal and seducing other people's wives and daughters."[5] On the other hand, Edward Thaden writes that the St. Petersburg aristocracy "dominated, even into the twentieth century, Russian politics and government to a degree unknown in any other major European country."[6] Ivan Berend argues that the Austrian grandees surmounted every challenge and monopolized national power. Things only began to change after universal suffrage was introduced in 1907.[7]

The balance between eagles and peacocks began to alter during the later nineteenth century. The capacity to clothe themselves in gorgeous raiment and lord it over the ballroom dance floor was not the same as being able to enact legislation beneficial to their class interest. The spread of democracy was very dangerous and, indeed, fatal to the aristocracy. In the twentieth century many peacocks still strutted petulantly about the landscape squawking but fewer and fewer eagles sailed across the skies making their prey tremble and scurry for cover.

Aristocrats faced both familiar threats and new challenges. The decline of Christian faith and the slower but persistent shrinkage of established churches weakened their rule. The rootlessness of a progressively larger population in the industrialized West also menaced them. However, the two most direct threats that had been gathering force for centuries accelerated rapidly in the nineteenth century: consolidation of state power and nationalism.

* * *

The modern bureaucratic state was far more injurious to aristocratic power than absolutist monarchs had been. The latter sought compromise and cooperation. The former grew like the "Blob": unstoppable, enveloping everything in its path. In Prussia the number of higher officials increased threefold between 1821 and 1901. The French bureaucracy sextupled during the nineteenth century. Many functions once conducted by the landed elite were engrossed by the state: tax operations, public health, police, military recruitment, and justice. New services such as railways, factory inspections, supervision of insurance, elevator safety, pensions, and the like added to the number of officials.[8] Bureaucracies grew so large that there were not enough nobles to fill many of the leadership posts. Nevertheless we must guard against making the same mistake historians did about absolutism in the seventeenth and eighteenth centuries, forgetting that elites still controlled the highest levels of these organizations. Many senior policy-making positions in the bureaucracy and the political command structure remained firmly in the grasp of aristocrats, especially in Austria, Germany, and Britain.

The presence of so many indolent peacocks can easily mislead observers into making the assumption that professionalization led to the withdrawal of the aristocracy from political control. Dominic Lieven writes: "Society was becoming too complicated for aristocrats to manage."[9] In fact, they did quite well staying on top of the latest changes in military technology and organization. Aristocrats were among the first to embrace innovations such as motorized transportation and airplanes. General Staffs dominated by the old elite managed vast citizen armies that dwarfed even major corporations in terms of size and complexity. Aside from the clergy, aristocrats were usually the best-educated segment of nineteenth-century society. A far larger proportion of nobles achieved university degrees than any other social class, and the numbers increased rapidly with time.[10]

The stereotypical view of aristocrats falling by the wayside due to the institution of meritocratic examination systems is mythic. Competitive examinations had been used since the seventeenth century in some bureaucracies in Northern Italy.[11] As early as 1808 and 1809 Russia and Prussia required candidates for certain positions to pass tests. It is true that governments increasingly searched for efficiency and professionalism, but landed elites were perfectly capable of meeting the expectations established by most states in the nineteenth century. Furthermore, examinations were usually established only for entry-level positions, while many aristocrats leapfrogged over competitors by taking office, often while still young, in senior ranks. Monarchs waived entrance qualifications altogether for members of old court families.[12]

Aristocrats also had the advantage of parents who could afford whatever tutoring and coaching might be required to gain entrance to exclusive academic or military schools, and independent incomes allowed them to survive the early years of state service before salaries became substantial in the higher ranks. In Finland restricting entrance to the University of Helsinki by competitive entrance examinations largely excluded commoners from government, for which an academic degree was a prerequisite. Only the nobility could afford the preparation necessary to pass the tests.[13] In Britain Gladstone's replacement of patronage with fitness-based selection was designed to preserve the role of the aristocracy by forestalling radical demands for a purge of blue bloods from government.[14] Even in France nobles remained ubiquitous among the senior posts in the army and diplomatic corps, while in England the Cabinet was dominated by the aristocracy throughout the nineteenth century.

Nationalism was one of the most dangerous and transformative forces of modern times. It proved a doubled-edged sword for the aristocracy. On the one hand, military victories, newfound independence, and triumphal unifications were rewarded by heightened prestige and power. The Belgian elite in 1830 and the Prussian Junkers in 1870 were beneficiaries of such achievements. The Swedish nobility won popular acclaim in 1912 when they spearheaded a public collection to build warships for which a Liberal government refused to budget funds.[15] The Hungarian elite was considered the core of the "historic nation," which sustained their power into the 1930s.

Jingoistic imperialism shored up flagging status, and shared patriotism brought classes together against common enemies. Powerful and emotive ideas of nationhood and empire could be used to persuade newly enfranchised masses to follow aristocratic leadership.

"We are all brothers of the same blood" is a dangerously egalitarian concept, however, for a class that believed in lineage and exclusivity. Nationalism stripped aristocrats of their identity and vital memories of separateness and honor. Estonian and Latvian peasants felt no common bond with their Germanic overlords, and similar ethnic and religious divisions left the Transylvanian and Irish elites in deep difficulties.[16] Their enemies used the myth that the Danish nobility were "outsiders" who came from Germany – though not accurate – effectively against them.[17] A number of Bohemian magnates were authentically Czech in origin but nationalists increasingly saw them as an elite imposed by the alien Habsburg dynasty. Only the Swedish-speaking Finnish nobility were able to surmount such a challenge, through a daring strategy of deliberately guiding the growth of Finnish national consciousness. [18] Numerous Czartoryskis, Radziwills, and Zamoyskis were forced to flee Poland into long years of exile after the failed risings against the Russians. If they later regained their land, estates divided among two or even three states made it virtually impossible for them to find a focus of loyalty. The Polish elite of Lithuania was swept away by Alexander II after the failed revolt of 1863, leaving the way clear for the development of Lithuanian national feeling without aristocratic leadership.[19] Old Italian families with close ties to the Vatican, "the black nobility," withdrew completely from public life upon the usurpation of Papal authority in Rome by the house of Savoy. The Risorgimento destroyed their ability to function as political leaders. Some still held a grudge as late as 1946, when they felt the overthrow of the royal family was just punishment for past misdeeds. Revived national feeling among the mass of the people largely undermined the Welsh landed elite.[20] After a period of central control by Vienna, Hungary gained a substantial measure of independence in 1867. However, the Magyar elite in turn suppressed other ethnic groups so that Romanian, Croat, and Serbian nationalism became a dangerous threat to Budapest's authority and left parliament deeply divided, indeed paralyzed, by issues of self-determination. The aristocracy acted, Count Bánffy observed, "as if they inhabited a world that contained nothing but Hungarians."[21]

Pan-Germanism in Austria emerged in the second half of the nineteenth century.[22] Many magnates, including some Hungarian ones, tried to remain above the fray and serve the empire and dynasty. A long-time acquaintance of the Habsburg prime minister and Bohemian grandee wrote in 1898: "Count Taaffe was born so to speak without a clear nationality," and he was thus "to a certain degree objective and unbiased with regard to national strivings."[23] Such Habsburg patriots were out of touch with reality, and nationalism would destroy them.

* * *

New threats to aristocratic rule emerged in the eighteenth and nineteenth centuries. Demographic factors challenged the landed elite's suzerainty in a variety of ways. Populations soared. Between 1800 and 1990 the United Kingdom expanded from 16 million to nearly 42 million while European Russia went from 35 to 103 million. Cities mushroomed. Between 1800 and 1910 Moscow grew from 250,000 to 1,481,000, Vienna from 247,000 to 2,030,000, and Berlin from 172,000 to 3,730,000. In spite of many new creations, the aristocracies of Europe became an ever-thinner layer at the top.

Even more dramatic was the shift of employment from the agricultural sector to industry, with all its implications for lost aristocratic ascendancy. In 1770 agriculture formed about half of the English national product, in 1811 36 percent; by 1851 it stood at only 20 percent. However, this was the earliest and most extreme case. In many countries the rural shrinkage was much slower than urban expansion. In Denmark in 1850 nearly four-fifths of the population still lived in the countryside. In the same year two-thirds of Germany's population was rural. On the eve of World War I country dwellers still made up 42 percent of Germans, 56 percent of the French, 81 percent of Hungarians and Romanians, and 86 percent of Russians.[24] One has to be careful in assessing the statistical evidence. Britain was the first to industrialize and urbanize heavily, yet its aristocracy remained powerful into the twentieth century. However, the diminishing proportion of national wealth derived from agriculture affected the balance between the aristocracy and the rest of society. The emergence of trade unions and working-class parties challenged the hegemony of the landed elite.[25]

Until 1789 the chief rival of the aristocracy was monarchy. After 1815 it was the people. Free speech, a free press, an educated citizenry, mass-circulation newspapers, constitutions, extension of suffrage, the secret ballot, and party politics, which diminished the independence and importance of individual politicians, were all threats to aristocratic rule. Intimidation of voters gained a bad name and limits were set on election expenses. Letters from beyond the seas began to reach the urban and rural poor of the European homeland with news of democracy and more prosperous lives. Even conservative parties tended to recruit more heterogeneous leadership.[26] During the nineteenth century the aristocracy as a class lost the initiative in politics.

Noble bashing became a staple of radical and even some middle-class politicians. In France republicans were highly successful in presenting the nobility to the electorate as grasping, reactionary, and desirous of restoring the monarchy and feudalism.[27] Lloyd George ("oh these dukes, how they oppress us") and even Winston Churchill, in his Liberal phase, aimed their fire at the peerage. In a mass democracy the candidate had to appear to share and experience the concerns of the voter.[28] A title of honor could become a liability. In an electoral campaign for a seat in the new German Reichstag in 1871, plain Eduard Müller defeated Viktor, Duke of Ratibor and Prince zu Hohenlohe-Schillingfürst. Müller's slogan was, "Why do you want to vote for the *Duke*? What does someone like that know of the interest of the *people*? Even the name of a man like 'miller' offers a greater guarantee."[29] The British elite lost control of many of its safe seats in 1832 and became dangerously vulnerable in elections in Wales and Ireland after the mid-century. The franchise extensions of 1867 and 1884 left traditional parliamentary families in a minority among MPs for the first time.[30]

Another danger for the nobility was becoming out of touch with mainstream political sentiment. The French aristocracy, riven by internal conflicts, not only wasted time and energy on issues irrelevant to most of their countrymen, but also the Legitimist loyalty to the exiled pretender Henry V was a huge boulder hung around their necks as they tried to swim in contemporary political life. Their strict adherence to Catholicism was also a liability among the urban lower classes increasingly indifferent to religious faith.[31] In Britain the decision by the Whig magnates to desert the Liberal Party over the issue of Home Rule for Ireland in the 1880s was not only damaging to both groups, but also created more candidates for fewer seats as the Whigs now had to compete with established Tory families for conservative nominations.[32] "Diehard" resistance to reform of the House of Lords in the early twentieth century was another failure of leadership. The "black nobility's" support for Pope Benedict XV's pacifism in the face of World War I put them further out of touch with national feeling.[33]

*   *   *

The role of aristocratic women in political life was challenged during the nineteenth century. In the eighteenth century women in Britain were active participants in the electoral system, both as influential owners in their own right of landed estates and through canvassing for friends, family, and protégés.[34] Aristocratic ambassadresses became famous. The role of women as political hostesses and *salonnières* is well known. Miklós Bánffy's novel about pre-1914 Transylvania is filled with formidable women interested in politics, most notably old Countess Sarmasaghy, before whom male politicians quailed.[35] Tolstoy's books not only contain many women with serious intellectual interests, but also figures such as Countess Lydia Ivanovna in *Anna Karenina*, who moved in the highest political circles and exercised influence. Westphalian and Piedmontese ladies were jailed for subversion.[36]

Evidence suggests that the participation of aristocratic women in elections declined as political power ceased to be regarded as property. The rise of party organizations, meritocracy, and public accountability is also seen to have limited the role of women in influencing national events through personal contacts and entertainment.[37] The links between "Society" and politics slowly weakened. As Amanda Vicary, James McCord, and K. D. Reynolds have demonstrated, however, the concept of separate spheres for different genders does not fit easily into the world of landed society.[38] Property and rank trumped gender. While female aristocrats had to be more circumscribed in public during the nineteenth century, their private activities and influence remained important. Even today much of the business of politics is done behind closed doors where personal relationships can have significance. Politicians continued to be drawn to salons in order to meet powerful people. It was the great ladies of the Faubourg Saint-Germain who made the decision in 1849 that it was acceptable to enter into relations with the newly elected President, Prince Louis Napoleon.[39]

Parisian salons were fully engaged in the political activities of the Second Empire and the Dreyfus Affair in the 1890s. The Duchess de Doudeauville and the Duchess de Polignac worked to bury the hatchet between Orleanists and Legitimists. The Countess de Loynes, who also subsidized journals, held the most famous of the right-wing salons. The Duchess d'Uzés partly financed the Boulanger coup attempt. In 1915 the Duchess de la Trémoille was still holding receptions that attracted senior members of the War Cabinet and leading figures in French journalism and politics.[40] In London great political hostesses also continued to exercise considerable social and political power. Female grandees corresponded with party managers, newspaper editors, and prime ministers and were married to Cabinet members. Even in the stodgy old Germanic Baltic provinces Countess Benedikte von Stackelberg and Baroness von Krüdener played a prominent role in nationalist politics in the years before World War I.[41]

In mid-nineteenth-century France noble girls surged into the regular orders during the Catholic revival and played a more important role than at any time since the seventeenth century as intermediaries between the state and the poor and in shaping the Church's response to social concerns. Florence, Lady Harberton became the President of the Rational Dress Society in Britain in 1883, which championed split skirts or knickerbockers for women, and she cycled about the country with groups of followers to demonstrate the efficacy of her cause. Even in relatively primitive countries such as Romania aristocratic women influenced the political process through cultural leadership and journalism.[42]

* * *

Aristocrats had traditionally split into multiple groups in debates over political issues. However, once socialist and radical parties emerged a smaller proportion of blue bloods found their way into positions of leadership in organizations patently hostile to aristocratic interests. The Count de Saint Simon was an important figure in the early socialist movement. Prince Peter Kropotkin was a leading anarchist. Even Marx married the daughter of a nobleman who served as a royal councilor in Brunswick. Countess Sophie Panine

was a minister in Kerensky's Provisional Government. Several grandees claimed the title "red prince," including Prince Hubertus
Löwenstein, an ardent radical during the same period, the Sicilian
Prince Allessandro Filangeri di Cutò who was a socialist deputy in
parliament in the early twentieth century, and Prince Jan Sapieha,
who aroused the ire of his Polish neighbors by driving his servants
to the movies.[43] "Red counts" abounded.

Aristocrats regularly led protests and revolutions during the nineteenth century: in 1818 in the Rhineland, in 1821 in Piedmont, and
in 1825 in Russia. In the 1830s the Italian Prince Luigi Spada was
active in secret societies and carried a dagger ready for quick assassination attempts, but he may just have been deranged.[44] The Polish
insurrections of 1830 and 1863 have already been mentioned. Prince
Adam Czartoryski led the earlier revolt. Prince Roman Sanguszko
walked to Siberia in chains for his part in the affair. The prison
encampments there became crowded with Russian and Polish grandees. The Catholic aristocracy of Belgium led the successful insur-
rection against the Protestant King of the Netherlands in 1830.
Young Romanian aristocrats were heavily involved in the 1848 rising,
and several Magyar magnates were executed in the aftermath of the
Hungarian revolt in the same year.[45]

More dangerous were the revolts that were aimed directly at aristocratic power led by members of the lower classes. Increasingly
revolutionaries questioned not just the political but also the social
order. In Germany the 1848 revolutions were implicitly more anti-
aristocratic than anti-monarchical.[46] During the 1905 revolution the
Baltic barons faced fearsome unrest. One hundred and eighty-four
manor houses were burned to the ground and many more were
damaged. At least 90 Germans, not all nobles, were murdered, including two barons.[47]

An aristocracy without political clout is not really an aristocracy at
all. Many lost the ambition necessary to struggle for the highest
political jobs or no longer enjoyed the self-confidence necessary to
get there. Marcel Proust's celebrated novel noted the French nobility's loss of self-confidence in the years before World War I. Some were
crippled by a new aversion to undeserved privilege. Unable to project
an image of modernity and benevolence required by expanding
electorates, many aristocrats turned inward, worshipping their ancestors rather than striking out for new achievements to add luster to
the family name. The vogue for family history and genealogy turned

out to be a dangerous sign of decay. Demoralization was deep-seated in St. Petersburg. The Council of the United Nobles formed in 1906 to obstruct constitutional government called themselves "aurochs," nearly extinct European wild oxen.[48]

* * *

One can easily exaggerate the degree to which aristocratic influence was waning during the nineteenth century. It is well to remember that in the aftermath of the French Revolution both the British and French aristocracies emerged in reasonably good shape. Monarchies created new titles and promoted talented men to bind the aristocracy more tightly to their service; lords tried to make themselves appear more useful.[49] The ethos of paternalism often produced a broader and more sympathetic outlook on social problems than is often remembered. The national memorial to the philanthropic work of the Earl of Shaftesbury that stands in the center of London's Piccadilly Circus should remind us of that fact and the appreciation it evoked. Enough reforms were enacted to diffuse social and political tensions, so successfully in fact that monarchs and aristocracies in Sweden, the Netherlands, Spain, and Britain weathered the violent storms of the twentieth century still in possession of their property and titles.

Nobles often served as bishops in both Catholic and Protestant countries, though not usually in Orthodox ones. They still made up 34 percent of the bishops in France in 1847, though this fell later in the century.[50] During the first three-quarters of the nineteenth century half the Anglican bishops were of patrician background or connections.[51] In 1800 aristocrats dominated the Roman Catholic College of Cardinals. Of the 99 cardinals created by Pius VII (1800–23) at least 40 were titled and another 16 were nobles. Under each of his successors this proportion declined, however.[52] All the popes between 1800 and 1903 were noblemen, and two came from comital families (Pius VII and Leo XIII). Some nineteenth-century aristocratic cardinals were major figures: the Prince of Schwarzenberg was one of the leading opponents of the new definition of the dogma of Papal infallibility, while the Prince of Hohenlohe-Schillingfürst was a central figure in the *Kulturkampf*.[53] Church leadership remained a key element in the power of landed elites in the twentieth century.

The aristocracy still largely dominated nineteenth-century diplomacy, while the proportion of patricians in Cabinets stood steady or even rose in Italy, Russia, Germany, Sweden, Finland, Holland, and Britain.[54] Even after the invention of the telegraph enabled home governments to play a more immediate role in forming foreign policy, the importance of ambassadors and their staffs did not diminish significantly until after World War I. Princes and counts dominated almost all the big embassies – London, St. Petersburg, Vienna, Paris, Berlin, and Rome – while commoners were relegated to Bogata, Washington, and other tropical or out-of-the-way places. Unreliable noblemen were assigned to posts where they could do comparatively little damage, although the Austrian Count Koziebrodzki had to be recalled from Lisbon after he climbed over a wall into the locked gardens of the royal palace and fought with a guard who challenged him.[55] Between 1815 and 1914 all but two of the British Foreign Secretaries were peers.[56]

In the crucial years 1859–60, as Piedmont took the lead in Italian unification, 36 of the 43 ranking members of the diplomatic corps were titled.[57] The German Foreign Office in 1914 was served by eight princes, 29 counts, 20 barons, 54 ordinary nobles, and 11 bourgeois. The proportion of noble envoys in the diplomatic corps actually increased between 1888 and 1914.[58] Austria-Hungary experienced a similar upwards trend.[59] The Swedish and Dutch foreign services remained dominated by counts and barons throughout the nineteenth century. In Holland being a mere jonkheer was hardly good enough.[60] Only in the decade just before the Great War did the French government make serious reforms that led to fewer noblemen in the service.[61] Even then men such as the Marquis de Breteuil were senior officials at the Quai d'Orsay when war broke out in 1914.

The great political figures of the age were largely drawn from the landed elite. The French court aristocracy ultimately rallied to each new regime like the English Vicar of Bray. David Higgs argues: "Nobles continued to set the tone on how to rule."[62] The Duke de Broglie became the French premier in 1873, contributing to what became known as "the republic of dukes" because of the extraordinary number of those elevated noblemen dominating politics in the 1870s. He worked to achieve an aristocratic republic with a parliamentary upper house of peers, separating the conservative cause from the lost monarchist one.[63] The shrewd and flexible Baron Louis DeGeer, Chancellor of Sweden, managed the passage of the parliamentary reform act of 1866–7 by seeking broad support and through willingness to compromise.[64] In Britain Wellington, Grey, Melbourne, Aberdeen, Palmerston, Derby, and Salisbury formed a chain of outstanding aristocratic leadership. Cavour and Bismarck built great modern nations. In 1848 Prince Metternich was forced to flee Vienna and Minister of War Count Baillet de la Tour was hanged from a lamppost, but the key figures in restoring Habsburg rule that would last another 70 years were Princes Schwarzenberg and Windisch-Graetz and Count Radetzky.

It is also important to note that a majority of titled aristocrats participated actively in national government. In 1885, of the 431 peers at Westminster who had inherited their titles, almost two-thirds held an elected or appointed office of note at some stage in their careers. The rate was still half in 1914.[65] Britain had a number of major governorships overseas that were almost invariably filled by aristocrats. Some of these were relatively untaxing, such as in Canada and Australia, but the Viceregal offices in Ireland and India were political posts of the first rank.

In some countries, however, decline in office holding contrasted with the successes mentioned above. Although the first commoner to hold the premiership in Sweden did not do so until 1883, aristocratic representation in government began to decline from mid-century onwards. In Spain ministers were largely drawn from a class of bureaucrats and professionals and in Portugal and Belgium signs of aristocratic retreat at the top appeared early.[66]

* * *

For centuries an important lever of aristocratic power was control over diets and parliaments. Here more than anywhere aristocracies performed a useful function as buffers between aspirations to absolute power by monarchs and the grievances and needs of the people. As privileges were shed over the nineteenth century participation in legislatures remained one of the most enduring rights held by the elite. The establishment of new parliaments in Prussia in 1848 and Russia in 1906 created fresh opportunities for aristocratic leadership that had hitherto not existed in those countries. Reforms diminished their role over time, but parliaments remained an important forum for mediating aristocratic leadership and the popular will without resort to violence.[67]

The study of upper chambers of parliaments is much neglected, yet it was here that aristocratic power was most secure and durable. A veto over legislation helped preserve landed authority even in the most advanced industrialized states.[68] The special place of nobles in parliaments survived in Finland until 1906, Portugal 1910, the German states 1918, Spain 1931, Hungary 1944, and in Britain continues to exist even today, though with major restrictions after 1911 and 1999.

Nobles in France, Holland, Belgium, Spain, and Denmark gained disproportionate access to upper chambers until the late nineteenth or early twentieth century through various inequitable selection systems.[69] Monarchs appointed aristocrats in large numbers to senates in Piedmont and later the united Italy. In Sweden the elite had their own chamber and also chaired all joint standing committees in the legislature until 1867. After reform, three-fifths of the new First Chamber was noble. Only after 1918–21, when universal suffrage was enacted, was the number of nobles significantly reduced. Over three-quarters of the Austrian upper chamber were nobles between 1861 and 1918. Similar conditions existed in many of the German principalities and kingdoms, including Prussia, until the end of the Great War. The Russian constitution of 1906 included a special place for nobles in the State Council, which became a key power center.[70]

The British House of Lords, which was composed of bishops and all of the hereditary peers, remained a strong institution throughout the nineteenth century. Even the Chartists did not call for its abolition. It successfully vetoed Gladstone's attempts to enact Home Rule for Ireland. The Marquis of Salisbury still found it possible to serve as Prime Minister while sitting there as late as 1902. After the loss of its veto power in 1911, the chamber could still delay legislation and many senior politicians continued to serve in office from its benches. However, the most potent aristocratic parliament that retained full powers and an exclusive membership existed in Hungary. The titled nobles had dominated the estates before 1848 and ensured that the upper chamber established after the revolution would belong to them. Between 1886 and 1918 membership was largely restricted to the magnates.[71]

The range of elective franchises to lower chambers was extraordinarily diverse. In 1890 the number of voters per thousand inhabitants ranged from 48 in Hungary to 271 in France.[72] Changes in suffrage occurred frequently. In most countries it was limited, and in some elaborate systems of indirect voting made it difficult for the masses to gain purchase on the electoral system even when much of the male population was granted the vote. Landowners could exercise control because ballots were often cast publicly. Voting in secret came to Britain only in 1872 and not until 1901 in Denmark. Aristocrats continued to serve in elective bodies, but a marked decline took place over the course of the nineteenth century, well before the outbreak of World War I. Most of the data relating to representation in parliaments, as with military officers, includes all nobles. However, in the late nineteenth and early twentieth century, increasingly only those from the upper levels of the elite could afford to get elected and serve in legislatures.

In many countries, including France, Portugal, Holland, Italy, Prussia, Spain, and Britain, noble representation in lower chambers was quite robust during the nineteenth century.[73] In Italy ten Princes and Dukes of Colonna served as either deputies or senators in the century after 1848.[74] In Britain 19 Cecils (Marquises of Exeter and of Salisbury) sat in parliament during the same period. Gradually, however, decline set in almost everywhere. The decisive year or decade differs, but the story is always the same.[75] Wider franchises, slackening aristocratic ambition, and progressively larger radical parties eroded elite representation.[76] In most countries fewer than one in five elected deputies were noble by 1914. Only in Russia, where changes in electoral rules favored the titled elite after 1907, did the trend reverse itself.[77] By 1919 most countries had fewer than one in ten legislators who were noble in their lower chambers.

The Prince de Polignac, head of Charles X's last ministry, hoped it would be possible "for us to return someday to a system which incorporates aristocratic principles and closes the door of the chamber of deputies to mediocre men driven by turbulent and revolutionary passions."[78] His optimism proved unjustified. The lid of Pandora's box had been forced open in 1789; egalitarian and democratic ideas could not be restored to their resting place. Franchise reform, combined with an increasingly literate and sophisticated electorate, socialist and radical parties, and articulate and forceful popular leaders, altered the political dynamic of European societies.

The fateful decision to pay legislators was made by the Dutch in 1798.[79] Although in other countries this practice would not commence for another century (Italy and Spain only in 1912), once legislators were salaried or were funded by unions or parties, a fundamental barrier protecting privilege disappeared. Only relatively modest extensions of the franchise could do severe damage. The serious decay in noble participation in the Italian parliament came after the reform of 1882 that increased the size of the electorate from 7 to 28 percent. The Dutch elite began to disappear in the legislature when those eligible to vote doubled to what was still less than half the male population in 1887. In the last decades of the nineteenth century the dykes burst. Universal male suffrage was established in Germany in 1871, Spain 1890, Russia 1906, Austria 1907, Italy in 1912, and Denmark in 1915. Immediately after World War I countries such as Holland and Sweden finally enacted universal suffrage and women were increasingly granted the vote as well.

Heinrich Best argues that the legislative importance of the traditional upper classes was still great in the nineteenth and early twentieth centuries. "The most traditional basis of authority – hereditary transmission – was, in fact, quite successful in passing the 'legitimacy test' of elections." The aristocracy showed great staying power and adaptability. "Deference for the old upper class remained significant," Best's data suggest, "and was confirmed via the ballot box until the late 1950s."[80]

Such statements paint too glowing a picture. By halting steps constitutional changes gradually excluded aristocrats from legislative participation. No straight line can be drawn from apogee to nadir in the story of decline. Franchise reform, however, meant that, to the horror of men such as the Swedish Baron Klinckowström, servants could now outvote their masters.[81]

* * *

The European aristocracies were complicit in their own demise. Many embraced a more advanced view of the world prompted by an understanding that the clock could not be turned back and out of sincere enthusiasm for a liberal ideology. This sometimes actually enhanced their power in the short term, but the long-term consequences were fatal. Extension of the franchise in England in 1832 or Sweden in 1866–7 was clearly led by – and possible only because of – the cooperation of the elite itself. The House of Lords and the Ridderhus reluctantly but effectively won friends and respect from those eager to join the political nation but at the price of a slow form of suicide.

The British were the most successful of all aristocracies in the nineteenth and twentieth centuries in sustaining their legitimacy because they governed the nation in a liberal and open spirit. Many reasons explain this phenomenon. Some are simple: the ruling elite lacked the military and police resources Continental states possessed to repress opposition from below. They also managed to be on the winning side in 1918 and 1945. A more complex but important reason was the aristocracy's relationship with electoral politics. The elite had long had to practice the political arts in an open arena in which many seats in the Commons could only be won by determined exertion and continuous attention to the interests of voters over successive generations.[82] The aristocracy was obliged to win popular support to preserve their power. In addition, love of liberty, which they associated with the quality of honor, inhered in the collective mentality of the English landed elite itself. Rather than being forced by a new class to be libertarian, the English landed elite was fundamentally disposed to be so. Historically it had defined itself against the crown, against the principles of autocracy, and against the maintenance of large standing armies. At bottom, this is what parliament, a landowner's assembly, stood for. Parliament, in turn, helped school the nation in liberal practices and a liberal spirit.[83] The great historian of Victorian England, George Kitson Clark, judged that "Britain was Liberal because many of the nobility were Liberal."[84] When the time came to surrender their legislative ascendancy, Tocqueville noted, the aristocracy submitted "to the force of argument."[85] Even in the twentieth century the elite injected liberal sinews into the political process as the nation experienced extreme economic and military stress.

During the 1848 revolution in Hungary the nationalist firebrand, Louis Kossuth, worked closely with the titled elite, led by Count Lajos Batthyány, one of Hungary's richest landowners, who became the first prime minister. Count István Széchenyi and Prince Pál Esterházy also entered the revolutionary government. In March 1848 the Upper House of the Diet accepted without debate the taxation of the nobility, suppression of feudal dues and services (with compensation to be paid to landowners), political rights for the urban middle class and the peasants, and a Hungarian government responsible to parliament.[86] Leading Hungarian magnates in gala dress with feathers and jewel-studded swords went to Vienna by steamer to present their demands in person to the Emperor. The Finnish nobility sought to find legitimacy among the bulk of the population by being responsive to the cultural demands of the peasantry.[87] A number of important aristocrats in late imperial Russia, such as the Benckendorffs and Obolenskys, favored the creation of a parliament with a democratic franchise. Count Cavour was the leading Italian liberal of the nineteenth century.

The shadow of the guillotine hung over Europe. Many nobles had come to believe that it was better to make voluntary concessions than be forced to sacrifice everything in a bloody revolution. The Hessian hereditary knight Wilhelm von Buttlar-Elberberg wrote to a noble deputy during a discussion of reform in 1830: "The present moment certainly must be used wisely. It is much better for us to act with honor for the benefit of all by giving up obsolete things voluntarily rather than have them taken from us by force."[88] Lord Grey was thinking in the same way when he said of his Reform Act of 1832, "the more it is considered, the less it will be found to prejudice the real interests of the aristocracy."[89] Lampedusa's Prince of Falconeri accepted the revolution in Italy with equanimity: "If we want things to stay as they are, things will have to change."[90] This formula, however, which had once served the aristocracy well, no longer worked in the later nineteenth century. A universal franchise was antithetical to the foundation of aristocratic power. The elite became progressively weaker. Their wealth and titles survived intact, but from the 1880s political authority ebbed away.

*   *   *

Many scholars have tried to establish explanatory models for the transition from traditional to modern societies, but "modernization" is a slippery term that means many different things to different observers. To economists it may connote industrialization; to political scientists, centralization, bureaucracy, and mass politics; to sociologists, the end of society based on legal orders; and to anthropologists, the adoption of the values of Western culture.[91] Prominent analysts such as Max Weber, Barrington Moore, and Samuel Huntington argue that the landed elites were a key part of the process.[92] They see aristocracies as "backward," working to build coalitions against peasants and workers, and shunting development down unprogressive roads.[93]

The deviations from these theories, of which Sweden is a particularly striking example, indicate how unhelpful the straitjackets of such model building can be.[94] The notion of a single "landed upper class," usually posited by the theorists, does violence to the relationship between the aristocracy and the lesser nobility, as well as failing to recognize the different historical traditions of elites as diverse as the Russian and British aristocracies.[95] No uniform path from the traditional to modern societies can easily be discerned.

It is worth considering the possibility that aristocrats created more progressive and humane societies than revolutionaries. The outcomes of major political upheavals led by landed elites in modern times, as opposed to movements led by progressive bourgeois and peasants, offer food for thought. The Whig grandees in 1688, Washington and Jefferson in 1776, Cavour and Bismarck in the 1860s, and the aristocratic leaders of the Meiji Restoration in Japan in 1867 created societies that were comparatively sane, safe, and civilized, launched on paths of constitutional development and the rule of law. Robespierre, Lenin, Hitler, and Mao built with other tools and inflicted unprecedented suffering on humanity. It is also worth remembering that it was Whig aristocrats who pressed hard to abolish the slave trade in 1807 and that the grandees at the Congress of Vienna endorsed that decision. Another Whig government top-heavy with magnates abolished slavery in the British Empire in 1833. On the other hand, the inhuman slave masters of the twentieth century were the communists and fascists who pursued their genocidal policies from Poland to Cambodia.

A classless society leaves the mass of the population without any defense against tyrants.[96] The struggles over religion and with absolutist monarchs had led many nobles to embrace an identity as defenders of the body politic and a bulwark against arbitrary rule.[97] This enabled aristocrats to pursue selfish interests while convincing themselves that they were acting nobly. It also led them to swallow many of the ideals of the Enlightenment, restrained their worst impulses, and except in Russia prevented over-mighty monarchs from establishing omnipotence.[98]

Arno Mayer has proposed that the European aristocracies turned to war in a desperate bid to reverse their losses to encroaching industrial capitalism. He argues that between 1905 and 1914, the old elites proceeded to reaffirm and tighten their political hold in order to bolster material, social, and cultural pre-eminence. In the process they intensified the domestic and international tensions that produced the Great War. Unfortunately, by labeling the elite "pre-

modern" and "feudalistic" he establishes an artificial distinction
between aristocracy and modernity. [99] In any case the elite had
already lost hegemony over the political process. The peacock
plumage that he so carefully delineated dazzled Mayer. He rightly
identified the cultural and social primacy of the elite in 1914, but he
could not see that their political authority and their will to rule had
been irreparably damaged before 1900. No convulsive or premedi-
tated reassertion of control was possible. The extent to which aristocrats welcomed war in 1914 was governed by how far nationalism had
bewitched them. This mass ideology had further diminished their
political role as they were swamped by an upwelling of forces that
allowed them at best to be figureheads – peacocks and not eagles.
The outbreak of World War I was due to an extremely complex set
of diplomatic, economic, and accidental circumstances that involved
everything from the personalities of monarchs to Social Darwinism.[100] Aristocrats played a role, but not a decisive one.

Nobles corporately and as a class were losing political power from
the eighteenth century onwards. Sometimes this was simply due to
gradual centralization. More significant was their changing place in
the economic structure of Europe. Cheap food had the progressive
effect of lessening economic inequality by redistributing income
from landowners to the rest of society.[101] Rising living standards and
educational levels led to what José Harris has called "an invisible
revolution in the structure of class power."[102] The diminished price
of agricultural land left aristocrats whose wealth was concentrated
exclusively in rural property poorer and less influential. Nonetheless
their economic, cultural, and social positions in 1914 were still potent.
It was the rise of egalitarian and democratic values that dissolved
aristocratic rule. This process occurred in reactionary Russia as well
as republican France, and meant that by the early twentieth century
only a few places such as Hungary still were literally in the hands of
the nobles. That is not to say that the landed elite ceased to be an
important component of government. Individuals remained mighty,
locally as heads of estate communities and nationally as holders of
great offices of state. However, by and large the aristocrats in government had to respond to popular opinion, and fewer and fewer of
them lived by the values of duty, honor, and memories of lineage that
had made the elite distinctive in the past.

In the mid-nineteenth century Alexis de Tocqueville found it much
easier to deal with the aristocrat, the Count de Falloux, with whom

he disagreed than with the liberal bourgeois politicians who were his political associates. Even though the French Revolution had abolished nobility, he wrote, it had not wiped out the invisible signs by which members recognized each other. He knew what language to speak to the nobleman; he felt instinctively what to say and when to remain silent. With men from other classes he felt no such assurance.[103] This was a fatal handicap.

9

ARISTOCIDE, 1917–1945

We, who spent the sunny side of life before the war, have been left with nothing but unappeasable regret, . . . our world had broken to pieces.

> Countess Nora Wydenbruck, 1932, in
> *An Austrian Background*[1]

Communism we dread more than Nazism, because under the German system some of us might survive for better days; under Bolshevism all of us will be strung up on the lamp posts.

> Count Pál Teleki, Prime Minister of Hungary,
> May 1940[2]

The Stauffenberg family was not Prussian, as many people assume, but from southern Germany, and they rose in the service of the Kings of Bavaria and Württemberg. The family had emerged during the thirteenth century as cupbearers to the Counts of Zollern and gained a barony from Emperor Leopold I in 1698. Leopold II raised the main line of the family to the rank of imperial counts, while another branch became Bavarian counts in 1874. Alfred Schenk, Count von Stauffenberg served as Lord Chamberlain at the royal court at Stuttgart from 1908. After the abdication of the King of Württemberg in November 1918 he managed the private estates of the royal family. His wife, Countess von Üxküll-Gyllenband, gave her sons a descent from the great Prussian Field Marshal Count von Gneisenau.

The couple's three sons, Berthold, Alexander, and Claus were raised in the country at Schloss Lautingen and in the prewar grandeur of the royal court. The family was not rich due to repeated past divisions of property among various branches. Nonetheless, Lautingen was a handsome estate, and the boys were surrounded by an intricate web of royalty and titled kinfolk. They were also a highly cultured family. Claus played the cello and among his closest associates in later life were a sculptor and a poet. His brothers studied law and classical literature. In spite of his love for the arts and music, Claus chose the army as a career. He believed passionately in the aristocratic tradition of public service, and at a time when his country lay in crisis and danger he felt it a duty to make a contribution to its defense. He and Berthold came finally to stand at the center of the most famous conspiracy of the twentieth century, aimed at the destruction of fascism. Claus became one of the last aristocrats, fully conscious of his honor and duty as a nobleman, to bid to play a decisive role in European history.[3]

Count von Stauffenberg was born into a shattered society. Between 1914 and 1918 Europe experienced extreme trauma. Its youth suffered unimaginable horrors and from that crucible came the crisis of capitalism and the triumph of two of the most influential political ideologies of the interwar years, communism and fascism. These in turn plunged the world into an even more horrific war. Ironically, men from humble or bourgeois backgrounds – Hitler, Stalin, Mussolini, Chamberlain, Dalladier – brought on the conflict, but aristocrats emerged for a final time to lead the fighting. Many of the generals on both the Allied and Axis sides were of noble birth, and more would have been had Stalin not murdered most of his top soldiers before the outbreak of hostilities. The two great democracies that survived the initial onslaught and fought back to win the war also turned to political leaders who were patricians – Roosevelt, as blue-blooded as American society could manage, and Churchill, a man spurred to excel by his ducal lineage.

Aristocrats also played a major role in the fruitless attempts to promote international peace both before and after the 1914 conflagration. The Austrian Baroness von Suttner (neé Countess Kinsky von Chinic und Tettau) and the French Baron d'Estounelles de Constant de Rebecque won the Noble Peace Prize in 1905 and 1909 respectively and Carl von Ossietzky and Lord Robert Cecil in 1936 and 1937, equally fruitlessly, the next time round. Many aristocrats, both conservative and liberal, saw a continued justification for their leadership in the spirit of honor, courage, loyalty, and family that resisted the modern challenge of materialism.

Aristocrats lost their political dominance as a class before World War I commenced, but as individuals bearing distinctive methods of thought and living in a traditional style they remained ubiquitous in the upper reaches of European politics and society until 1945, and some lingered on even beyond that date. One may ask whether democracy could have survived after 1939 without them.

As late as September 1939 old chivalric virtues could still be witnessed in the new war that overwhelmed Europe. Prince Arthur Radziwill was killed at the battle of Kuno where Polish cavalrymen were ordered to charge German tanks.[4] Hitler, however, made it clear to his generals in an order issued 17 March 1941 that the war against Russia "cannot be conducted in a knightly fashion."[5] Those who obeyed him lost their connection with the traditions that were used to justify the continued leadership of the European aristocracy in modern times. The elite had never lived as chivalrously as Burke had hoped, but now even the pretense of honor died on the Eastern Front.

* * *

In World War I young cavalry officers rode into battle with flowers in their horses' bridles, emblems taken from their coats of arms.[6] Many aristocrats welcomed the war both because they were caught up in the nationalistic frenzy that swept the Continent and because it offered them an opportunity to demonstrate their courage and utility to a society that seemed increasingly skeptical about their usefulness. Even modern technology offered opportunities for adventure and chivalric combat. What they had not counted on was a war of attrition, one in which economic resources outweighed skill on the battlefield; one in which governments turned to the concept of "Total War," where aristocrats were reduced to mere cogs in a machine. The dukes and earls of England were active in the early days of military recruitment. They held rallies at their houses and offered the deaths of their sons as examples of sacrifice. The introduction of conscription made their work irrelevant, and they were marginalized in an area where their influence had been extensive and important.[7] The Irish peerage rallied to serve the king and died in disproportionate numbers to others who fought; yet they gained nothing.[8] They had been abandoned by the English ruling class before the war, and after it their service was despised, country houses were looted and burned down, and nobles in the new "Free State" became disposable.

Statistical analysis shows that officers died at a higher rate than enlisted men in Russia, Italy, France, and Britain.[9] Almost half (44 percent) of the Irish peers and their sons who served were killed or wounded.[10] Added to the horrors of the war for Russian families were the deaths suffered in the revolution and civil war that followed. Countless stories of the loss of fathers, husbands, brothers, fiancés, uncles, and friends shadowed the lives of those who survived.

More serious for the long-term health of landed families was the loss of wealth as a result of higher income taxes, death duties, inflation, and diminished income. Further special exactions were imposed on large landowners in countries such as Poland to help with reconstruction. Wages rose as more and more laborers disappeared into the army or urban factories. A freeze on rents seriously injured the finances of the Italian aristocracy. In Russia, Poland, Lithuania, Romania, Belgium, and northern France country houses and forests were burned or destroyed in the fighting.[11] Sales and confiscations of land were precipitated across Europe. Big estates became substantially smaller almost everywhere in the wake of war.

French and Belgian aristocrats who had invested heavily in Russian bonds lost everything. Closed-off opportunities for military careers and court offices took its toll financially on modestly endowed families in Germany and the Habsburg Empire. Many landed estates ceased to be economically viable. Non-agricultural revenue was also greatly reduced. Of a gross income in mineral royalties of £82,450 in 1918, the Duke of Northumberland netted only £23,890 after tax. By 1924 he was receiving less than one-seventh of his gross mining royalties as disposable income.[12]

Of course, concessions were made and good lawyers could contrive complex systems of trusts and private companies to keep the taxman at bay.[13] Sales of land were not all due to the need for cash. Peers were advised to sell land to buy stocks. The continued devaluation of the lira in Italy during the 1920s and a flood of eager buyers from the ranks of the tenants drove up the value of farmland to the point where price had little relationship to profitability. Some Piedmontese families transferred virtually all their wealth to urban real estate and investments.[14]

In Britain probably more than one million acres changed hands during the first year after the war. The next few years exceeded this total. Perhaps up to six to eight million acres were sold. About half the estates of 3000 acres or more in a sample of six counties in 1873 had been disposed of by 1941.[15] In southern Ireland the final divestment of landed estates was comparable in its totality to the Bolshevik confiscations in Russia.[16] Auction prices for art and heirlooms soared. Town houses and their contents were discarded. Country houses were reduced in size, demolished, or rented out to American plutocrats. For the squires and gentry this era was far more devastating than for the great landowners. They were much more likely to lose everything.[17] Across the Continent the lesser nobility all but disappeared from the countryside.

Nobles in neutral countries also suffered. World War I brought massive economic dislocation and social distress to Spain that in turn generated unprecedented levels of popular antagonism against the established regime and the government of the pro-Entente Prime Minister, the Count of Romanones. He was not only the target of a fierce campaign by the Austrian and German ambassadors to oust him, but also he suffered from the acceleration of pre-existing social and political discontent. At his fall in April 1917 he left behind turmoil generated by rapid economic, social, and ideological changes that threatened to bring down the entire political order.[18]

In the 1920s and 1930s, when a wider range of career paths were open to young aristocrats, they often entered the business world, as employees and salaried managers, not partners. Few magnates still had the resources or chutzpah to initiate large new enterprises as they had in the past. Except for some merchant bankers in the City of London, aristocrats were largely excluded from increasing their fortunes on a grand scale through business ventures.[19]

Apprehension suffused aristocratic households. The families of the lost were bereft. Many survivors from the trenches were never the same again. The cowardice or ineptitude displayed by the Emperors of Germany, Austria, and Russia struck at the heart of traditional noble values. Royal families with which aristocrats had been associated for centuries disappeared overnight. In central Europe it was difficult for the aristocracy to sustain their multi-national, imperial loyalties, once the Habsburg monarchy disappeared. Across Europe disillusionment and cynicism could be found among the younger generation that tended to sever the emotional bonds that linked them to the past. A new indifference to tradition arose, and an erosion of aristocratic taboos.[20]

The German elite had failed to win the war.[21] Now they faced the problem the Legitimist aristocracy in France had confronted a century before. Did they owe loyalty to the state, even if it was a republic, or should they stand aloof and disengaged? In the latter case they would have no control over what the state did to them and their possessions, and they would lose access to the occupation that had given so many a sense of purpose. Like all Germans they deeply felt the humiliation of the Versailles Treaty. Like their Austro-Hungarian peers, many were transferred to new jurisdictions such as Poland or Czechoslovakia. The Habsburg elite suffered even more seriously. If they found themselves in the successor states other than Austria and Hungary, they faced massive expropriation of their estates. Such a nobleman described his family as amputated from the core of their identity: "We were like those British colonials who remained in India after the end of the Raj."[22] Hyperinflation soon threw their finances into chaos.

Some noblemen went off the rails under the stress of defeat and disintegration. The Baltic Count Hermann Keyserling moved to Germany and founded a "School of Wisdom" that encouraged yoga, contemplation, Oriental philosophy, and spiritual exercises.[23] The French nobleman de Boeldieu, a member of a comital family in Jean Renoir's 1938 film about the war, *Grand Illusion*, commits a suicidal act of bravery because he decides that to survive even as a victor would be futile for his class.

Nevertheless aristocrats continued to hold high office in a number of countries during the interwar years. They dominated the diplomatic scene at the ambassadorial level, if for no other reason than the years of experience and expertise they had accumulated before the war. The Hungarian, Italian, and Spanish foreign services were heavily supplied with dukes and counts, but aristocrats were also to be found frequently among the diplomats sent out by more democratic Sweden, Denmark, and Holland. Count Brockdorff-Rantzau, Minister of Foreign Affairs in the immediate postwar German government, served as Berlin's first ambassador to Moscow in 1922. Contrary to expectation, his cold and autocratic bearing found a warm response among the communist leadership and the successful conduct of German–Soviet relations for the ensuing six years was in part due to his ability and statesmanship.[24] In spite of the fact that the new Austrian republic had made it a legal offense to use a title, Baron Franckenstein, from an old and distinguished aristocratic family, played a critical role in gaining economic and political relief from the strictures of the postwar treaties as ambassador to London between 1920 and 1938.[25]

Another nook where nobles continued to play a significant role was in the leadership of the Roman Catholic Church. In the twentieth century three popes were of noble birth: Benedict XV, Pius XII, and Paul VI. Two of the most notable aristocrats to wear red birettas in the mid-twentieth century were the German Counts, Konrad von Preysing Lichtenegg (Bishop of Berlin from 1935 to 1950) and his cousin Clemens August von Galen (Bishop of Munster from 1933 to 1946). They spoke out with varying degrees of courage against the Nazi regime.[26]

British politicians continued to be drawn in large numbers from the landed gentry and aristocracy, although the Labour Party attracted only a few titled supporters. Aristocratic hostesses in London and Paris during the interwar period were still closely integrated into diplomatic, social, cultural, and political worlds. At a ball commemorating the Congress of Vienna held at the Austrian embassy in 1935 Lady Londonderry wore in her hair the same Order of the Garter that her predecessor had worn at the *bal masque* given by Prince Metternich in 1814.[27]

Noblewomen also took a more dynamic part in politics as opportunities for advancement gradually appeared. Revolver blazing, Countess Markievicz (née Gore-Booth) participated in the Easter Rising in Dublin and was condemned to death for treason (the sentence was eventually reduced). Later she became the first female Cabinet minister in Western Europe.[28] Women such as Lady Cynthia Curzon and the Duchess of Atholl were elected to the House of Commons. The daughter of one English peer grazed Mussolini with a bullet in an assassination attempt while a daughter of Lord Redesdale became one of Hitler's companions and shot herself when war broke out in 1939.

During the interwar years magnates among the central European aristocracy, Prince Michael Radziwill remembered, still "traveled from capital to capital, surrounded by a staff of butlers, menservants, chefs and nannies, who tended to make each stop similar to the last one, except for the climate."[29] More dashing French and English noblemen traveled by air in their own "machines." They skied at

Gastaad, did the Cresta run at St. Moritz, raced at Deauville, competed in polo at Hurlingham, and played *chemin-de-fer* on the Côte d'Azur.[30] Newspapers and magazines chronicled their scandals and successes with a seriousness and deference hardly credible today. Outstanding photographers such as Cecil Beaton snapped their portraits. The number of servants supporting country house life remained more stable than is often assumed. The Duke de Lorge had a staff of 28 in 1932, while the Earl of Lichfield had 30 indoors and 20 more in the garden. Blenheim Palace took a ton of coal a day to heat.[31]

American heiresses such as Barbara Hutton continued to marry titled Europeans.[32] The Baltimorean Mrs. Simpson married the King of England. Big shoots were still held at Czechoslovakian castles and big balls in Roman palaces. In Kenya an eighteenth-century world with a large serf population attached attracted British and Continental aristocrats attempting to escape "Bolshevik" Europe. "Adulteries, arson, bankruptcies, insanity, suicides, even duels" at 8000 feet above the steaming seaboard, Evelyn Waugh gleefully reported.[33] Life there was perhaps best captured by the Danish writer Baroness Blixen-Finecke, known as Isak Dinesen, in her celebrated book, *Out of Africa* (1937), about her relationship with the son of the Earl of Winchelsea. She saw the country estate as rooted in eternal values and Africa as a Garden of Eden untrammeled by bourgeois materialism.[34] Nevertheless, the old style of life limped along back in Europe as well. "I . . . have just been home to help celebrate my Father's [3rd Baron Cottlesloe] 80th birthday," reported Dr. Margaret Jennings, one of the discoverers of penicillin, in February 1940. "The best part of the meager celebrations permitted by the war was the entirely feudal presentation of an address by the four leading farmers in their best suits and ties; with shuffling of feet and expression of loyalty to the family."[35] But this was a pale imitation of what once had been. As Michael Thompson observed: "The popping of champagne corks is no substitute for the roasting of oxen."[36]

* * *

In analyzing the interwar aristocracies some broad categories can be discerned. Countries that more or less completely eradicated landed elites, physically or psychologically – Russia, the Baltic provinces, and Ireland – fall into one group. Italy, Spain, Portugal, and Germany constitute the states that adopted some form of fascist dictatorship. In Austria, Poland, Hungary, Czechoslovakia, Romania, and parts of Yugoslavia aristocrats survived and even prospered, at least for a time. In Scandinavia, Belgium, the Netherlands, and France the old elite seemed to slip into a semi-comatose state, still propertied but largely marginalized in spite of the continued existence of royal courts. Finally, England and Scotland achieved a unique mixture of democracy and aristocracy.

Prince G. E. Lvov, an admirable and liberal man, headed the first Provisional Government of Russia in 1917 after the overthrow of Nicholas II. Unfortunately, he lacked the skill and allies necessary to win enthusiastic support. Some patricians continued to participate in Kerensky's successor administration, though its comparatively radical nature alienated many of them, blind as they were to what would follow. When the blow fell in October 1917, few were prepared for the catastrophe. Many sat frozen by indecision. Others continued to live on their estates, hoping things would settle down. The wise fled. Some nobles like Count Mouraviev associated themselves with the Bolshevik regime, while the well-connected nobleman G. V. Checherin became, in the best aristocratic tradition, Commissar for Foreign Affairs. In spite of bouts of imprisonment by the secret police, a number of titled officers served on the staffs of the army and navy, not always willingly. One of them was referred to as General Count Citizen Ignatieff. Famously, the nobleman Marshal Tukhachevsky helped rebuild the Soviet military but perished along with most of the senior military leadership in a Stalinist purge in 1937.[37]

As "former persons," aristocrats were prevented by decrees from gaining employment. They did manual labor or became beggars, living on the streets. Some changed their names and acquired forged documents. Hundreds ended in the gulags. Many met savage ends.[38] All estate land was confiscated. Commissars forced families to leave their houses with breakfast still on the table, the building sailing on empty with everything in place like the *Mary Celeste*. In the maelstrom virtually all the great estates of Russia were physically damaged or totally destroyed, and the records and possessions of generations of owners scattered or obliterated. Those houses left standing were put to public uses as schools, sanatoriums, museums, agricultural institutes, or recreational facilities. Many were left to decay.[39]

The émigrés fled all over the world. Paris was the center of "white" Russian life from the 1920s until World War II. Famously, many of the exiles became waiters and taxicab drivers. Most had only a Nansen (League of Nations) passport. The young were resilient and spoke numerous foreign languages. Their university educations often helped them rise to prominent positions in business and the professions in Canada, the United States, and Britain.[40] The old felt unrelieved tragedy.[41]

The Baltic barons did not suffer immediate immolation in 1917 thanks to German protection. However, once the Estonians and Latvians gained independence, no friendly treatment could be expected. Most noble land was expropriated with little compensation.[42] After Hitler completed the agreement with the Soviet Union in 1939, the Nazi government urged all persons of German origin in the Baltic States to liquidate their interests as quickly as possible and leave, since the area was allotted to the Soviet sphere of influence. Lithuania expropriated estates of "foreign" (Polish, German, and Russian) aristocrats. Landowners were stripped of their property and became isolated and helpless. Most did not speak Lithuanian and retreated into what was left of their manors, where even titled families lived essentially like peasants or fled.[43]

The nationalist movement in Ireland finally succeeded in wresting independence for much of the island from the British in 1922. Country houses were burned, although the number destroyed has been exaggerated. The total lost between 1920 and 1923 was less than 200 out of at least 2000 in existence.[44] In addition, after the war there was much non-payment of rent, land was occupied without compensation, timber stolen, salmon dynamited, farm buildings destroyed, and cattle poisoned.[45] Peers likened the state of the country to "virtually a form of Bolshevism," but few were personally attacked. The Earl of Ossory was in residence at Kilkenny Castle in 1922 when his butler informed him: "Excuse me disturbing your Lordship, but the Republicans have taken the Castle." The Free State forces in turn besieged them. The family stayed on in order to try to preserve the house, crawling around on hands and knees in the long corridors still served by the footmen. An armored car crashing through the gateway finally ended the siege.[46]

In total between 1880 and the 1930s some 15 million out of 17 million acres were transferred from landlords to tenants in Ireland. Compensation was set at about half the real value. The 1922 constitution excluded further creation of titles and ended the parliamentary rights of Irish peers. Titles continued to be recognized by courtesy, however, and an office of heraldry was set up to keep records of chiefs of native clans. Surviving houses became educational centers, hotels, hospitals, industrial sites, and religious foundations, or were left as ruins or torn down. Like the Russian nobility, the Irish Ascendancy survived only in literature.[47]

*   *   *

There is no doubt the aristocracies of Italy, Portugal, Spain, and Germany were the fellow travelers of fascism. Some saw it as a way to suppress the class conflicts generated by modern Western society. The most common and serious motive for supporting the ideology, as the epigraph by Count Teleki suggests, was fear of communism. Fascism did not, however, find universal favor with the elite. It was the gentry not the magnates who became fascists in Hungary. Aristocrats who honored traditional social and political conventions found Mussolini and Hitler vulgar and repellant. Most found the mass aspects of fascism threatening.[48] The German elite became increasingly estranged by the failure of the Nazis to restore the Hohenzollern dynasty, which, before coming to power, Hitler had hinted he might do in order to win their support. Men as diverse as Stauffenberg and Lampedusa could hardly conceal their contempt.[49]

Radical fascism preached the destruction of the aristocracy and establishment of a classless national state. However, once in power, the fascists usually found it easier to accommodate themselves with the landed elite. The alliance between reaction and fascism was most successful in Spain and Portugal. In Italy and Germany things came unstuck. Hitler succeeded in depriving his conservative supporters of authority but Mussolini was never able to do the same.[50] It eventually became impossible to ignore the depraved aspects of Hitler's regime. In Italy the King and his courtiers revolted against the doomed military strategy of the Duce.

Many of the problems facing the Italian polity and rural society began long before 1914, but the war galvanized "supercharged expectations" among the peasantry.[51] In 1919 the situation became revolutionary. The government proved unable to guarantee the lives or property of landowners. Fascism offered the only visible safe harbor.

The elite looked for a strong government that could restore order, reduce taxes, crush the unions, rescind the promises of land reform, and subsidize agricultural growth. Mussolini was their man. Responses varied among the regions, with the haughty Piedmontese holding aloof from the black shirts while the Tuscans enthusiastically embraced them.[52] Few anywhere condemned the excesses of the regime.

Respect for the monarchy survived in muted form. Efforts to expel the anti-fascist Count Sforza from the Senate failed in 1938 and 1941 because monarcho-fascists opposed it as an attack on the royal prerogative.[53] The coup of 1943 was the last time the Italian aristocracy, recent and old, played a decisive role in national politics. Count Grandi, the fascist elder statesman, secretly organized a repudiation of Mussolini by the Grand Council, which allowed the Duke of Acquarone, the minister closest to the King, to nudge Victor Emmanuel III into action. The Marquis Lanza d'Ajeta was sent as a secret emissary to the Allies while the newly minted Duke of Addis Ababa (Marshal Badaglio) was appointed as the Duce's replacement. Due to the cowardice and incompetence of the King, however, Mussolini was able to make a brief comeback.[54]

Dictatorial arrangements progressed much more successfully in Portugal. The republic established in 1910 was overthrown in a military coup in 1926. Antonio Salazar became Finance Minister from 1928 and dictator between 1932 and 1968. Like his compatriots in Italy and Germany, he came from a lower-middle-class background. Salazar restored the use of titles and gave judicious help to the nationalists in the Spanish Civil War. It was not for nothing that exiled princes began to congregate in droves at Estoril. A dwindling band of patricians held office under the dictator's administration, most notably the Count of Lumbralles, who was Salazar's "number two" man in the regime in the early 1950s.[55] No significant land reform took place. Sons of families with coats of arms still formed 91 percent of the intake of cadets in the naval academy in 1941.[56]

Between 1936 and 1939 Spain experienced one of the most harrowing civil wars of the twentieth century, and the aristocracy was in the middle of it. The monarchy was overthrown in 1931, and an aggressively anti-elitist republic established. A coup plotted in the Seville house of the Marquise de Esquivel launched an attempt to overthrow the new regime in 1932. Two princes were among the 145 nobles and army officers deported to a penal colony after it failed. Prime Minister Azaña's agrarian reform law introduced soon afterwards was intended to punish the *grandes*, many of whom had sympathized with the coup. Thirty of them still owned more than 10,000 acres apiece, mostly in the south where a vast and angry rural proletariat, deeply affected by collapsing cereal prices, had already begun to strike and launch land invasions. No compensation was offered, and the Prime Minister followed the bill with a promise of further confiscations. Titles were abolished and postmen forbidden to deliver mail to people so addressed.[57]

In 1936 a policeman killed the fascist Marquis of Heredia. The monarchists, led by the Count of Vallellano, abandoned parliament and fled Madrid. Soon an army putsch led to war. Both sides dealt out brutal treatment to their opponents. Aristocrats were murdered or fled into exile. Many fought for what became the fascist cause. The Duke of Sevilla was a distinguished Nationalist general, and, while the Duke of Alba acted as Franco's representative in London, his brother the Duke of Peñaranda died on the battlefield. Not surprisingly, a count became foreign minister. Franco had a sincere admiration for the aristocracy and believed that large numbers of them fought heroically in supporting his cause. His new political and social order was "aimed mainly at the winning back of power by those who had lost it in 1931."[58] Redistribution of land ceased and that confiscated from the aristocracy was returned.

*   *   *

The battering taken by the German aristocracy in November 1918 cannot be exaggerated. The army had suffered a humiliating defeat. At home anarchy seemed imminent. The key decisions restoring order were made through an alliance of Fritz Ebert, a tailor's son who headed the interim government in Berlin, and General Wilhelm Gröner, the son of a non-commissioned officer.[59] Junkers felt scorn and loathing for such a republic and its agents. Count Arco-Valley assassinated the Independent Socialist head of the Bavarian government 1919. Nobles were never reconciled to the loss of the monarchy and the abolition of titles that followed the revolution, even though personal property survived the cataclysm and they retained considerable status and some power in the new society. A Junker even became president. They were legally able to continue to use their honorifics as part of their proper names, and in a sense they became an even more exclusive group because no new nobles were created.[60] The lower and poorer nobles were particularly vulnerable to economic depression and loss of employment in the military. Many became radicalized, joined the Free Corps, and later became Nazis.

The German nobility continued to play a dominant role in the diplomatic corps and army. The agrarian structure remained largely unreformed, but they had little influence in the Reichstag. In the von Papen "Cabinet of the barons" in 1932, formed shortly before Hitler came to power, seven of the nine ministers were nobles. In the dictator's first Cabinet Baron von Neurath continued as Foreign Minister and Count Schwerin von Krosigk as Finance Minister. In rebuilding the officer corps in the 1920s particular efforts were made to attract the sons of the aristocracy and military caste. Close links were maintained between new regiments and the old elite traditions of the Prussian army.[61]

In 1941 270 members of princely houses were members of the Nazi Party, and many others from families of lesser rank also joined.[62] But relatively few aristocrats embraced Nazism with enthusiasm. The appeal was strongest in the north among the Junkers for the same reason that fascism gained the support of Italian and Spanish nobles – fear of Bolshevism and disorder. It should be noted, however, that the desperation of agricultural laborers, peasants, civil servants, and shopkeepers struggling to keep their heads above water in the collapsing Prussian agricultural economy also played a large role in Hitler's rise. The Junkers alone were incapable of placing anyone in power.[63]

* * *

The fragments of the shattered Habsburg Empire were jigged into shape at Versailles. Reconstituted Poland became a super-state in size though not in power. Invented countries such as Yugoslavia and Czechoslovakia emerged on the European stage for the first time. Romania also became a giant at the expense of a shrunken Hungary. Austria was a pygmy. The experience of the aristocracies in each of these countries was different although, save in Yugoslavia, they remained a significant and in one case dominant force in each as politicians and electorates sought to gain a footing in the new arena.

In November 1918 the Habsburg Emperor Karl abdicated and for the first time in many centuries Vienna was without a monarch. All honors were abolished. It was not the loss of property or princely denominations, however, that changed things. What was mourned was the disappearance of a great state. A Lithuanian princess noted in her diary during World War II:

> There is an enormous difference, I find, between that generation of Austrian aristocrats, who still ran their Empire, and the present generation, who grew up in an amputated, stunted little country with no future. The latter are, nearly all of them, basically provincial and even when there is still plenty of money around, they can barely speak a foreign language and few of them have been outside Austria for any length of time. Moreover, though full of charm and delightful company, they are, by and large, lightweights. . . .[64]

In the 1919 election not a single nobleman gained a seat in parliament.[65]

Laws of entail were abolished. Some estates were sold off to small farmers. The elite did not work for a restoration of the monarchy, but contented themselves with boycotting the republic. Only in the diplomatic corps did nobles continue to predominate.[66] In Austria, as in Britain but nowhere else, the fascist movement was actually led by an aristocrat. The *Heimwher* (Home Guard) was founded by Prince Ernst von Starhemberg, who used his personal wealth to pay troops to maintain order and protect property in the chaotic situation immediately after the end of the war, and he rode the movement nearly to the top.[67] He was an extreme nationalist and fascist, though was not interested in merging with Germany, and ultimately became a victim of the Nazi aggression. Starhemberg became Minister of the Interior in 1930 and later Vice Chancellor and Minister of Security under Dolfuss until dismissed in 1936. He was willing to work within the context of coalition governments in what became called a Patriotic Front. He labeled Nazism "brown Bolshevism" but may have been closer to Hitler than he admitted. He had to flee the country after the *Anschluss* in 1938.[68]

The hero of the new republic in Poland was Marshal Pilsudski, the son of an impoverished noble family. Prince Janusz Radziwill was one of his close associates and other magnates rallied to his regime.[69] Titles were abolished but remained in common use.[70] In the 1920s aristocrats opened up their Warsaw palaces for the winter season and the capital revived as a center of Polish society. The top 500 landowners in interwar Poland included 12 Potockis, 12 Lubomirskis, ten Radziwills, ten Zamoyskis, eight Tarnowskis, seven Czartoryskis, six Sapiehas, and many other members of the titled nobility. The top ten families owned three and a half million acres in 1922. Men such as Count Alfred Potocki controlled vast financial and industrial empires. Entails were not abolished until 1939 and even then the old ones associated with great families were protected and could only be ended with the consent of the parliament.[71]

Some agrarian reform took place but did not bring about much change. Four and a half million acres of property taken from large estates was subdivided, but much of this divestment was prompted by indebtedness, restructuring of assets, or punishment of Prussian landowners.[72] Aristocrats were found everywhere in the administrative and governmental functions of the Republic.[73] Much of the military officer class was drawn from the lower nobility, but the command of the army fell to a succession of titled generals.

In the east, when the Soviet troops entered Poland in September 1939, those landowners in residence were murdered by the peasants – if they were lucky – or fell into the hands of the NKVD (People's Commissariat for Internal Affairs), where they disappeared into the maw of prisons and gulags, few ever to surface again. The nobles in the officer corps were slaughtered in the Katyn Forest. Estates east of the Ribbentrop–Molotov line were taken over by the Soviets. West of the line the Nazis originally intended to exterminate the Polish nobility and settle deposed Baltic Germans on the emptied estates.[74] However, the grandees were left unmolested. In 1944 the remaining estates were doomed as the Red Army spread over the country. Leading aristocrats such as Count Jan Zamoyski were imprisoned. Those who could, fled. Count Alfred Potocki escaped to the West with railway cars full of his possessions.[75] Count Edward Raczynski became the Polish Ambassador to Britain for the government in exile in London in 1940, perhaps the most important post in that doomed ghost state.

In 1919 Bohemia and Moravia, with its small group of Polish, Hungarian, German, Austrian, and Czech magnates, was shaped into an independent state of Czechoslovakia. The new Republic abolished titles, yet more than one-third of the soil belonged to fewer than 100 aristocrats. The celebrated Czech nationalists Masaryk and Benes hated the old ruling class and implemented land redistribution, although proprietors were allowed to retain all of their business properties. In actuality only 16 percent of arable land was redistributed. Ten years after the war large estates still covered 40 percent of the land, although further reform was speeded up in the 1930s. Most big estates lost a third to a half of their land at worst. Only aristocrats who were deemed Germanophile or were Hungarian suffered badly. The Schwarzenbergs gave up barely a tenth of their holdings of over 500,000 acres.[76]

However, unlike the Polish elite, with a few exceptions the aristocracy played little direct role in government during the 1920s and 1930s. Prince Franz Schwarzenberg, a Czech patriot, was prominent. A group of 12 great noblemen pledged loyalty to the President of the Republic in the crisis of 1938, and the Nazis immediately confiscated their estates after Bohemia was occupied. Sixty-nine nobles signed a second declaration of support for the Czech cause in September 1939 after the German occupation, which was honorable and courageous.[77] A number of grandees were sent to concentration camps.

Among the successor states aristocrats were least well treated in Romania, even though it retained a monarchy. Out of fear of a Bolshevik revolt most of the agricultural land was redistributed to the peasants with some compensation after World War I, although estates of up to 1200 acres survived.[78] Aristocrats retained their business interests, which in some cases were considerable. They also used their compensation money to invest in banking and other commercial activities. The ethnically Hungarian landowners in Transylvania and the Russians in Bessarabia suffered serious setbacks and rarely showed themselves in Bucharest. The stranded Transylvanians, struggling to keep afloat with their small farms and big houses, were reminiscent of the surviving Anglo-Irish elite in County Cork.[79]

Up to 1914 most of the big estates in Croatia, Bosnia, and Slovenia were held by Hungarian, German, Italian, or Serbian nobles. The land tenure system was among the most archaic in Europe. At the outbreak of war nearly 100,000 peasant families were still held in a form of feudal service. In the newly constructed Yugoslavia, really a giant Serbian empire, serfdom was ended, and much land was taken from nobles and given to peasants in the vigorous agrarian reform scheme put into effect by the King to win the loyalty of his diverse and poverty-stricken subjects. Since most of the owners were foreigners, confiscation with little compensation was easy and widespread.[80]

The initial period at the end of the war appeared threatening to the Hungarian aristocracy, even though at first a nobleman was in charge. Count Mihály Károlyi, a member of one of the greatest families of the kingdom, headed the newly independent country. He lacked the political skills to hold together a diverse coalition in virtually impossible circumstances and soon resigned. A communist regime headed by Béla Kún came to power. During his reign estates were confiscated and aristocrats were attacked and imprisoned. Many went into hiding in fear for their lives.[81] The Kún regime collapsed, partly because his confiscation of land from prosperous peasants made him unpopular with key elements in the countryside, and partly thanks to a Romanian/Czech/French invasion followed by a "white" armed force led by Admiral Horthy, a lesser noble connected to the magnates by friendship and marriage. He arrived in Budapest in November 1919. Horthy's Prime Minister, Count Bethlen, came from an old Transylvanian family. He restored the aristocratic House of Magnates, giving great political power back to the aristocracy. Horthy's kingless kingdom was anti-democratic but relatively moderate. About one-tenth of the available arable land was redistributed in the 1920s, but more than one-third of the fertile areas remained owned by the Church and 1500 magnates. Prince Esterházy retained some 180,000 acres of good land.[82]

Bethlen's regime was undermined by the world depression. Several Hungarian aristocrats were among the founders of fascist parties, but control passed quickly to more aggressive leaders. Grandees were inclined to recoil from the excesses of National Socialism. The head of the strongest fascist group, the Arrow Cross, had a social background similar to Hitler's. When the war came, Count Pál Teleki, the last titled Prime Minister, whose fear of both communism and fascism noted in the eipgraph was shared by aristocrats across the Continent, hoped for a victory by the Western democracies over Hitler. He committed suicide in April 1941 to protest the transit of German forces through Hungarian territory in their attack on Yugoslavia. Advised by Count Bethlen, in 1944 Horthy tried to open secret negotiations with the Allies, but the Germans arrested the Regent.[83]

* * *

In many respects Scandinavia and the Low Countries began to advance at a more rapid pace in terms of social and political development than the rest of Europe after 1918. Here the landed elites tended to become marginalized without rancor. After putting up often spirited opposition in the later nineteenth century they seem to have accepted their fate in the twentieth without much anguish. However, in traditional places in the community, the diplomatic corps, the armed services, the court, and on their estates the aristocracy continued to fulfill its traditional functions. The survival of monarchies in Denmark, Sweden, Belgium, Luxemburg, and Holland provided some support for a titled elite. In Denmark no new titles had been granted since 1849. Sweden took longer to abolish the process, and the last nobleman there was created in 1902.

The landowning aristocracy of Belgium played a diminishing role in the political arena. In the mid-nineteenth century they were able to block the passage of a law in parliament on land credit. A vote on farm leases in 1926 demonstrated that they were no longer able to contest a policy directed against their economic privileges.[84] Some titles continued to be created and the aristocracy played a special role in "Society," but they ceased to be of much national importance. No new titles have been created in the Netherlands since 1940. Dutch diplomats continued to be drawn from the titled aristocracy, and a few noblemen served in Cabinets after the war. For all practical purposes the political life of the nation became fully democratic.

France also witnessed the atrophy of the aristocracy in the early twentieth century. Action Française, the royalist party, had fascist overtones, but it was distinct from most other such movements due to the central place given to royalism. This, combined with identification with Catholicism and the broad support it held among the nobility, distinguished it from more plebian and more secular fascist movements.[85] Increasingly aristocratic estates were broken up among multiple heirs, which diminished further the landholdings of an elite that had always been more modestly endowed than in other countries. The percentage of nobles among conservative deputies in parliament dropped precipitously at the end of World War I.

The last prominent blue blood in French life was General Maxime Weygand, Commander-in-Chief of the army in 1940, although mystery shrouds the exact nature of his origins. It seems likely that he was the illegitimate son of a Belgian prince, but it is possible his well-funded childhood that took him to St. Cyr and then the elite cavalry School at Samur could have been paid for by a less exalted source. He owned no landed estate but emphatically embraced the traditional conservative views of the old elite.[86]

High Society in Paris during the interwar years still had a strongly aristocratic tinge, but Café Society emerged as peripatetic, open, and *louche*. The Duchess de Clermont-Tonnerre complained *c*.1930: "I went to a costume ball recently. Russians ruined by the revolution, ostentatious Argentines, olive-skinned Syrians were strutting about to the sound of a saxophone, and drinking cocktails."[87] Exotics such as the Duke of Windsor, the Aga Khan, and the horde of white Russians meshed with the traditional elite of French dukes and counts and Romanian princes. Society also now contained celebrities of the stage and screen with literature and bohemia sprinkled in.

Most of the old elite acquiesced to the Vichy regime in 1940, relieved that the threat of radical socialism seemed to have been eradicated. Some enthusiastically endorsed it.[88] They emerged after the war much as they had been before it, still moderately prosperous and politically irrelevant. However, a few members of the old aristocracy saw honor in resistance to the invaders and traitors. Baron Henri d'Astier de la Vigerie organized the assassination of Admiral Darlan in 1942, while his brother, Baron Emmanuel, was leader of one of the most important underground groups, the Libération Resistance.[89]

* * *

On the occasion of a state visit to London by the President of France in March 1939, the King and Queen took him to Covent Garden. One observer noted: "Almost everyone in the Opera House was in Court dress or uniform; half the women wore tiaras; it was a brave sight . . . The ancien régime dies hard in England."[90] The prevailing view is that Britain's elite was much weaker during the interwar period than they had been before 1914. The Great War is seen as a breakpoint of the most fundamental kind. The 1920s and 1930s were characterized by a disintegrating empire and economic depression. However, there are historians such as W. D. Rubinstein who argue that Britain's mainstream elites "were *not* weakened by the First World War or by any of its attendant changes. During the interwar years, and especially during the 1930s, they were in fact stronger than ever before."[91] No expropriation of property took place. Landed families who relied purely on agricultural income were in decline, but those with substantial revenues from urban property, mineral royalties, and stocks and bonds stayed rich.[92] Fascism and communism never seriously threatened the state. The popularity of the monarchy, the survival of the House of Lords, the continued creation of hereditary titles, membership of old families in the Cabinet and high military posts, willingness to merge into a more open "Establishment," and the respect accorded to traditional institutions and rituals sustained elite power and privilege. New men from both the political and commercial spheres were anxious to acquire the trappings of a peerage and acreage.[93]

This view may be something of an exaggeration. Mineral royalties, for example, were in decline in the 1920s and 1930s. Many large estates were sold after the war and even more reduced in size. Paintings and manuscripts went to rich Americans or museums. Though eminent and able, Curzon was considered debarred in the 1920s from serving as prime minister by his seat in the House of Lords, and the presence of the landed elite in parliament became a shadow of its former self.[94] Further reform of the county councils in 1933 made them more open to a wider range of candidates. Welfare legislation and rural labor unions gradually replaced landlord paternalism in the countryside.

The elite survived longest at the top level of politics. Every Earl of Derby in the century from 1830 to 1948 sat in the Cabinet, and all but one of the Marquises of Salisbury between 1852 and 2005. Stanley Baldwin's Cabinet in 1935 included a Percy and a Stanley, families prominent in British life since the Middle Ages, several old-line marquises, and a number of titled men with large landed estates. Grandees of very modest ability, such as the 7th Marquis of Londonderry, were promoted to key positions in the Cabinet for little reason other than their lineage and wealth.[95] Even Labour administrations featured titled politicians.[96] Key governorships and ambassadorial posts went to aristocrats. The Marquis of Lothian and the Earl of Halifax served in Washington during the 1940s when the relationship with the Roosevelt administration and American public opinion was critical to national survival. In 1939 Viscount Gort was Commander-in-Chief of the British army in France. Admiral the Earl of Cork and Orrery was put in charge of the first naval action at Narvik.

David Cannadine's massive study of the decline of the British aristocracy is full of shrewd observation and elegant analysis, but he offers definitions and measures that impose unrealistic standards of who was or was not an aristocrat. He also calls Churchill's contribution to the war effort a "largely accidental" exception.[97] To call Lord Halifax a marginal figure in politics and government seriously overstates the case.[98] Recent research has shown how influential the old elite could be. We now know that a cabal of aristocrats, led by the 4th Marquis of Salisbury, engineered the toppling of Neville Chamberlain in May 1940.[99]

Faith in the traditional system wobbled among a portion of the elite. Sir Oswald Mosley, 6th Baronet, headed the British Union of Fascists. He gained support from the 2nd Duke of Westminster and 12th Duke of Bedford. Other grandees, such as Lord Londonderry, sought closer relations with Nazi Germany as a way to avoid war. This was of major consequence not only because of the seniority these men held in the Conservative Party, but also because Londonderry was in charge of rearmament as Secretary of State for the Air Force. As late as 1940 Halifax was receiving letters from many aristocrats imploring a negotiated peace.[100]

On the other hand, many members of the aristocracy were psychologically robust and confident. The 8th Earl of Berkeley undertook a massive and expensive restoration of 900-year-old Berkeley Castle between 1920 and 1929. The Earl of Jersey completed a new and sumptuous country house designed by Edwin Lutyens in 1938.[101] The English establishment was still strong enough in its traditions and values to force Edward VIII off the throne. When invited to propose a toast at a reception at the German Embassy in the spring of 1939, the 73-year-old Countess of Airlie turned to the Ambassador with a raised glass: "To Hell with Hitler and the German Army."[102]

Scotland was perhaps the most desirable place in Europe for an aristocrat to live during the interwar years. More than anywhere else the great names in national history, like the Ramsays, were still found among the landed elite in modern times. The 1930s witnessed a revival in the number of sons of Scottish peers elected to the House of Commons. Many of the grandees began to reassociate themselves in the public mind with the historic traditions of a nation increasingly concerned about drawing distinctions between itself and England. Anti-landlord feelings declined as farmers and lairds aligned themselves together to secure better treatment from the government. Dukes and earls served as members or chairs of virtually every important commission or organization in the country from the National Library to the Medical Research Council. Many county councils were chaired by peers and more lord lieutenancies remained in the hands of great lairds in Scotland than among nobles in England. During the war Lord Lovat won regard by his bravery and perhaps also for landing on the beaches at Normandy accompanied by his personal piper.

* * *

The last act in the history of the European aristocracy opened in 1939. The loss of life among the German elite reached an unprecedented level, as they perished in the snow at Stalingrad and in Soviet prisoner-of-war camps. When killed in action the young counts and princes were brought home for burial in the family vaults at their ancestral castles. This gave rise to local manifestations of sympathy on a scale that was interpreted as anti-Nazi demonstrations. A decree was issued discharging "undependable elements" from the army, specifying sons of ex-reigning families and mediatized princes.[103]

The British elite suffered many casualties, although not on the German scale.[104] The French officer corps failed in its duty to defend the nation, except for a small group who fled with Charles de Gaulle to London. Admiral Count Jean de Laborde, the Toulon commander, ordered the sinking of the fleet in harbor so that it would not fall into British hands.[105] Many of the *noblesse* relished the fascist victory.

The scale of the tragedy of World War II was so grand and vast that individual contributions, except in a few cases, are hard to identify. The remaining eagles were lonely if imperial birds. Nonetheless, a number of aristocrats played a decisive role in the unfolding of events after 1939. The flame flared up with astonishing brightness before twilight became evening. Aristocrats, most notably in Finland, Germany, and Britain, made extraordinary contributions to leadership during the war.[106]

Baron Gustav Mannerheim became the most important Finnish leader of modern times. His family had been ennobled in Sweden in 1693 and made barons in 1768. They bought an estate in Finland in the 1790s, and were created counts by Tsar Alexander I.[107] The father of the famous baron was in straitened circumstances, which made it difficult for Mannerheim to enter the Tsarist army, yet he managed to serve in a Guards regiment and personally escorted Nicholas II at the coronation in Moscow in 1896. By 1917 he was a lieutenant general. Mannerheim demonstrated superb leadership in the crisis that ensued after the Russian Revolution. With very little in the way of equipment he managed to crush the Soviet attempts to reabsorb newly independent Finland. The Baron's refusal to embrace the fascist Lapua movement blocked it from destroying the fledgling democracy, and he helped suppress further communist agitation. Mannerheim's brilliant management of the "Winter War" of 1939–40, again with wholly inadequate numbers of men and equipment against a giant foe, at first achieved considerable success and then, though the war cost Finland territory, managed to save the country from destruction.[108]

Finland had to balance as delicately as it could between Nazi Germany and Stalinist Russia, with little or no help from the Allies. The Soviets made impossible demands, and a "continuation" war followed between 1941 and 1944. As the war neared its end, once again the nation made use of Mannerheim's international stature and independent position to extricate them from guilt by association with the Germans in the eyes of the Allied powers. The Baron was chosen as President in August 1944 when an old and tired man. He managed to salvage Finnish independence and democracy before stepping down due to ill health in 1946.[109]

*   *   *

It was hard to preserve one's honor inside Hitler's Reich. Most of the senior military leadership failed to do so. They were grateful for the restored and expanded army and air force that the Führer built in defiance of the Versailles diktat and impressed by the success he had in using it. The thrill of easy conquests appealed to their patriotism. Most were anti-Semites and all feared communism. They became technocrats who carried out orders, however abominable or horrific. They also claimed to be tied by their oath of personal loyalty sworn to Hitler, and as servants of the state found it impossible to commit treason in time of war. By 1939 few of the top men were nobles, let alone aristocrats. Of the 12 field marshals created in July 1940 only one was a hereditary knight, and none held the title baron or count.[110]

Resistance was not easy in a totalitarian state. The risks to one's own career and life were great and punishment for disobedience was also imposed on innocent members of a traitor's family. Moreover, Hitler was surrounded by elaborate systems of security that required

even field marshals to remove their weapons before gaining access
to his presence. Only a small body of men and women had the
courage to defy Nazism. Some of these were ordinary citizens such
as the heroic students of the White Rose movement. Communists
and socialists were sent to concentration camps for opposition activities, but most of them never had a realistic opportunity to inflict
mortal damage on the regime. A few resisters were soldiers such as
the middle-class General Ludwig Beck, a unique figure who more
fully embodied the old traditions of military honor than most of his
colleagues who were noble by birth. Others who paid with their lives
included Catholic priests, a former mayor of Leipzig, trade union
leaders, and Protestant pastors, but only one commoner, Georg Elser,
came close to killing Hitler, with a bomb in Munich in 1939. Once
war began the dictator was all but inaccessible.

It was aristocrats who led the only truly dangerous internal attack
on the Nazi regime during the war. This was due to the fact that they
could construct a broad conspiracy involving hundreds of people
who could trust each other because of their close family ties and
strict code of honor, and because only they could get hold of the
weapons and access to Hitler's person that made an assassination
practicable.[111]

The core of the movement came from comital families who bore
celebrated names – Bismarck, Yorck of Wartenburg, and Moltke –
along with Junker grandees such as Dohna, Lehndorf, Dönhoff, and
Schwerin-Schwanenfeld. The arrests, suicides, trials, and executions
that unfolded after July 20, 1944 affected directly and indirectly
thousands of members of the aristocracy. Due to the intervention of
his commanding officer, Baron Saurma von der Jeltsch suffered
only dismissal from the army after he was heard announcing when
the coup attempt failed: "Better luck next time!"[112] Most were not
so lucky. Ten members of the Stauffenberg family were sent to
Buchenwald.[113]

The main aristocratic conspiracy had two centers, although the
judge at the subsequent trials, the fanatical Nazi Roland Freisler,
lumped them together as "the Counts' Circle."[114] One group, led by
Count Moltke, focused on proposals for restructuring postwar
Germany. The other broader resistance movement had a number of
leaders, including Beck, in the early stages though eventually it was
Count Claus von Stauffenberg who became the moving force. After
much bad luck and failed attempts, the climactic attack came on July

20, 1944 when Stauffenberg's bomb detonated during a staff meeting, killing several of those present but leaving Hitler alive because of the accidental movement of the Count's briefcase shortly before it exploded.[115] Twenty counts, ten barons, and two knights were executed, some of them after extensive torture. Others died in prison or escaped death only by accident. Dozens of nobles were also arrested, among whom at least 25 were killed or committed suicide. It is incorrect to say that resistance was widespread among the German nobility. However, a substantial number of men and women from the titled elite were willing to defy Hitler at great personal risk. The Gestapo was stunned at the extent of the conspiracy as the investigation unfolded, and the aristocratic nature of the final surge of resistance confirmed Hitler's distrust and loathing for the old elite.[116]

Few nobles opposed the new regime from the start. Most of them swallowed the conquest of innocent nations calmly or even with enthusiasm. Many were anti-Semitic, although it was ultimately the monstrous treatment of the Jews, especially on the Eastern Front, that swung many into opposition.[117] For men such as Moltke the moral depravity of the regime was central to his stand against Nazism.[118] However, for most of the aristocrats involved honor and service were the heart of the matter. Their noble lineage and family traditions transformed them into agents of national salvation. By 1944 they realized that the war was lost. Earlier they had been blinded by patriotism and wishful thinking. As the full horror of the situation, their own complicity and that of the nation became obvious, they set a course of atonement and expiation in which they understood their own lives were likely to be forfeit. They were human enough to fantasize about a better end. Adam Trott persisted in thinking he could convince the Allies of their *bona fides*.[119] Stauffenberg had a plan to establish an interim government. Moltke held seminars about public policy. In 1944, however, they could only hope that the Allies would reach Berlin before the Red Army, and that the conditions of surrender might to some degree be mitigated by their sacrifice. As Prince Metternich, who was connected with many of the conspirators, noted, "however it ends, people like us will lose everything."[120]

On his deathbed in 1936 Stauffenberg's father had made his sons promise to uphold the honor and greatness of the family. The old Count told them: "It does not matter what you do, only that you act

decently and that you bring honour to your name." In his draft proc-
lamation to the nation, to be issued after the coup took place, the
young Count wrote: "We should be unworthy of our fathers, we
should deserve the contempt of our children, if we had not the
courage to do all we could to avert this fearful danger and regain
our self-respect."[121] These were not idyll words, which with Hitler
safely dead we should parse with too cynical an eye. Stauffenberg
had demonstrated great personal courage in battle, where he lost an
eye and had a hand amputated. His brother wrote days before the
failed coup: "The most terrible thing is knowing that we cannot
succeed, and yet we have to do it, for our country and our children."[122] Count Schwerin von Schwanenfeld wrote his father before
the attack that he fully realized that a violent overthrow of the Nazis
could not save Germany from catastrophe, but that a failed attempt
would help free Germany from the spiritual disease of National
Socialism.[123] Counts Yorck, Bismarck, and Moltke were fully aware
that they bore some of the most famous names in modern German
history and risked their lives further to honor that tradition. The
stoicism with which they met their outrageous trials and horrible
deaths, late as they were in making the sacrifice, was majestic.[124]
Count Yorck told his wife hours before his execution: "I can stand
proudly with my ancestors, with my father and brothers."[125]

Stauffenberg and his associates still possessed an unthinking
assumption of the right to lead, and proved they were capable of
taking audacious action.[126] Under the most difficult conceivable conditions they functioned for the last time in modern history as an
aristocratic force to be reckoned with. In the end, the generals failed
to act, the communists failed to act, and the churches failed to act.
It was aristocrats who risked their lives, families, and estates for the
sake of honor.[127]

* * *

The British aristocracy was also given one more outing on the world
stage during World War II, and it performed well. The British army
was led largely by men from landed backgrounds, some from the
lesser gentry like Montgomery, and some from the aristocracy such
as Lord Gort and Harold Alexander, a younger son of the Earl of
Caledon. The top commander, Alan Brooke, was also the younger
son of a magnate family from Northern Ireland. The Cabinet was

filled with landed gentlemen and grandees. Churchill was born at Blenheim Palace, and for a time he was the heir to the dukedom of Marlborough; he married the granddaughter of a Scottish earl.

As we have seen, some historians suggest that Winston Churchill's role was almost "accidental," and his aristocratic colleagues "marginal men." Cannadine claims that Churchill was a "half-breed," poor, and irrelevant in 1930s. Once in office his aristocratic friends provided a dignified façade while others did the work.[128] This overstates the case. Churchill was no more a half-breed than hundreds of other sons of peers from the most ancient and distinguished families with American mothers. He was never genuinely poor. His sense of style was that of a grandee, which made his bank balances frightening to contemplate, but he continued to live like a lord and even managed to buy a country house with money gained from the sale of an Irish landed estate that he inherited. As for his political isolation in the 1930s, we now can see both the profound nature of his insights into Nazism and that he was no more at a disadvantage than his Whig ancestors had been in the 1820s.

It was clear that in May 1940 the most difficult decision confronting twentieth-century Britain was made by a small group of men. The question of whether to negotiate a peace with Hitler or to fight to the death lay in the hands of Winston Churchill and the Earl of Halifax. The latter's decision to retire from contention for the premiership and Churchill's masterful political skill obliged the appeasers in the Cabinet to accept the policy of death or victory.[129]

Churchill was dubious about giving every man and woman the vote; he was a champion of free societies led by aristocrats. It was the fate suffered by the nobility that upset him most about the Russian Revolution.[130] Isaiah Berlin believed Churchill remained, even in the 1940s, "a European of the nineteenth century."[131] His swashbuckling faith in the empire amazed even his aristocratic colleagues. The Marquis of Linlithgow wrote to him in 1933, "you are hanging, hairy, from a branch, while you sputter the atavistic shibboleths of an age destined very soon to retreat into the forgotten past."[132] They were right and Churchill was wrong, but as a warrior organizing Britain's survival his atavistic instincts proved superbly suited to the crisis. Like Stauffenberg and Yorck, honor was vital to his sense of being and his service to the country.[133] He told the House of Commons in 1940 of the importance of bearing rectitude and sincerity as a shield. "It is very imprudent to walk through life without this shield, because we are so often mocked by the failure of our hopes and the upsetting of our calculations: but with this shield, however the fates may play, we always march in the ranks of honour."[134]

On that great day in London in May 1945 after victory was announced massive crowds spontaneously moved down the Mall to cheer the King and Queen along with Churchill as they stood on the balcony of the battle-scarred palace. The British people generously acknowledged leadership drawn from the most traditional of sources. King George VI and Queen Elizabeth embodied the nation, and in thanking them the people thanked themselves, but Churchill was another matter. He stood for valor. He was a warrior and the representative of a family who were princes of the Holy Roman Empire and English dukes. He made no apology for this. He reveled in his ancestry. The British people knew that and were respectful, but they would turn to new, meritocratic, socialist leaders to make the peace and build a new society.

Fortunately, the dogged devotion to freedom and humane culture of Britain allowed for a peaceful transition. Other societies were not so lucky. In an unparalleled case of aristocide Hitler and Stalin made it their object to liquidate landed society in the East as they pursued their depraved dreams. The dictators achieved what no previous revolutionaries had been able to accomplish, the overthrow of aristocratic privilege and wealth. It turned out, however, that in its place the masters of mass movements, the common men, had only war and suffering to offer humanity, and no honor.

10

WHERE ARE THEY NOW?
1945–2005

> Poor old dukes are considered more freakish by the day.
>
> 11th Duke of Devonshire, *Accidents of Fortune*, p. 15

Paul Ignatieff was the only son of a fort commander. As a 17-year-old ensign, he held his regimental colors aloft on the Champs Elysées when the Preobrajensky Guards rode as victors into Paris in 1815. During the Decembrist uprising in 1825, the first platoons to rally to the Tsar were led by Captain Paul Ignatieff. He was showered with imperial favor, married the daughter of a wealthy industrialist, and was created a count. His son, Nicholas, married a princess and became one of the architects of the Russian empire in Asia. In 1860 he negotiated the Amur–Ussuri Treaty that defines the border between Russia and China to this day and in 1878 the agreement that brought the Russo-Turkish War to a conclusion. As Minister of the Interior in the 1880s he enforced harsh measures of repression. His son, Paul, married Princess Natasha Mestchersky and served as Minister of Education in the last Cabinet of Tsar Nicholas II. His wife said of him: "My husband never belonged to himself, always serving the state and his countrymen."[1] Paul's brother Vladimir, a naval officer, was killed in 1905 at the Battle of Tsushima. His uncle Alexis, governor of Tver province, was assassinated during the revolution in early 1906. Count Paul was a liberal but party politics was anathema to him, a betrayal of the oath of service he had given to the Tsar personally. In early 1914 Paul was named joint heir (along with Prince Demidoff) of the Maltsev industrial empire, which employed over 20,000 workmen. The Count continued in government service while helping to run the factories. He also served as President of the Russian Red Cross under the Provisional Government. However, he was overwhelmed by depression and suffered a nervous collapse as the system he had been brought up to serve disintegrated. He retreated to "bed gazing at his inner wreckage."[2] The family fled to the Caucasus in July 1917 as things began to slip out of control in Petrograd, still accompanied by nannies, tutors, cooks, and lady's maids. Workers from the Maltsev factories regularly appeared, having traversed the war zone with business letters and cash in their boots. Both the Whites and Reds occupied the town where the Ignatieffs lived. Paul was arrested but saved from execution by his reputation as an educational reformer. The servants melted away, except for the English nanny who took command and engineered their escape through the Black Sea to London. Fortunately, a Liverpool cotton broker owed the Maltsev company £25,000. The family purchased a farm in England and tried to restore themselves to a landed exist-ence. Relatives and hangers-on joined them. Ex-judges minded the dairy herd, colonels drove the tractor, and a general managed the woods. Eventually they sold up. Paul went to Paris to head the Russian Red Cross in exile, and the rest of the family went to Canada seeking a new life. One son became a Rhodes Scholar, another studied law at McGill. They became engineers and professors. One served as a Canadian diplomat, and his son, Michael, became the distinguished director of an institute at Harvard. The Princess played the stock market and loved to rummage in the one-cent sale tubs at the local drugstore. She died 1944 and the Count, who had rejoined her, in 1945. The family's country house in Russia became a school. The graves of the counts and countesses, only slightly worse for wear, have survived to the present day in the crypt of the estate church.[3]

All over central Europe in the spring and summer of 1945 a great social revolution swept away families that had owned and ruled the countryside for centuries. Now the remaining landed elites suffered what the Ignatieffs had already experienced in 1917. Princes and counts fled. For those who failed to escape, rape, torture, murder, or long years of starvation in the gulags often followed.

By and large, the French, Italian, Austrian, and German elites, even though many died courageously on the battlefield, acted ignobly in the great testing moment of modern Western civilization. Despite the sacrifice of many sons, their military services led only to crushing defeat and moral ignominy. In the case of Germany this was for the second time in less than 30 years. Whatever remaining arguments there were that justified hereditary privilege went up in smoke. In France and Italy it was republicans and communists who most often led the resistance.

Only in Britain did Churchill and his political and military associates drawn from the old ruling class perform well. In command of a vast empire, creaking at every joint but still intact, the aristocracy demonstrated exceptional war-making capacities. Britain fought well above its weight, in part because the leadership functioned as if they were still in charge of a superpower. Only towards the end of the war did it become obvious to everyone that the illusion could no longer be sustained. The empire was a spent force, and the ferociously egalitarian Russians and Americans were now in charge of the world.

Without the opportunity to rule, did the word "aristocracy" have any remaining meaning? Something of importance lingered in the countryside, although with a smaller and smaller proportion of the populations of European countries living there, the significance of lords on the surviving landed estates has relatively little meaning in the context of national life. Yet, titled families of wealth and lineage still live in grand houses, occasionally lead political careers, and are an integral part of national history.

* * *

The eastern European lords stayed on their estates until the spring of 1945 when the Russian army approached. The Clarys were still at Teplitz, the Metternichs at Königswort, and the Dönhoffs at Friedrichstein. Great vintage wines were served with beets and potatoes by old retainers as the families worked their way through the cream of their cellars in the days remaining to them.[4] Refugees who had already fled the Soviets or the Nazis in 1939 were often trapped in what had appeared a safe haven. The Prince of Pless was imprisoned in Britain as an enemy alien.[5] Prince Peter Schönburg-Hartenstein fled Austria to South America just before the *Anschluss* and was obliged to find work as a surveyor in the Amazon.

In January 1945 Countess Marion Dönhoff, accompanied by a groom, rode on horseback from near Königsberg in East Prussia to the Rhine. Her harrowing description of the January escape, riding only a few miles ahead of the Russian army, is epic. On the way she visited Countess Bismarck, the Chancellor's aged daughter-in-law, who had ordered the Bismarck archive evacuated in horse-drawn wagons but refused to leave the family estate at Varzin herself. She had a grave dug in the garden while workers were still available, and then stoically awaited her fate.[6]

Princess Biron von Courland escaped from Silesia by climbing through the window of a train. Baroness Blumen fled with friends who had access to diplomatic vehicles. Countess Dohna was borne away with a few small suitcases in a truck filled with fleeing soldiers. Others used old carriages or were reduced to walking. As the guns boomed in the distance and flashes of light filled the horizons, great families "got up from tea in the library, where first editions and fine manuscripts remained on the shelves, and [went] out through warm rooms filled with beautiful furniture, down passages where cupboards contained silver and linen. When they drove off, the house's familiar aspect with its lighted windows shining peacefully in the dusk made it seem as if the family were going off for a weekend."[7]

Thirty von Armins died in the war, including a number who were Russian prisoners. The von der Schulenburgs lost 23 men. Princess Eleanore-Marie von Schönburg-Hartenstein's five brothers perished; the last, a wounded officer lying in a hospital in Prague, was dragged out his bed and murdered in April 1945. Only one of the six sons of Count Siegfried Lehndorf of Trakehenn survived the war. A number of French aristocrats were killed in the fighting during the spring of 1940. The Duke de Ayen died in Bergen-Belsen. Among the dozen English peers killed were the 9th Duke of Northumberland and the 7th Marquis of Lansdowne. Many heirs to peerages and younger sons also perished.[8]

After World War II the cost of physical reconstruction and rebuilding societies led to continued heavy taxation. Death duties were increased, and taxes became harder to avoid. The upkeep of many big houses, especially when compensation for war damage was inadequate, became an impossible burden.[9] Across Europe castles, palaces, and country houses that had survived the war intact were demolished. In Russia Khrushchev's onslaught on churches in the late 1950s led to the destruction of many surviving estate buildings as well.[10]

As the Soviet empire crumbled in 1989 Countess Dönhoff returned to Friedrichstein for the first time since 1945. Nothing remained standing, "not even rubble." The area had been entirely denuded of people and the Russians brought in new settlers from Smolensk and the Caucasus.[11] Across eastern Europe paintings, furniture, plasterwork, and archives were destroyed on a scale unprecedented in modern Western civilization. Great palaces such as Eszterháza in Hungary were damaged and looted. In East Prussia Stalin finished what Hitler began.

Even in victorious Britain up to a fifth of all important country houses were demolished, although some were replaced by smaller ones. Many large mansions lost wings or upper stories. The major period of destruction took place between 1946 and 1965. Among the survivors, many were opened to visitors or came into some form of public ownership.[12]

The British and Americans hatched plans to destroy the landowning class by breaking up big estates to help democratize West German society. But land reform ran out of steam very quickly and was largely abandoned.[13] In 1906 half of the land in Sicily was owned by 1000 landowners. In 1946 this had grown to 6000. Peasants invaded the remaining *latifundia* at the end of the war and the 1947 constitution pledged to transform large estates. A land reform scheme with compensation was launched in 1950. Nearly 20 million acres were to be redistributed, but by 1960 only about 8 percent had actually been expropriated and not much more in the next decade. Vested interests were able to slow the losses to a trickle.[14] In Finland, on the other hand, severe measures were necessary to provide for 425,000 refugees from territory confiscated by the Soviet Union. In Denmark by the 1960s, 19 out of 20 farms were owned by their operators.[15] In Portugal agricultural workers occupied over two million acres during the chaotic period immediately after the revolution in 1975. Legislation subsequently confirmed and extended this to nearly four million acres.[16]

Many aristocrats were either unable or too stupid to flee the Soviet advance in 1945. Perhaps some took the attitude: "If all is lost, there is nothing to lose."[17] They were wrong. The Russians launched a system of total expropriation in East Germany in July 1945.[18] In Czechoslovakia the estates of the nobles whose property had been confiscated by the Nazis in 1938, due to their support of the Republic, were returned to them in 1945, and a brief Indian summer with dozens of servants and shooting parties resumed, only to be quickly snuffed out in 1948 when the communists took full control of the government. In Romania, Hungary, and Poland nobles were declared a "parasite class" and their property seized.[19]

In May and June 1951 the Hungarian government forced members of the aristocracy to leave Budapest. According to official figures the resettlement included six princes, 52 counts, 41 barons, as well as many more untitled landowners. The nobles were obliged to earn a living as agricultural laborers, barred from leaving their assigned place of residence.[20] Some were sent off to be coalminers. Count Mátyás Esterházy worked as a road mender and parquet floor layer. Count Mihály Károlyi, the radical Prime Minister of Hungary in 1919, returned to Budapest in 1946. His wife, born an Andrássy and known as the "Red Countess," came with him. They went into exile again, but she returned after her husband's death in France in the 1950s and lived as a kind of communist *grande dame* in part of the family palace.[21] In Poland poor treatment of aristocrats eased after 1956, and a few members of the elite re-emerged. Prince Krzysztof Radziwill, who had made the acquaintance of subsequent communist leaders in the Nazi concentration camp of Mauthausen, joined the puppet Democratic Party and served as head of protocol in the Foreign Ministry. Well-educated aristocrats were eventually allowed to pursue professional careers. Count Ilya Tolstoy, grandson of the novelist, returned to Russia after World War II and became a professor at Moscow State University.[22] Prince Ion Mavrocordato was an engineer in Romania in the 1970s. Eighty-four-year-old Princess Ekaterina Meshcherskaya was allowed to publish her memoirs in the celebrated Soviet literary magazine *Novy Mir* in 1988, even though these reflected poorly on the regime, and she was interviewed on television.

In the West aristocrats also found they were living in a hostile environment. In Germany the reputation of the nobility who had served the Nazi state was irreparably stained. Aristocratic traditions were deliberately eradicated. In Italy the nobles tried to preserve elite status by distancing themselves from the monarchy and emphasizing the historically autonomous role of the Italian aristocracy. Despite these desperate efforts, the republican constitution of 1947 abolished all titles of distinction.[23] The countryside rapidly depopulated. It became hard to find labor for the estates and relationships with workers were sometimes decidedly unfriendly. The Marchesa di Origio wrote of her estate in Tuscany in the 1950s and 1960s: "We had become Enemies of the People, the abusers of the poor. The church was no longer attended, and in the school the children's essays stated, a little puzzled, that now all the *padroni* had become 'bad' . . . It was a painful, distressing period . . ."[24] The family began to think about selling out. The old, socially exclusive Società del Whist of Turin merged with the bourgeois club Accademia Filarmonica in 1948.[25]

Even where they retained wealth, aristocrats found themselves slipping in comparison to the *nouveaux riches*. In the 1980s it was estimated that approximately 3000 personal fortunes greater than ten million francs existed in France; most were in the hands of industrialists and people connected with the professions or entertainment.[26] The *Sunday Times* "Rich List" changed during the last decade of the twentieth century. In 1990 more than a third out of the top 100 were titled or from landed families, many of them authentic grandees. By 2003, although the Duke of Westminster was still number one, only 12 other aristocrats remained in the top group. Self-made businessmen, entertainers, sports figures, and film stars dominated the roster of wealth owners.[27]

To be sure, many grandees were able to sustain an aristocratic style of life. The Sykes baronets of Sledmere lived very much in the grand style in the 1960s and 1970s. Nannies and governesses raised children. The house continued to be run by an army of cooks, butlers, maids, footmen, and hall boys, to say nothing of a large outdoor staff of gardeners, gamekeepers, and grooms.[28] Guests brought their own valets and maids to house parties. The disappearance of domestic servants hit the middle classes and gentry hard, but in aristocratic households where incomes were still high it was more a question of footmen no longer wearing powdered wigs and knee breeches. Otherwise a genuinely stately way of life was maintained. Prince Serge Obolensky went to a white-tie ball in 1952 at Londonderry House where all the ladies wore tiaras.[29] The Queen did not stop the presentation of débutantes at Buckingham Palace until 1958.

In the 1950s smart aristocratic society survived in Rome, Paris, Madrid, and London, often blending with café society. France witnessed a brief blaze of splendor ignited by the son of an Austrian financier, Baron de Redé, and his ally, Baroness de Rothschild. They gave a series of glittering balls in the 1960s and 1970s in their contiguous houses carved out of the old Czartoryski palace in Paris and at Château Ferrières. One party appropriately took the Proust centennial as its theme while another embraced "modernism," where everyone wore Surrealist headdresses. The level of hospitality was quite in the old style, and dukes and princes were thick on the ground. However, celebrities such as Bianca Jagger, Brigette Bardot, Elizabeth Taylor, and Richard Burton became fixtures at these affairs.[30] Andy Warhol, also a guest, watched aristocrats get 15 minutes of fame. Gradually, café society transmogrified into Euro-trash, an amalgam of countesses, opera divas, bullfighters, Swiss bankers, Greek ship-owners, pop stars, sheiks, and soccer players. The marvelous ball scene in Visconti's version of *The Leopard,* filmed in 1963, was staged in the Gangi Palace in Palermo with hundreds of authentic Sicilian aristocrats as "extras." The Prince of Monaco shrewdly married the Irish-American film star Grace Kelly in order to put his casino business back on the map. Titles still had cachet, although fewer and fewer people understood the protocol of their use. British Airways recently issued a ticket to "Mr. Duke of Buccleuch and Mrs. Duchess of Buccleuch."[31]

All barriers restricting careers fell away. The 10th Duke of Beau-fort, who still lived in very grand style at Badminton, ran an art gallery. The banker and stockbroker Prince Rupert Löwenstein became the financial advisor to the Rolling Stones.[32] Thousands of men and women listed in the current editions of the *Almanach de Gotha* proudly call themselves businessmen, lawyers, doctors, archi-tects, journalists, engineers, and scholars. A study made in France in 1954 found that 29 percent of top positions in insurance and banking were in noble hands.[33] In the 1950s, daughters of the remnants of the Irish titled aristocracy still resident in the Republic posed for photographs to advertise Pond's cold cream in the *Irish Times.*[34] Vis-count De L'Isle, owner of the ancient great house at Penshurst, became executive director of Schwepps and chairman of Phoenix Assurance. The Earls of Verulam managed engineering companies and steel works in order to generate enough money to sustain their estate and country house.[35] Count Ivan Tolstoy was a distinguished geophysicist and his brother Paul a professor of anthropology. Prince Dimitri Obolensky, an Oxford professor, was knighted by the British government for scholarly distinction, and in 1997 he was elected to the Russian Academy of Sciences.[36] Spanish nobles not only invested in banks and industry but also became major figures in the financial world of Madrid.[37]

After the war the communists sought out Countess Yorck von Wartenburg to work for them in the Berlin city government. However, she began to feel manipulated and shifted back to her prewar interest in the law. The Countess entered the judicial service in West Berlin where she served until the 1960s, and she became the first female judge in German history to preside over a jury court.[38] In Portugal most of the owners of great estates moved to Lisbon and often took up careers in government bureaucracy, banking, or business. Literally thousands of aristocrats across Europe have turned their country houses into luxury accommodation and become hoteliers. Count Otto von Stolberg-Wernigerode (d. 1984), a professor at the University of Munich, became the editor of the *Neue Deutsche Biographie*, a national institution. His children are a patent lawyer, goldsmith, physiotherapist, and businessman. The Duke de Brissac, who married into the industrialist Schneider family, headed a complex of engineering, electrical, and steel companies while still retaining his magnificent château in the Loire.[39]

* * *

John Martin Robinson recently challenged David Cannadine's gloomy judgment about aristocratic decline in Britain: "The aristocracy rallied in the 20th century: they have secured their estates and great houses, maintained some degree of political influence in the Lords, in the Commons and at constituency level, and continued to fulfill their traditional ceremonial and public role in the counties, as well as developing new areas of activity in the city, 'the arts', as patrons of charities, and generally serving as model leaders of civil society."[40] Most English counties contain half a dozen large estates and 50 to 100 lesser ones. The new rich have been successfully absorbed. The compensation paid to coal owners after 1947 and the Labour government's decision to institute programs to subsidize historic houses helped the aristocracy recover successfully from the exigencies of war. These policies also removed landowners from ugly clashes with trade unions and made their homes holiday destinations for millions of their fellow citizens. Working-class kids could visit the lions at Longleat and their mothers could chat about the china at Woburn with the friendly Duke of Bedford.[41] No wonder a recent book by Peter Mandler, which discusses the benefits accruing to the British elite from government subsidies and popular support, was entitled *The Fall and Rise of the Stately Home.*[42] In France a move began in the 1960s to open châteaux to the public. Since 1964 100 percent of the cost of repairs and upkeep can be set against taxes if the house is available for visits 50 or more days a year. A 1988 law grants exemp-

tion from death duties on the condition that the heir opens his
château to the public.[43]

In the post-1945 period landowners began to benefit from a
variety of favorable trends. Sometimes tax burdens on agricultural
and forest land were eased. Land prices rose in Britain from £60 an
acre in 1945 to £2000 in the 1980s. Subsidies came from governments and through membership in the European Economic Community. Official policies also favored technological innovation and
large-scale agricultural production.[44] Unexpected windfalls came
the way of even wealthy aristocrats. The Duchess of Northumberland's new garden at Alnwick Castle received a grant from the
European Union of £8.8 million in 2004.[45] Not everyone was initially
so lucky. In 1946 the 10th Duke of Devonshire handed over Chatsworth to his son, along with 120,000 acres, and told him to tick off
each week when he went to church on Sunday to keep track of when
the estate would qualify for exemption from death duties. Alas, the
Duke died 14 weeks before the transfer met the five-year deadline.
The heir had to pay 80 percent of the value of the property and art
treasures. He mounted a battle to save Chatsworth, advised by the
best lawyers he could find. One of his three Rembrandts was sacrificed, but by delaying its sale for years while the art market rocketed
upwards great advantage was gained. Later the old master bought
by the National Gallery turned out not to be a Rembrandt at all,
while the two the Duke retained were declared to be genuine. Hard-
wick Hall was given to the National Trust, and Compton Place was
leased as a school. In the end 76,000 acres and several houses, in
addition to a refurbished Chatsworth still crammed with treasures,
remained.[46]

Owners of large estates continued to possess between a fifth and
a third of the whole area of England and Wales in the 1960s, while
in Scotland half the country belonged to 579 landowners.[47] Grandees
who owned property in London – the Duke of Westminster, Earl
Cadogan, Viscount Portman, Lord Howard de Walden and others –
were seriously rich and large holdings in provincial cities also survived. In the 1990s the Earl of Derby moved back into his vast palace
at Knowsley, which was redecorated and made functional again after
the Lancashire police force, to whom it had been leased by his father,
moved elsewhere. Similarly the Earl of Arundel renovated the gigantic Arundel Castle, abandoned as a residence in the 1960s, and
moved his family back to their seat of eight centuries' standing. The

Duke of Northumberland owns 120,000 acres and an art collection worth £200 million.[48]

Some French families managed to keep their patrimonies intact. However, the contents of most châteaux were not as valuable as their English counterparts and land became dispersed among multiple heirs.[49] In Italy aristocrats continued to own landed property, and in some regions such as Tuscany acreage remained concentrated in a small number of hands. In 1998 25 Danish families owned large estates, some of them over 10,000 acres.[50] In Spain the rural property structure remained unchanged into the 1970s and 1980s. Seven grandees still owned 658,000 acres in the south in the 1960s; the Duke de Medinaceli alone retained 235,000.[51] Three-quarters (74.1 percent) of the mediatized families of Germany listed in the edition of the *Almanach de Gotha* published in 1998 gave a country house as their address or lived in villages long associated with their families.[52]

*   *   *

After crawling across the blasted hulk of Germany in the spring of 1945, Prince and Princess Metternich reached the refuge of their bombed-out castle on the Rhine. They were greeted by servants with the cry: "Unsere Herrschaften sind da!" (Our masters are back!)[53] As late as the 1950s, farm laborers were expected to call Protestant landowners "Master" in southern Ireland.[54] When Lord Leconfield was out foxhunting on his estate in Sussex during the war and came across a village football match, he stood up in his stirrups and shouted, "Haven't you people got anything better to do in wartime than play *football?*" He then went on hunting.[55] Even the upheavals of the global conflict seemed not to shake the structure of relationships formed over centuries in the countryside. In 2002 the Duke of Buccleuch still provided 320 employees with free housing on his estates.[56]

The core group in subservience to the aristocracy continued to be servants. Both their rank in the hierarchy of household or estate life and their role as emblems of wealth and authority (demonstrated by their numbers and liveries) sustain the name and influence of great landowners in rural communities. Huntsmen wear family colors, butlers still look like the butlers, and maids still say, "Yes, your Ladyship," to their employers. The 6th Earl of Harwood kept 27 indoor staff and entertained house parties of up to 40 guests at a time in the 1950s. Twenty-one gardeners labored at Chatsworth in the 1960s. In the 1980s the Duke retained seven gamekeepers, three river-keepers, two telephonists, and a clock man who took four hours every Wednesday to wind the 63 clocks in the house. Archivists and secretaries scurried down basement corridors. In 2003 the Duke employed 286 full-time and 226 part-time workers including electricians, plumbers, painters, a mason, seamstresses, housekeepers, maids, foresters, gamekeepers, security men, and drivers. These were separate from another staff that served in the shops, restaurant, farmyard, adventure playground, and education service that were part of the tourist business.[57] At the funeral of the 11th Duke in 2004 more than 600 staff, dressed as chefs, gamekeepers, dairymen, maids, and carpenters, volunteered to line the funeral route between the house and the nearby family church.[58]

Many grandees remain active in philanthropy. In rural regions they can be the leading figures in charitable work. Local museums, hospitals, and other institutions often have a direct family connection that has been maintained over centuries. Apparently, English aristocrats will do almost anything to raise cash. In 1992 the 64-year-old Duchess of Beaufort agreed to abseil down the walls of the Gloucester Hospital for charity, ending up dangling upside-down.[59]

In Britain aristocrats continued to hold official positions in local government, some appointive and ceremonial, others elective and powerful. Lords Lieutenant were increasingly figureheads, and in England – though not so much in Scotland – fewer and fewer were drawn from the aristocracy. In the 1960s 30 of the 52 county councils in England and Wales had a titled person among the leadership, and some had several. This figure declined steadily, however, over the next 40 years.[60] In the 1960s and 1970s landowners continued to be a force in local elections. A study of Suffolk showed that the families who had long dominated the magistracy continued to have influence although they were increasingly obliged to share authority with other groups and individuals. The more rural the area, the more respect for leadership from the titled elite remained.[61] This suggests that broad national generalizations about aristocracies need to be qualified by recognition of regional variations. A Scottish duke cuts little ice in Glasgow these days, but in his fastness in the Highlands he is still a formidable figure.

The old landed elite played a notable role in Northern Ireland after the partition of 1922. Several of the leading Unionist politicians of the postwar era came from old landed families, notably the Prime Minister, Viscount Brookeborough, who ruled from 1943 to 1963, and the more appealing but ultimately unsuccessful Captain Terence O'Neill. Noble landlords remained targets of terrorist attacks. The Stronge baronets, father and son, were murdered and their great house in County Armagh burned down in 1981. Among the key figures in the rebuilding and economic development of Belfast, after the destruction wreaked by the IRA terror campaigns during the 1970s and 1980s, was a Tory aristocrat whose family had long held an estate in Ulster. Richard Needham, 6th Earl of Kilmorey, served as Secretary and later Minister in the Northern Ireland Office between 1983 and 1992. The Duke of Abercorn, whom he appointed the head of the Laganside Company, the main redevelopment agency, ably assisted him. Kilmorey also turned for assistance to other aristocrats such as Hugh O'Neill and the Marchioness of Dufferin.[62]

Serious salons in Paris in the 1950s and 1960s, attended by both society figures and Academicians, were still conducted by the Vicountess de Noailles, Countess de Polignac, and the Duchess de la Rochefoucauld.[63] Nobles continued to be elected as mayors in considerable numbers in the 1940s and 1950s.[64] In some regions they led the syndicalist and cooperative organizations after the war. In Brittany the man in charge was Hervé Budes de Guébriant, one of the largest landowners in the region and married to a daughter of the Duke of Trevise. He was thrown in jail for nine months after the Liberation for collaborating with the Germans but was released without being convicted and later was given 500,000 francs in compensation for "abusive and illegal internment" and awarded the Légion d'Honneur.[65] Syndical reforms in the 1950s and the rapidly shrinking proportion of the population engaged in agriculture, as well as the greater education and sophistication of the peasants, finally brought an end to aristocratic domination in rural regions.

In Piedmont many old families still own ancestral castles that bear their names. Even though the commercial and landowning elites of northern Italy increasingly mixed together socially and in business, the fusion has not been complete. Eight of 11 presidents of the merged Whist–Filarmonica between 1948 and 1977 were old-line nobles.[66]

*   *   *

The Princes of Liechtenstein and Monaco have entire small states under their direct rule. They appoint ministers, set the domestic agenda, and conduct foreign policy. None of their peers any longer enjoy that level of authority. Decolonization eliminated most of the governorships available to titled gentlemen in the interwar years. However, those willing to assay other routes still found the means to power.

The most natural place for continued participation of the old elite in statecraft has lain, unsurprisingly, in diplomacy. Almost all the leading democracies of Western Europe have fielded aristocrats in their embassies on numerous occasions since 1945. Famous names still pop up, such as Austria's Duke of Hohenberg (Archduke Franz Ferdinand's grandson), Count Folke Bernadotte for Sweden, and Count Bismarck for Germany. One-sixth of the German diplomatic corps in 1959 were nobles.[67] Although ambassadors currently exercise much less influence than they did 50 or 100 years ago, senior figures such the Earl of Cromer and Lord Harlech, who were the personal representatives of Prime Ministers Heath and Macmillan in the United States at the height of the "special relationship," were forces to be reckoned with in Washington.

Lord Cromer also served as Governor of the Bank of England. The 11th Earl of Drogheda became Managing Director of the *Financial Times*, and Charles Douglas-Home (nephew of the 14th Earl of Home) served as editor of *The Times* in the 1980s. Marion, Countess Dönhoff became a close associate of Chancellor Helmut Schmidt. She was also a strong advocate in her journalism of Willy Brandt's *Ostpolitik* of rapprochement with Germany's neighbors to the East.[68] Some aristocrats still reach senior ranks in the military. One of the sons of the Marquis de Monteforte was an admiral in the Italian navy after the war and his son is presently a Rear Admiral. Chancellor Adenauer appointed Count von Schwerin the first Security Advisor of the Federal Republic of Germany in 1950, and General Count von Kielmansegg was leader of NATO land forces in the 1960s.[69] General the Marquis de Pouilly, in command in western Algeria, stayed loyal to the French Republic, which contributed to the failure of the army putsch against the government in April 1961. However, by and large the officer class in Europe has relatively few members of the old elite still in it. The guards regiments in Britain and cavalry regiments in

France remain fashionable.[70] Increasingly, aristocratic young men have looked to improve their prospects by attending universities not military academies.

The Count de Cossé Brissac was appointed Director General of the European Community for Coke and Steel in the 1960s (as well as being the first man to climb Anapurna). The 8th Duke de Broglie served as President of the French Supreme Court of Justice from 1959 to 1961, while Prince Gabriele de Broglie was in Cabinets headed by Schumann and Couve de Murville. Princes and dukes served on the fringes of de Gaulle's administration.[71] Baron Olivier Guichard, the "eminence grise" of Gaullism, became chief of the General's personal staff in 1947, a post in which he later also served Pompidou. He held many senior Cabinet offices and died in 2004.[72] Members of the *noblesse*, such as Couve de Murville and the current Prime Minister, Dominique de Villepin, continue to emerge in French politics.

One of the most important Italian politicians of the late 1940s was Count Carlo Sforza, Foreign Minister during the critical years immediately after the end of the war. The conduct of Victor Emmanuel III had so disgusted him that he became head of the Republican Party. Francisco Franco excluded the nobility from the Falange Party in Spain. Only the Marquis Huétor de Santillán was among the entourage of the Caudillo. One-eighth of the West German Cabinet was noble in 1956.[73] A leading anti-Nazi, Count Richard von Matuschka-Greifenclau, survived the war and worked to help form the Christian Democratic Party in the aftermath of defeat.[74] A neo-Nazi group (Socialist Reich Party) was founded by Count Westarp, nephew of the veteran Conservative politician. Baron von Weizsäcker served as President of the Federal Republic between 1984 and 1994. Numerous aristocrats have been elected to the Bundestag, including Prince Bismarck. In 1996 there were three counts and three barons among the deputies. Count Otto Lambsdorff served in Helmut Schmidt's Cabinet during the coalition with the SPD and was Chairman of the Free Democratic Party from 1988 to 1993.

The British House of Lords survived, its existence prolonged by the institution of life peerages in 1964. Significant debates, such as the one on sanctions for Rhodesia in the 1960s, continued to take place there. About one in five of Conservative Cabinet ministers were members of the landed elite between 1955 and 1984.[75] Though thin on the ground, some peers from older families served in Labour governments.[76] Viscount Dilhorne, descended from an old landed family, served as Lord Chancellor from 1962 to 1964, while his daughter has been director of the Security Service since 2002 – an entirely appropriate occupation for a woman whose mother, the daughter of the 27th Earl of Crawford, was in charge of communications with secret agents in Europe during World War II through carrier pigeons with coded message strapped to their legs.[77]

David Cannadine overreaches to prove his thesis by calling the Tory governments between 1951 and 1964 "more patrician in façade than in substance."[78] This is an unhelpful way of describing administrations headed by Churchill, Eden, Macmillan, and the 14th Earl of Home. Cannadine's identification of Macmillan as "quintessentially middle class" is an error. Not only was "Super Mac" fully integrated into the old elite socially, but also his memoirs and conduct as Prime Minister revealed a cast of mind that was politically very much in tune with the aristocratic tradition.[79] Cannadine calls Home's appointment "a fluke."[80] In fact Macmillan and old-guard Tories such as the Marquis of Salisbury engineered it, in the traditional manner, from the inside. There are far too many exceptions to the rule to call the presence of these men accidental. Only when the Conservative Party adopted an electoral system for its leadership did recruitment at the top change. However, recent political figures continued to be drawn from the aristocracy, including William Waldegrave, Lord Carrington, Viscount Cranborne, and Michael Ancram. Their numbers were simply not sufficient, however, to allow them any longer to act in the way Lord Salisbury and his family party in parliament had in 1940.

It is worth reflecting for a moment, however, on the record of the Scottish peerage in government. Grandees and their brothers have continued to hold senior political positions for the last 60 years out of all proportion to the number of titled Scots available for service. The giant size of many remaining Scottish estates also suggests that the Caledonian aristocracy has remained robust in ways found nowhere else in Europe.[81]

Religious leadership continues to be provided by aristocrats. The Dukes of Norfolk are generally considered the secular leaders of the Roman Catholic Church in England and are consulted by popes about appointments. The French Rothschilds have stood at the head of the Jewish community in that country for most of the twentieth century. Perhaps the most remarkable appointment made by Pope

Pius XII was that of Prince Adam Sapieha, a member of one of the most historic families in Poland, as Archbishop of Cracow. He was made a cardinal in 1946 in direct defiance of the regime being imposed by the Soviet Union. He carried out clandestine religious activities during the German occupation, and allowed the production of false baptismal certificates to help save Jews from arrest. It was he who recruited and ordained as a priest Karol Wojtyla, his eventual successor at Cracow, better known as Pope John Paul II. Wojtyla remained deeply devoted to the Prince's memory. The role John Paul played in helping to undermine the Soviet empire in Eastern Europe during the 1980s would have gladdened Sapieha both as a churchman and a prince.[82] In recent years the best-known aristocrat among the College of Cardinals has been Count Christof Schönborn, Archbishop of Vienna, who received fast-track promotion from John Paul II. He is, perhaps, the most prominent titled nobleman now holding a major public office in Europe and was on the short-list to succeed as pope in 2005. He is the author of the new Catholic Catechism and recently launched a dramatic assault on current teaching about Darwinian evolution that has implications for the relationship between religion and science around the world. He is still young enough to be elected as the successor to Benedict XVI.

Many writers of the later twentieth century were noblemen or continued to place aristocrats at the center of their creative worlds. In the aftermath of World War II several important novels were published that looked back at aristocratic experiences in the early and mid-twentieth century. Evelyn Waugh's *Brideshead Revisited* (1945) and *Sword of Honour* (1965), Prince Lampedusa's *The Leopard* (1958), and Anthony Powell's *Dance to the Music of Time* (1951–75) were among the most important. Count Peter Esterházy's *Celestial Harmonies* (2003) and Edward St. Aubyn's *Some Hope* (1992–8) have achieved recent critical attention. The work of Nabokov, Rezzori, and Dinesen is also notable.

Nancy Mitford, the daughter of Lord Redesdale, became well known for publishing a humorous book in 1956 entitled *Noblesse Oblige: An Enquiry into the Identifiable Characteristics of the English Aristocracy*, which caused a huge stir. Mitford was also a gifted comic novelist. P. G. Wodehouse, one of the great masters of English prose in the twentieth century, was a cadet of the Earls of Kimberley and devoted his talents to the creation of comedies of enormous ingenuity and charm centered on the lives of English aristocrats and their servants. British writers found it hard to escape the theme of the landed elite in their work. A recent critic claims that the world of the aristocracy "suffused [Virginia Woolf's] imagination."[83]

Aristocracy remained an important theme in postwar film. Visconti's *The Leopard* (1963) improbably starred Burt Lancaster, who played the role of the Prince of Salina with extraordinary dignity. Count Luchino Visconti was the son of the Duke of Modrone. Though a professed communist, his images of the old Sicilian aristocracy were loving in their attention to Lampedusa's descriptions. Perhaps the most remarkable British film was Medak and Barnes's *The Ruling Class* (1972), starring Peter O'Toole as a wildly eccentric but genuinely terrifying mad earl. One of the greatest postwar comedy films, made by the celebrated Ealing Studio, was *Kind Hearts and Coronets* (1949), about a man who murders his way through multiple heirs to a dukedom. Wildly popular, if less esoteric, was the story of Baron von Trapp and his family in *The Sound of Music* (1965). Television sagas such as the series based on Trollope's Duke and Duchess of Omnium (1974) and Waugh's *Brideshead Revisited* (1981) became smash hits. In France Jean d'Ormesson's 1974 novel about a fictional noble family whose château was demolished to make way for an airport was made into a television serial that became a hugely popular success.[84] Even the Soviet regime produced a spectacular version of Tolstoy's *War and Peace* (1967), said to have been the most expensive film ever made.

Aristocrats also fulfilled other traditional cultural roles. Charles Viscount de Noailles was a celebrated patron of the arts and arbiter of taste and manners in Paris, as was his friend Prince Jean-Louis de Faucigny-Lucinge. The 11th Duke of Devonshire was a friend of Lucian Freud and systematically added the cream of twentieth-century British art to the collection at Chatsworth. Often modern aristocrats became experts on their own possessions, studied art history at university, and worked for auction houses or as curators. The Metropolitan Museum of Art in New York has been headed for decades by the enormously successful Count Philippe de Montebello. A son of Lord Moyne, Desmond Guinness, and the Knight of Glin not only saved several of the most important works of architecture in Ireland through their leadership of the Irish Georgian Society, but also helped slow down the wanton destruction of provincial towns and the rape of Dublin by unregulated development. The

Marchese di Origio and Vita Sackville-West created what are considered among the great gardens of the twentieth century.

Aristocrats continued to pursue important scholarly interests. The 3rd Earl Russell (Bertrand Russell of the ducal house of Bedford) was a distinguished mathematician and philosopher. The 7th Duke de Broglie, who had won a Nobel Prize in Physics for his work on the wave theory of matter, continued to lecture at the Sorbonne. In 1973 he established a foundation to promote the study of microphysics in France. The 12th Duke de la Force was elected a member of the French Academy. Lord David Cecil became a well-known literary critic, historian, and Professor at Oxford. Countess Anna de Noailles was a French poet, Lord Berners a composer, and Sir Thomas Beecham, a conductor. Princess Diane von Fürstenberg became a leading figure in fashion design. The list is almost endless and touches on virtually every aspect of modern culture.

* * *

Britain rewarded its generals and admirals after the war with peerages, and General Franco, who created four dukedoms, restored coats of arms and titles in Spain. The conferral of hereditary peerages ceased, however, in Britain in the 1960s. In 1968 the extinction of the Papal nobility was announced. Thus aristocracies have lost the power to restore and reinvigorate themselves. Monarchies, however, continue to recognize and sustain existing members of the elite. Titles are still legally held and used under the protection of constitutional laws, offices of heraldry, or government registries in Sweden, Denmark, the Netherlands, Belgium, Luxemburg, Spain, and the United Kingdom. Nobles retain public status in law in Finland, and the Gaelic chiefs in Ireland enroll in a special government registry. Most republics ceased to recognize titles and arms, but in Germany their use was not banned, France accepts and registers them, Italy throws up its hands.

The rate of endogamous marriage is still very high among mediatized families listed in 1998 edition of the *Almanach de Gotha*. Only 16 percent of heads of houses were married to someone who was not noble by birth and over 60 percent were married to countesses or princesses. Although a few of these marriages were contracted before World War II, most are post-1945 unions. For example, the present Prince von Quadt zu Wykradt und Isny married a princess of Bavaria in 1955. The three of their children who have married, in 1985, 1991, and 1992, all did so with counts, one of whom was a Stauffenberg. Of the eight children, grandchildren, and great-grandchildren of Count Ludwig von Waldburg und Waldsee, six espoused nobles, most recently Countess Elizabeth who married Prince von Löwenstein in 1987 and Count Hubertus who married Princess von Khevenhüller in 1993. Similar traditions can still be found in Italian, French, and Spanish families. In the 1960s 16 of 26 English dukes at one time married noble wives.[85] The children of French aristocrats went around together in Paris in curious social groups known as *rallyes*, or gathered in huge house parties for holidays, dances, and weddings in the summer. According to opinion polls, most French nobles say they would be most comfortable marrying another noble.[86]

Despite the Duke of Devonshire's somewhat disingenuous observation about his order noted in the epigraph, his case offers an interesting example of the intermarriage of great aristocratic families with the twentieth-century power elite. His mother was a Cecil, granddaughter of the prime ministerial 3rd Marquis of Salisbury. His brother married "Kick" Kennedy, who is buried at Chatsworth, sister of President John F. and Senators Robert and Edward Kennedy. The Devonshires maintained good relations with the family and visited the White House a number of times during "Camelot." The Duke's wife, "Debo" Mitford, is yet another daughter of Lord Redesdale and the sister of Unity, an intimate friend of Adolf Hitler. Another of her sisters married Sir Oswald Mosley. The Duke's aunt married Prime Minister Harold Macmillan. An uncle married Adele Astaire, so the dancer Fred was also a relative. Who else in the twentieth century could have been connected in this way with Hollywood, Hitler, the White House, and 10 Downing Street?

* * *

Signs that the communist regimes in the East were softening cropped up here and there. When Count George Ignatieff returned to the USSR as a Canadian diplomat in 1955, the Soviet officials, led by Nikita Khrushchev, called him "Graf" (Count) and took him aside and asked, apparently in all sincerity, why he did not come "home" and continue the diplomatic work of his grandfather.[87] In 1989 the Hungarian government allowed the publication of a book that was something of a rehabilitation of the nobility.[88]

After the Berlin Wall collapsed and the Soviet empire evaporated, Eastern bloc countries responded differently to the return of old aristocratic families. No restitutions for former owners took place in Hungary, although the government is offering some compensation.[89] East Elbians attempting to regain expropriated land after German reunification have met with little success, but a restitution law was passed in Czechoslovakia in 1990. In the first three years 785,000 acres of farm and forest was claimed. In Slovakia a special law was enacted recently to extend the period when claims can be made until the end of 2004.[90] Not only property but also art and family archives have been returned. Prince Martin Lobkowicz regained nine castles in the 1990s along with paintings by Rubens, Cranach, Veronese, Brueghel, and Canaletto and a 65,000-volume library containing autograph scores by Mozart and Beethoven. Many of the estates of Prince Karl Schwarzenberg were returned to him.[91] He was active in helping Czech dissenters against the communist regime and served between 1985 and 1990 as Chairman of the Helsinki Human Rights Federation. After the "Velvet" Revolution he became *chef du Cabinet* to President Vaclev Havel.

In 2001 a bill for restitution to former owners passed through the Polish parliament but former communist President Alexander Kwaniewski vetoed it, even though restitution of possessions confiscated by the Nazis or communists was a condition for the country's 1997 entry into the European Union. Legal challenges are being pursued in Brussels.[92] More than anywhere else, aristocrats have re-entered public life in Poland. A number of princes and counts now work in parliament and the diplomatic corps. In East Germany Prince Georg zur Lippe-Weissenfeld returned in 1990 to revive an old family vineyard, while Count Heinrich von Bassewitz built an ecological farm on dynastic property. In 1994 Baron Helmuth von Maltzahn, after a tussle with the Church of Scientology who wanted it as a retreat, repurchased a family castle that had been used by East German tanks for target practice. The family now employs 30 people in the castle's restaurant and hotel business.[93]

Some of the Romanian aristocracy regained property, but at least one count raised in the West believes "their spirit has been broken." Count Tibor Kalnoky argues that only those who escaped and then returned have the will to restore old country houses and build businesses. It took eight years of legal wrangling for him to get his family castle back. He has opened a guesthouse and plans to settle in a wing of the old building.[94]

A Nobles Assembly in Moscow was organized in 1990, headquartered in an eighteenth-century mansion that had formerly been a museum dedicated to Marx and Engels. Prince Andrei Galitzine spearheaded the organization. In 2003 it had attracted 6000 members.[95] Russia has not passed a restitution law, but a few nobles have seized abandoned houses that once belonged to their families and have begun to restore them.[96]

* * *

The final moment of the European aristocracy can best be dated to the day in 1954 when Queen Elizabeth II offered the departing Prime Minister Churchill a dukedom, which he declined. The monarch acted without the advice of a democratically elected official and with the full expectation (thanks to consultations with another aristocrat, John Colville, the Prime Minister's private secretary) that Sir Winston would refuse. She had concluded that such a reward was no longer appropriate but wanted to please the old man with a private gesture of thanks. He declined because he understood that without a parliamentary grant to support the dignity of the kind made to Marlborough and Wellington, a dukedom would be a hollow coronet, even undignified, a burden for his descendants. He also knew that the political careers he hoped his progeny might choose could only be sustained in the House of Commons.[97]

Evelyn Waugh believed that World War II destroyed the traditional conception of honor. When heroes were needed for propaganda purposes, his character Ian Kilbannock, a Scottish peer who had become a cog in the "information" bureaucracy, wanted plebeian soldiers to hold up as examples to encourage morale. The aristocratic commandos, fine flower of the nation, were "the Wrong Period. Last-war stuff . . . Went out with Rupert Brooke." "This is a People's War, and the People won't have poetry and they won't have flowers. Flowers stink. The upper classes are on the secret list. We want heroes of the People. . . ."[98]

The Sword of Honour in Waugh's eponymous novel echoed King George VI's gift to the Russian people to celebrate the heroism of the proletarian victory at Stalingrad. The author would have relished the story that only later became known of how, after Churchill made the presentation in Moscow, Stalin passed the blade to his inept crony Marshall Voroshilov, who reversed the scabbard, either ignorant of how to hold a sword or assuming that it was a fake. The blade crashed to the floor. The King's gift honoring the sacrifice of millions of human lives was cast away carelessly by a communist courtier.[99]

In so far as aristocracy survived after the war, it was likely to be invisible on the surface. By the 1960s the Earl of Home found his title a liability both constitutionally and electorally. Michael Ancram, a former Chairman of the Conservative Party, candidate for the premiership, and presently Shadow Foreign Secretary, concealed his courtesy title of earl while his father was alive and now the marquisate (of Lothian) after he succeeded in 2004. One baronet whose family has lived in the same castle for seven centuries recently complained that listing "landowner" as one's status on immigration forms when traveling results only in shoes being "removed and sprayed with something horrible to deter land-based bugs and insects."[100] A nobleman standing for the position of French Deputy may call himself an "agricultural developer."[101] On the national stage, in order to exist, remnants of the aristocracy must conceal themselves.

11

VITAL MEMORIES

I am just a small part of a long chain. But the spirit of the whole chain is in me.

Count Tibor Kalnoky, 2004[1]

It's differences of attitude, not estates and feudal rights, which make a noble.

The Prince of Lampedusa, *The Leopard*, p. 230

The Tomasi family arose in Tuscany in the twelfth century. One of them went to England as a papal legate in the dispute between Henry II and Thomas Beckett, while another was Patriarch of Constantinople. From Siena Ludovico Tomasi went south to Naples and the family reached Sicily in the sixteenth century. In about 1580 Mario Tomasi, a military officer in the Spanish service, married a local heiress who brought him the barony of Montechiaro. In 1638 the family became Dukes of Palma and in 1667 Princes of Lampedusa, a barren island halfway to Africa that they never inhabited. Their coat of arms sported a rampant leopard. Later Lampedusas served the Bourbon kings in administrative roles and constructed a massive palazzo in Palermo, which was destroyed by American bombs in 1943. They continued to play a role in public life but struggled financially in the nineteenth century and began to sell land. Prince Giulio died in 1885 without leaving a will. The estate was divided equally among ten adult children. The siblings demonstrated utter disregard for maintaining loyalty to the lineage in the pursuit individual interests. Even childless heirs left their portions, traditionally given back to the head of the house, to strangers not related to the family. Only one subsequent Tomasi, Pietro, Marquess of Torretta, took an active part in public life as Italian ambassador to St. Petersburg and London and Foreign Minister before Mussolini gained power. He was removed from the diplomatic service by the Duce for his anti-fascism but became President of the Senate in 1944.

The last prince was left with only the great palazzo, a large part of which was leased to the local gas board as office space, and a fragment of the landed inheritance that gradually disappeared during his lifetime. He was also the end of the line, for none of the other heirs produced sons. He married a baroness from the Baltic nobility, served as an officer during World War I, traveled widely, and spoke many languages. Lampedusa moved at the highest levels in London society during his uncle's ambassadorship at the Court of St. James's, and after World War II he headed the Sicilian Red Cross during the years of reconstruction. His wife lost her castle near Riga and he the palazzo. The Prince spent his final years writing at tables in cafés in Palermo, pouring all his anguish and intelligence into what became the most celebrated novel written in modern Italian. He died of cancer in 1958, soon after receiving news that several publishers had rejected his manuscript. Only after his death was it finally accepted. Since publication it has sold well over 1,000,000 copies. The leading French critic, Louis Aragon, declared *The Leopard* "one of the great novels of this century, one of the great novels of all time."[2]

*   *   *

Marx was wrong to dismiss the aristocracy, once the French Revolution was over, as the mere dancing masters of Europe. We now recognize that they were far more formidable for far longer than he imagined. Ironically, what gave them strength was the Marxist idea that possession of a distinctive group consciousness matters. Fewer and fewer of them, however, retained in their minds and characters what made them special. In the twentieth century sightings of the authentic article became increasingly rare. At the same time fascination with them seemed to linger. Like unicorns, they incarnated a mystery, a lost world, a different way of looking at life gone beyond redemption yet still with us in fairy tales. Why "Count" Basie and "Duke" Ellington? Why tailcoats at weddings and at concerts? Why is visiting country houses still occupied by titled families more popular than touring those in public ownership? Why did coats of arms survive almost universally as a language of civic or corporate identity? What injected the passion into the recent debate about whether to abolish foxhunting in England? Oddly enough, democracies seem to find it comforting to live with well-known families in politics. Even egalitarian America has repeatedly turned to dynastic rule: Adamses, Roosevelts, Tafts, Kennedys, and Bushes. There is something enduringly attractive about choosing leaders who do not need to make their fortunes out of office holding and who embrace a tradition of public service. Familiar faces and names are also a way to assuage the anxiety that rapid change can engender. In Britain "life" peerages continue to confer unique social prestige, while egalitarian Australians tack the initials of "honors" after the end of their names with as much pride as English dukes used to enjoy on having the letters of orders of knighthood strung after theirs.

Alexis de Tocqueville was right in 1856 when he observed: "all the men of our day are driven, sometimes slowly, sometimes violently, by an unknown force – which may possibly be regulated or moderated, but cannot be overcome – toward the destruction of aristocracies."[3] The Enlightenment and the French Revolution undermined aristocratic power. The process accelerated in the 1830s and 1840s and reached full flood in the second half of the century. The size of the agricultural sector in an increasingly industrial world shrank. Estates were sold or confiscated. In the process the elite lost the anchor that tied them to honor and lineage. An Irish earl wrote in the 1930s: "I always think it rather pathetic when I see people who have been turned out of their country houses by taxation stick up their family portraits in small London flats. They are clinging to the past and will not realize that an old family only remains such as long as it continues to own the family home and landed property."[4]

The hero of Lampedusa's novel, the leopard-like Prince of Salina, talking of his dim, horse-mad, and incompetent son, Paolo, the Duke of Querceta, sees the boy as fundamentally unaristocratic.[5] As he lies dying in the 1880s, he reflects:

It was useless to try to avoid the thought, but the last of the Salinas was really himself . . . For the significance of a noble family lies entirely in its traditions, that is in its *vital memories*; and he was the last to have any unusual memories, anything different from those of other families. [His grandson] Fabrizietto would only have banal ones like his schoolfellows, of snacks, of spiteful little jokes against teachers, horses bought with an eye more to price than to quality; and the meaning of his name would change more and more to empty pomp embittered by the gadfly thought that others could outdo him in outward show. . . . The tapestries of Donnafugata, the almond groves of Ragattisi, even, who knows, the fountain of Amphitrite, might suffer the grotesque fate of being transmuted into pots of quickly swallowed *foie gras*, into noisy little women as transient as their rouge, from the age-old things of patina that they'd been.[6]

Internal decay, the loss of a distinctive attitude towards life, noted in the epigraph, was the final enemy. A sad old age often tints yesteryear with a golden glow, but in this case Lampedusa was right.

William Godsey and other historians of European aristocracies argue that we need to focus more on the "residue of noble identity." "Deep into the nineteenth century and beyond, nobles successfully maintained many pivotal elements of a specific and separate self-understanding."[7] The Baroness von Campenhausen observed in 1887: "In the education of one's sons, one has to know above all one's family history – in order to educate them in the feeling of respect and duty which they owe former times . . ."[8] In the early twentieth century, as the world the Baroness had known crumbled around her, crushed between the pincers of the Tsar's Russification program and aggressive nationalism of the Estonian and Latvian peasantry, her fellow members of the Baltic German nobility focused intensively on writing family histories. Honored first names of distinguished ancestors were given more frequently upon the birth of children. The barons collected documents, worked on genealogical registers, and formed historical societies. Family foundations were created whose purpose was to promote dynastic consciousness.[9] All this was part of a convulsive struggle to stay separate and hold on to vital memories. Even in recent times men such as Count Kalnoky still feel deeply connected to their aristocratic past.

Veneration of lineage was vital to the continued existence of aristocracies, but it was a pointless gesture unless accompanied by the concept of contributing additional luster to the family's store of honor. Tocqueville, who dissolved into soppy sentimentality at the thought of his château at Tocqueville, "the ancient abode of my forefathers," not only composed one of the greatest books written in the nineteenth century but also pursued a career as a legislator and Foreign Minister.[10] At the turn of the twentieth century the 5th Duke de Broglie wrote to his grandson, who was thinking of resigning from military service to pursue what appeared to the old man a mere hobby, that the young prince must think first about the traditions of the family "of which you must be worthy."[11] The young Stauffenberg counts were deeply influenced by their noble lineage, with its traditional forms and values anchored in their estates in Swabia and Franconia and their father's service at the royal court of Württemberg. They were highly distinct from most of their contemporaries even in the army, and they were aware of themselves as being unlike other people because of their aristocratic backgrounds. This did not lead to snobbery but to holding themselves to the very highest standards of honor.[12] The aristocrats who led the resistance against Hitler were deeply rooted in the land and held vibrant memories of lineage.[13] Stauffenberg, Yorck, and Moltke had remained convinced they were a race apart from the mass of ordinary people, and that this imposed on them the obligation to make their mark, to shape the course of Germany.[14]

Not all examples of this phenomenon were so efficacious. Vital memories worked against the French aristocracy in the nineteenth century because too much attention was focused on loss and recrimination. This isolated the elite from the ongoing concerns of the rest of society. The memories of the Revolution were so traumatic that they became part of dynastic lore, and thus acted to weaken rather than to strengthen aspirations to rule. The 7th Marquis of Londonderry, who served in the British Cabinet during the 1930s and conducted what amounted to a personal foreign policy with Nazi Germany, was destroyed by his ambition to emulate his great ancestor, Viscount Castlereagh, Metternich's colleague at the Congress of Vienna. In a moment of rare self-perception he wrote to Stanley Baldwin in 1939, "I sometimes feel rather shamefaced vis-à-vis my ancestors. I feel that they are murmuring, 'Well, he might have done better than that.' "[15]

Almost every European country has produced families such as the Salisburys, Dalhousies, Lothians, Broglies, Lambsdorffs, Schönborns, Esterházys, Schwarzenbergs, Hammarskjölds, and Albas who, generation after generation, continued to aspire to national leadership deep into the twentieth century and resist absorption into the mass.

For them, like Count Paul Ignatieff, life had "meaning only within the terms of fidelity to his family's tradition of service."[16] By 1914, however, aristocrats as a group had lost their ascendancy except in the localities surrounding their estates. Even robust vital memories were insufficient to surmount the shift in attitude toward inherited power that arose out of the Enlightenment. Constitutional reforms were halting and often half-baked, but assumptions about justice and merit became so deeply ingrained in the mass of society that they were ineradicable. By prodigious acts of individual will, members of the old elite such as Mannerheim, Stauffenberg, Churchill, and Lampedusa sustained aristocratic values for another half century, but vital memories were not being renewed. Revolutionaries plotted to extirpate landed society, and democratic politicians had a more generous and humane vision of the world to offer than most aristocrats could understand.

Even though the aristocracies of Europe faded from the scene in the twentieth century, they have left an indelible impression on our culture and traditions. John Stevenson wrote that still in 1945 the aristocracy "represented an important component of British society, less through their possession of great wealth than through their powerful hold over its ethos."[17] Periodically during the last decades of the twentieth century unexpected pomp and pageantry has been summoned up by modern republics to honor almost forgotten imperial figures from the past. The Presidents of Austria and Russia presided over the funerals of Empress Zita in 1989 and Tsar Nicholas II in 1998. No such memorials have been arranged for the European aristocracies. We are left only with haunting images like Sokurov's *The Russian Ark* and Visconti's *The Leopard* and such memories as historians are able to evoke.

NOTES

INTRODUCTION

1. Eisenstein chose not to use the actual staircase that featured in the attack on the Palace and falsified history by filming his scene on the Jordan staircase. Figes 460. Sokurov, on the other hand, used the site with respect and honesty.
2. Cannadine (2001) xiii–10.
3. Bramsted 10.
4. Cannadine (1990) 236; Dewald 7–9.
5. Godsey (2002) 512–13, citing a speech by Reif in 1997.
6. A number of historians have posited revivals in aristocratic consciousness, prestige, and power deep into the twentieth century: Rubinstein (1998) 1–18; Hutchinson 131–48; McCrone and Morris 170–85; Baranowski (1996b) 228.
7. For example, DeNora 310–46.
8. Cannadine (1990) 4, 31.
9. Stern 45–46; Godsey (1999b) 56–57; Deme 581; Berend (1998) 24–25.
10. See works listed in the bibliography. Spring's introduction to a collection of essays on nineteenth-century European aristocracies is a brief but seminal work (D. Spring 1977).
11. Mayer 4–5, 133–34.
12. Lieven (1992).
13. Where the only source for material is in German or French, I have cited material in those languages. I have also included some books and articles in other languages when it seemed particularly important to do so.
14. For landowners in Greece and Bulgaria, see Mouzelis. A largely Muslim feudal noble class existed in Bosnia and Herzegovina in the nineteenth century, but it had little historic continuity and did not last for long. Tomasevich 97–104.
15. The Norwegian nobility had declined and virtually disappeared during the sixteenth and seventeenth centuries. The remnant was officially abolished in 1821. A handful of families continued to use their titles informally. A few served in government or the diplomatic

corps. The modest stock of Norwegian country houses, almost all no larger than manors elsewhere, may be viewed in Valebrokk et al.
16. Sinclair 182.

1 DEFINING ARISTOCRACY

1. Cardoza (1988) 596–7; see also Montroni 267–8.
2. Beckett (1986) 20–1; Powis 7–8; Scott, I, 21; Goodrich 15–21.
3. Cardoza (2002) 163. In Hungary the term had a strictly technical meaning of titled nobility. Lukacs (1993) 132.
4. For the difficulties, see: Reddy 13–25; Romanelli (1991) 717–39.
5. Bourne 383.
6. On the development of the legal concept of the nobility, see: Zmora 2–54.
7. More subtle signifiers were also used. Leigh Fermor (2004a) 213.
8. G. Best 34.
9. Mack Smith (1968) 470; Roszkowski (1991) 110.
10. Carsten (1989) 84; see also Halévy 121.
11. Higgs (1987) 70; Worsthorne 2–3.
12. Harris and Thane 218.
13. Mosse (1981) 607.
14. Aron (1950) 142; Dore 298–300.
15. Lieven (1992).
16. Frost, II, 199–202.
17. Tocqueville 183.
18. Augustine (2004) 1328.
19. Bush (1983) 17; Bush (1988) 26, 94; Zaniewicki 71–5; Scott, I, 21.
20. Scott, I, 32–5; J. V. H. Melton, II, 117–18; Asch 39–48; Bush (1988) 131; F. M. L. Thompson (1969) 34–5; Fonseca 216.
21. Torov 14–15; Whelan 40; Blum (1978) 26.
22. Thaden (1984b) 33.
23. Berend (2003) 188; Verdery 196.
24. Lukowski 156–7.
25. Beevor and Cooper 11.
26. Gross 139; Bush (1988) 70; Lieven (1992) 182; Becker 171.
27. Yorck von Wartenburg 23.
28. Lieven (1992) xv. I do not agree with Lieven's assertion that the Junkers lacked an aristocratic tier. See contra: E. Melton, II, 91. Eddie equates Prussian Junkers with titled Hungarian nobles: Eddie (1994) 109–31.
29. Stone and Stone 403.
30. Montagu of Beaulieu 82; Bánffy (1999) 121.
31. Castellane 169, 171.
32. Egremont 57.
33. Le Roy Ladurie 58–61.
34. Rezzori (1994) 63.

35. Bourdieu 18–24.
36. In Hesse–Cassel beneath the five mediatized families were the lower nobility who were divided between those who were part of the Ritterschaft (knighthood) and those who were not. In general the families in the corporate body of knights had enjoyed noble status much longer and owned more land than did lower nobles. They formed less than half of the total number of nobles in the state. They were a highly exclusive group, and the German emperors seem later to have accorded them the right to use the title "baron" when traveling abroad. The knights of the corporations (barons), like the mediatized princes and counts, were granted special representation in the Hessian legislature and 11 of the 40 families were raised to the rank of baron officially. In Hesse–Darmstadt the hereditary knights bore the title "baron." Many more Baltic families were titled, but hereditary membership in the nobiliar corporations was the key distinction. Pedlow (1988) 17–26.
37. Goodwin 100; Lieven (1992) 63. A similar process took place in Denmark: Jensen 41.
38. Cardoza (2002) 40.
39. Confino 47–58.
40. This began in the seventeenth and eighteenth centuries. Scott, I, 10.
41. A split between the *noblesse d'épée* and *noblesse de robe* existed in France and other countries such as Piedmont: proud old feudal aristocrats and those whose titles originally derived out of tenure of office rather than patent or prescription and were usually of more recent origins. In Italy some nobilities arose from merchant elites such as those that dominated Milan, Venice, Genoa, and Florence. Sword and robe families tended to merge fairly quickly after a couple of generations. Fusion led to a shared sense of loyalty to the dynasty and tradition of service, and they closed ranks against newcomers. Cardoza (2002) 15–18. France was also beset with conflicts between Napoleonic vs. pre-Revolutionary nobles and Orleanists vs. Legitimists.
42. Fugger von Babenhausen 157–9.
43. Ceased publication in 1944 after Gotha fell under Soviet control. Resumed publication in 1998. The *Genealogisches Handbuch des Adels* (1951 onwards) filled the gap.
44. Published until 1970, resumed 1999, and now on-line.
45. Higgs (1987) 20.
46. Farrelly 87–90.
47. Scott I, 32–5; J. V. H. Melton, II, 117–18, 121; Eddie (1967) 297.
48. F. M. L. Thompson (2001) 47; see also Carr (1953) 48; Verdery 378; Cardoza (2002) 8.
49. Becker 38–9; Cardoza (2002) 94–5; for Prussia see: Baranowksi (1996b) 212; only 15 percent of the English peerage had estates of less than 10,000 acres in 1880. Clemenson 27.
50. Macartney (1968) 53; Becker 37–8.

51. Higgs (1987) 54; this was not a new development. D. Sutherland (2003) 34.
52. Schimert, II, 173–5; Jensen 41.
53. Lesniakowska 35.
54. Torov 12–13.
55. Roosevelt 159.
56. Channon 219.
57. Wrangel 113, 115–16.
58. Kenez 137.
59. Montroni 274.
60. Berdahl 26–7; Muncy (1970) 130–4, 144, 151; E. Melton, II, 74. Swedish counts and barons also married commoners less frequently than untitled nobles. Carlson 600.
61. Armstrong 121; Scott, I, 32–5.
62. J. Lewis (1998) 28, 52.
63. LeDonne (1987) 233–93; Blum (1977) 77.
64. Franckenstein 332–3.
65. Farrelly 71.
66. Mosse (1981) 623–4; D. Obolensky xiv; Higgs (1987) 11, 103; Nowak 89–90.

2 THE *ANCIEN RÉGIME*

1. See John W. Coogan, who rightly takes authors and publishers to task for this kind of error. Coogan 367.
2. Lach-Szyrma 96.
3. Here and there exceptions to these rules can be found among royalty, issue of morganatic marriages, or a few other odd cases, which I ignore for the sake of clarity.
4. Higgs (1987) 17.
5. Blum (1977) 68–9.
6. The work of J. H. Pinches is a good place to start in mastering the intricacies of titles.
7. Benckendorff 11.
8. The term derives from the Latin root *media* (between) coming from their position within the layers of allegiance in the Holy Roman Empire. Their annexation began in 1804 in Bavaria and Württemberg. The Treaty of Vienna did not specify which houses were to qualify as equal to the reigning ones, but left that to the individual states to decide. *Almanach de Gotha* (2001) Part III, 773–89.
9. Higgs (1987) 1–2, 28. Even in Sweden, which has good records and where it is relatively easy to count, various historians give differing estimates for the mid-nineteenth century. Verney 14–15; Anderson and Anderson 24; Kopczynski 112–13; Carlson 576–7.
10. This number seems to have stayed fairly steady between 1789 and 1990. Forster (1976) 185–6; Mayer 106; Bartillat 554. Michael Thomp-

son estimates a similar number for London "Society" in the mid-nineteenth century. F. M. L. Thompson (1995) 67–78.

11. Higgs (1981) 30; Tudesq (1973) 202.
12. Becker 18.
13. Hoensch 36–7.
14. F. M. L. Thompson (1977) 31–2; Beckett (1986) 36–9; Wasson (2000) 41.
15. Bush (1988) 7–29; Dewald 22–5; Havránek 219; Alapuro (1988) 38; Kabuzan 153–69; Lukowski 12–13; Berend (2003) 187.
16. Pinches 246; Herr 99.
17. One expert counted 474 "court" families in the whole of the Austro-Hungarian Empire in the late nineteenth and early twentieth centuries. Godsey (1999b) 62.
18. Nicholas Henshall estimates 550 politically prominent families in old regime France, Henshall 21–2; 492 families had been "presented" at court between 1715 and 1790, Lukowski 38; Forster estimated several hundred families in the court nobility before 1789, Forster (1971) 210.
19. These estimates are based on a wide array of sources. For data on titles see Pinches. Also helpful were Petersen 251; Ilincioiu 11; Pedlow (1988) 17; Gross 137–9; Whelan 7; Jespersen, II, 60–1; Verney 14–15; Herr 99; Beckett (1986) 486–8; Wasson (2000) 57, 175; Higgs (1987) 11, 28; James 89.
20. Cardoza (2002) 72.
21. D'Azeglio 199–200.
22. Loewenstein 259–62.
23. Cannadine (1990) 5; Wasson (2000) 145–8.
24. J. M. Roberts 62.
25. Georgescu 40.
26. Toumanoff passim.
27. Rosenberg 61–2, 144.
28. Asch 88; Zmora 76–8, Dewald 122–32; Adamson 9.
29. Adamson 7–11, 39, 72–3, 290; Asch 2–3, 7, 93, 125; Dewald 59, 151–7, 183; Zmora 2, 72–82, 89; Henshall 51; Schissler (1986) 28; Meyer passim; Labatut passim.
30. Bush (1988) 31; Asch 11–12; Jespersen, II, 56–62.
31. Some stayed loyal, however: Lobkowicz, Schwarzenberg, Harrach, Kinsky, Liechtenstein. The traitors were eventually pardoned. Odlozilik 26–7.
32. Zmora 4, 6–7, 35, 57–61, 65, 87, 89–90, 108; Asch 4, 133, 142–3; Dewald 140–8; E. Melton, II, 98.
33. Blum (1978) 440–1.
34. Pedlow (1988) 122; Blum (1978) 227.
35. Bairasauskaite 48–73; Blum (1948) 200, 209–46; Devine (2001) 185–6.
36. Levinger 267; Schissler (1986) 33–4; Wank (1992b) 135–6; I. A. A. Thompson, I, 223–4; Higgs (1987) 52–4.

37. Christiannsen 474–5; Berend (2003) 109, 163; Becker 200; Lieven (1992) 81–2.
38. Brakensiek 137–79.
39. Kriegel (1980a) 347.
40. D. M. G. Sutherland (2003) 29.
41. Mansel 35–6.
42. Chaussinand-Nogaret 85–7. Many embraced the notion of a moral service obligation of the aristocracy to the state. Kann 5.
43. Dewald 184–6; Blum (1978) 220, 248–57, 266–88, 312, 316, 324–5.
44. Tillyard 321–2.
45. Jespersen, II, 68.
46. D. M. G. Sutherland (2003) 28, 68–72.
47. Swann, I, 172–3; Lukowski 185–6.
48. A network of complicities defended noble patrimonies. Wives stayed at home to preserve estates when husbands fled abroad. Unremitting legal chicanery was practiced. Gibson (1981) 11ff.; P. M. Jones 71; Higgs (1987) 52–4.
49. Forster (1976) 185–9, 192, 203.
50. McCahill and Wasson 1–38.
51. Harling 87.
52. Cardoza (2002) 26, 30–1; Capra 12–42.
53. Higgs (1987) 51–3.
54. Forster (1967) 72; Serna 31–2, 73, 77.
55. Kahan 26.
56. Zmora 103.

3 WEALTH

1. *New York Times*, June 28, 2004; *The Economist*, December 18, 2004.
2. Horstmann 60–1. The reader is referred to the exhaustive analysis of aristocratic wealth in Britain, Germany, and Russia in Lieven (1992) 21–133.
3. Tolstoy 657; Roszkowski (1991) 15.
4. Kale (1992) 6; F. M. L. Thompson (1969) 5; R. Gibson (1981) 30–1; Zamagni 133, 136; Baranowski (1996b) 217.
5. Snowden (1986) 11–14.
6. Carsten (1989) 127.
7. Lukowski 91; Carr (1953) 48; Villani 66–81.
8. Blum (1978) 25; Eidelberg 32; Stekl 163; Cannadine (1990) 9–10; Mayer 27; Lieven (1992) 49–50.
9. Cardoza (2002) 107–8.
10. Berend (1998) 25; Stekl 163; Gross 163, 173–4.
11. Lieven (1992) 35, 49; Bateman; Becker 38; Gross 163, 173–4; Pratt 49; Roszkowski (1983) 281–99; Sinclair 145; Malefakis 71–2; Carsten (1989) 127; Godsey (1999a) 62, 64–5; Macartney (1968) 623; Cardoza

(2002) 107–8; Eddie (1994) 124; Eidelberg 200; Lévêque 56, 60–1; Pedlow (1988) 95–6; Dallas 223.

12. Devine (2001) 449–50; Mack Smith (1968) 470; Zamagni 160; Rees 236; Hoppen 168; Berend (2003) 163; Callander 60.

13. Blum (1978) 437; D. Spring (1977) 3, 6; Dipper 194; Pedlow (1988) 9, 95; Berend (2003) 159, 184; Ames 2–3; Roszkowski (1991) 52–3; Eidelberg 32; Eddie (1989) 232–5, 247; Lieven (1992) 14; B. Dooley 326.

14. Malefakis 71–2; Dipper 194; E. Melton, II, 104; Muncy (1970) 79; Carsten (1989) 127–8.

15. Whelan 14, 292. The average size of an estate in southern Latvia was 6701 acres. Pistohlkors 173.

16. Cardoza (2002) 25, 106–8. Only four titled families in nineteenth-century Piedmont held more than 5000 acres and none above 11,000.

17. Lévêque 56, 60–1; Zeldin (1977) 129.

18. Lieven (1992) 89; R. Gibson (1981) 16–24; Carlson 598; Cardoza (1982) 29; Jensen 96–7; O'Brien and Keyder 130, 134; Ciuffetti 5–24; Berend (2003) 186.

19. Dewald xv; Janos 344; I. A. A. Thompson, I, 223, 229–30.

20. D. Spring (1980) 129.

21. Romanelli (1991) 726; J. V. H. Melton, II, 128–9; Dewald 68–70; Swann, I, 151–2; I. A. A. Thompson 223, 229–30; Wank (1992b) 135ff.; Dodgshon; Macinnes 1–42; Beckett (1986) 157–8, 159–205; Schissler (1991) 101; Schissler (1978); Hagen; Finlay 291–2; Stern 51–2; Blum (1977) 85.

22. Kállay 349–51.

23. D. Spring (1963); Beckett (1986) 156; F. M. L. Thompson (1969) 177; Beckett (1994).

24. Blum (1948) 129–44; Canciullo 629–54; Wasson (1978) 89–99; Blum (1978) 289–92; Jardin and Tudesq 220, 226–7, 236, 257, 330; Berend (2003) 90–1.

25. Blum (1978) 283.

26. Blum (1977) 84–5; Becker 7–14, 41–2; Lieven (1992) 78–80.

27. J. A. Davis (1994) 295–6; Cardoza (1982) 39; Cardoza (2002) 108–9; Romanelli (1991) 736.

28. Hoppen 164–77.

29. Lalliard 67–92; Kale (1992) 210–32; Dallas 74, 81; Higgs (1987) 65, 68, 110; Cardoza (1991) 183; Whelan 84, 88, 100, 294; Berend (2003) 159–62; Blum (1948) 101, 155, 159.

30. Blum (1948) 103–6; Finlay 291–2.

31. Blum (1948) 111–12; J. M. Roberts 68; Cardoza (2002) 108–9.

32. Lieven (1992) 103; Blum (1977) 86; Clemenson 76; Pedlow (1988) 133–5; Blum (1978) 295–7.

33. Verdery 91; Sykes 313, 342; Benckendorff 100–11; Whelan 295; Blum (1948) 166.

34. Whelan 101; Mack Smith (1965) 87.

35. Carmona Pidal 63–88.

36. Beckett (1986) 180–3.

37. Blum (1978) 301; Bush (1988) 138–52; Bush (1984) 173, 187–8, 196; Higgs (1987) 123; Cardoza (2002) 169; D. Spring (1960) 61. Sometimes the English elite is mentioned as the exception to the general rule, (M. B. Brown 25) but the usual story is that they, too, were averse to direct involvement with industry, and newcomers who made their money in commerce hurried to withdraw from active involvement. Wiener, *passim*; Beckett (1986) 134–5; Bush (1992) 38.

38. Tolstoy 170–2, 722.

39. Stone and Stone 285–6; Higgs (1987) 105–6, 111; Swann, I, 156–8; I. A. A. Thompson, I, 229–30; B. Dooley 326–30; Cummings 43–61; Devine (2001) 114–15; Christiannsen 266; Dowden 23–37; Klima 67–8, 85, 91–2; Berend (2003) 144–5; Blum (1978) 297–301; J. V. H. Melton, II, 136; Madriaga, II, 258; Beloff 176, 178, 184; Roosevelt 235–6; Lukowski 85; J. M. Roberts 142–3; Beckett (1986) 238–42; F. M. L. Thompson (2001) 21; Serna, 45; Chaussinand-Nogaret (1985) 84–116; Dewald 96–7.

40. Lieven (1992) 127, 130–1; Jacob 273–330; Berghoff (2000) 233–71; Malinowski 143; Pedlow (1988) 91–2.

41. Blum (1978) 423; Klima 150–1; 184; Verdery 147, 172–3; Blum (1977) 87; Locke (1974) 101, 112–14; Lalliard 67–92; Kale (1992) 26, Higgs (1987) 111, 113–19, 126; R. Gibson (1981) 30–1; Romanelli (1995) 15–16; Cannadine (1982) *passim*; Ward and Wilson *passim*.

42. Carsten (1989) 123–4; D. Spring (1977) 13; Baranowski (1995) 25; Higgs (1987) 110.

43. Snowden (1989) 126; Lieven (1992) 48; Higgs (1987) 110, 118–19; Jardin and Tudesq 333.

44. D. Spring (1977) 13. In some countries nobles did not exploit their mineral resources because the crown retained the rights either to some or all the products of the subsoil or to a share of the profits. Bush (1988) 147–9. In Spain when the revolution of 1868 led to a law for the auction of mineral rights, foreign investors obtained the richest mines. In this area Spaniards who had capital had little experience or economic commitment. Herr 110.

45. E. J. Evans 153.

46. Sturgess 6; Raybould (1984) 65; Raybould (1968) 529–44; Beckett (1986) 208–21.

47. Verney 16, 32, 79.

48. Higgs (1987) 110, 119–20; Berend (2003) 152; F. M. L. Thompson (1969) 263; Beckett (1986) 243–55, 260; Adonis (1993) 178; Cannadine (1994) 58–60.

49. C. Sutherland (1996) 21, 32; S. Obolensky 55; Sinclair 144.

50. Cardoza (2002) 204–5; S. Obolensky 35; Becker 43.

51. E. J. Evans 152; J. A. Davis (1988) 272.

52. Mansel 177; McReynolds 174–6; Beckett (1986) 262–86; Fletcher 522, 528.

53. Higgs (1987) 119; Zamagni 128.

54. Vassili 346; Botticelli 501–12; Cannadine (1994) 63–7; F. M. L. Thompson (2001) 37; Cardoza (2002) 165, 170–1.

55. Lieven (1992) 119; Higgs (1987) 114–15; Freudenberger 349; Klima 162–3; Szczepanski 61–71; Berend (2003) 145. Several great English peers owned textile mills, although their activity was relatively minor. Beckett (1986) 225–7.
56. Lieven (1992) 129–32; Higgs (1987) 119.
57. Locke (1977) 268–81; Higgs (1987) 121; Blum (1978) 422–3; Forster (1976) 199; Becker 115; Berend (2003) 186; Stern 58; S. Clark (1984) 151–3; Zamagni 145, 152; Whelan 297; F. M. L. Thompson (1969) 307; Beckett (1986) 120; Harris 105.
58. Becker 115; Stern 58; Wrangel 211; Cardoza (2002) 169–70; Farrelly 87–90, 99–100.
59. Lanier 5–28.
60. Gross 148, 155; Higgs (1987) 120–1.
61. Wank (1992b) 135–6; Whelan 298; Verney 16; Becker 52–3; Cardoza (2002) 169–70.
62. Cardoza (2002) 113–14, 169–70, 206–7; Moroni 255–92.
63. Lieven (1992) 120–7; Higgs (1987) 115–17. The Earls of Crawford, however, remained at the helm as colliers well into the twentieth century. So too did the Earls of Dudley and Ellesmere and the Marquis of Londonderry, even after 1918.
64. Raybould (1968) 529–44.
65. Windischgraetz 8–9, 11; D. Obolensky 11, 13; S. Obolensky 138; Benckendorff 100; Blum (1978) 423; Whelan 297.
66. Count Chotek established an exhibition of industrial products in Prague in 1828. Klima 147. Count Joseph Kinsky in the 1860s served as President of the Bohemian Commercial Council. He founded diverse enterprises and made huge investments in industry and encouraged fellow magnates to do the same. Freudenberger 342, 345–8.
67. Cannadine (1977) 643–5; Beckett (1988) 286; F. M. L. Thompson (2001) 23–44.
68. Beckett (1988) 287; Mee xi–xii.
69. Klima 157; Berend (2003) 185; King 78.
70. Roosevelt 235–6.
71. Cardoza (2002) 171.
72. M. L. Anderson 101; Beckett (1986) 232–4; Lieven (1992) 53–4; Wank (1992b) 136.
73. Pratt 210; Lampedusa 31; Bence-Jones and Massingberd 84.
74. Lukowski 97–9.
75. D. and E. Spring (1996) 377–94; Cannadine (1977) 624–33; Lieven (1992) 52; Cardoza (2002) 94–5, 199–200; Adonis (1988) 883.
76. Devine (2001) 455.
77. Cardoza (2002) 109–10, 197–200; Zanetti 749; Cardoza (1982) 47–9; J. A. Davis (1994) 301; Whelan 297–300; Christiannsen 457–60.
78. Farrelly 25, 116–51.
79. D. Spring (1984) 19, 22, 24–5; Farrelly 92; It is true that the Duke of Devonshire was spending 17 percent of his disposable income on interest payments on debt in 1874 but 60 percent by 1880. However,

this was partly due to investments in relatively unprofitable business ventures as well as to declining agricultural revenue. Cannadine (1990) 94.

80. Becker 41–2; Carsten (1989) 129; Lieven (1992) 98; Berend (2003) 185; Verdery 196–7, 205; Godsey (1999b) 85; Herr 110.
81. Beckett (1986) 87; Cannadine (1990) 112–15; Pagano 189–231.
82. Cardoza (1982) 47–9; Dallas 202.
83. Cannadine (1990) 105–7.
84. Cannadine (1990) 110; D. Spring (1984) 42; Farrelly 145–7.
85. Devine (2001) 449, 455.
86. Godsey (1999b) 87; Mack Smith (1965) 94; Becker 41–2; Pedlow (1988) 88–91, 95; Pratt 98–103.
87. Eddie (1967) 296–7.
88. Mack Smith (1968) 470.
89. Cardoza (2002) 109–10; Blum (1977) 87; Herr 106–7; R. Gibson (1981) 29; Pedlow (1988) 95, 100.
90. Cardoza (1982) 42–3, 81, 127; Corner 1–5.
91. Devine (2001) 118–19, 176–82; Rees 236–42.
92. Higgs (1987) 61, 68–9; Gibson and Blinkhorn 25.
93. Godsey (2002) 508–9; Finlay 283–4, 288, 290.
94. Höbelt (1996) 295.
95. Schissler (1978).
96. Fugger von Babenhausen 238.

4 FAMILY AND HONOR

1. Dönhoff 88–9, 109–28, 130.
2. Bánffy (1999) 455.
3. Cardoza (2002) 129.
4. Esterházy 458.
5. Whelan 154.
6. For cousinhoods, see Cohen 110–14.
7. Whelan 149.
8. Kiernan 258.
9. Fugger von Babenhausen 142, 157–69.
10. E. Spring (1993) 176–9.
11. Scott, II, 289; Tovrov 336; Whelan 143–5; Higgs (1987) 191.
12. Pedlow (1988) 41–3, 46–7.
13. Whelan 137.
14. Baranowski (1996b) 212. Berdahl (data page 27) suggests that it was declining even in the nineteenth century. Higgs (1987) 193–4, 268 fn 58; Cardoza (2002) 177–81.
15. D. Thomas 102, 109; Hollingsworth 8–10; Lieven (1992) 37–8; Lukowski 161–2.
16. The rise was even more dramatic among untitled nobles. Carlson 600.
17. Reynolds 11–12; Tillyard 91.

18. Staves 203.
19. Youssoupoff 29.
20. Verdery 164–5; Berdahl 23–4.
21. Higgs (1987) 176, 196; Cardoza (2002) 98–9.
22. Tillyard 289–90; Whelan 122–3.
23. C. Sutherland (1996) 27–9.
24. Abrams 41–55.
25. C. Sutherland (1985); Nye 405.
26. Whelan 134.
27. Reynolds 32–3, 42–70. They could run up against determined opposition of male trustees, but even then ways could be found around this sort of obstruction. Mitson 547–63.
28. Torov 263; Turgenev 123.
29. Lukowski 172–3.
30. Dönhoff 42.
31. Clermont-Tonnerre 26.
32. J. S. Lewis (1998) 52; Zanetti 752, 756; Stone and Stone 282; Whelan 11, 168, 251–2; Muncy (1970) 98–9; Cardoza (2002) 209–10.
33. Tillyard 79, 213–23.
34. Torov 348; Whelan 164–5.
35. Higgs (1987) 179, 222; Cardoza (2002) 135–7; Dönhoff 51.
36. Dönhoff 52–3, 57–65; Starhemberg 3; Airlie 28, Rezzori (1991) 159.
37. W. Churchill 2–14, 72–3; Rezzori (1991) 3–54; Figes 121–30.
38. Beckett (1986) 23–4; Stone and Stone 229–39.
39. Whelan 155.
40. Loewenstein 189.
41. Higgs (1987) 125.
42. Frost, II, 197; Schimert, II, 173. There were countries where lesser nobles managed to survive without practicing strict primogeniture such as Hesse-Cassel and the Baltic provinces. Pedlow (1988) 55–8.
43. Bush (1988) 28; Cardoza (2002) 211.
44. A plethora of devices were used. Some tied estates directly to titles while others were linked simply to families in one way or another. They went under names such as: *mayorazgo* in Spain; *majorat* in France; *majorate* in the Baltic German states; *maioraty* in Russia; *fideikommiss* in Germany and Austria; *maiorascato* and *fedecommisso* in Italy; in Poland-Lithuania *ordynacje*; strict settlement in England and Wales.
45. Desan 597–634; Swann, I, 160; Blum (1978) 429; Romanelli (1995) 16; Whelan 136–9.
46. Whelan 130–1; Berdahl 23–5; Pedlow (1988) 46–7, 62–3.
47. Dönhoff 130–1.
48. Reif (1979) 224; Whelan 289; Carsten (1989) 43; Blum (1978) 428–9; Berend (2003) 186; Habbakuk (1994) 6, 14; Cooper 285, 297–8. Unlike in Prussia entails did not increase much in Austria in the decades before 1914 because the law was changed to require parliamentary sanction for new creations that the assembly grew reluctant to grant.

49. Higgs (1987) 15; D. Spring (1977) 9; Becker 70–1.
50. E. Spring (1993); Beckett (1986) 58–65; Stone and Stone 73–86; Habakkuk (1994) 1–76.
51. Berend (2003) 185; Becker 70–1; Blum (1978) 428–9; Eddie (1967) 298; Jespersen, II, 61; F. M. L. Thompson (1969) 68; Roszkowski (1991) 17.
52. I. A. A. Thompson, I, 226; Herr 106.
53. Cruz (1996b) 100–101; Godsey (1999b) 84; Cardoza (2002) 21.
54. Higgs (1987) 72–8.
55. Grimaldi 435–49; Scott, II, 288; Cardoza (2002) 4; Mack Smith (1965) 93; Higgs (1987) 18, 31, 273; Daumard (1988) 85.
56. Malefakis 68; Scott, II, 287. A practice similar to that in Piedmont after 1814. Cardoza (2002) 118.
57. Cruz (1996b) 5, 268; D. Spring (1977) 8; I. A. A. Thompson, I 193–4, 223–4; Herr 111; Goujard 559–84.
58. Forster (1971) 194; Higgs (1987) 176–7, 215.
59. Petiteau 731–45.
60. Zanetti 749, 752–3; Cardoza (2002) 133, 208–9; E. Spring (1977) 40–59; Harris 105.
61. Scotland ended the establishment of new entails in 1914. Count Helmut James von Moltke apparently had found a way legally to pass on the Kreisau estate to his eldest son in the 1940s. Moltke 333.
62. F. L. Hansen 2–3, 26, 116.
63. Cruz (1996b) 200.
64. Dewald 11.
65. Roth 265.
66. Higgs (1987) 174.
67. Kriegel (1980b) 267.
68. Cardoza (1988) 597.
69. Tolstoy 170–1; Powis 4–5, 30.
70. Lampedusa 289.
71. Girouard (2000) 21–2; Stone and Stone 117–18.
72. Bánffy (1999) 292–3.
73. Andrew 413; Kiernan 12.
74. Kiernan 265; Frevert 128, 136; McAleer 7, 183.
75. Kelly 30; McCord (2000) 91–2, 113–14; McAleer 190–3.
76. Leigh Fermor (2004b) 57.
77. McAleer 75; Kiernan 260–1.
78. Bánffy (1999) 232–42.
79. McAleer 69, 91; Becker 118; Deák (1990) 130–8; Cardoza (2002) 168; Frevert 61–2.
80. S. Obolensky 69–70; Youssoupoff 123–4; Windischgraetz 50.
81. Reck-Malleczewen 64.
82. Deák (1990) 137; Leigh Fermor (2004a) 30. Marshal Pilsudski fought a duel with General Szeptycki in 1923. Potocki 147.
83. Shovlin 35–6; Lieven (1992) 191–2.
84. Cannadine (1990) 276.

85. S. Obolensky 121.
86. Geyer (1990) 185.
87. Storrs and Scott 3, 23.
88. Starhemberg 1–3. Many other aristocratic children, perhaps most famously, Winston Churchill, commanded massive toy armies. R. Churchill, I, 41, 120–1, 132, 165; Loewenstein 82.
89. Higham 47.
90. Baranowski (1995) 58; Carsten (1989) 113.
91. Bush (1988) 129.
92. Deák (1990) 97–8; Kann 10; Godsey (1999a) 73.
93. Burgos 96; Baquer 105–35; Lazo Diaz 53–61.
94. Dönhoff 4.
95. Service in the navy was never as popular among landed families as in the army. The meritocratic reputation of navies had some truth to it, although from the time of the Spanish Armada, senior commanders were often noblemen or from old landed families. This was particularly true in Sweden, Portugal, and England. Some aristocratic families in Britain had strong ties with the navy, and admirals continued to come from the hereditary peerage in the nineteenth and twentieth centuries.
96. Sources present different numbers: Serman (1988) 554; Serman (1979) 305–6; Serman and Bertard 566; Stimmer 84; Craig 233; Janowitz 94; Blum (1978) 421; Kenez 131; J. A. Davis (1994) 306; Razzell 253.
97. Otley (1968) 104; Craig 238; Messerschmdit 54–6; Kenez 132; Hildermeirer 209; L. Cecil (1970) 794; Cardoza (2002) 72, 150. In Austria the figure was dropping rapidly before the War. Deák (1990) 163; Stimmer 84.
98. Ambler 23; Serman (1988) 556; Tudesq (1988) 131; Serman and Bertard 566.
99. Castellane 70.
100. Petersen 249; Janowitz 94; Otley (1968) 99, 104; Razzell 254; Carlson 585, 589–91; Linz 395.
101. Stoneman 32; Kenez 127, 132, 136–7, 144; Serman (1979) 208; Becker 109–11, 120–1; Deák (1990) 95.
102. Powis 98.
103. Vassiltchikov 140–1, 144.
104. Bertaud 91–111.
105. Whelan 44, 56–7.
106. F. M. L. Thompson (2001) 26–30; Hilton; Brent 259–77.
107. McCahill and Wasson 1–38; Higgs (1987) 7–8, 25; Mayer 111; Cardoza (1988) 598–9; Weber 647.
108. Higgs (1987) 246 fn 79; Tudesq (1988) 124–6; Montroni 268, 272.
109. D'Azeglio xvi.
110. Lampedusa 286.
111. Forster (1967) 83–4.
112. Kiernan 5.
113. Dönhoff 41.

5 THE BEAU MONDE: CULTURE AND SOCIETY

1. See also Márai (2002) 18–19.
2. Bánffy (2003) xv.
3. Thursfield 44–6; "Transylvania Trust" www.artnouveau.org consulted 12/2/03.
4. Plumb (1979) 887–911; Jones and Retallack 29.
5. Mayer 190; Cardoza (2002) 4–5.
6. Deák (1990) 79–84; Higham 47.
7. Rubinstein (1993) 102–39; F. M. L. Thompson (2001) 124.
8. Knoll 457–62.
9. Parouchéva 34–7.
10. Muncy (1970) 100–1; Pedlow (1988) 156–62; Godsey (1999a) 41.
11. Loewenstein 55.
12. Blum (1977) 81.
13. Potocki 31–42.
14. *Lietuvos Architektúros Istorija*, II, 166–72. The Potocki counts retained town palaces in Lvov, Cracow, and Warsaw into the 1940s. Potocki *passim*.
15. Youssoupoff 71; Tolstoy 71, 728, 730; Nabokov (1981) 146.
16. Bánffy (1999) 321–2.
17. D. Spring (1977) 11.
18. Roosevelt 32; Riker 4.
19. Schmemann 9–10; Fonseca 216.
20. Roosevelt 97, 112; Higgs (1987) 40.
21. Brewer 628–9.
22. Stone and Stone 373–5; Higgs (1987) 45; Girouard 297–331.
23. Purtscher-Wydenbruck 50; Higgs (1987) 48.
24. Roosevelt xii–xiii, 29, 83; Whelan 50–3, 304–5; Tenno and Maiste; T. Dooley (2001) 28–9, 31, 34, 42; Wasson (2006) 13–18.
25. Bánffy (1999) 495.
26. Sinclair 41.
27. Dönhoff 7.
28. Dönhoff 59, 63; D. Spring and E. Spring (1975) 65–7.
29. Girouard (2000) 257, 259, 313. However, at Ferrières *c.*1850 the Rothschilds employed 100 servants and 50 gardeners. Rothschild 21; Cardoza (2002) 98; Roosevelt 103–5; Fugger von Babenhausen 166–7.
30. Youssoupoff 152.
31. Nabokov (1951) 45.
32. Sykes 130.
33. Metternich 132; Bánffy (2001) 42–3; Cardoza (2002) 134–5; Baranowski (1995) 65.
34. Lampedusa 111–56.
35. Mangin 649–75; Spencer and Spencer.
36. McReynolds 174; Higgs (1987) 38–9.
37. Reynolds 14.
38. Egremont 60.
39. Harper 41.

40. Windischgraetz 45–6.
41. Bailey 131.
42. Mannerheim 9; Windischgraetz 68; Roszkowski (1991) 119; Leigh Fermor (2004a) 78; Cannadine (1994) 68–72.
43. Saint Martin 22–32.
44. McReynolds 87–8.
45. Buruma 150–79.
46. MacAloon 3, 7; Guttman 122.
47. Christiannsen 31–5; Fugger von Babenhausen 35–6; Bánffy (2000) 131–44; Benckendorff 14.
48. Rothschild 30–2; Benckendorff 133–7; Radziwill 75–9.
49. Cannadine (1990) 364–5.
50. Lieven (1992) 154.
51. Fugger von Babenhausen 129–31.
52. Portland 228–9.
53. Batcheller 161–6.
54. Clermont-Tonnerre 218.
55. Bánffy (2001) 95–6; Esterházy 408.
56. Bánffy (2000) 149, 302, 307; Youssoupoff 62; Nabokov (1951) 17, 51; Potocki 17–27.
57. Buruma 86–110; *Country Life* February 15, 2001, 62–5; Bánffy (1999) 137; Turgenev 123; J. Richardson 239–46; Girouard (2000) 307–10; Pratt 91–9, 131–2.
58. Leigh Fermor (2004b) 202.
59. Tolstoy 621.
60. Clermont-Tonnerre 14–15.
61. Montagu of Beaulieu 75; Luke 36; Bánffy (1999) 90–5, 109, 111, 114, 296; Lampedusa 144; Rezzori (1991) 146, 149; D. Obolensky 94; Lermontov 96.
62. D'Azeglio 3.
63. Turgenev 43, 66; Esterházy 408.
64. *Oxford Dictionary of National Biography*, 29, 426–7.
65. Airlie 56.
66. Tenno and Maiste; Leigh Fermor (2004a and b).
67. Irving.
68. Wasson (2005) 73–6.
69. Kale (2004) 212; Clermont-Tonnerre, *passim*.
70. Cardoza (2002) 71, 73; Cardoza (1991) 184.
71. Dal Lago 375–7; Lambert, *passim*.
72. *Country Life* January 1, 2004, 54–7; Bailey 54.
73. Fugger von Babenhausen 94–5, 155–6.
74. Waterfield 47–66.
75. Roosevelt 59, 70.
76. Painting was one of the few areas where aristocrats were rarely creators themselves as opposed to collectors. Only the French Count Toulouse-Lautrec achieved the front rank. However, Prince Pavel Trubetskoy was the greatest Russian sculptor of the late Imperial era, and the 8th Duchess of Rutland was a gifted amateur sculptor.

77. Kelsall, *passim.*
78. Weintraub 47–63; Szelle 113–24; Vassili 187, 190–1.
79. Vassili 337–8; Harsanyi 501–2, 505–6.
80. Rantzau 394–446.
81. Zelechow 261–6; Cardoza (2002) 39.
82. DeNora 310–46; Kale (2004) 144; Schmemann 110; C. Sutherland (1996) 64; Lukacs (1990) 177.
83. Benckendorff 36, 313; S. Obolensky 51.
84. Roosevelt 129–53; Pratt 130; Girouard (2000) 197–217.
85. Wasson (1978) 89–99.
86. Nye 397–421; Schaffer 178.
87. Fugger von Babenhausen 146.
88. *Oxford Dictionary of National Biography,* 19, 940–2.
89. *Oxford Dictionary of National Biography,* 42, 947–50; J. S. Lewis (1995) 387–94.
90. Robins, *passim.*
91. Bánffy (1999) 298, 310, 314–15, 336.
92. Kale (2004) 10.
93. Montgomery 76; K. Clark 180; Ellenberger 633–53; F. M. L. Thompson (1977) 28.
94. Castellane 188; Potocki 55–6.
95. Vassili 168–9, 350–1; Halévy 69–70.
96. Cardoza (1988) 604.
97. Reynolds 15.
98. Simoni 349–54.

6 SWALLOWING THE TOAD: THE ARISTOCRACY AND THE MIDDLE CLASSES

1. Fugger von Babenhausen 42.
2. Price 84–5.
3. Dewald xv, 13; Wasson (2000) 65–92.
4. Asch 166; Fitzsimmons 418–31; McCahill (1999) 599–629; Higgs (1987) 1.
5. Cardoza (2002) 16–17; Lieven (1992) 43, 51; M. Roberts 143; E. Melton, I, 90, 103; Godsey (1999b) 56–104; Berkis 220–99.
6. Stone and Stone 197, 206–10, 221, 403.
7. Unfortunately, most scholars now agree the Stones misinterpreted their own data. F. M. L. Thompson (2001) 53, 57, 143; Wasson (2000) 69–79, 86–90; E. Spring (1999) 86; D. and E. Spring (1986) 333–51; D. and E. Spring (1985) 149–80, 393–6; D. Brown 122–54; Halliday 61; McCahill (1999) 618–20. Moreover, their system failed to incorporate the regular interpenetration of business and land among the gentry families from whom the peerage was drawn in subsequent generations.
8. Godsey (1999a) 22; Cardoza (1982) 28; Von Laue 25–46; S. Clark (1984) 169; McCragg (1971) 13; Wasson (2000).

9. Wende 51; Bush (1988) vii; Jespersen, II, 69.
10. F. M. L. Thompson (1977) 23; Perkin 436–7.
11. Wiener, *passim*.
12. Romanelli (1995) 4.
13. Thane 94; F. M. L. Thompson (2001) 21–44.
14. Stern 61–2.
15. Vassili 343.
16. Lampedusa 93, 144, 148–52.
17. Even in quarterings-obsessed Austria: Godsey (1999a) 61, 96; Godsey (1996) 155–77; J. A. Davis (1988) 272–3; Pedlow (1988) 44; Baranowski (1995) 32; Girouard (2000) 320–1.
18. Rubinstein (1980) 19.
19. Hartzell, *passim*.
20. Cannadine (1990) 347. Montgomery and Davis do not believe financial issues were necessarily the prime motivator, and indeed, fashion, romantic notions of love, and admiration for the education and vitality of American women may have been key aspects of a complex process. Montgomery 138; R. W. Davis 140–99.
21. St. Aubyn 89; Vassili 185.
22. Bánffy (2003) 125.
23. Corner 127–8; Bánffy (1999) 27.
24. McClelland 192–3.
25. Kale (2004) 9–10, 139.
26. Mack Smith (1968) 479.
27. Montagu of Beaulieu 59.
28. Roosevelt 205.
29. Cardoza (2002) 185–6.
30. Lach-Szyrma 99.
31. Muncy (1970) 119–21; Moncure 58–68.
32. Aliberti 211–26.
33. Cox 295–98.
34. Cardoza (1982) 49, 53–4, 82–6, 115–16, 122, 142–3, 149, 200.
35. M. Davis 40, 47–8.
36. F. M. L. Thompson (1988) 107; D. Thomas 102–3.
37. Adonis (1993) 12; Beckett (1986) 120.
38. R. Gibson (1981) 24, 29; Daumard (1980) 105; R. Gibson (1991) 86–7; Higgs (1981) 46; Kale (1992) 24.
39. Cardoza (2002) 11, 92; Cardoza (1991) 182.
40. Carsten (1989) 124; Pedlow (1991) 112.
41. Rubinstein (1980) 21–2, 54–5, 74.
42. Mayer 36, 45, 57, 77.
43. Cardoza (2002) 90, 202; Cardoza (1988) 595.
44. S. Clark (1984) 153.
45. Camplin 35–6 and *passim*.
46. Daumard (1980) 105–6.
47. Godsey (1999a) 60; Whelan 303.
48. Lieven (1992) 52.
49. Farrelly 94–5, 100–101.

50. Bourdieu 95.
51. Stern 60–1, 67.
52. Craig 238; Geyer (1990) 185.
53. Beckett (1986) 3–5; Arnstein (1975a) 205–21; Struve 61–2; Stone and Stone 3–5, 28.
54. Higgs (1981) 46; Augustine (1994) 46–7; McCragg (1971) 14–15; Cardoza (1988) 599; Becker 105–7, 216; Lukacs (1990) 95; Hoensch 37; Ilonzski 203–4.
55. Buruma 194.
56. Anderson and Anderson 195; Berghoff (1994) 153–5; Pedlow (1988) 25; Beckett (1986) 120–1.
57. Tudesq (1988) 124–6.
58. Leigh Fermor (2004b) 247–59, (2004a) 60; McCragg (1972) 75, 77; Roszkowski (1991) 36; Cardoza (1988) 600–2; Cardoza (1991) 182–3; Gross 163, 173–4; Pedlow (1988) 65–9; Mikulski 38–51.
59. I. A. A. Thompson, I, 191, 227–8; Linz 396; Herr 107.
60. Cardoza (1988) 600–2; Snowden (1989) 127–8; Cardoza (1991) 182–3.
61. F. M. L. Thompson (2001); Stone and Stone; E. Spring (1999) 77–91; D. Brown 122–54.
62. Roszkowski (1991) 36.
63. Lieven (1992) 49; Roszkowski (1991) 19.
64. McCragg (1971) 16, 22; Augustine (1994) 46, 81, 190, 200, 202–4, 208.
65. Harris and Thane 226.
66. Augustine (1994) 158–9.
67. Among the best summaries are to be found in Kocka 3–16; R. J. Evans 67–94; Jones and Retallack 8–9; Stern 45–6; Baranowski (1995) 195; Carsten (1989) 126–7; Rosenberg passim.
68. Finlay 280–1, 283–4, 288, 290.
69. Perkins 79–81, 96, 111, 114, 116. France and Italy also raised tariffs on imported grain in the later nineteenth century without a Sonderweg.
70. Schissler (1978); Hagen, passim; Finlay 291–3, 301–2.
71. Eley 47; Jones and Retallack 8–14.
72. Eley 85, 95–6, 99, 102; Hagen 653.
73. Best et al. 139, 189–90; H. Best 6–7.
74. See particularly Augustine (1994) 4–8, 27, 38, 46, 53, 144, 158–9, 162–88, 212–13, 226, 239, 243–6, 254; Gillis (1971) 11; Bratvogel 404–28; Kaelble 451–60. Lieven's assessment can hardly be bettered for balance and judgment. Lieven (1992) 228, 252, 281.
75. Cruz (1996b) 4.
76. Cruz (1996b) 55–7, 119, 123, 129, 144–5, 159–60, 164, 172, 210–11, 257.
77. Tudesq (1964), I, 8–9, 99, 422–31; Locke (1974) 81, 146; Kale (1992) 26–7; LeBozec 35–45; R. Gibson (1981) 7–8, 30–1.
78. P. M. Jones 73, 75; R. Gibson (1981) 7–11; R. Gibson (1991) 84–5; Higonnet and Higonnet 217, 222; Higgs (1987) xii, xvi, 45, 108, 129.

79. Cardoza (2002) 26, 163, 180; Cardoza (1982) 31, 37; M. Malatesta
     179–82; Laroche 81–91; Romanelli (1995) 4.
80. Cardoza (2002) 8–9, 163, 169, 185–9, 195; J. A. Davis (1994) 301, 305;
     Schwetje 288–361; Macry 339–83.
81. Daalder and van den Berg 220.
82. Wiener 13.
83. F. M. L. Thompson (2001) 23–44, 101–42, 154–5; F. M. L. Thompson
     (1984) 211; Smith 767–76; Harris and Thane 227. W. D. Rubinstein
     has also delivered some hefty blows against Wiener based on extensive
     statistical analysis. Rubinstein (1993) 21–4, 45–101.
84. Thane 93–100.
85. G. R. Searle 321.
86. Cardoza (2001) 8–9.
87. Mayer 21–2; Schumpeter; D. Brown 136.
88. Marburg and Matzerath 6; Godsey (2002) 507.
89. Cardigan 25.

7   THE HABIT OF AUTHORITY: LOCAL POWER

1.   J. V. H. Melton, II, 126.
2.   Stilling 21.
3.   Christiannsen 414–15.
4.   Christiannsen 578 and *passim*.
5.   Christiannsen 295–6.
6.   Forster (1976) 200.
7.   Jardin and Tudesq 235; Mack Smith (1968) 438; Whelan 54; Gilmour
     24.
8.   Blum (1948) 215–17; Blum (1978) 412–13; Whelan 219–22.
9.   Zeldin (1959) 54.
10. Becker 149; Wank (1992b) 138; Gillis (1971) 254.
11. Verney 16; Alapuro (1993) 152.
12. Muncy (1970) 175–90; Muncy (1973) 299–308.
13. Cardoza (2002) 87; Cardoza (1991) 184; Higgs (1987) 144–5.
14. Lévêque 75; Cannadine (1990) 559–72; Zangerl 114–15.
15. D. Spring (1960) 58.
16. Emmons 182; Becker 144–5, 168, 170; Blum (1977) 73, 89–92, 95–6;
     D. Obolensky 29–30; Benckendorff 124.
17. Anderson and Anderson 143–51; Wank (1992b) 137; Berend (2003)
     109–10, 187; Beckett (1986) 393–5; Dubabin 357, 371; Newby et al.
     225; Adonis (1993) 189–91. Only in Wales was the elite virtually
     eliminated in the first election. Howell et al. 64.
18. Higgs (1987) 127; D. Sutherland (1991) 45; Lévêque 74; R. Gibson
     (1981) 7, 26.
19. D'Azeglio 37.
20. I came across this incident while doing research for another project
     and cannot now find the reference.

21. See Gibson and Blinkorn 3–16; Márai (2000) 167; Figes 196.
22. Baranowski (1995) 53–4.
23. Tocqueville 113.
24. Lévêque 66; P. M. Jones 263.
25. Baranowski (1995) 76.
26. Lévêque 75–7; Berger 13, 45–7, 59–82, 119; Dallas 275–9.
27. D. Spring (1977) 14; Herr 114–19; Anderson and Anderson 159.
28. Christiannsen 398–9, 403, 406.
29. Snowden (1989) 9–14, 43.
30. Eidelberg 38–9; Berend (2003) 163–4, 198.
31. Blinkorn 223; Cardoza (1991) 182.
32. Snowden (1989) 14–15.
33. Blum (1978) 340; Whelan 78–80, 219; Pedlow (1988) 128–31; Gibson and Blinkhorn 90–1.
34. Wasson (2000) 144.
35. Cannadine (1990) 65, 65, 67.
36. Berend (2003) 250–2; Eidelberg 1–2, 230.
37. Whelan 2; Lieven (1992) 96; Schmemann 141; Roosevelt 227; Blum (1978) 333.
38. Cardoza (1991) 184–96; Snowden (1989) 20–33.
39. Snowden (1991) 200; Mack Smith (1965) 99–100; Mack Smith (1968) 466, 468, 490, 502, 509.
40. Whelan 286–8; E. J. Evans 175–6.
41. Christiannsen 491.
42. Whelan 33–4, 219, 228.
43. R. Gibson (1991) 87, 91; R. Gibson (1981) 24, 32–7; Dallas 223; Lévêque 61.
44. Blinkhorn 226; Cardoza (1982) 35; Roszkowski (1983) 281–99.
45. Beckett (1986) 12; Lieven (1992) 203–4; E. J. Evans 145–61.
46. R. W. Johnson 18.
47. Baranowski (1995) 28–9; Dipper 194; Eddie (1994) 124–5.
48. Lieven (1992) 221–2.
49. Cardoza (2002) 55, 87, 212.

8   EAGLES AND PEACOCKS: NATIONAL POWER

1. Forster (1976) 192.
2. Mannheim 98; Weber 626–32; Goodrich 29–55.
3. Daalder (1966a) 197.
4. Blum (1977) 73; Becker 6–7.
5. Macartney (1968) 620.
6. Thaden (1984b) 196.
7. Berend (2003) 184–5.
8. Anderson and Anderson 167, 189–91; Forster (1976) 190; Steiner 3–4.
9. Lieven (1992) 4.

10. Whelan 258–9, 267; Godsey (1999a) 41, 45–6.
11. Brizzi 249–65.
12. Godsey (1999a) 225; Cecil (1976) 26–36.
13. Konttinen 201–20; Rosenberg 180.
14. Greenaway 159–69; Gowan 4–34.
15. Witte 226–52; Thorson 48.
16. Godsey (2002) 516–17; Whelan 9, 58–60, 210–13, 235–7.
17. Jespersen, II, 63–70.
18. Thaden (1984a) 221; Thaden (1984b) 201–30; Alapuro (1988) 92, 146–7, 188; Thaden (1995) 10–11.
19. Trumpa 115–22.
20. Cragoe 250–2; Wasson (2000) 99–101.
21. Bánffy (2003) 59, 235; Deák (1990) 34–5; Andics 51–64.
22. The movement was initially led by Georg Ritter von Schönerer, one of the first politicians in Europe to talk of direct action, racial purity, and the inevitability and usefulness of conflict. He urged the abandonment of traditional civilized behavior, calling for the destruction of the Habsburg state, presenting an apocalyptic vision that Hitler admired and followed. He had been born into a wealthy industrial family that was granted a hereditary knighthood in 1860, but the family was making its way up the traditional social ladder from the "second society." His father purchased a 3000-acre landed estate. He and his sisters married into recently ennobled families; the eventual heir was absorbed into the aristocracy. Whiteside 3, 6–7, 64–6, 78, 139.
23. King 55.
24. Spring and Spring (1975) 69; Tilton 563; Blum (1978) 418–19; Harrison 86; Anderson and Anderson 23.
25. Amizade 492.
26. Czudnowski 5–6.
27. R. Gibson (1981) 31–6.
28. Cannadine (1990) 49.
29. M. L. Anderson 98, 103.
30. Wasson (2000) 149–57.
31 Higgs (1987) 174.
32. Cannadine (1990) 502–16.
33. Phillips; Rossi 309–38.
34. Judith Lewis discovered that over a quarter of the county elections in England, Scotland, and Ireland in the period 1790–1820 recorded a woman participating in the process. J. S. Lewis (2003) 21–2, 40, 44, 75, 244–51.
35. Bánffy (1999) 26, 447, 564.
36. Pedlow (1988) 206, 226; Lieven (1992) 150; D'Azeglio 28–9.
37. J. S. Lewis (2003) 125; Kale (2002) 54–80; Kale (2004) 152, 165, 226; Augustine 13–14.
38. Vicary; Reynolds 153–87; McCord (2002) 24–55.
39. Kale (2004) 8, 150, 172, 204.
40. Kale (2004) 210–11; Vassili 248–51; C. Sutherland (1996) 102.

41. Henricksson 213–28.
42. Higgs (1987) 166–8, 175; *Oxford Dictionary of National Biography*, 44, 789–90; Harsanyi 497–511; Roskowski (1991) 92.
43. Loewenstein 303–85; Gilmour 23; Roszkowski (1991) 129.
44. Weitz 201–73; Cardoza (2002) 47–8; D'Azeglio 254–9.
45. Pauls 785–811; Witte 226–52; Campbell 181–90.
46. Stern 55.
47. Whelan 2, 305–12; Pistohlkors 191–2; Lundin 234–5.
48. Blum (1978) 424–5; Phillips, *passim*.
49. Colley 177–92; McCahill and Wasson; Higgs (1987) 8–15.
50. Higgs (1987) 165–6; Boudon cited in Plamper 30; R. Gibson (1981) 27.
51. Cannadine (1990) 257.
52. Gregory XVI (1831–46) appointed only 13 titled and 11 nobles out of 75, while Pius IX (1846–78) elevated only seven titled and 18 nobles out of 123. By the reign of Benedict XV (1914–22) numbers were down to only two untitled nobles out of 32.
53. Weber 607–57.
54. Cardoza (2002) 6, 35–6, 58; Stimmer 86, 458; Wank (1992b) 135–9; Berend (2003) 185; Godsey (1999a) 39–40; Becker 12, 109; Hildermeier 211; Lieven (1987) 430; Mosse (1979) 242; Pedlow (1988) 195–6; Gillis (1971) 212; Anderson and Anderson 195–6; H. Best 7, 14; Muncy (1970) 28–9, 104–10, 202–3; R. Jones 52–6, 63; Arnstein (1975b) 210; F. M. L. Thompson (1977) 27–9; Wasson (2000) 47–9; Guttsman (1951) 125; Carlson 583; Verney 103; Boogman 143–5; Slavolainen 173–210.
55. Godsey (1999a) 183–6.
56. Steiner 2, 16; Godsey (1999a) 10, 17, 24, 31–2; Nightengale 313–14.
57. Cardoza (2002) 62; Petersen 250.
58. Anderson and Anderson 196; Dönhoff 4; L. Cecil (1976) 66.
59. Godsey (1996) 156.
60. Boogman 145; Carlson 583.
61. Godsey (1999a) 102; Osborne 112.
62. Higgs (1987) 132, 137–8; Forster (1976) 203.
63. Halévy 121–3.
64. Nilsson 198–297.
65. Adonis (1993) 203.
66. Cruz (1996b) 87, 157–8; Monteiro (1999) 185–210; S. Clark (1984) 166.
67. Tilton 569; Lieven (1992) 220–1.
68. Löffler 29–76.
69. Higgs (1987) 23, 134–6; Zeldin (1977) 137; Anderson and Anderson 56–7; Daalder and van den Berg 219–29; I. Secker 281; Beekler and de Schepper 279–87; S. Clark (1984) 166; Blum (1978) 430–1; Linz 374–9.
70. Cardoza (2002) 65; Stjernquist 424–6; Verney 89; Stimmer 459; Jenks 127–34; Warren 18, 22–3; Bush (1983) 101–2; Lieven (1992) 33; Dönhoff 24; Emmons 211.

71. Péter 80.
72. Anderson and Anderson 319–20, 328.
73. Higgs (1987) 136, 140; R. Gibson (1981) 25; Zeldin (1973), I, 424; Magone 346; I. Secker 281–5, 303; Muncy (1970) 73–4; Cruz (1996b)148; Linz 380.
74. A. Malatesta, I, under Colonna.
75. Best and Glaxie 99, 102, 110; Locke (1974) 56–9, 70, 225; H. Best 6; R. Gibson (1981) 25–6; Dogan 73, 84–5; Cardoza (2002) 66–70; Cotta et al. 230, 233–4; Linz 395–6; Magone 346; S. Clark (1984) 165; Carlson 622; Ruostetsaari 62–3; Stimmer 459; Luft 16–25; Best et al. 153; Rus and Cromwell 463; Wasson (2000) 149–58; Cromwell 386.
76. Ferraboschi 435–60.
77. Anderson and Anderson 335–6.
78. Spitzer 221.
79. I. Secker 276.
80. Best and Cotta 499, 507–8, 513, 521.
81. Verney 73.
82. Wasson (2000) 4.
83. D. Spring (1977) 16; Kriegel (1980a) 337–46; Rose 32; Kahan 5, 16, 32, 47.
84. Kitson Clark 51.
85. D. Spring (1977) 17.
86. Deák (1976) 320–61.
87. Alapuro (1993) 145–7, 162.
88. Pedlow (1988) 221, 224.
89. Beckett (1986) 452.
90. Lampedusa 40.
91. Herr 105; Dore 295.
92. Moore xiv; Berend (2003) 238–9.
93. Best and Cotta 495.
94. Tilton 561–71; Rojas 64–74; Rothstein 149–71.
95. Dore 298–300; Moore xiv.
96. Aron (1950) 131.
97. Zmora 70–1; Blum (1948) 30–1.
98. Dewald 151–7.
99. Mayer 4–5, 9, 15.
100. Wank (1981) 1–16; Lieven (1992) 243–4.
101. Offer, III, 694–5.
102. Harris 5.
103. Tocqueville 242–3; Anderson and Anderson 384.

9 ARISTOCIDE, 1917–1945

1. Purtscher-Wydenbruck 52–3.
2. Listowel 207.
3. Hoffmann chapter 1.
4. Radziwill 112–13.

5. Wheeler-Bennett 513.
6. Leigh Fermor (2004a) 128.
7. Graves 55–7, 65–9.
8. Martin (2002a) 28–48.
9. Winter 85; Beckett (1986) 473; Beard 25–6.
10. Martin (2002a) 39–40; Bartillat 439.
11. Roszkowski (1991) 51–2; Cardoza (2002) 214; Alexander 7–8.
12. Cannadine (1990) 97–8; Beard 40.
13. Cannadine (1990) 132; Clemenson 112; Beckett (1986) 477.
14. Cardoza (2002) 216, 218–19.
15. Clemenson 11, 115, 127; Cannadine 111–18. Of course, some of this attrition would have occurred naturally without taking the war into account.
16. Cannadine (1990) 105–9. In 1923 the Irish Free State introduced compulsory purchase of remaining estate property.
17. Cannadine (1990) 125–7.
18. Salvadó 893–914.
19. Cardoza (2002) 1–12.
20. Cardoza (2002) 220; Godsey (1999a) 164; Rezzori (1991) 28, 136.
21. Dissow 9.
22. Rezzori (1991) 35.
23. Struve 274–316; Novella 333–49.
24. Wheeler-Bennett 49, 124–5.
25. Franckenstein 219–321.
26. Cornwell 145, 197–9.
27. Franckenstein 280; Bartillat 157.
28. *Oxford Dictionary of National Biography*, 36, 700–2. Countess Sophie Panine became the first woman minister in Eastern Europe when she joined the Russian Cabinet in 1917.
29. Radziwill 21.
30. Rezzori (1985) 142, 149, 154, 170, 189.
31. Girouard (2000) 262; *Historic Houses* 117, 178; Channon 30.
32. She became Countess Haugwitz-Reventlow.
33. Waugh 113.
34. F. L. Hansen 22.
35. Lax 200.
36. F. M. L. Thompson (1969) 76.
37. Benckendorff 246, 249, 251, 298; Ignatiev 145–6, 179; Mackintosh 21–2, 93; Erickson 464. A number of Soviet leaders such as Malenkov were of noble descent. Lenin's father had earned the rank of an official, and his mother came from a genuinely landed family.
38. Meshcherskaya 10–19, 92–3.
39. Schmemann 204; Roosevelt xiv, 330–1.
40. D. Obolensky 197, 211–15.
41. Ustinov 12.
42. Lipping 35, 99, 204, 279, 302; Harpe 669–72; Bilmanis 280–329; Woodward and Butler 4–5, 26–7; Pistohlkors 193, 198–200; Alexander 73.

43. Whelan 313–14; Metternich 60.
44. Bence-Jones 195; T. Dooley (2001) 172–207. My own research suggests that about 120 houses were deliberately destroyed between 1919 and 1924. Wasson (2005) 19–22.
45. Martin (2002b) 159; T. Dooley (2001) 130–1, 233.
46. Bence-Jones 219–22.
47. Cannadine (1990) 105; T. Dooley (2001) 13, 131–3; Cleary 271–3; Kreilkamp 175–6, 179.
48. Rezzori (1991) 188; Reck-Malleczewen 34–5 and *passim*; Horstmann 11; Simms 258, 267; Baranowski (1995) 162–3.
49. Simms 259; Fromm 64; Gilmour 35, 37.
50. Schieder 39–65.
51. Cardoza (1982) 47, 55–67, 235, 245–9; Snowden (1989) 33–49.
52. Corner 107–8, 123–4, 135–6, 261; Cardoza (1982) 4–11, 115–16, 122, 142–3, 149, 398, 434–5, 451–4; Cardoza (2002) 222; Romanelli (1995) 19; Snowden (1989) 33–41, 57–9, 60–9, 122–3, 226; Reece (1973) 265, 269–70; Mack Smith (1965) 120–2.
53. De Grand 523.
54. Katz *passim*. Count Ciano, the Foreign Minister, who had turned on his father-in-law, was shot, while Count Cini, the Finance Minister, ended up in Dachau.
55. P. H. Lewis 622–47; De Meneses 153–63; Sinclair 90; Gallagher 83–4; Magone 350–2.
56. Machado 148–9.
57. I. A. A. Thompson, I, 235; Malefakis 179–235; Harrison 92–3; Sinclair 92; Montagu of Beaulieu 79.
58. Cenarro 462; Preston (1994) 283–4.
59. Wheeler-Bennett 20–5.
60. The state governments in Germany such as Prussia and Bavaria continued to legally recognize and regulate titles and noble law. Loewenstein 21.
61. Messerschmidt 64; Janowitz 94; Stimmer 84; Wheeler-Bennett 31–45, 99–100; Carsten (1990) 123; Carsten (1989) 161–2.
62. Malinowski 570, 573.
63. Baranowski (1993) 409–32; Vascik 229–30.
64. Vassiltchikov 254.
65. Anderson and Anderson 384.
66. Stimmer 879; Sinclair 80.
67. Of the 29 leading members of the *Heimwehr*, 55 percent were from the titled nobility. Stimmer 837.
68. Starhemberg 82, 112–13; Leigh Fermor (2004b) 127–8; Stadler 104–5; Edmondson 109.
69. Berend (1998) 197–8; Roszkowksi (1991) 97–9.
70. In 1935 the law could again be invoked to regulate their protection. Pinches 187.
71. Roszkowski (1991) 18–19, 33; Polonsky 12.
72. Radziwill 82; Roszkowski (1991) 45, 56–8, 104; Berend (1998) 290; Maczak 289; Luke 88, 104–8.

73. Radziwill 56; Roszkowski (1991) 96–7.
74. Roszkowski (1991) 112, 134; Mitchell 34–5.
75. Potocki 283.
76. Berend (1998) 291; Pratt 49, 98–103; Sternberg 16.
77. Godsey (2002) 520; Listowel 145–6. Due to technical problems I was unable to gain access to Eagle Glassman's doctoral dissertation on the Czech nobility and nationality politics 1918–48 before this book went to press, but those interested in the topic should consult it.
78. Berend (1998) 289; I. L. Evans 125, 128, 179.
79. Bánffy (2003) 373; Leigh Fermor (2004a) 97.
80. Tomasevich 65, 108–9, 204–5, 366–7, 377; West 75.
81. Listowel 23–6.
82. Ilonzski 205; Romsics 271–89; Berend (1998) 141–2; Z. Harsányi 95.
83. Erös 132, 136–7; Lengyel 166–91; Hoensch 128, 142–3, 150; Sinclair 83, 85; Lukacs (1993) 133.
84. Delfosse 53–90.
85. Warner 309.
86. Bankowitz 225: Ambler 37, 58–9; Müller 21. Another aristocrat who emerged in the critical months of early 1940 was Helène Countess de Porte, mistress and "evil genius" of Prime Minister Paul Reynaud, who was besotted with her. She had close associates in anti-war and defeatist circles, influenced his appointments, passed British and French state secrets to the Italians, and urged surrender. J. Jackson 126, 140–1; Listowel 216–17.
87. Clermont-Tonnerre 68.
88. Berger 134, 139.
89. Beevor and Cooper 15, 21, 148–9, 186, 190–1.
90. Channon 234.
91. Rubinstein (1998) 1–18.
92. In 1922 the 7th Marquis of Londonderry held £439,000 in Victory bonds and was making further similar investments. De Courcy 194.
93. Rubinstein (1998) 1–18; Beard 47; Farrelly 163.
94. Wasson (2000) 157–8, 165–71, 175–6, 178.
95. Rubinstein (1998) 16; Wasson (2000) 47–8; Kershaw, xv, 9, 12.
96. For example, Sir Charles Trevelyan, 3rd Baronet, the 9th Earl De La Warr, and the 7th Earl of Longford.
97. Cannadine (1990) 607–8.
98. Cannadine (1990) 233.
99. Witherell 1134–66; Kershaw 315. Cannadine, (1990) 572–88, also exaggerates the newness of their leadership role in "good" causes, museums, and associations. The elite had regularly helped to form and lead such organizations since the time of the founding of the Royal Society in the later seventeenth century, and the Oxford and Cambridge colleges before that. It is true, however, that the aristocracy sustained its prestige into the mid-twentieth century by taking on ceremonial positions with wide public exposure and doing good works rather than by controlling a majority of seats in the House of Commons.

100. Many appeasers weeded out their papers after the war so insufficient evidence exists about their numbers. Lukacs (2001) 56–8.
101. *Country Life*, December 9, 2004, 56–60; Aslet 323.
102. Airlie 211.
103. Metternich 152.
104. Cannadine (1990) 625–34.
105. Ambler 76–7.
106. In this connection mention should be made of Charles de Gaulle. He was not an aristocrat by the definition in this book, yet one cannot overlook the importance of his self-perception, which was profoundly tied to a noble past. De Gaulle descended from a genuine old line, although no longer landed. He was raised in a conservative, royalist, and Catholic tradition, fully conscious of his ancestry, and he acted with all the arrogance and style of a nobleman.
107. The title passed by primogeniture to the heir while younger sons became barons.
108. Jägerskiöld *passim*; Siaroff 107–9.
109. Jägerskiöld 181.
110. Wheeler-Bennett 497.
111. Schlabrendorff 120–1.
112. Vassiltchikov 234.
113. Wheeler-Bennett 685.
114. Moltke 400.
115. Hoffmann 162–3, 185, 229–40; Kane 185; Wheeler-Bennett 561–4, 589, 591.
116. Mommsen 30.
117. Hoffmann 27, 105, 107, 133, 151–2, 283; Mommsen 238–76.
118. Fest 240; Moltke *passim*.
119. Vassiltchikov 186, 190.
120. Metternich 118.
121. Hoffmann 93, 210.
122. Hoffmann 243.
123. Whalen 119–20; Hoffman 238.
124. Mommsen 7.
125. Whalen 60.
126. Mommsen 45, 47–8, 83.
127. Executed or committed suicide post July 20: (Wheeler-Bennett 744–52 with my additions). Nobles: Blumenthal, Börsig, Dohanyi, H. B. Haeften, W. Haeften, Halem, Harnack, Hase, Hassell, Hayessen, Hofacker, Kleist-Schmenzin, Linstow, Mumm von Schwarzenstein, Oertzen, Rabenau, Stülpnagel, Thadden, G. Tresckow, H. Tresckow, Voss, Witzleben. Ritters: Mertz von Quirnheim and Scholz-Babisch. Barons: Boeselager, Breitbach-Bürresheim, Freytag-Loringhoven, Guttenberg, Leonrod, Lüninck, Plettenberg, Roenne, Thüngen, Trott zu Solz. Counts: Bernstorff, Blumenthal, Dohna-Tolksdorf, Drechsel, Helldorf, Lehndorff-Steinort, Lynar, Margona-Redwitz, Matuschka, Moltke, Salviati, Schack, F. D. Schulenburg, F. W. Schulenburg, Schwerin-Schwanenfeld, B. Stauffenberg, the younger, C. Stauffen-

berg, Sponeck, Üxküll, Yorck von Wartenburg. Berthold, Count von Stauffenberg, the elder, died in prison. Georg Kissling and Wentzel-Teutschenthal, estate owners, were also executed. Count Gottfried von Bismarck was tried and convicted but survived. Count Carl Hans von Hardenberg attempted to commit suicide before his arrest, was gravely wounded, and placed in a concentration camp. Ritter von Niedermayer was condemned to death, but died in a Russian camp. Baron von Falkenhausen and Fabian von Schlabrendorff were sent to Dachau. Dozens of princes, counts, barons, and other nobles also supported the coup but escaped death sentences. Many wives, children, and cousins of the Stauffenbergs were arrested and held in prison. The property of the conspirators was confiscated, and they had to struggle with the German bureaucracy after the war to get it back and get widows' pensions. Hoffmann 280.

128. Cannadine (1990) 617–24.
129. Lukacs (2001) 113–30, 146–57, 182–6.
130. Addison 23–47; G. Best 97.
131. Berlin 32; G. Best 31.
132. Gilbert, V, 401, 482.
133. Colville 182.
134. A. Roberts 179.

10 WHERE ARE THEY NOW? 1945–2005

1. Ignatieff 69–70.
2. Ignatieff 114–17.
3. Ignatieff *passim.*
4. Vassiltchikov 274–302.
5. Luke 151–211.
6. Dönhoff 173–204.
7. Horstmann 40, 53, 56.
8. Sinclair 134; Vassiltchikov 267; Beard 81–5.
9. Mandler 312–19.
10. Roosevelt 332; Littlejohn 39.
11. *New York Times*, December 12, 1990, A4.
12. Clemenson 133, 135; S. Jenkins, *The Spectator*, October 18, 2003, 24.
13. Farquharson 35–6, 44–5, 49; Bauerkämper 623–4.
14. Zamagni 160; Mack Smith (1965) 123.
15. Christiannsen 46–7, 121; Sinclair 171.
16. R. A. H. Robinson 266.
17. Esterházy 670.
18. Nettl 78, 85, 172, 176.
19. H. L. Roberts 296; Pratt 291. Oddly, the Magyar elite more than any other Eastern aristocracy, chose not to flee the communist takeover in 1945, perhaps due to their intense nationalism or to a misguided assumption that they might yet be considered worthy of service by the new regime. Lukacs (1993) 134.

20. Hoensch 200; Esterházy 707.
21. Lukacs (1990) 87. She died in the 1980s.
22. Roszkowski (1991) 136; Sinclair 169.
23. Rossi 309–38.
24. Origio et al. 46; Moorehead 296.
25. Cardoza (2002) 223–4.
26. Daumard (1980) 120.
27. Beresford; *The Sunday Times Rich List 2003*, April 27, 2003.
28. Sykes 342–51.
29. S. Obolensky 320.
30. Redé 69–79, 80, 96, 127–49; Rothschild 272, 275–82.
31. *The Spectator*, June 12, 2004, 34.
32. Redé 103–4.
33. Higgs (1987) 126–7.
34. Potterton 106–7.
35. Perrott 49–52.
36. D. Obolensky 184, 244.
37. Herr 122; Sinclair 139–40.
38. Yorck 72–7.
39. Sinclair 159.
40. J. M. Robinson 9.
41. J. M. Robinson 9–10; Littlejohn 79–90.
42. Mandler; Christiannsen 283; Roosevelt 332.
43. *Country Life*, July 2, 1998, 76–9; Girouard (2000) 29, 337.
44. Devine (2001) 459; Christiannsen 528–30; Beard 159.
45. *The Economist*, June 19, 2004, 57; Littlejohn 69.
46. Devonshire 45–8. Some estimates put his fortune in 2004 at £1.6 billion. *The Economist*, May 15, 2004, 83.
47. Callander 9–10.
48. Sinclair 149–50; *Country Life*, April 22, 2004, 140–5; Clemenson 116–20, 214; Perrott 151–6, 160; Beckett (1986) 470; F. M. L. Thompson (1990) 14–15; *Country Life*, July 1,1999, 93–7 and April 23, 1998, 94–9.
49. *Country Life*, July 2, 1998, 76–9; Girouard 335.
50. Zamagni 141; Stilling 20–1.
51. Preston (1984) 179; Sinclair 140–1; Montagu of Beaulieu 79–80; Malefakis 14, 19, 29.
52. The rate is much lower, however, for less exalted princely and ducal families. In the 2001 edition only 39 percent were still at their seats in Britain, France, Belgium, Italy, Austria, and Germany.
53. Metternich 270.
54. Potterton 104.
55. Egremont 63.
56. *Country Life*, December 19/26, 2002, 65.
57. *Historic Houses* 158; Lees-Milne (2004) 18; Ingilby 114–16; Devonshire 89, 121. When working in the archives at Chatsworth in the 1970s, I was amazed by the number of people one encountered in the base-ment of the house. Researchers in those days, before most papers

were deposited in public archives, often saw the inner workings of fully operational big estates, and my conversations with estate workers in a variety of venues confirmed that aristocratic country houses still formed large and loyal communities.

58. *Country Life*, May 20, 2004, 220; *The Spectator*, June 12, 2004, 52; *The Economist*, May 15, 2004, 83.
59. Lees-Milne (2004) 320, 325.
60. F. M. L. Thompson (1990) 5; Newby et al. 225–6; Beckett (1986) 473; Perrott 189.
61. R. W. Johnson 18; Woods 453–78; Newby et al. 108, 112, 196–7.
62. Brett 88; Needham 145–6, 180–3.
63. Redé 12, 60–8.
64. D. Sutherland 45; Beevor and Cooper 102.
65. Berger 65, 72–4, 80, 101, 107, 133, 138, 281, 285.
66. Cardoza (2002) 224–5.
67. Sinclair 161.
68. *New York Times*, March 12, 2002, A27.
69. A. Searle 9, 50.
70. Ambler 138, 143; Razzell 253–4; Sinclair 161; Macdonald 635; Otley (1970) 218.
71. Higgs (1987) 218–19; Best and Gaxie 99.
72. *New York Times*, January 27, 2004.
73. Sinclair 161.
74. Vassiltchikov 302.
75. Burch and Moran 15.
76. Including the 6th Earl of Lucan and 5th Earl of Listowel. The 7th Earl of Longford was a Cabinet minister and the leading speaker for the Labour Party in the Lords for 40 years.
77. *New York Times*, April 2, 2004.
78. Cannadine (1990) 638.
79. Cannadine (1990) 666.
80. Cannadine (1990) 667.
81. Hutchinson 131–48; McCrone and Morris 170–85; Jarvie and Jackson 1–22; Rosie 22–40. The best place to start to understand the extraordinary size and durability of great estates in Scotland is Wightman, *Who Owns Scotland*, and Callander. Cahill, *Who Owns Britain*, is also useful. He includes Ireland.
82. Szulc 104, 121, 125–33, 138, 142, 147, 165, 194.
83. Rudikoff 6, 8.
84. Higgs (1987) 223.
85. Sinclair 209; F. M. L. Thompson (1990) 7.
86. Girouard 28–9; Dewald 10; Mension-Rigau 28, 50–1.
87. Ignatieff 11.
88. Lukacs (1993) 131–4.
89. *Country Life*, November 11, 1999, 46–50, 60–1.
90. *The Slovak Spectator*, February 9–15, 2004.
91. *Country Life*, June 6, 2002, 148–53; *The Economist*, December 6, 2003; www.radio.cz/en/article/62325, accessed January 14, 2005; www.

prague.tv//pill/article.php?name=nobility-on-trial, accessed June 20, 2003.
92. *Country Life*, December 11, 2003, 40–2.
93. *Wall Street Journal*, May 15, 2002.
94. "Count Tibor Kalnoky," www.earthfoot.org/guides/kalnoky.htm, accessed August 1, 2004.
95. *Russian Life*, February 1996, 4.
96. *Business Week*, October 26, 1998.
97. Gilbert (1988) 1123–5.
98. Waugh 309.
99. Alanbrooke 485.
100. Ingilby 7.
101. Dogan 64.

11   VITAL MEMORIES

1. www.earthfoot.org/guides/kalnoky.htm. 1/8/04.
2. Gilmour 7–14, 188–9, 192.
3. Cannadine (1990) 698–9.
4. Airlie 191–2; Dewald 11.
5. Lampedusa 59.
6. Lampedusa 286 – my italics.
7. Godsey (2002) 507.
8. Whelan 238.
9. Whelan 232–3, 239–40; Godsey (2002) 513. Obsession with "olden days" was not necessarily a sign of decay. European aristocrats were fascinated with medieval chivalry throughout the nineteenth century. Girouard (1981) *passim*.
10. Tocqueville 102–3.
11. Nye 404.
12. Hoffmann xiii, xv, 39, 46–7.
13. "In my thoughts I am always at Kreisau," wrote Count Helmuth James von Moltke in 1941, ". . . wondering how everything looks and planning all that might be done." Moltke 133.
14. Hoffmann 103; Yorck 86; Moltke 212, 289.
15. Kershaw 10, 259, 288, 350.
16. Ignatiev 94. Dag Hammarskjöld, Secretary-General of the United Nations, was the son of one of the last noblemen to be prime minister of Sweden. He wrote: "From generations of soldiers and government officials on my father's side I inherited a belief that no life was more satisfactory than one of selfless service to your country or humanity. This service required a sacrifice of all personal interests, but likewise the courage to stand up unflinchingly for your convictions." www.nobelprize.org/peace/laureates/1961/hammarskjold-bio/, April 29, 2004/accessed February 28, 2005.
17. Stevenson 465; Adonis (1993) 244–72, 275; F. M. L. Thompson (1969) 1.

References

Abrahamsson, Bengt, "The Ideology of an Elite: Conservatism and National Insecurity – Some Notes on the Swedish Military," in Jacques van Doorn (ed.), *Armed Forces and Society* (The Hague: Mouton, 1968), pp. 71–83.

Abrams, Lynn, "The Personification of Inequality: Challenges to Gendered Power Relations in the Nineteenth-Century Divorce Court," *Archiv für Sozialgeschichte*, 38 (1998) 41–55.

Adamson, John (ed.), *The Princely Courts of Europe, 1500–1750* (London: Seven Dials, 2000).

Addison, Paul, "The Political Beliefs of Winston Churchill," *Transactions of the Royal Historical Society*, 30 (1980) 23–47.

Adonis, Andrew, "Aristocracy, Agriculture and Liberalism: the Politics, Finances and Estates of the Third Lord Carrington," *Historical Journal*, 31 (1988) 871–97.

Adonis, Andrew, *Making Aristocracy Work: The Peerage and the Political System in Britain, 1884–1914* (Oxford: Oxford University Press, 1993).

Agnew, Hugh LeCaine, "Noble Nation and Modern Nation: the Czech Case," *Austrian History Yearbook*, 23 (1992) 50–71.

Airlie, Mabell, Countess of, *Thatched with Gold* (London: Hutchinson, 1962).

Alanbrooke, Viscount, *War Diaries, 1939–1945* (London: Phoenix Press, 2002).

Alapuro, Risto, *State and Revolution in Finland* (Berkeley, CA: University of California Press, 1988).

Alapuro, Risto, "Peasants in the Consolidation of the Finnish State," in David Howell, Gert von Pistohlkors, and Ellen Wiegandt (eds.), *Roots of Rural Ethnic Mobilisation: Comparative Studies on Governments and Non-Dominant Ethnic Groups in Europe, 1850–1940*, vol. VII (New York: New York University Press, 1993), pp. 145–68.

Alexander, Tania, *Tania: Memories of a Lost World* (Bethesda, MD: Adler and Adler, 1988).

Aliberti, Giovanni, "Elites e Modello Nobiliare nel Secolo XIX," *Storia Contemporanea*, 26 (1995) 211–26.

Almanach de Gotha (Gotha and London: various editions).

Ambler, John Stewart, *The French Army in Politics, 1945–1962* (Athens, OH: Ohio State University Press, 1966).

245

Ames, Ernest O. F. (ed.), *The Revolution in the Baltic Provinces of Russia* (London: Independent Labor Party, 1907).

Amizade, Ronald, "Breaking the Chains of Dependency," *Journal of Urban History*, 3 (1972) 485–500.

Anderson, Eugene N. and Pauline R. Anderson, *Political Institutions and Social Change in Continental Europe in the Nineteenth Century* (Berkeley, CA: University of California Press, 1967).

Anderson, Gordon K., "Old Nobles and *Noblesse d'Empire*, 1814–1830: in Search of a Conservative Interest in Post-revolutionary France," *French History*, 8 (1994) 149–66.

Anderson, Margaret Lavinia, "The Kulturkampf and the Course of German History," *Central European History*, 19 (1986) 82–115.

Andics, Erzsébet, "Die Konterrevolutionäre Tätigkeit der Ungarischen Konservativen Aristokratie in Siebenbürgen im Jahre 1848," *Annales Universitatis Scientiarum Budapestienensis, Sectio Historica*, 20 (1980) 51–64.

Andrew, Donna T., "The Code of Honour and its Critics: the Opposition to Dueling in England, 1700–1850," *Social History*, 5 (1980) 409–34.

Armstrong, John A., "Acculturation to the Russian Bureaucratic Elite: the Case of the Baltic Germans," *Journal of Baltic Studies*, 15 (1984) 119–29.

Arnstein, Walter L. (1975a) "The Myth of the Triumphant Victorian Middle Class," *The Historian*, 37 (1975) 205–21.

Arnstein, Walter L. (1975b) "The Survival of the Victorian Aristocracy," in F. C. Jaher (ed.), *The Rich, the Well Born, and the Powerful* (Secaucus, NJ: Citadel Press, 1975), pp. 203–57.

Aron, Raymond, "Social Structure and the Ruling Class," *British Journal of Sociology*, 1 (1950) 1–16 and 126–43.

Aron, Raymond, "The Revolt of the Masses," *Partisan Review*, 55 (1988) 359–70.

Aronsson, Peter, "Swedish Rural Society and Political Culture," *Rural History*, 3 (1992) 41–57.

Asch, Ronald G., *Nobilities in Transition, 1550–1700: Courtiers and Rebels in Britain and Europe* (London: Edward Arnold, 2003).

Aslet, Clive, *The Last Country Houses* (New Haven, CT: Yale University Press, 1982).

Augustine, Dolores L., *Patricians and Parvenus: Wealth and High Society in Wilhelmine Germany* (Oxford: Berg, 1994).

Augustine, Dolores L., "Review," *American Historical Review*, 109 (2004) 1328.

Bailey, Suzanne et al., *A Brush with Grandeur: Philip Alexis de László (1869–1937)* (London: Paul Holberton Press, 2004).

Bairasauskaite, Tamara, "1817 Metu Vilniaus Gubernijos Bajoru Seimelis," *Lietuvos Istorijos Metrastis* (1998) 48–73.

Banac, Ivo and Paul Bushkovitch (eds.), *The Nobility in Russia and Eastern Europe* (New Haven, CT: Yale Concilium, 1983).

Bánffy, Count Miklós, *The Writing on the Wall: The Transylvanian Trilogy*, 3 vols (London: Arcadia Books, [1934, 1937, 1940] 1999, 2000, 2001).

Bánffy, Count Miklós, *The Phoenix Land: The Memoirs of Count Miklós Bánffy* (London: Arcadia Books, 2003).

Bankowitz, Philip C. F., "Maxime Weygand and the Fall of France," *Journal of Modern History*, 31 (1959) 225–47.

Banti, Alberto Mario, "Elites Agrarie e Organizzazione Delgi Interessi in Prussia e in Val Padana 1880–1914," *Annali dell'Instituto Storico Italo-Germanico in Trento*, 14 (1988) 413–60.

Baquer, Miguel Alonso, "La Selección de la Élite Militar Española en el Siglo XIX," *Revista de Historia Militar*, 24 (1980) 105–35.

Baranowski, Shelley, "Continuity and Contingency: Agrarian Elites, Conservative Institutions and East Elbia in Modern German History," *Social History*, 12 (1987) 285–308.

Baranowski, Shelley, "Convergence on the Right," in Larry Eugene Jones and James Retallack (eds.), *Between Reform, Reaction, and Resistance* (Oxford: Berg, 1993) pp. 407–32.

Baranowski, Shelley, *The Sanctity of Rural Life: Nobility, Protestantism and Nazism in Weimar Prussia* (Oxford: Oxford University Press, 1995).

Baranowski, Shelley (1996a) "Conservative Elite Anti-Semitism from the Weimar Republic to the Third Reich," *German Studies Review*, 19 (1996) 525–37.

Baranowski, Shelley (1996b) "East Elbian Landed Elites and Germany's Turn to Fascism: the *Sonderweg* Controversy Revisisted," *European History Quarterly*, 26 (1996) 209–40.

Bartillat, Christian de, *Histoire de la Noblesse Française de 1789 à Nos Jours*, vol. 2: *Les Nobles du Second Empire à la fin du XXe Siècle* (Paris: Albin Michel, 1991).

Batcheller, Tryphosa Bates, *Italian Castles and Country Seats* (London: Longmans, 1911).

Bateman, John, *The Great Landowners of Great Britain and Ireland*, ed. David Spring (Leicester: Leicester University Press, [1883] 1971).

Bauerkämper, Arnd, "Der Verlorene Antifaschismus," *Zeitschrift für Geschichtswissenschaft*, 42 (1994) 623–34.

Beard, Madeleine, *Acres and Heirlooms: The Survival of Britain's Historic Estates* (New York: Routledge, 1989).

Becker, Seymour, *Nobility and Privilege in Late Imperial Russia* (Dekalb, IL: Northern Illinois University Press, 1985).

Beckett, J. V., *The Aristocracy in England, 1660–1914* (Oxford: Basil Blackwell, 1986).

Beckett, John V., "The Aristocratic Contribution to Economic Development in Nineteenth-Century England," in *Les Noblesses Européennes au XIXe Siècle, Collection de L'École Française de Rome 107* (Milan and Rome: Università di Milano and École Française de Rome, 1988) pp. 281–96.

Beckett, John, *The Rise and Fall of the Grenvilles* (Manchester: Manchester University Press, 1994).

Beekler, Gerhard A. M. and Hugo de Schepper, "The First Chamber in the Netherlands, 1815–1848," in H. W. Blom, W. P. Blockmans, and H. de Schepper (eds.), *Bicameralism: Tweekamerstelset Vroeger En Nu* (Gravenhage: SUK, 1992) pp. 279–89.

Beevor, Antony and Artemis Cooper, *Paris after the Liberation, 1944–1949* (London: Penguin, rev. edn., 2004).

Beloff, Max, "Russia," in A. Goodwin (ed.), *The European Nobility in the Eighteenth Century* (London: Adam and Charles, 1953) pp. 172–89.

Ben-Ami, Shlomo, *Fascism from Above* (Oxford: Oxford University Press, 1983).

Bence-Jones, Mark, *Twilight of the Ascendancy* (London: Constable, 1987).

Bence-Jones, Mark and Hugh Montgomery-Massingberd, *The British Aristocracy* (London: Constable, 1979).

Benckendorff, Count Constantine, *Half a Life* (London: Richards Press, 1954).

Berdahl, Robert M., *The Politics of the Prussian Nobility: The Development of a Conservative Ideology, 1770–1848* (Princeton, NJ: Princeton University Press, 1988).

Berend, Ivan T., *Central and Eastern Europe, 1944–1993* (Cambridge: Cambridge University Press, 1996).

Berend, Ivan T., *Decades of Crisis: Central and Eastern Europe before World War II* (Berkeley, CA: University of California Press, 1998).

Berend, Ivan T., *History Derailed: Central and Eastern Europe in the Long Nineteenth Century* (Berkeley, CA: University of California Press, 2003).

Beresford, Philip, *The Book of the British Rich* (New York: St. Martin's Press, 1990).

Berger, Suzanne, *Peasants against Politics: Rural Organization in Brittany, 1911–1967* (Cambridge, MA: Harvard University Press, 1972).

Berghoff, Hartmut, "Aristokratisierung des Bürgertums?," *Vierteljahrschrift für Sozial und Wirtschaftsgeschichte*, 81 (1994) 153–5.

Berghoff, Hartmut, "Adel und Industrielkapitalismus im Deutschen Kaiserreich," in Heinz Reif (ed.), *Adel und Bürgertum in Deutschland*, vol. I (Berlin: Akademie Verlag, 2000) pp. 233–71.

Berkis, Alexander V., *The History of the Duchy of Courland (1561–1795)* (Towson, MD: Paul M. Harrod, 1969).

Berlin, Isaiah, *Mr. Churchill in 1940* (Boston, MA: Houghton Mifflin, 1949).

Bertaud, Jean-Paul, "Napoleon's Officers," *Past & Present*, 112 (1986) 91–111.

Best, Geoffrey, *Churchill* (New York: Hambeldon and London, 2001).

Best, Heinrich, "Elite Structure and Regime (Dis)continuity in Germany, 1867–1933: the Case of Parliamentary Leadership Groups," *German History*, 8 (1990) 1–27.

Best, Heinrich and Maurizio Cotta, *Parliamentary Representatives in Europe, 1848–2000: Legislative Recruitment and Careers in Eleven European Countries* (Oxford: Oxford University Press, 2000).

Best, Heinrich and Daniel Gaxie, "Detours to Modernity: Long-Term Trends of Parliamentary Recruitment in Republican France, 1848–1999," in H. Best and M. Cotta (eds.), *Parliamentary Representatives in Europe, 1848–2000* (Oxford: Oxford University Press, 2000) pp. 88–137.

Best, Heinrich, Christopher Hausmann, and Karl Schmitt, "Challenges, Failures, and Final Success: the Winding Path of German Parliamentary Leadership Groups towards a Structurally Integrated Elite, 1848–1999," in H. Best and M. Cotta (eds.), *Parliamentary Representatives in Europe, 1848–2000* (Oxford: Oxford University Press, 2000) pp. 138–95.

Bilmanis, Alfred, *A History of Latvia* (Princeton, NJ: Princeton University Press, 1951).

Birke, Adolf M. and Lothar Kettenacker (eds.), *Bürgertum, Adel und Monarchie* (Munich: K. G. Saur, 1989).

Birmingham, David, *A Concise History of Portugal*, 2nd edn. (Cambridge: Cambridge University Press, 2003).

Biskupski, M. B., "A Prosopographical Analysis of the Polish Naval Elite, 1918–1945," *Journal of Slavic Military Studies*, 12 (1999) 166–79.

Blackbourn, David and Geoff Eley, *The Peculiarities of German History: Bourgeois Society and Politics in Nineteenth-Century Germany* (Oxford: Oxford University Press, 1984).

Blinkhorn, Martin, "Land and Power in Arcadia: Navarre in the Early Twentieth Century," in Ralph Gibson and Martin Blinkorn, *Landownership and Power in Modern Europe* (London: HarperCollins, 1991) pp. 216–34.

Blok, L., "Van Een Wettelijke Fictie tot Eene Waarheid," *Tijdschrift voor Geschiedenis*, 92 (1979) 391–412.

Blom, H. W., W. P. Blockmans, and H. de Schepper (eds.), *Bicameralism: Tweekamerstelsel Vroeger En Nu* (Gravenhage: SUK, 1992).

Blum, Jerome, *Noble Landowners and Agriculture in Austria, 1815–1848* (Baltimore, MD: The Johns Hopkins University Press, 1948).

Blum, Jerome, "Russia," in David Spring (ed.), *European Landed Elites in the Nineteenth Century* (Baltimore, MD: The Johns Hopkins University Press, 1977) pp. 68–97.

Blum, Jerome, *The End of the Old Order in Rural Europe* (Princeton, NJ: Princeton University Press, 1978).

Boogman, J. C., "Background and General Tendencies of the Foreign Policies of the Netherlands and Belgium in the Middle of the 19th Century," *Acta Historiae Neerlandica*, 1 (1966) 132–58.

Boswell, A. Bruce, "Poland," in A. Goodwin (ed.), *The European Nobility in the Eighteenth Century* (London: Adam and Charles, 1953) pp. 154–71.

Botticelli, Peter, "Rolls–Royce," *The American Scholar*, 66 (1997) 501–12.

Jacques-Oliver Boudon, "L'épiscopat français à l'époque condordataire (1802–1905): Origins, formation, nomonation" (Paris, 1996) pp. 56–8, cited in Plamper.

Boulton, D'Arcy Jonathan Dacre, "A Fair Field Full of Folk: the Study of the Nobilities of Latin Europe," *Historically Speaking* (November 2002) 5–7.

Bourdieu, Pierre, *Distinction: A Social Critique of the Judgement of Taste* (Cambridge, MA: Harvard University Press, 1984).

Bourne, J. M., "The Decline and Fall of the British Aristocracy," *Twentieth Century British History*, 2 (1991) 380–6.

Brakensiek, Stefan, "Agrarian Individualism in North-Western Germany, 1770–1870," *German History*, 12 (1994) 137–79.

Bramsted, Ernest K., *Aristocracy and the Middle-Classes in Germany: Social Types in German Literature, 1830–1900*, rev. edn. (Chicago, IL: University of Chicago Press, 1964).

Bratvogel, Friedrich W., "Landadel und Ländliches Bürgertum: Mecklenburg-Strelitz und Oberschwaben, 1750–1850," *Geschichte und Gesellschaft*, 25 (1999) 404–28.

Brent, Richard, *Liberal Anglican Politics: Whiggery, Religion and Reform, 1830–1841* (Oxford: Oxford University Press, 1987).

Brett, C. E. B., *Buildings of County Armagh* (Belfast: Ulster Architectual Heritage Society, 1999).

Brewer, John, *The Pleasures of the Imagination* (London: HarperCollins, 1997).

Brizzi, Gian Paolo, "Aux Origines du Systeme de Merite," *Paedagogica Historica*, 30 (1994) 249–65.

Brombert, Beth Archer, *Cristina: Portrait of a Princess* (New York: Alfred A. Knopf, 1977).

Brose, Eric Dorn, *The Kaiser's Army: The Politics of Military Technology in Germany during the Machine Age, 1870–1918* (Oxford: Oxford University Press, 2001).

Brown, David, "Equipoise and the Myth of an Open Elite: New Men of Wealth and the Purchase of Land in the Equipoise Decades, 1850–1869," in Martin Hewitt (ed.), *An Age of Equipoise?* (Aldershot: Ashgate, 2000) pp. 122–54.

Brown, Michael Barratt, "Away with All the Great Arches," *New Left Review*, 167 (1988) 22–51.

Burch, Martin and Michael Moran, "The Changing British Political Elite, 1945–1983," *Parliamentary Affairs*, 38 (1985) 1–15.

Burdiel, Isabel, "Myths of Failure, Myths of Success: New Perspectives on Nineteenth-Century Spanish Liberalism," *Journal of Modern History*, 70 (1998) 892–912.

Burgos, Manuel Espadas, "The Spanish Army During the Crisis of the Old Régime," in Raphael Bañón Martínez and Thomas M. Barker (eds.), *Armed Forces and Society in Spain Past and Present* (New York: Columbia University Press, 1988) pp. 81–103.

Burke's Peerage and Baronetage (London: Burke's Peerage Ltd., various editions).

Buruma, Ian, *Voltaire's Coconuts or Anglomania in Europe* (London: Weidenfeld and Nicolson, 1999).

Bush, M. L., *Noble Privilege* (Manchester: Manchester University Press, 1983).

Bush, M. L., *The English Aristocracy: A Comparative Synthesis* (Manchester: Manchester University Press, 1984).

Bush, M. L., *Rich Noble, Poor Noble* (Manchester: Manchester University Press, 1988).

Bush, M. L. (ed.), *Social Orders and Social Classes in Europe since 1500* (London: Longman, 1992).

Butler, R., "Historical Dimensions of the Comédie Humaine – Bourgeoisie and Aristocracy under the Revolution and Empire," *European Studies Review*, 5 (1975) 147–70.

Cahill, Kevin, *Who Owns Britain* (Edinburgh: Canongate, 2001).

Callander, Robin Fraser, *A Pattern of Landownership in Scotland* (Finzean: Haughend Publications, 1987).

Campbell, John C., "Eighteen Forty-Eight in the Rumanian Principalities," *Journal of Central European Affairs*, 8 (1948) 181–90.

Camplin, Jamie, *The Rise of the Plutocrats: Wealth and Power in Edwardian England* (London: Constable, 1978).

Canciullo, Giovanna, "La Nobilita Siciliana tra Rivolte e Restaurazione," *Studi Storici*, 37 (1996) 629–54.

Cannadine, David, "Aristocratic Indebtedness in the Nineteenth Century: the Case Reopened," *Economic History Review*, 30 (1977) 624–50.

Cannadine, David (ed.), *Patricians, Power and Politics in Nineteenth-century Towns* (New York: St. Martin's Press, 1982).

Cannadine, David, *The Decline and Fall of the British Aristocracy* (New Haven, CT: Yale University Press, 1990).

Cannadine, David, *Aspects of Aristocracy: Grandeur and Decline in Modern Britain* (New Haven, CT: Yale University Press, 1994).

Cannadine, David, *Ornamentalism: How the British Saw their Empire* (New York: Oxford University Press, 2001).

Capra, Carlo, "Nobili, Notabili, Elites: Dal 'Modello' Francese al caso Italiano," *Quaderni Storici*, 13 (1978) 12–42.

Cardigan, Countess of, *My Recollections* (New York: John Lane, 1909).

Cardoza, Anthony L., *Agrarian Elites and Italian Fascism* (Princeton, NJ: Princeton University Press, 1982).

Cardoza, Anthony L., "The Enduring Power of Aristocracy: Ennoblement in Liberal Italy, 1861–1914," in *Les Noblesses Européennes au XIXᵉ Siècle, Collection de L'École Française de Rome 107* (Milan and Rome: Università di Milano and École Française de Rome, 1988) pp. 595–605.

Cardoza, Anthony L., "Commercial Agriculture and the Crisis of Landed Power: Bologna, 1880–1930," in Ralph Gibson and Martin Blinkorn, *Landownership and Power in Modern Europe* (London: HarperCollins, 1991) pp. 181–98.

Cardoza, Anthony L., "The Long Goodbye: the Landed Aristocracy in North-Western Italy, 1880–1930," *European History Quarterly*, 23 (1993) 323–58.

Cardoza, Anthony L., *Aristocrats in Bourgeois Italy: The Piedmontese Nobility, 1861–1930* (Cambridge: Cambridge University Press, 2002).

Carlson, Sten, "The Dissolution of the Swedish Estates, 1700–1865," *Journal of European Economic History*, 1 (1972) 574–624.

Carmona Pidal, Juan, "Las Estrategias Economicas de la Vieja Arsitocracia Española y el Cambio Agrario en el Siglo XIX," *Revista de Historia Económica*, 13 (1995) 63–88.

Carr, Raymond, "Spain," in A. Goodwin (ed.), *The European Nobility in the Eighteenth Century* (London: Adam and Charles, 1953) pp. 43–59.

Carr, Raymond, *English Fox Hunting: A History* (London: Weidenfeld and Nicolson, 1976).

Carsten, Francis L., *A History of the Prussian Junkers* (Aldershot: Scolar Press, 1989).

Carsten, Francis L., "Der Preussische Adel und Seine Stellung in Staat und Gesellschaft bis 1945," in Hans-Ulrich Wehler (ed.), *Europäischer Adel, 1750–1950* (Göttingen: Vandenhoeck & Ruprecht, 1990) pp. 112–25.

Castellane, Marquis de, *Men and Things of My Time* (London: Chatto & Windus, 1911).

Cazacu, Matei, "Familles de la Noblesse Roumaine au Service de la Russie XVe–XIXe Siècles," *Cahiers du Monde Russe et Soviétique*, 34 (1993) 211–26.

Cecil, Lamar, "The Creation of Nobles in Prussia 1871–1918," *American Historical Review*, 75 (1970) 757–95.

Cecil, Lamar, *The German Diplomatic Service, 1871–1914* (Princeton, NJ: Princeton University Press, 1976).

Cenarro, Angela, "Elite, Party, Church, Pillars of the Francoist 'New State' in Aragon, 1936–1945," *European History Quarterly*, 28 (1998) 461–86.

Ceva, Lucio, "Il Problema dell'Alto Comando Militare in Piemonte durante la Prima Guerra d'Indipendenza," *Risorgimento*, 37 (1985) 143–83.

Channon, Sir Henry, *Chips: The Diaries*, ed. Robert Rhodes James (London: Penguin, 1984).

Charle, Christophe, "The Present State of Research on the Social History of Elites and the Bourgeoisie," *Contemporary European History*, 1 (1992) 99–112.

Chaussinand-Nogaret, Guy, *The French Nobility in the Eighteenth Century* (Cambridge: Cambridge University Press, 1985).

Chaussinand-Nogaret, G., J. M. Constant, C. Durandin, and A. Jouanna, *Histoire des Élites en France du XVIe au XXe Siècle* (Paris: Tallandier, 1991).

Cheschebec, Roxana Lucia, "The Unholy Marriage of Feminism and Nationalism in Interwar Romania: the Discourse of Princess Alexandrina Cantacuzino," www.wome.it/cyberarchive/files/chesbebec.htm.

Christiannsen, Palle Ove, *A Manorial World: Lord, Peasants and Cultural Distinctions on a Danish Estate, 1750–1980* (Oslo: Scandinavian University Press, 1996).

Churchill, Randolph S., *Winston S. Churchill, Youth, 1874–1900*, vol. I (Boston, MA: Houghton Mifflin, 1966).

Churchill, Winston S., *My Early Life* (New York: Simon and Schuster, [1930] 1996).

Ciano, Count Galeazzo, *Diary, 1937–1943* (London: Phoenix Press, 2002).

Ciuffetti, Augusto, "La Nobilta Dall 'Ancien Regime' all'eta Contemporanea: Appunti sulle Dinamiche Familiari in Area Umbra," *Risorgimento*, 50 (1998) 5–24.

Clark, Kenneth, *Another Part of the Wood* (London: John Murray, 1974).

Clark, Samuel, "Nobility, Bourgeoisie and the Industrial Revolution in Belgium," *Past & Present*, 105 (1984) 140–75.

Clark, Samuel, *State and Status: The Rise of the State and Aristocratic Power in Western Europe* (Montreal: McGill-Queen's University Press, 1995).

Cleary, Joe, "Postcolonial Ireland," in Kevin Kenny (ed.), *Ireland and the British Empire* (Oxford: Oxford University Press, 2004) pp. 251–88.

Clemens, Gabriele B., "Ancestors, Castles, Tradition: the German and Italian Nobility and the Discovery of the Middle Ages in the Nineteenth Century," *Journal of Modern Italian Studies*, 8 (2003) 1–15.

Clemenson, Heather A., *English Country Houses and Landed Estates* (New York: St. Martin's Press, 1982).

Clermont-Tonnerre, Elizabeth, Duchess de, *Years of Plenty* (London: Jonathan Cape, 1931).

Cohen, Abner, *Two-Dimensional Man* (London: Routledge & Kegan Paul, 1974).

Colley, Linda, *Britons: Forging the Nation, 1707–1837* (New Haven, CT: Yale University Press, 1992).

Colville, John, *The Fringes of Power: 10 Downing Street Diaries, 1939–1955* (New York: W. W. Norton, 1985).

Confino, Michael, "A Propos de la Notion de Service dans la Noblesse Russe aux XVIIIᵉ et XIXᵉ Siècles," *Cahiers du Monde Russe et Soviétique*, 34 (1993) 47–58.

Coogan, John W., "Review," *Albion*, 36 (2004) 367.

Cooper, J. P., "Patterns of Inheritance and Settlement by Great Landowners from the Fifteenth to the Eighteenth Centuries," in Jack Goody et al. (eds.), *Family and Inheritance: Rural Society in Western Europe, 1200–1800* (Cambridge: Cambridge University Press, 1976) pp. 192–327.

Corner, Paul, *Fascism in Ferrara, 1915–1925* (Oxford: Oxford University Press 1975).

Cornwell, John, *Hitler's Pope* (New York: Viking, 1999).

Cotta, Maurizio, Alfio Mastropaolo, and Luca Verzichelli, "Parliamentary Elite Transformation along the Discontinuous Road to Democratization: Italy, 1861–1999," in H. Best and M. Cotta (eds.), *Parliamentary Representatives in Europe, 1848–2000* (Oxford: Oxford University Press, 2000) pp. 226–69.

Country Life (London, various editions).

Cox, Marvin R., "Tocqueville's Bourgeois Revolution," *Historical Reflections*, 19 (1993) 279–307.

Cragoe, Matthew, *An Anglican Aristocracy: The Moral Economy of the Landed Estate in Carmarthenshire, 1832–1895* (Oxford: Oxford University Press, 1996).

Craig, Gordon A., *The Politics of the Prussian Army, 1640–1946* (Oxford: Oxford University Press, 1955).

Cromwell, Valerie, "Peers and Personal Network," in H. W. Blom, W. P. Blockmans, and H. de Schepper (eds.), *Bicameralism: Tweekamerstelset Vroeger En Nu* (Gravenhage: SUK, 1992) pp. 383–93.

Cruz, Jesús (1996a) "An Ambivalent Revolution: the Public and the Private in the Construction of Liberal Spain," *Journal of Social History*, 30 (1996) 5–27.

Cruz, Jesus (1996b) *Gentlemen, Bourgeois, and Revolutionaries: Political Change and Cultural Persistence among the Spanish Dominant Groups, 1750–1850* (Cambridge: Cambridge University Press, 1996).

Cummings, A. J. G., "The Business Affairs of an Eighteenth Century Lowland Laird: Sir Archibald Grant of Monymusk, 1696–1778," in T. M. Devine (ed.), *Scottish Elites* (Edinburgh: John Donald, 1994) pp. 43–61.

Czudnowski, Moshe M. (ed.), *Does Who Governs Matter?* (DeKalb, IL: Northern Illinois University Press, 1982).

Daalder, Hans (1966a) "The Netherlands," in Robert A. Dahl (ed.), *Political Oppositions in Western Democracies* (New Haven, CT: Yale University Press, 1966) pp. 188–236.

Daalder, Hans (1966b) "Parties, Elites, and Political Developments in Western Europe," in Joseph LaPalombara and Myron Weiner (eds.), *Politi-*

cal Parties and Political Development (Princeton, NJ: Princeton University Press, 1966) pp. 43–77.

Daalder, Hans and Joop Th. J. van den Berg, "Members of the Dutch Lower House: Pluralism and Democratization, 1848–1967," in Moshe M. Czudnowski (ed.), *Does Who Governs Matter?* (DeKalb, IL: Northern Illinois University Press, 1982) pp. 214–42.

Dal Lago, Enrico, "The City as Social Display: Landed Elites and Urban Images in Charleston and Palermo," *Journal of Historical Sociology*, 14 (2001) 374–96.

Dallas, Gregor, *The Imperfect Peasant Economy: The Loire Country, 1800–1914* (Cambridge: Cambridge University Press, 1982).

Danhofer, W., "Das Wiederaufleben des Rittertums in der Romantik," *Blätter für Heimatkunde*, 37 (1963) 62–6.

Daumard, Adeline, "Wealth and Affluence in France since the Beginning of the Nineteenth Century," in W. D. Rubinstein (ed.), *Wealth and the Wealthy in the Modern World* (New York: St. Martin's Press, 1980) pp. 90–121.

Daumard, Adeline, "Noblesse et Aristocratie en France au XIXᵉ Siècle," in *Les Noblesses Européennes au XIXᵉ Siècle, Collection de L'École Française de Rome 107* (Milan and Rome: Università di Milano and École Française de Rome, 1988) pp. 81–104.

Davis, John A., *Conflict and Control: Law and Order in Nineteenth-Century Italy* (London: Macmillan, 1988).

Davis, John A., "Remapping Italy's Path to the Twentieth Century," *Journal of Modern History*, 66 (1994) 291–320.

Davis, John A. (ed.), *Italy in the Nineteenth Century, 1796–1900* (Oxford: Oxford University Press, 2000).

Davis, Mike, *Late Victorian Holocausts* (New York: Verso, 2001).

Davis, Richard W., "'We Are All Americans Now!' Anglo-American Marriages in the Later Nineteenth Century," *Proceedings of the American Philosophical Society*, 135 (1991) 140–99.

D'Azeglio, Marchese Massimo, *Things I Remember* (Oxford: Oxford University Press, 1966).

Deák, István, "Reform Triumphant: Hungary's Self-Assertion during the Springtime of the Peoples (March–April 1848)," in Jaroslav Pelenski (ed.), *The American and European Revolutions, 1776–1848: Sociopolitical and Ideological Aspects* (Iowa City: University of Iowa Press, 1976) pp. 320–61.

Deák, István, *Beyond Nationalism: A Social and Political History of the Habsburg Officer Corps, 1848–1918* (Oxford: Oxford University Press, 1990).

De Courcy, Anne, *Society's Queen: The Life of Edith, Marchioness of Londonderry* (London: Phoenix, 2004).

De Grand, Alexander, "Cracks in the Façade: the Failure of Fascist Totalitarianism in Italy 1935–39," *European History Quarterly*, 21 (1991) 515–35.

Delfosse, Pascale, "La Terre contra l'Etat? Pouvoir d'Etat et Resistances traditionelles en Belgique (1851–1929), *Mouvement Social*, 166 (1994) 53–90.

Delille, Gérard (ed.), *Les Noblesses Européennes au XIXᵉ Siècle, Collection deL'École Française de Rome 107* (Milan and Rome: Università di Milano and École Française de Rome, 1988).

Deme, Laszlo, "From Nation to Class: the Changing Social Role of the Hungarian Nobility," *International Journal of Politics*, (Summer 1988) 568–84.

De Meneses, Filipe Ribeiro, "The Origins and Nature of Authoritarian Rule in Portugal, 1919–1945," *Contemporary European History*, 11 (2002) 153–63.

DeNora, Tia, "Musical Patronage and Social Change in Beethoven's Vienna," *American Journal of Sociology*, 97 (1991) 310–46.

Desan Suzanne, "'War between Brothers and Sisters'," *French Historical Studies*, 20 (1997) 597–634.

Deutsch, Phyllis, "Moral Trespass in Georgian London: Gaming, Gender, and Electoral Politics in the Age of George III," *Historical Journal*, 39 (1996) 637–56.

Devine, T. M., *Scottish Elites* (Edinburgh: John Donald, 1994).

Devine, T. M., *The Scottish Nation, 1700–2000* (New York: Penguin, 2001).

Devonshire, Andrew, Duke of, *Accidents of Fortune* (Norwich: Michael Russell, 2004).

Dewald, Jonathan, *The European Nobility, 1400–1800* (Cambridge: Cambridge University Press, 1996).

Dipper, Christoph, "La Noblesse Allemande à L'Époque de la Bourgeoisie," in *Les Noblesses Européennes au XIXe Siècle, Collection de L'École Française de Rome 107* (Milan and Rome: Università di Milano and École Française de Rome, 1988) pp. 165–97.

Dissow, Joachim von, *Adel im Übergang* (Stuttgart: W. Kohlhammer Verlag, 1961).

Dodgshon, Robert A., *From Chiefs to Landlords: Social and Economic Change in the Western Highlands and Islands, c.1493–1820* (Edinburgh: Edinburgh University Press, 1998).

Dogan, Mattei, "Political Ascent in a Class Society: French Deputies, 1870–1958," in Dwaine Marvick (ed.), *Political Decision-Makers* (Glencoe: The Free Press, 1961) pp. 57–90.

Donati, Claudio, "The Italian Nobilities in the Seventeenth and Eighteenth Centuries," in H. M. Scott (ed.), *The European Nobilities in the Seventeenth and Eighteenth Centuries*, 2 vols. (New York: Longman, 1995) vol. I, pp. 237–68.

Dönhoff, Countess Marion, *Before the Storm: Memories of My Youth in Old Prussia* (New York: Alfred A. Knopf, 1990).

Dooley, Brendan, "Crisis and Survival in Eighteenth-Century Italy: the Venetian Patriciate Strikes Back," *Journal of Social History*, 20 (1986) 323–34.

Dooley, Terence, *The Decline of the Big House in Ireland: A Study of Irish Landed Families, 1860–1960* (Dublin: Wolfhound Press, 2001).

Dooley, Terence, *A Future for Irish Historic Houses?* (Dublin: Irish Georgian Society, 2003).

Dore, Ronald P., "Making Sense of History," *Archives Européenes de Sociologie*, 10 (1969) 295–305.

Dowden, M. J., "Land and Industry: Sir Charles Morgan, Samuel Homfray and the Tredegar Lease of 1800," *The National Library of Wales Journal*, 28 (1993) 23–37.

Drescher, Seymour, "Who Needs *Ancienneté*? Tocqueville on Aristocracy and Modernity," *History of Political Thought*, 24 (2003) 624–46.

Dubabin, J. P. D., "Expectations of the New County Councils and their Realization," *The Historical Journal*, 8 (1965) 353–79.

Duindam, Jeron, *Myths of Power: Norbert Elias and the Early Modern European Court* (Amsterdam: Amsterdam University Press, 1996).

Duma, Jean, "A Propos des Élites: Approche Historiographique," *Cahiers d'Histoire: Revue d'Histoire Critique*, 73 (1998) 7–17.

Eastwood, David, *Government and Community in the English Provinces, 1700–1870* (London: Macmillan, 1997).

Eckardt, Hans Wilhelm, *Herrschaftliche Jagd Bäuerliche not und Bürgerliche Kritik* (Göttingen: Vandenhoech & Ruprecht, 1976).

Eddie, Scott M., "The Changing Pattern of Landownership in Hungary, 1867–1914," *Economic History Review*, 20 (1967) 293–310.

Eddie, Scott M., "The Social Distribution of Landed Wealth in Hungary ca. 1910," *Research in Economic History*, Supplement 5, Part A, (1989) 219–49.

Eddie, Scott M., "Junkers and Magnates: the Social Distribution of Landed Wealth in Pomerania and Transdanubia, 1893," *Österreichische Osthefte*, 36 (1994) 109–31.

Edmondson, C. Earl, *The Heimwehr and Austrian Politics, 1918–1936* (Athens, GA: University of Georgia Press, 1978).

Egremont, Lord, *Wyndham and Children First* (London: Macmillan, 1968).

Eidelberg, Philip Gabriel, *The Great Rumanian Peasant Revolt of 1907* (Leiden: E. J. Brill, 1974).

Eley, Geoff, *From Unification to Nazism* (Boston, MA: Allen & Unwin, 1986).

Eliassen, Kjell A. and Mogens N. Pedersen, "Professionalization of Legislatures: Long-Term Change in Political Recruitment in Denmark and Norway," *Comparative Studies in Society and History*, 20 (1978) 286–318.

Ellenberger, Nancy W., "The Transformation of London 'Society' at the End of Victoria's Reign," *Albion*, 22 (1990) 633–53.

Emmons, Terence, "The Russian Nobility and Party Politics before the Revolution," in Ivo Banac and Paul Bushkovitch (eds.), *The Nobility in Russia and Eastern Europe* (New Haven, CT: Yale Concilium, 1983) pp. 177–220.

English, Barbara, *The Great Landowners of East Yorkshire, 1530–1910* (London: Harvester, 1990).

Erauw, Willem, "Musica Morale, Miracolo Musicale," *Bulletin de L'institute Historique Belge de Rome*, 66 (1996) 171–99.

Erickson, John, *The Soviet High Command: A Military-Political History, 1918–1941* (London: Frank Cass, 2001).

Erös, J., "Hungary," in S. J. Woolf (ed.), *Fascism in Europe* (London: Methuen, 1981) pp. 117–50.

Esterházy, Count Péter, *Celestial Harmonies* (New York: HarperCollins, 2004).

Evans, Eric J., "Landownership and the Exercise of Power in an Industrializing Society: Lancashire and Cheshire in the Nineteenth Century," in Ralph Gibson and Martin Blinkorn, *Landownership and Power in Modern Europe* (London: HarperCollins, 1991) pp. 145–63.

Evans, Ifor L., *The Agrarian Revolution in Roumania* (Cambridge: Cambridge University Press, 1924).

Evans, Richard J., "The Myth of Germany's Missing Revolution," *New Left Review*, 149 (1985) 67–94.

Farquharson, John, "Land Reform in the British Zone, 1945–1947," *German History*, 6 (1988) 34–56.

Farrelly, Robert James, "The Large Landowners of England and Wales, 1870–1939: An Elite in Transition," unpublished Ph.D. dissertation, University of Toronto, 1980.

Fernández González, A., "Los Grupos de Poder Local en Galicia, 1750–1850," *Noticiario de Historia Agraria*, 5 (1995) 129–53.

Ferraboschi, Alberto, "Le 'Regole' della Rapresentanza: L'elite Amministrativa a Reggio Emilia," *Rassegna Storica del Risorgimento*, 84 (1997) 435–60.

Fest, Joachim, *Plotting Hitler's Death* (London: Weidenfeld and Nicolson, 1996).

Figes, Orlando, *Natasha's Dance: A Cultural History of Russia* (New York: Henry Holt, 2002).

Finer, S. E., *The Man on Horseback* (London: Pall Mall Press, 1962).

Finlay, Mary, "New Sources, New Theses, and New Organizations in the New Germany," *Agricultural History*, 75 (2001) 279–307.

Fitzsimmons, Michael P., "New Light on the Aristocratic Reaction in France," *French History*, 10 (1996) 418–31.

Fletcher, Allan, "The Role of Landowners, Entrepreneurs and Railways in the Urban Development of the North Wales Coast during the Nineteeth Century," *Welsh History Review*, 16 (1993) 514–41.

Fonseca, Helder Adegar, "Agrarian Elites and Economic Growth in Nineteenth-Century Portugal," *Social History*, 28 (2003) 202–26.

Forster, Robert, "The Survival of the Nobility during the French Revolution," *Past & Present*, 37 (1967) 71–86.

Forster, Robert, *The House of Saulx-Tavanes, Versailles and Burgundy, 1700–1830* (Baltimore, MD: The Johns Hopkins University Press, 1971).

Forster, Robert, "The French Revolution and the 'New' Elite, 1800–50," in Jaroslav Pelenski (ed.), *The American and European Revolutions, 1776–1848: Sociopolitical and Ideological Aspects* (Iowa City: University of Iowa Press, 1976) pp. 182–207.

Franckenstein, Baron Georg, *Facts and Features of My Life* (London: Cassell, 1939).

Frankl, P. J. L., "The Early Years of the Mombasa Club," *History of Africa*, 28 (2000) 71–81.

Fraser, Derek, "Voluntaryism and West Riding Politics in the Mid-Nineteenth Century," *Northern History*, 13 (1977) 199–231.

Freudenberger, Herman, "An Industrial Momentum Achieved in the Habsburg Monarchy," *Journal of European Economic History*, 12 (1983) 339–50.

Frevert, Ute, *Men of Honour: A Social and Cultural History of the Duel* (Cambridge: Polity Press, 1995).

Fromm, Bella, *Blood and Banquets: A Berlin Diary, 1930–38* (New York: Simon and Schuster, 1990).

Frost, Robert I., "The Nobility of Poland-Lithuania, 1569–1795," in H. M. Scott (ed.), *The European Nobilities in the Seventeenth and Eighteenth Centuries*, 2 vols. (New York: Longman, 1995) II, pp. 183–222.

Fugger von Babenhausen, Princess Nora, *The Glory of the Habsburgs* (London: George G. Harrap, 1932).

Gallagher, Tom, *Portugal* (Manchester: Manchester University Press, 1983).

Georgescu, Vlad, "The Romanian Boyars in the 18th Century," *East European Quarterly*, 7 (1973) 31–49.

Gerschenkron, Alexander, *Bread and Democracy in Germany* (Berkeley, CA: University of California Press, 1944).

Geyer, Michael, "The Past as Future: The German Officer Corps as a Profession," in Geoffrey Cocks and Konrad H. Jaravsch, *German Professions, 1800–1950* (Oxford: Oxford University Press, 1990) pp. 183–212.

Geyer, Michael, "Professionals and Junkers: German Rearmament and Politics in the Weimar Republic," in Richard Bessel and E. J. Feuchtwanger (eds.), *Social Change and Political Development in Weimar Germany* (London: Croom Helm, 1981) pp. 77–133.

Gibson, Ralph, "The French Nobility in the Nineteenth Century – Particularly in the Dordogne," in Jolyon Howorth and Philip G. Cerny (eds.), *Elites in France* (London: Frances Pinter, 1981) pp. 5–45.

Gibson, Ralph, "The Périgord: Landownership, Power and Illusion," in Ralph Gibson and Martin Blinkorn, *Landownership and Power in Modern Europe* (London: HarperCollins, 1991) pp. 79–98.

Gibson, Ralph and Martin Blinkhorn, *Landownership and Power in Modern Europe* (London: HarperCollins, 1991).

Gibson, William, "The Social Origins and Education of an Elite: The Nineteenth-Century Episcopate," *History of Education*, 20 (1991) 95–105.

Gilbert, Martin, *Winston S. Churchill: The Prophet of Truth, 1922–1939*, vol. V (Boston, MA: Houghton Mifflin, 1977).

Gilbert, Martin, *Winston S. Churchill: Never Despair, 1945–1965*, vol. VIII (Boston, MS: Houghton Mifflin, 1988).

Gillis, John R., "Aristocracy and Bureaucracy in Nineteenth-century Prussia," *Past & Present*, 41 (1968) 105–29.

Gillis, John R., *The Prussian Bureaucracy in Crisis, 1840–1860* (Stanford, CA: Stanford University Press, 1971).

Gilmour, David, *The Last Leopard: A Life of Giuseppe Tomasi di Lampedusa* (New York: Pantheon, 1988).

Girouard, Mark, *The Return to Camelot: Chivalry and the English Gentleman* (New Haven, CT: Yale University Press, 1981).

Girouard, Mark, *Life in the French Country House* (London: Cassell, 2000).

Glassman, Eagle, "Crafting a Post-Imperial Identity: Nobles and Nationality Politics in Czechoslovakia, 1918–1948," unpublished Ph.D. dissertation, Columbia University, 2000.

Godsey, William D., "The Nobility, Jewish Assimilation, and the Austro-Hungarian Foreign Service in the Late Imperial Era," *Austrian Yearbook*, 27 (1996) 155–80.

Godsey, William D. (1999a), *Aristocratic Redoubt: The Austro-Hungarian Foreign Office on the Eve of the First World War* (West Lafayette: Purdue University Press, 1999).

Godsey, William D. (1999b), "Quarterings and Kinship: the Social Composition of the Habsburg Aristocracy in the Dualist Era," *Journal of Modern History*, 71 (1999) 56–104.

Godsey, William D., "Nobles and Modernity," *German History*, 20 (2002) 504–21.

Goodrich, Amanda, *Debating England's Aristocracy in the 1790s* (London: Royal Historical Society, 2005).

Goodwin, A., *The European Nobility in the Eighteenth Century* (London: Adam and Charles, 1953).

Goujard, Philippe, "Une Révolution Agraire Manquée: L'Espagne au XIXᵉ Siècle," *Annales Historiques de la Révolution Française*, 52 (1980) 559–84.

Gowan, Peter, "The Origins of the Administrative Elite," *New Left Review*, 162 (1987) 4–34.

Graves, Keith, "'Lowther's Lambs': Rural Paternalism and Voluntary Recruitment in the First World War," *Rural History*, 4 (1993) 55–75.

Gray, Marion, "Bureaucratic Transition and Accommodation of the Aristocracy in the Prussian Reform Year of 1808," *Consortium on Revolutionary Europe: Proceedings* (1981) 86–92.

Greenaway, John R., "Parliamentary Reform and Civil Service Reform," *Parliamentary History*, 4 (1985) 157–69.

Grimaldi, Luigi Buccino, "La Legislazione Fedecommissaria Nell'Italia del Sud Dal 1806 Fino All'Unità," in *Les Noblesses Européennes au XIXᵉ Siècle, Collection de L'École Française de Rome 107* (Milan and Rome: Università di Milano and École Française de Rome, 1988) pp. 435–49.

Gross, Mirjana, "The Position of the Nobility in the Organization of the Elite in Northern Croatia," in Ivo Banac and Paul Bushkovitch (eds.), *The Nobility in Russia and Eastern Europe* (New Haven, CT: Yale Concilium, 1983) pp. 137–76.

Grubb, Alan, *The Politics of Pessimism: Albert de Broglie and Conservative Politics in the Early Third Republic* (Newark: University of Delaware Press, 1996).

Guttman, Allen, *Games and Empires: Modern Sports and Cultural Imperialism* (New York: Columbia University Press, 1994).

Guttsman, W. L., "The Changing Social Structure of the British Political Elite, 1886–1935," *British Journal of Sociology*, 2 (1951) 122–34.

Guttsman, W. L., *The British Political Elite* (New York: Basic Books, 1963).

Habakkuk, H. J., "England," in A. Goodwin (ed.), *The European Nobility in the Eighteenth Century* (London: Adam and Charles, 1953) pp. 1–21.

Habakkuk, H. J., *Marriage, Debt and the Estates System: English Landownership, 1650–1950* (Oxford: Oxford University Press, 1994).

Hagen, William W., *Ordinary Prussians: Brandenburg Junkers and Villagers, 1500–1840* (Cambridge: Cambridge University Press, 2002).

Halévy, Daniel, *The End of the Notables* (Middletown: Wesleyan University Press, [1930], 1974).

Halliday, S., "Social Mobility, Demographic Change and the Landed Elite of County Durham, 1610–1819: An Open or Shut Case?," *Northern History*, 30 (1994) 49–63.

Hamburg, G. M., "Portrait of an Elite: Russian Marshals of the Nobility, 1861–1917," *Slavic Review*, 40 (1981) 585–602.

Hamerow, Theodore S., "The Conservative Resistance to Hitler and the Fall of the Weimar Republic, 1932–34," in Larry Eugene Jones and James Retallack (eds.), *Between Reform, Reaction, and Resistance* (Oxford: Berg, 1993) pp. 433–63.

Hansen, Ernst Willi, "The Military and the Military-Political Breakdown in Germany 1918 and France 1940," in Klaus-Jürgen Müller (ed.), *The Military in Politics and Society in France and Germany in the Twentieth Century* (Oxford: Berg, 1995) pp. 89–109.

Hansen, Frantz Leander, *The Aristocratic Universe of Karen Blixen* (Brighton: Sussex Academic Press, 2003).

Harling, Philip, "Bolstering Elite Authority in the Age of Revolution," *Consortium on Revolutionary Europe: Proceedings* (1995) 86–94.

Harpe, Werner von, "Auf Einem Rittergut in Estland," *Osteuropa*, 17 (1967) 669–72.

Harper, Marjory, "Aristocratic Adventurers: British Gentlemen Emigrants on the North American Frontier, ca. 1880–1920," *Journal of the West*, 36 (1997) 41–52.

Harris, José, *Private Lives, Public Spirit: Britain, 1870–1914* (London: Penguin, 1994).

Harris, José and Pat Thane, "British and European Bankers, 1880–1914: An 'Aristocratic Bourgeoisie'?" in Pat Thane, Geoffrey Crossick, and Roderick Floud (eds.), *The Power of the Past* (Cambridge: Cambridge University Press, 1984) pp. 215–34.

Harrison, Joseph, *The Spanish Economy in the Twentieth Century* (London: Croom Helm, 1985).

Harsanyi, Doina Pasca, "Blue Blood and Ink: Romanian Aristocratic Women before and after World War I," *Women's History Review*, 5 (1996) 497–511.

Harsányi, Zsolt, "A Hungarian Magnate," *Hungarian Quarterly*, 5 (1939) 90–8.

Hartley, Anthony, "O! What a Fall was There," *The National Interest*, 35 (1994) 36–45.

Hartzell, A. E., *Titled Americans* (New York: 1915).

Havránek, Jan, "The University Professors and Students in Nineteenth-century Bohemia," in Mikuláš Teich (ed.), *Bohemia in History* (Cambridge: Cambridge University Press, 1998) pp. 215–28.

Hayne, M. B., *The French Foreign Office and the Origins of the First World War, 1898–1914* (Oxford: Oxford University Press, 1993).

Henricksson, Anders, "Minority Nationalism and the Politics of Gender: Baltic German Women in the Late Imperial Era," *Journal of Baltic Studies*, 27 (1996) 213–28.

Henshall, Nicholas, *The Myth of Absolutism: Change and Continuity in Early Modern European Monarchy* (New York: Longman, 1992).

Herr, Richard, "Spain," in David Spring (ed.), *European Landed Elites in the Nineteenth Century* (Baltimore, MD: The Johns Hopkins University Press, 1977) pp. 98–126.

Higgs, David, "Social Mobility and Hereditary Titles in France, 1814–1830," *Histoire Sociale*, 14 (1981) 29–47.

Higgs, David, *Nobles in Nineteenth-Century France: The Practice of Inegalitarianism* (Baltimore, MD: The Johns Hopkins University Press, 1987).

Higham, Robin, "The Selection, Education, and Training of British Officers, 1740–1920," in Béla K. Király and Walter Scott Dillard (eds.), *The East Central European Officer Corps, 1740s–1920s: Social Origins, Selection, Education, and Training* (New York: Columbia University Press, 1988) pp. 39–56.

Higonnet, Patrick L-.R. and Trevor B. Higonnet, "Class, Corruption, and Politics in the French Chamber of Deputies, 1846–1848," *French Historical Studies*, 5 (1967) 204–24.

Hildermeier, Manfred, "Der Russische Adel von 1700 bis 1917," in Hans-Ulrich Wehler (ed.), *Europäischer Ade,l 1750–1950* (Göttingen: Vandenhoeck & Ruprecht, 1990) pp. 166–216.

Hilton, Boyd, *The Age of Atonement* (Oxford: Oxford University Press, 1988).

Historic Houses: Conversations in Stately Homes (London: Condé Nast, 1969).

Höbelt, Lothar, "'Verfassungstreue' und 'Feudale': Die Beiden Österreichen Adelsparteien, 1861–1918," *Etudes Danubiennes*, 7 (1991) 103–14.

Höbelt, Lothar, "The Discreet Charm of the Old Regime," *Austrian History Yearbook*, 27 (1996) 289–302.

Hoberman, John, "Toward a Theory of Olympic Internationalism," *Journal of Sport History*, 22 (1995) 1–37.

Hoensch, Jörg K., *A History of Modern Hungary, 1867–1986* (London: Longman, 1984).

Hoffmann, Peter, *Stauffenberg, a Family history, 1905–1944* (Cambridge: Cambridge University Press, 1995).

Hollingsworth, T. H., "The Demography of the British Peerage," *Population Studies*, 18 supplement, (1964) 3–108.

Hoppen, K. Theodore, "Landownership and Power in Nineteenth-Century Ireland: The Decline of an Elite," in Ralph Gibson and Martin Blinkorn, *Landownership and Power in Modern Europe* (London: HarperCollins, 1991) pp. 164–80.

Horstmann, Lali, *Nothing for Tears* (London: Weidenfeld and Nicolson, 1953).

Howard, Michael, "War and the Nation State," *Daedalus*, 108 (1979) 101–10.

Howell, David, Gert von Pistohlkors, and Ellen Wiegandt, *Roots of Rural Ethnic Mobilisation: Comparative Studies on Governments and Non-Dominant Ethnic Groups in Europe, 1850–1940*, vol. VII (New York: New York University Press, 1993).

Hroch, Miroslav, "Social and Territorial Characteristics in the Composition of the Leading Groups of National Movements," in Andreas Kappler (ed.), *The Formation of National Elites, Comparatve Studies of Governments and Non-Dominant Ethnic Groups in Europe, 1850–1940*, vol. VI (New York: New York University Press, 1992) pp. 257–76.

Hryniuk, Stella, "Polish Lords and Ukranian Peasants," *Austrian History Yearbook*, 24 (1993) 119–32.

Huntington, Samuel P., *Political Order in Changing Societies* (New Haven, CT: Yale University Press, 1968).

Hutchinson, I. G. C., "The Nobility and Politics in Scotland, c. 1880–1939," in T. M. Devine (ed.), *Scottish Elites* (Edinburgh: John Donald, 1994) pp. 131–51.

Ignatieff, Michael, *The Russian Album* (London: Penguin, 1988).

Ilincioiu, Ion (ed.), *The Great Romanian Peasant Revolt of 1907* (Bucharest: Editura Academiei Romane, 1991).

Ilonszki, Gabriella, "Belated Professionalization of Parliamentary Elites: Hungary 1848–1999," in H. Best and M. Cotta (eds.), *Parliamentary Representatives in Europe, 1848–2000* (Oxford: Oxford University Press, 2000) pp. 196–225.

Ingilby, Sir Thomas, *Yorkshire's Great Houses* (Skipton: Dalesman, 2005).

Irving, Robert Grant, *Indian Summer, Lutyens, Baker and Imperial Delhi* (New Haven, CT: Yale University Press, 1981).

Jackson, Alvin, "Ireland, the Union, and the Empire, 1800–1960," in Kevin Kenny (ed.), *Ireland and the British Empire* (Oxford: Oxford University Press, 2004) pp. 123–53.

Jackson, Julian, *The Fall of France: The Nazi Invasion of 1940* (Oxford: Oxford University Press, 2003).

Jacob, Thierry, "Das Engagement des Adels der Preussischen Provinz Sachsen in der Kapitalistischen Wirtschaft, 1860–1914/18," in Heinz Reif (ed.), *Adel und Bürgertum in Deutschland* (Berlin: Akademie Verlag, 2000) pp. 273–330.

Jägerskiöld, Stig, *Mannerheim: Marshall of Finland* (London: C. Hurst, 1986).

James, Francis G., *Lords of the Ascendancy: The Irish House of Lords and Its Members, 1600–1800* (Dublin: Irish Academic Press, 1995).

Janos, Andrew C., "The Politics of Backwardness in Continental Europe, 1780–1945," *World Politics*, 41 (1989) 325–58.

Janowitz, Morris, *The Professional Soldier* (Glencoe: Free Press, 1960).

Jardin, Andre and Andre-Jean Tudesq, *Restoration and Reaction, 1815–1848* (Cambridge: Cambridge University Press, 1983).

Jarvie, Grant and Lorna Jackson, "Deer Forests, Sporting Estates and the Aristocracy," *British Society of Sports History*, www2.umist.ac.uk/sport/jarvie.html., accessed June 1, 2004.

Jenks, William Alexander, *The Austrian Electoral Reform of 1907* (New York: Columbia University Press, 1950).

Jensen, Einar, *Danish Agriculture: Its Economic Development* (Copenhagen: J. H. Schultz Forlag, 1937).

Jespersen, Knud J. V., "The Rise and Fall of the Danish Nobility, 1600–1800," in H. M. Scott (ed.), *The European Nobilities in the Seventeenth and Eighteenth Centuries*, 2 vols. (New York: Longman, 1995) II, pp. 41–70.

Johnson, Richard, "Moore, Anderson, and English Social Developments," in S. Hall et al. (eds.), *Culture, Media, Language* (London: Hutchinson, 1980) pp. 61–70.

Johnson, R. W., "The Nationalisation of English Rural Politics: Norfolk South West, 1945–1970," *Parliamentary Affairs*, 26 (1973) 8–55.

Jones, Larry Eugene, "Nazis, Conservatives and the Establishment of the Third Reich, 1932–34," *Tel Aviver Jahrbuch für Deutsche Geschichte*, 23 (1994) 41–64.

Jones, Larry Eugene and James Retallack (eds.), *Between Reform, Reaction, and Resistance: Studies in the History of German Conservatism from 1789 to 1945* (Oxford: Berg, 1993).

Jones, P. M., *Politics and Rural Society: The Southern Massif Central c. 1750–1880* (Cambridge: Cambridge University Press, 1985).

Jones, Ray, "The Social Structure of the British Diplomatic Service, 1815–1914," *Histoire Sociale*, 14 (1981) 50–66.

Jonsson, Ulf and Janken Myrdal, "Den Jordägande Aristokratin och Moderniteten I Europa under 1800 – och Början av 1900," *Historisk Tidskrift*, 4 (1997) 655–84.

Jussila, Osmo, "Finlands Steg fran Provins till Stat," *Historisk Tidskrift för Finland*, 72 (1987) 437–55.

Kabuzan, V. and Troitski S. M., "Izmeneniia v Chislennosti, Udel'nom Vese I Razmeshchenii Dvorianstva v Rossii v 1782–1858," *Istoriia SSSR*, 4 (1971) 153–69.

Kaelble, Hartmut, "Le Modele Aristocratique dans le Bourgeoisie Allemande," *Francia*, 14 (1986) 451–60.

Kahan, Alan S., *Aristocratic Liberalism: The Social Thought of Jacob Burckhardt, John Stuart Mill, and Alexis de Tocqueville* (Oxford: Oxford University Press, 1992).

Kale, Steven D., *Legitimism and the Reconstruction of French Society, 1852–1883* (Baton Rouge: Louisiana State University Press, 1992).

Kale, Steven D., "Women, Salons, and the State in the Aftermath of the French Revolution," *Journal of Women's History*, 13 (2002) 54–80.

Kale, Steven D., *French Salons: High Society and Political Sociability from the Old Regime to the Revolution of 1848* (Baltimore, MD: Johns Hopkins University Press, 2004).

Kállay, "Management of Big Estates in Hungary between 1711 and 1848," in *Etudes Historiques Hongroises* (Budapest: Akademiai Kindo, 1980) I, pp. 339–61.

Kane, Robert B., *Disobedience and Conspiracy in the German Army, 1918–1945* (Jefferson, NC: McFraland & Co., 2002).

Kann, Robert, "Aristocracy in the Eighteenth Century Habsburg Empire," *East European Quarterly*, 7 (1973) 1–13.

Kappler, Andreas, Fikret Adanir, and Alan O'Day (eds.), *The Formation of National Elites, Comparatve Studies of Governments and Non-Dominant Ethnic Groups in Europe, 1850–1940*, vol. VI (New York: New York University Press, 1992).

Katz, Robert, *The Fall of the House of Savoy* (London: George Allen and Unwin, 1972).

Kelly, James, "The Duel in Irish History," *History Ireland*, 2 (1994) 26–30.

Kelsall, Malcolm, *Literary Representations of the Irish Country House* (London: Palgrave Macmillan, 2003).

Kenez, Peter, "A Profile of the Prerevolutionary Officer Corps," *California Slavic Studies*, 7 (1973) 121–58.

Kennedy, Paul, *The Rise and Fall of the Great Powers* (New York: Vintage Books, 1989).

Kershaw, Ian, *Making Friends with Hitler: Lord Londonderry and Britain's Road to War* (London: Allen Lane, 2004).

Kieniewicz, Stefan, "The Revolutionary Nobleman: An East European Variant of the Liberation Struggle in the Restoration Era," in Jaroslav Pelenski (ed.), *The American and European Revolutions, 1776–1848: Sociopolitical and Ideological Aspects* (Iowa City: University of Iowa Press, 1976) pp. 268–86.

Kiernan, V. G., *The Duel in European History: Honour and the Reign of Aristocracy* (Oxford: Oxford University Press, 1988).

King, Jeremy, *Budweisers into Czechs and Germans, a Local History of Bohemian Politics, 1848–1948* (Princeton, NJ: Princeton University Press, 2002).

Király, Béla K., and Walter Scott Dillard (eds.), *The East Central European Officer Corps, 1740s–1920s: Social Origins, Selection, Education, and Training* (New York: Columbia University Press, 1988).

Kitson Clark, G., *The Making of Victorian England* (London: Methuen, 1970).

Kleine, Georg H., "Adelsgenossenschaft und Nationalsocialismus," *Vierteljahrshefte für Zeitgeschichte*, 26 (1978) 100–43.

Klima, Arnost, *Economy, Industry and Society in Bohemia in the 17th–19th Centuries* (Prague: Charles University, 1991).

Knoll, Werner, "Zur Entwicklung von Offiziersschulen und Militärakademien in Deutschland anfang des 19. Jahrhunderts," *Militärgeschichte*, 17 (1978) 457–62.

Kocka, Jürgen, "German History before Hitler: the Debate about the German *Sonderweg*," *Journal of Contemporary History*, 23 (1988) 3–16.

Kolegar, Ferdinand, "The Elite and the Ruling Class: Pareto and Mosca Re-Examined," *Review of Politics*, 29 (1967) 354–69.

Konttinen, Esa, "Central Bureacracy and the Restricting of Education in Early Nineteenth-Century Finland," *Scandinavian Journal of History*, 21 (1996) 201–20.

Kopczynski, Michael, "The Nobility and the State in the 16th–18th Centuries: The Swedish Model," *Acta Poloniae Historica*, 77 (1998) 111–26.

Koralka, Jiri, "The Czechs, 1840–1900," in Andreas Kappler (ed.), *The Formation of National Elites, Comparatve Studies of Governments and Non-Dominant Ethnic Groups in Europe, 1850–1940*, vol. VI (New York: New York University Press, 1992) pp. 77–103.

Kreilkamp, Vera, "Fiction and Empire: the Irish Novel," in Kevin Kenny, *Ireland and the British Empire* (Oxford: Oxford University Press, 2004) pp. 154–81.

Kriegel, Abraham D. (1980a), "Edmund Burke and the Quality of Honor," *Albion*, 12 (1980) 337–49.

Kriegel, Abraham D. (1980b), "Liberty and Whiggery in Early Nineteenth-Century England," *Journal of Modern History*, 52 (1980) 253–78.

Krueger, Rita Arlene, "From Empire to Nation: The Aristocracy and the Formation of Modern Society in Bohemia, 1770–1848," unpublished Ph. D. dissertation, Harvard University, 1997.

Labatut, Jean-Pierre, *Les noblesses européennes de la fin du XVe siècle à la fin du XVIIIe siècle* (Paris: Presses Universitaires de France, 1978).

Lach-Szyrma, Krystyn, *From Charlotte Square to Fingal's Cave: Reminiscences of a Journey through Scotland, 1820–1824*, ed. Mona Kedslie McLeod (East Linton: Tuckwell Press, 2004).

Lalliard, François, "Proprieté Arsitocratique et Innovation Agronomique en Ile-de-France au XIXe Siècle," *Histoire et Sociétés Rurales*, 13 (2000) 67–92.

Lalumia, Matthew, "Realism and Anti-aristocratic Sentiment in Victorian Depictions of the Crimean War," *Victorian Studies*, 27 (1983) 25–51.

Lambert, Angela, *Unquiet Souls: The Indian Summer of the British Aristocracy, 1880–1914* (London: Macmillan, 1984).

Lampedusa, Giuseppe, Prince di, *The Leopard* (New York: Pantheon [1958] 1988).

Langford, Paul, *Public Life and the Propertied Englishman, 1689–1798* (Oxford: Oxford University Press, 1991).

Lanier, Amelie, "Die Partialobligationen," *Bankhistorisches Archiv*, 21 (1995) 5–28.

"La Noblesses de Bohème et de Moravie au XIXe Siècle," *Etudes Danubiennes*, 19 (2003) 1–206.

Laroche, Pierre, "Mutations du Consensus en Italie du Liberalisme au Fascisme," *Pensée*, 284 (1991) 81–91.

Lässig, Simone, "Stagnation or Reform? The Political Elites in the Federal States of Wilhelmine Germany," *Parliaments, Estates & Representation*, 17 (1997) 195–208.

Lawes, Kim, *Paternalism and Politics: The Revival of Paternalism in Early Nineteenth-Century Britain* (London: Macmillan, 2000).

Lax, Eric, *The Mold in Dr. Florey's Coat* (New York: John Macrae, 2004).

Lazo Diaz, A., "La Lucha contra los Privilegios Estamentales en las Cortes de Cádiz," *Atlántida*, 49 (1971) 53–61.

Lazuga, Waldemar, "The Formation of Polish Political Elites in Austria during the Pre-Constitutional Era," *Polish Western Affairs*, 34 (1993) 41–60.

LeBozec, Christine. "Elites – Revolution – Transition (1760–1830)," *Cahiers d'Histoire: Revue d'Histoire Critique*, 73 (1998) 35–45.

LeDonne, John P., "Ruling Families in the Russian Political Order, 1689–1825," *Cahiers du Monde Russe et Sovietique*, 28 (1987) 233–322.

LeDonne, John P., "The Ruling Class: Tsarist Russia as the Perfect Model," *International Social Science Journal*, 45 (1993) 285–300.

Lees-Milne, James, *Ancestral Voices* (London: Faber and Faber, 1984).

Lees-Milne, James, *Ceaseless Turmoil: Diaries, 1988–1992* (London: John Murray, 2004).

Leigh Fermor, Patrick (2004a), *Between the Woods and the Water* (London: John Murray, 2004).

Leigh Fermor, Patrick (2004b), *A Time of Gifts* (London: John Murray, 2004).

Lengyel, György, "Von der Gelenkten Wirtschaft zur Kriegswirtschaft: Institutionen, Eliten, Ideologien in Ungarn," *Österreichische Zeitschrift für Geschichteswissenschaften*, 3 (1992) 166–91.

Lermontov, M. Yu., *A Hero of Our Time* (London: Penguin, 1966).

Le Roy Ladurie, Emmanuel, *Saint-Simon and the Court of Louis XIV* (Chicago, IL: University of Chicago Press, 2001).

Lesniakowska, Marta, "The Manor House – Toward a Retrospective Utopia," *Polish Art Studies*, 13 (1992) 31–41.

Lévêque, Pierre, "Large Landed Property and Its Influence in Nineteenth-Century Burgundy," in Ralph Gibson and Martin Blinkorn, *Landownership and Power in Modern Europe* (London: HarperCollins, 1991) pp. 53–78.

Levinger, Matthew, "The Prussian Reform Movement and the Rise of Enlightened Nationalism," in Philip G. Dwyer, *The Rise of Prussia, 1700–1830* (London: Longman, 2000) pp. 259–77.

Lewis, Edward G., "Social Backgrounds of French Ministers, 1944–1967," *The Western Political Quarterly*, 23 (1970) 564–78.

Lewis, Judith S., "Political Behavior of Elite Women in England, 1774–1832," *Consortium on Revolutionary Europe, 1750–1850: Proceedings* (1983) 242–70.

Lewis, Judith S., "Princess of Parallelograms and Her Daughter: Math and Gender in the Nineteenth-Century English Aristocracy," *Women's Studies International Forum*, 18 (1995) 387–94.

Lewis, Judith S., " 'Tis a Misfortune to Be a Great Ladie': Maternal Mortality in the British Aristocracy, 1558–1959," *Journal of British Studies*, 37 (1998) 26–53.

Lewis, Judith S., *Sacred to Female Patriotism: Gender, Class, and Politics in Late Georgian Britain* (London: Routledge, 2003).

Lewis, Paul H., "Salazar's Ministerial Elite, 1932–1968," *Journal of Politics*, 40 (1978) 622–47.

Lietuvos Architektúros Istorija, vol. II (Vilnius, 1994).

Lieven, Dominic, "The Russian Ruling Elite under Nicholas II," *Cahiers du Monde Russe et Sovietique*, 28 (1987) 429–54.

Lieven, Dominic, *The Aristocracy in Europe, 1815–1914* (London: Macmillan, 1992).

Linz, Juan, Pilar Gangas, and Miguel Jerez Mir, "Spanish *Diputados*: From the 1876 Restoration to Consolidated Democracy," in H. Best and M. Cotta (eds.), *Parliamentary Representatives in Europe, 1848–2000* (Oxford: Oxford University Press, 2000) pp. 371–462.

Lipping, Imre, "Land Reform Legislation in Estonia and the Diestablishment of the Baltic German Rural Elite, 1919–1939," unpublished Ph.D. dissertation, University of Maryland, 1980.

Listowel, Judith, Countess of, *This I Have Seen* (London: Faber and Faber, 1943).

Littlejohn, David, *The Fate of the English Country House* (New York: Oxford University Press, 1997).

Liveanu, Vasile and Irina Gavrila, "Political Elite in an Agrarian Country: Romania in 1866–1916," *Historical Social Research*, 33 (1985) 92–105.

Locke, Robert R., *French Legitimists and the Politics of Moral Order in the Early Third Republic* (Princeton, NJ: Princeton University Press, 1974).

Locke, Robert R., "A Method for Identifying French Corporate Businessmen (The Second Empire)," *French Historical Studies*, 10 (1977) 261–92.

Loewenstein, Prince Hubertus, *Conquest of the Past* (London: Faber and Faber, 1938).

Löffler, Benhard, "Die Ersten Kammern und der Adel in den Deutschen Konstitionellen Monarchien," *Historische Zeitschrift*, 265 (1997) 29–76.

Lovell, Mary S., *The Sisters: The Saga of the Mitford Family* (New York: W. W. Norton, 2003).

Luft, Robert R., "Sociological Structures of Czech Political Elites before World War I," *East Central Europe*, 19 (1992) 16–25.

Lukacs, John, *Budapest, 1900: A Historical Portrait of a City and Its Culture* (New York: Grove Press, 1990).

Lukacs, John, "Noblesse Oblige," *The Hungarian Quarterly*, 34 (1993) 131–4.

Lukacs, John, *Five Days in London: May 1940* (New Haven, CT: Yale University Press, 2001).

Luke, Michael, *Hansel Pless: Prisoner of History* (London: The Cygnet Press, 2001).

Lukowski, Jerzy, *The European Nobility in the Eighteenth Century* (London: Palgrave Macmillan, 2003).

Lundin, C. Leonard, "The Road from Tsar to Kaiser: Changing Loyalties of the Baltic Germans, 1905–1914," *Journal of Central European Affairs*, 10 (1950) 223–55.

McAleer, Kevin, *Dueling: The Cult of Honor in Fin-de-Siècle Germany* (Princeton, NJ: Princeton University Press, 1994).

MacAloon, John J., *This Great Symbol: Pierre de Coubertin and the Origins of the Modern Olympic Games* (Chicago, IL: University of Chicago Press, 1981).

Macartney, C. A., "Hungary," in A. Goodwin (ed.), *The European Nobility in the Eighteenth Century* (London: Adam and Charles, 1953) pp. 118–35.

Macartney, C. A., *The Habsburg Empire, 1790–1918* (London: Weidenfeld and Nicolson, 1968).

McCahill, Michael W., "Open Elites: Recruitment to the French *Noblesse* and the English Aristocracy in the Eighteenth Century," *Albion*, 30 (1999) 599–629.

McCahill, Michael and Ellis Archer Wasson, "The New Peerage: Recruitment to the House of Lords, 1704–1847," *The Historical Journal*, 46 (2003) 1–38.

McClelland, Charles, E., "Structural Change and Social Reproduction in German Universities, 1870–1920," *History of Education*, 15 (1986) 177–93.

McCord, James N., Jr., "Politics and Honor in Early-Nineteenth-Century England: The Dukes' Duel," *Huntington Library Quarterly*, 62 (2000) 89–114.

McCord, James N., Jr., "Taming the Female Politician in Early Nineteenth-Century England: John Bull Versus Lady Jersey," *Journal of Women's History*, 13 (2002) 31–55.

McCragg, William O., Jr., "Ennoblement in Dualistic Hungary," *East European Quarterly*, 5 (1971) 13–26.

McCragg, William O., Jr., "Hungary's 'Feudalized' Bourgeoisie," *Journal of Modern History*, 44 (1972) 65–78.

McCrone, David and Angela Morris, "Lords and Heritages: The Transformation of the Great Lairds of Scotland," in T. M. Devine (ed.), *Scottish Elites* (Edinburgh: John Donald, 1994) pp. 170–86.

Macdonald, K. M., "The Persistence of an Elite: The Case of British Army Officer Cadets," *Sociological Review*, 28 (1980) 635–9.

Machado, Diamantino P., *The Structure of Portuguese Society* (New York: Praeger, 1991).

Macinnes, Allan I., "Landownership, Land Use and Elite Enterprise in Scottish Gaeldom: From Clanship to Clearance in Argyllshire, 1688–1858," in T. M. Devine, *Scottish Elites* (Edinburgh: John Donald, 1994) pp. 1–42.

Mackintosh, Malcolm, *Juggernaut: A History of the Soviet Armed Forces* (New York: Macmillan, 1967).

McMahon, Deirdre, "Ireland, the Empire, and the Commonwealth," in Kevin Kenny (ed.), *Ireland and the British Empire* (Oxford: Oxford University Press, 2004) pp. 182–219.

McReynolds, Louise, *Russia at Play: Leisure Activities at the End of the Tsarist Era* (Ithaca, NY: Cornell University Press, 2003).

Maczak, Antoni, "Vicissitudes of Feudalism in Modern Poland," in Pat Thane, Geoffrey Crossick, and Roderick Floud (eds.), *The Power of the Past* (Cambridge: Cambridge University Press, 1984) pp. 283–97.

Mack Smith, Denis, "The Latifundia in Modern Sicilian History," *Proceedings of the British Academy*, 51 (1965) 85–124.

Mack Smith, Denis, *A History of Sicily: Modern Sicily after 1713* (New York: The Viking Press, 1968).

Mack Smith, Denis, *Cavour* (London: Methuen, 1985).

Macry, Paolo, "Borghesie, Citta e Stato. Appunti e Impressioni su Napoli, 1860–1880," *Quaderni Storici*, 19 (1984) 339–83.

Madariaga, Isabel de, "The Russian Nobility in the Seventeenth and Eighteenth Centuries," in H. M. Scott (ed.), *The European Nobilities in the Seventeenth and Eighteenth Centuries*, 2 vols. (New York: Longman, 1995) II, pp. 223–73.

Magone, José M., "Political Recruitment and Elite Transformation in Modern Portugal 1870–1999," in H. Best and M. Cotta (eds.), *Parliamentary Representatives in Europe, 1848–2000* (Oxford: Oxford University Press, 2000) pp. 341–70.

Malatesta, Alberto, *Ministri, Deputati, Senatori dal 1848 al 1922* (Milan: Instituto Editoriale Italiano, 1940) 3 vols.

Malatesta, Maria, "Amministrazioni ed Elites Locali. La Padania fra Otto e Novecento," *Italia Contemporranea*, 176 (1989) 179–82.

Malefakis, Edward E., *Agrarian Reform and Peasant Revolution in Spain* (New Haven, CT: Yale University Press, 1970).

Malinowski, Stephan, *Vom König zum Führer* (Berlin: Akademie Verlag, 2003).

Mandler, Peter, *The Fall and Rise of the Stately Home* (New Haven, CT: Yale University Press, 1997).

Mangin, Nathalie, "Les Relations Franco-Allemandes et les Bains Mondains d'Outre-Rhin," *Histoire, Economie et Société*, 13 (1994) 649–75.

Mannerheim, Baron Gustaf, *Memoirs* (New York: Dutton, 1954).

Mannheim, Karl, *Essays on Sociological Social Psychology* (London: Routledge and Kegan Paul, 1953).

Mansel, Philip, *Prince of Europe: The Life of Charles Joseph de Ligne* (London: Weidenfeld and Nicolson, 2003).

Márai, Sándor, *Embers* (New York: Vintage, [1942] 2002).

Márai, Sándor, *Memoir of Hungary, 1944–1948* (Budapest: Central European University Press, 2000).

Marburg, Silke and Josef Matzerath (eds.), *Der Schritt in die Moderne: Sächsischer Adel zwischen 1763 und 1918* (Cologne: Böhlau, 2001).

Martin, Benjamin F., *Count Albert de Mun* (Chapel Hill: University of North Carolina Press, 1978).

Martin, Peter (2002a), *"Dulce et Decorum*: Irish Nobles and the Great War, 1914–19," in Adrian Gregory and Senia Paseta (eds.), *Ireland and the Great War* (Manchester: Manchester University Press, 2002) pp. 28–48.

Martin, Peter (2002b), "Unionism: The Irish Nobility and Revolution, 1919–23," in Joost Augusteijn (ed.), *The Irish Revolution, 1913–1923* (New York: Palgrave, 2002) pp. 151–67.

Mayer, Arno J., *The Persistence of the Old Regime: Europe to the Great War* (New York: Pantheon, 1981).

Mayzel, Matitiahu, *Generals and Revolutionaries* (Osnabrück: Biblio Verlag, 1979).

Mee, Graham, *Aristocratic Enterprise: The Fitzwilliam Industrial Undertakings, 1795–1857* (Glasgow: Blackie, 1975).

Melton, Edgar, "The Prussian Junkers, 1600–1786," in H. M. Scott (ed.), *The European Nobilities in the Seventeenth and Eighteenth Centuries*, 2 vols (New York: Longman, 1995) II, pp. 71–109.

Melton, James Van Horn, "The Nobility in the Bohemian and Austrian Lands, 1620–1780," in H. M. Scott (ed.), *The European Nobilities in the Seventeenth and Eighteenth Centuries*, 2 vols (New York: Longman, 1995) II, pp. 110–43.

Mension-Rigau, Eric, *Aristocrates et Grands Bourgeois* (Paris: Plon, 1994).

Meshcherskaya, Princess Ekaterina, *A Russian Princess Remembers: The Journey from Tsars to Glasnost* (New York: Doubleday, 1989).

Messerschmidt, Manfred, "The Military Elites in Germany since 1870: Comparisons and Contrasts with the French Officer Corps," in Klaus-Jürgen Müller (ed.), *The Military in Politics and Society in France and Germany in the Twentieth Century* (Oxford: Berg, 1995) pp. 43–72.

Metternich, Tatiana, Princess, *Tatiana: Five Passports in a Shifting Europe* (London: Heinemann, 1976).

Meyer, Jean, *Noblesses et pouvoirs dans l'Europe d'Ancien Régime* (Paris: Hachette Litterature, 1973).

Mikulski, Krzysztof, "Adel und Patriziat im Königlichen Preussen vom 15. bis 18. Jahrhundert," *Zeitschift für Ostmitteleuropa-Forschung*, 49 (2000) 38–51.

Mishkova, Diana, "Modernization and Political Elites in the Balkans before the First World War," *East European Politics and Societies*, 9 (1995) 63–89.

Mitchell, Alan, "Nazi Occupation Policies and the Response of Polish, Dutch, and French Elites," *The Wiener Library Bulletin*, 32 (1979) 34–40.

Mitson, Anne, "An Exchange of Letters: Estate Management and Lady Yarborough," *Women's History Review*, 7 (1998) 547–63.

Moltke, Helmut James, Count von, *Letters to Freya: 1939–1945* (New York: Vintage, 1995).

Mommsen, Hans, *Alternatives to Hitler: German Resistance under the Third Reich* (Princeton, NJ: Princeton University Press, 2003).

Moncure, John, "The Royal Prussian Cadet Corps, 1871–1918: A Prosopographical Approach," in Béla K. Király and Walter Scott Dillard (eds.), *The East Central European Officer Corps, 1740s–1920s: Social Origins, Selection, Education, and Training* (New York: Columbia University Press, 1988) pp. 57–70.

Montagu of Beaulieu, Lord, *More Equal than Others: The Changing Fortunes of the British and European Aristocracies* (New York: St. Martin's Press, 1971).

Monteiro, Nuno Gonçalo, "Os Rendimentos da Aristocracia Portuguesa na Crise do Antigo Regime," *Análise Social*, 26 (1991) 361–84.

Monteiro, Nuno Gonçalo, "Noblesse et Aristocratie au Portugal sous l'Ancien Régime (XVIIe–debut du XIXe Siècle)," *Revue d'Histoire Moderne et Contemporaine*, 46 (1999) 185–210.

Monteiro, Nuno Gonçalo, *Elites e Poder: Entre o Antigo Regime e o Liberlismo* (Lisbon: ICS, 2003).

Montgomery, Maureen E., *"Gilded Prostitution": Status, Money, and Transatlantic Marriages, 1870–1914* (New York: Routledge, 1989).

Montroni, Giovanni, "Aristocracy and Professions," in Maria Malatesta (ed.), *Society and the Professions in Italy, 1860–1914* (Cambridge: Cambridge University Press, 1995) pp. 255–75.

Moore, Barrington, Jr., *Social Origins of Dictatorship and Democracy: Lord and Peasant in the Making of the Modern World* (London: Penguin, [1966] 1984).

Moorehead, Caroline, *Iris Origio, Marchesa of Val d'Orcia* (Boston: David Godine, 2002).

Moroni, Andrea, "Le Ricchezze dei Corsini: Struttura Patrimoniale e Vicende Familiari tra Sette e Ottocento," *Società e Storia*, 9 (1986) 255–92.

Mosse, W. E., "Aspects of Tsarist Bureaucracy: Recruitment to the Imperial State Council, 1855–1914," *The Slavonic and East European Review*, 57 (1979) 240–54.

Mosse, W. E., "Bureaucracy and Nobility in Russia at the End of the Nineteenth Century," *The Historical Journal*, 24 (1981) 605–28.

Mouzelis, Nicos P., *Politics in the Semi-Periphery* (London: Macmillan, 1986).

Müller, Klaus-Jürgen (ed.), *The Military in Politics and Society in France and Germany in the Twentieth Century* (Oxford: Berg, 1995).

Muncy, Lysbeth Walker, "The Junkers and the Prussian Administration from 1918 to 1939," *The Review of Politics*, 9 (1947) 482–501.

Muncy, Lysbeth Walker, *The Junker in the Prussian Administration under William II, 1888–1914* (New York: Howard Fertig, 1970).

Muncy, Lysbeth Walker, "The Prussian *Landräte* in the Last Years of the Monarchy: 1890–1918," *Central European History*, 6 (1973) 299–338.

Nabokov, Vladimir, *Speak, Memory* (London: Victor Gollancz, 1951).

Nabokov, Vladimir, *Lectures on Russia Literature* (London: Weidenfeld and Nicolson, 1981).

Needham, Richard, *Battling for Peace* (Belfast: Blackstaff Press, 1998).

Nettl, J. P., *The Eastern Zone and Soviet Policy in Germany, 1945–50* (Oxford: Oxford University Press, 1951).

Newby, Howard, Colin Bell, David Rose, and Peter Saunders, *Property, Paternalism and Power: Class and Control in Rural England* (London: Hutchinson, 1978).

Nicholls, David, "Fractions of Capital," *Social History*, 13 (1988) 71–83.

Nightengale, Robert T., "The Personnel of the British Foreign Office and Diplomatic Service, 1851–1929," *The American Political Science Review*, 24 (1930) 310–31.

Nilsson, Göran B., "Den Samhällsbevarande Representationsreformen," *Scandia*, 35 (1969) 198–297.

Novella, Vittorio, "Un Grand Seigneur," *Synthèses*, 16 (1962) 33–49.

Nowak, Joanna, "The Elitism of Polish 1831 Emigrés," *Polish Western Affairs*, 34 (1993) 81–96.

Nye, Mary Jo, "Aristocratic Culture and the Pursuit of Science: The De Broglies in Modern France," *Isis*, 88 (1997) 397–421.

O'Brien, Patrick and Caglar Keyder, *Economic Growth in Britain and France, 1780–1914* (London: George Allen and Unwin, 1978).

Obolensky, Prince Dimitri, *Bread of Exile: A Russian Family* (London: Harvill Press, 1999).

Obolensky, Prince Serge, *One Man in His Time* (London: Hutchinson, 1960).

Odlozilik, Otakar, "The Nobility of Bohemia, 1620–1740," *East European Quarterly*, 7 (1973) 15–27.

Offer, Avner, "Cost and Benefits, Prosperity and Security," in Andrew Porter (ed.), *The Nineteenth Century*, vol. III, *The Oxford History of the British Empire* (New York: Oxford University Press, 1999) pp. 690–711.

Origio, Benedetta, Morna Livingston, Laurie Olin, and John Dixon Hunt, *La Foce: A Garden and Landscape in Tuscany* (Philadelphia: University of Pennsylvania Press, 2001).

Osborne, Thomas R., *A Grande Ecole for the Grand Corps* (New York: Columbia University Press, 1983).

Otley, C. B., "Militarism and Social Affiliations of the British Army Elite," in Jacques van Doorn (ed.), *Armed Forces and Society* (The Hague: Mouton, 1968) pp. 84–108.

Otley, C. B., "The Social Origins of British Army Officers," *Sociological Review*, 18 (1970) 213–39.

Oxford Dictionary of National Biography (Oxford: Oxford University Press, 2004).

Pagano, Sergio, "Archivi di Famiglie Romane e non Romane nell'Archivo Segreto Vaticano," *Roma Moderna e Contemporanea*, 1 (1993) 189–231.

Page, Stanley W., "Lenin, Turgenev and the Russian Landed Gentry," *Canadian Slavonic Papers*, 18 (1976) 442–56.

Palla, Marco, "Sul Regime Fascista Italiano," *Italia Contemporanea*, 169 (1987) 17–35.

Parouchéva, Dobrinka, "L'elite Gouvernmentale en Bulgarie et en Roumanie a la Fin du XIXe et au Debut du XXe Siecle, et la France," *Etudes Balkaniques*, 35 (1999) 34–7.

Parry, Geraint, *Political Elites* (New York: Frederick A. Praeger, 1969).

Pauls, Georg, "'Das de Pottersche Viehstück': Heine, Börne und die Belgische Revolution von 1830," *Revue Belge de Philologie et d'Histoire*, 65 (1987) 785–811.

Paxton, Robert O., *Parades and Politics at Vichy: The French Officer Corps under Marshal Pétain* (Princeton, NJ: Princeton University Press, 1966).

Pedersen, Mogens N., "The Personal Circulation of a Legislature: The Danish Folketing 1849–1968," in William O. Aydelotte (ed.), *The History of Parliamentary Behavior* (Princeton, NJ: Princeton University Press, 1977) pp. 63–101.

Pedersen, Mogens N., "The Incremental Transformation of the Danish Legislative Elite," in H. Best and M. Cotta (eds.), *Parliamentary Representatives in Europe, 1848–2000* (Oxford: Oxford University Press, 2000) pp. 29–49.

Pedlow, Gregory W., *The Survival of the Hessian Nobility, 1770–1870* (Princeton, NJ: Princeton University Press, 1988).

Pedlow, Gregory W., "The Landed Elite of Hesse-Cassel in the Nineteenth Century," in Ralph Gibson and Martin Blinkorn, *Landownership and Power in Modern Europe* (London: HarperCollins, 1991) pp. 111–30.

Pelenski, Jaroslav, "The *Haidamak* Insurrections and the Old Regimes in Eastern Europe," in Jaroslav Pelenski (ed.), *The American and European Revolutions, 1776–1848: Sociopolitical and Ideological Aspects* (Iowa City: University of Iowa Press, 1976) pp. 228–47.

Perkin, Harold, *The Origins of Modern English Society, 1780–1880* (London: Routledge & Kegan Paul, 1969).

Perkins, J. A., "The Agricultural Revolution in Germany, 1850–1914," *Journal of European Economic History*, 10 (1981) 71–118.

Perrott, Roy, *The Aristocrats* (London: Weidenfeld and Nicolson, 1968).

Péter, László, "The Aristocracy, the Gentry and Their Parliamentary Tradition in Nineteenth-Century Hungary," *Slavonic and East European Review*, 70 (1992) 77–110.

Petersen, Jens, "Der Italienische Adel von 1861 bis 1946," in Hans-Ulrich Wehler (ed.), *Europäischer Adel, 1750–1950* (Göttingen: Vandenhoeck & Ruprecht, 1990) pp. 243–59.

Petiteau, Natalie, "Homogamie et Conflits dans la Noblesse d'Empire," *Cahiers d'Histoire*, 45 (2000) 731–45.

Petter, Wolfgang, "Der Kompromiss zwischen Militaer und Gesellschaft im Kaiserlichen Deutschland, 1871–1918," *Revue d'Allemagne*, 11 (1979) 346–62.

Phillips, Gregory D., *The Diehards: Aristocratic Society and Politics in Edwardian England* (Cambridge, MA: Harvard University Press, 1979).

Pinches, J. H., *European Nobility and Heraldry* (Ramsbury: Heraldry Today, 1994).

Pistohlkors, Gert von, "Inversion of Ethnic Group Status in the Baltic Region," in David Howell, Gert von Pistohlkors, and Ellen Wiegandt, *Roots of Rural Ethnic Mobilisation: Comparative Studies on Governments and Non-Dominant Ethnic Groups in Europe, 1850–1940*, vol. VII (New York: New York University Press, 1993) pp. 169–220.

Plamper, Jan, "The Russian Orthodox Episcopate, 1721–1917: A Prosopography," *Journal of Social History*, 34 (2000) 5–34.

Plumb, J. H., "The Edwardians," *Horizon*, 13 (1971) 18–41.

Plumb, J. H., "La Diffsione della Modernità," *Quaderni Storici*, 14 (1979) 887–911.

Poensgen, Ruprecht, "Die Schule Schloss Salem im Dritten Reich," *Vierteljahrshefte für Zeitgeschichte*, 44 (1996) 25–54.

Polonsky, Antony, *Politics in Independent Poland, 1921–1939* (Oxford: Oxford University Press, 1972).

Pope-Hennessy, James, *Anthony Trollope* (London: Phoenix Press, 2001).

Porter, J. H., "Tenant Rights: Devonshire and the 1880 Ground Game Act," *Agricultural History Review*, 34 (1986) 188–97.

Portland, Duke of, *Men, Women, and Things* (London: Faber and Faber, 1937).

Potocki, Count Alfred, *Master of Lancut* (London: W. H. Allen, 1959).

Potterton, Homan, *Rathcormick: A Childhood Recalled* (London: Vintage, 2004).

Powis, Jonathan, *Aristocracy* (Oxford: Basil Blackwell, 1984).

Pratt, Lord Michael, *The Great Country Houses of Central Europe* (New York: Abbeville Press, 1991).

Preston, Paul, *Revolution and War in Spain, 1931–1939* (London: Methuen, 1984).

Preston, Paul, *Franco* (New York: Basic Books, 1994).

Price, J. L., "The Dutch Nobility in the Seventeenth and Eighteenth Centuries," in H. M. Scott (ed.), *The European Nobilities in the Seventeenth and Eighteenth Centuries*, 2 vols. (New York: Longman, 1995) I, pp. 82–113.

Purtscher-Wydenbruck, Nora, *An Austrian Background* (London: Methuen, 1932).

Radziwill, Prince Michael, *One of the Radziwills* (London: John Murray, 1971).

Raeff, Marc, "The Russian Nobility in the Eighteenth and Nineteenth Centuries," in Ivo Banac and Paul Bushkovitch (eds.), *The Nobility in Russia and Eastern Europe* (New Haven, CT: Yale Concilium, 1983) pp. 99–121.

Randolph, John, "The Old Mansion: Revisiting the History of the Russian Country Estate," *Kritika: Explorations in Russian and Eurasian History*, 1 (2000) 729–49.

Rantzau, Johann Albrecht von, "Zur Geschichte der Sexuellen Revolution: Die Gräfin Franziska zu Reventlow und die Münchener Kosmiker," *Archiv für Kulturgeschichte*, 56 (1974) 394–446.

Raybould, T. J., "The Development and Organization of Lord Dudley's Mineral Estates, 1774–1845," *Economic History Review*, 21 (1968) 529–44.

Raybould, Trevor, "Aristocratic Landowners and the Industrial Revolution: The Black Country Experience c. 1760–1840," *Midland History*, 9 (1984) 59–86.

Razzell, P. E., "Social Origins of Officers in the Indian and British Home Army: 1758–1962," *British Journal of Sociology*, 14 (1963) 248–60.

Reck-Malleczewen, Friedrich, *Diary of a Man in Despair* (London: Duckworth, 2000).

Reddy, William D., "The Concept of Class," in M. L. Bush (ed.), *Social Orders and Social Classes in Europe since 1500* (London: Longman, 1992) pp. 13–25.

Redé, Alexis, Baron de, *Alexis, the Memoirs of the Baron de Redé* (Wimborne Minster: Dovecote Press, 2005).

Reden-Dohna, Armgard von and R. Melville (eds.), *Der Adel an der Schwelle des Bürgerlichen Zeitalters* (Stuttgart: Franz Steiner Verlag, 1988).

Reece, Jack E., "Fascism, the Mafia, and the Emergence of Sicilian Separatism (1919–43)," *Journal of Modern History*, 45 (1973) 261–76.

Reece, Jack E., "Sicilian Autonomists and the Sicilian Revolution of 1848 in Palermo," *Consortium on Revolutionary Europe 1750–1850: Proceedings* (1979) 104–23.

Rees, Tim, "Agrarian Power and Crisis in Southern Spain: The Province of Badajoz, 1875–1936," in Ralph Gibson and Martin Blinkorn, *Landownership and Power in Modern Europe* (London: HarperCollins, 1991) pp. 235–53.

Reif, Heinz, *Westfälischer Adel 1770–1860, Vom Herrschaftsstand zur Regionalen Elite* (Göttingen: Vandenhoeck & Ruprecht, 1979).

Reif, Heinz, *Adel im 19. und 20. Jahrhundert* (Munich: R. Oldenbourg Verlag, 1999).

Reif, Heinz (ed.), *Adel und Bürgertum in Deutschland*, I (Berlin: Akademie Verlag, 2000).

Reynolds, K. D., *Aristocratic Women and Political Society in Victorian Britain* (Oxford: Oxford University Press, 1998).

Rezzori, Gregor von, *The Death of My Brother Abel* (New York: Penguin, 1985).

Rezzori, Gregor von, *The Snows of Yesteryear* (New York: Vintage, 1991).

Rezzori, Gregor von, *Oedipus at Stalingrad* (New York: Farrar Straus Giroux, 1994).

Richardson, Joanna, "'Hunting, Fishing and Crikett': Anglomania under the Second French Empire," *History Today*, 21 (1971) 239–46.

Richardson, Nicholas, *The French Prefectorial Corps, 1814–1830* (Cambridge: Cambridge University Press, 1966).

Riker, T. W., *The Making of Roumania, 1856–1866* (Oxford: Oxford University Press, 1931).

Ringrose, David R., *Spain, Europe, and the "Spanish Miracle," 1700–1900* (Cambridge: Cambridge University Press, 1996).

Rioux, Jean-Pierre, "A Changing of the Guard? Old and New Elites at the Liberation," in Jolyon Howorth and Philip G. Cerny (eds.), *Elites in France* (London: Frances Pinter, 1981) pp. 78–92.

Rioux, Jean-Pierre, "Les Deux Cents Familles," *Histoire*, 84 (1985) 20–24.

Riska, Cecilia, "Koti ja Koulu Säätyaseman Turvaajina," *Historiallinen Aikakauskirja*, 91 (1993) 121–9.

Robb, George, *British Culture and the First World War* (London: Palgrave, 2002).

Roberts, Andrew, *Hitler and Churchill* (London: Weidenfeld and Nicolson, 2003).

Roberts, Henry L., *Rumania* (New Haven, CT: Yale University Press, 1951).

Roberts, J. M., "Lombardy," in A. Goodwin (ed.), *The European Nobility in the Eighteenth Century* (London: Adam and Charles, 1953) pp. 60–82.

Roberts, Michael, "Sweden," in A. Goodwin (ed.), *The European Nobility in the Eighteenth Century* (London: Adam and Charles, 1953) pp. 136–53.

Robichez, Jacques, "Prost et l'Aristocratie," *Revue des Travaux de l'Académie des Sciences Morales et Politiques*, 134 (1981) 261–77.

Robins, Joseph, *Champagne and Silver Buckles: The Viceregal Court at Dublin Castle 1700–1922* (Dublin: The Lilliput Press, 2001).

Robinson, John Martin, "Still the Top Class," *The Spectator*, November 16, 1996, pp. 9–10.

Robinson, R. A. H., *Contemporary Portugal* (London: George Allen and Unwin, 1979).

Rojas, Mauricio, "The 'Swedish Model' in Historical Perspective," *Scandinavian Economic History Review*, 39 (1991) 64–74.

Romanelli, Raffaele, "Political Debate, Social History, and the Italian *Borghesia*: Changing Perspectives in Historical Research," *Journal of Modern History*, 63 (1991) 717–39.

Romanelli, Raffaele, "Urban Patriciates and 'Bourgeois' Society: A Study of Wealthy Elites in Florence, 1862–1904," *Journal of Modern Italian Studies*, 1 (1995) 3–21.

Romano, Sergio, "Niedergang und Ende der Risorgimentalen Ideologie," *Quellen und Forschungen aus Italienische Archiven und Bibliotheken*, 75 (1995) 427–44.

Romsics, Ignác, "Graf István Bethlens Politische Anschten (1901–1921)," *Acta Historica*, 32 (1986) 271–89.

Roosevelt, Priscilla, *Life on the Russian Country Estate: A Social and Cultural History* (New Haven, CT: Yale University Press, 1995).

Rose, Kenneth, *The Later Cecils* (New York: Harper and Row, 1975).

Rosenberg, Hans, *Bureaucracy, Aristocracy, and Autocracy: The Prussian Experience, 1660–1815* (Boston, MA: Beacon Press, 1966).

Rosie, G., "The Establishment and the Aristocracy," in M. Linklater and R. Denniston (eds.), *Anatomy of Scotland: How Scotland Works* (Edinburgh: Chambers, 1992) pp. 26–42.

Rossi, Luigi, "La *Rivista Araldica* e la Corporazione Nobiliare nella Prima Meta del XX Secolo," *Nuova Rivista Storica*, 82 (1998) 309–38.

Roszkowski, Wojciech, "Lista Najwiekszych Wlascicieli Ziemskich w Polsce w 1922r.," *Przeglad Historyczny*, 74 (1983) 281–99.

Roszkowski, Wojciech, *Landowners in Poland, 1918–1939* (New York: Columbia University Press, 1991).

Roth, Joseph, *The Radetzky March* (New York: Alfred A. Knopf, [1932] 1996).

Rothschild, Baron Guy de, *The Whims of Fortune* (New York: Random House, 1985).

Rothstein, Bo, "State Structure and Variations in Corporatism: The Swedish Case," *Scandinavian Political Studies*, 14 (1991) 149–71.

Rubinstein, W. D. (ed.), *Wealth and the Wealthy in the Modern World* (New York: St. Martin's Press, 1980).

Rubinstein, W. D., "The Structure of Wealth-Holding in Britain, 1809–39: A Preliminary Anatomy," *Historical Research*, 65 (1992) 74–89.

Rubinstein, W. D., *Capitalism, Culture and Decline: 1750–1990* (London: Routledge, 1993).

Rubinstein, W. D., "Britain's Elites in the Inter-War Period, 1918–39," *Contemporary British History*, 12 (1998) 1–18.

Rudikoff, Sonya, *Ancestral Houses: Virginia Woolf and the Aristocracy* (Palo Alto, CA: Society for the Promotion of Science and Scholarship, 1999).

Ruiz Torres, Pedro, "L'Aristocrazia Valenzana," *Quaderni Storici*, 21 (1986) 415–34.

Ruostetsaari, Ilkka, "From Political Amatuer to Professional Politician and Expert Representative: Parliamentary Recruitment in Finland since 1863," in H. Best and M. Cotta (eds.), *Parliamentary Representatives in Europe, 1848–2000* (Oxford: Oxford University Press, 2000) pp. 50–87.

Rus, Michael and Valerie Cromwell, "Continuity and Change: Legislative Recruitment in the United Kingdom, 1868–1999," in H. Best and M. Cotta (eds.), *Parliamentary Representatives in Europe, 1848–2000* (Oxford: Oxford University Press, 2000) pp. 463–92.

Saccone, Eduardo, "Nobility and Literature: Questions on Tomasi di Lampedusa," *MLN*, 106 (1991) 159–78.

St. Aubyn, Edward, *Some Hope* (New York: Open City Books, [1992–8], 2003).

Saint Martin, Monique de, "La Noblesse et les 'Sports' Nobles," *Actes de la Recherche en Sciences Sociales*, 80 (1989) 22–32.

Salvadó, Francisco J. Romero, "The Great War and the Crisis of Liberalism in Spain, 1916–1917," *Historical Journal*, 46 (2003) 893–914.

Salzar, Fernando de, "Estabilidad de la Nobleza a Traves del Siglo XIX y de Toda la Historia," *Hoja Informative del Instituto Internacional de Genealogía y Heráldica*, 9 (1962) 87–8.

Schaffer, Simon, "Physics Laboratories and the Victorian Country House," in Crosbie Smith and Jon Agar (eds.), *Making Space for Science* (New York: St. Martin's Press, 1998) pp. 149–80.

Schenk, H. G., "Austria," in A. Goodwin (ed.), *The European Nobility in the Eighteenth Century* (London: Adam and Charles, 1953) pp. 102–17.

Schieder, Wolfgang, "La Germania di Hitler e l'Italia di Mussolini," *Passato e Presente*, 9 (1985) 39–65.

Schimert, Peter, "The Hungarian Nobility in the Seventeenth and Eighteenth Centuries," in H. M. Scott (ed.), *The European Nobilities in the Seventeenth and Eighteenth Centuries*, 2 vols. (New York: Longman, 1995) II, pp. 144–82.

Schissler, Hanna, *Preussiche Agragesellschaft im Wandel Wirtshaftliche, Geseelschaftliche, und Politische Transformationsproszesse von 1763 bis 1847* (Göttingen: Vandenhoesch & Ruprecht, 1978).

Schissler, Hanna, "The Junkers: Notes on the Social and Historical Significance of the Agrarian Elite in Prussia," in Robert G. Moeller (ed.), *Peasants and Lords in Modern Germany* (London: Allen and Unwin, 1986) pp. 24–51.

Schissler, Hanna, "The Social and Political Power of the Prussian Junkers," in Ralph Gibson and Martin Blinkorn, *Landownership and Power in Modern Europe* (London: HarperCollins, 1991) pp. 99–110.

Schlabrendorff, Fabian von, *The Secret War against Hitler* (London: Hodder and Stoughton, 1966).

Schmemann, Serge, *Echoes of a Native Land: Two Centuries of a Russian Village* (New York: Alfred A. Knopf, 1997).

Schumpeter, Joseph, *Capitalism, Socialism, and Democracy*, 3rd ed. (New York: Harper, 1962).

Schwetje, Burkhard, "Adlige Lebensform und Sozialer Wandel im Risorgimento," *Quellen und Forschungen aus Italienischen Archives und Bibliotheken*, 77 (1997) 288–361.

Scott, H. M. (ed.), *The European Nobilities in the Seventeenth and Eighteenth Centuries*, 2 vols. (New York: Longman, 1995).

Searle, Alaric, *Wehrmacht Generals, West German Society and the Debate on Rearmament, 1949–1959* (Westport, CT: Praeger, 2003).

Searle, G. R. *Entrepreneurial Politics in Mid-Victorian Britain* (Oxford: Oxford University Press, 1993).

Secker, Ineke, "Representatives of the Dutch People: The Smooth Transfromation of the Parliamentary Elite in a Consociational Democracy, 1849–1998," in H. Best and M. Cotta (eds.), *Parliamentary Representatives in Europe, 1848–2000* (Oxford: Oxford University Press, 2000) pp. 270–309.

Secker, Wilhelmina P., "Political-Administrative Elites in The Netherlands," *Historical Social Research*, 20 (1995) 61–86.

Serman, William, *Les Origines des Officers Français, 1848–1870* (Paris: Publications de la Sorbonne, 1979).

Serman, William, "La Noblesse dans L'Armée Française au XIXe Siècle (1814–1900)," in *Les Noblesses Européennes au XIXe Siècle, Collection deL'École Française de Rome 107* (Milan and Rome: Università di Milano and École Française de Rome, 1988) pp. 551–7.

Serman, William and Jean-Paul Bertard, *Nouvelle Historie Militaire de la France, 1789–1919* (Paris: Fayard, 1998).

Serna, Pierre, "The Noble," in Michel Vovelle (ed.), *Enlightenment Portraits* (Chicago, IL: University of Chicago Press, 1997) pp. 30–84.

Servadio, Gaia, *Luchino Visconti* (New York: Franklin Watts, 1988).

Shaw, Tony, "Cadogan's Last Fling: Sir Alexander Cadogan, Chairman of the Board of Governors of the BBC," *Contemporary British History*, 13 (1999) 126–45.

Shovlin, John, "Toward a Reinterpretation of Revolutionary Antinoblism: The Political Economy of Honor in the Old Regime," *Journal of Modern History*, 72 (2000) 35–66.

Siaroff, Alan, "Democratic Breakdown and Democratic Stability: A Comparison of Interwar Estonia and Finland," *Canadian Journal of Political Science*, 32 (1999) 103–24.

Siegert, Heinz, *Adel in Österreich* (Vienna: Verlag Kremayr, 1971).

Simms, Brendan, "Prussia, Prussianism and National Socialism, 1933–47," in Philip G. Dwyer (ed.), *Modern Prussian History, 1830–1947* (London: Longman, 2001) pp. 253–73.

Simoni, Pierre, "*Reproduction Sociale* and Elite Values: Obituaries and the Elite of Apt (Vacluse) 1840–1910," *Histoire Sociale*, 16 (1983) 331–58.

Sinclair, Andrew, *The Last of the Best: The Aristocracy of Europe in the Twentieth Century* (New York: Macmillan, 1969).

Sked, Alan, *The Decline and Fall of the Habsburg Empire, 1815–1918* (London: Longman, 1989).

Slavolainen, Raimo, "Släktsenaten, 1809–1870," *Historisk Tidskrift för Finland*, 77 (1992) 173–210.

Smith, Julia A., "Landownership and Social Change in Late Nineteenth-Century Britain," *Economic History Review*, 53 (2000) 767–76.

Snowden, Frank M., *Violence and Great Estates in the South of Italy: Apulia 1900–1922* (Cambridge: Cambridge University Press, 1986).

Snowden, Frank M., *The Fascist Revolution in Tuscany, 1919–1922* (Cambridge: Cambridge University Press, 1989).

Snowden, Frank M., "The City of the Sun: Red Cerignola, 1900–15," in Ralph Gibson and Martin Blinkorn, *Landownership and Power in Modern Europe* (London: HarperCollins, 1991) pp. 199–215.

Spectator, The (London: various numbers).

Spencer, Raine, Countess and John, Earl Spencer, *The Spencers on Spas* (London: Weidenfeld and Nicolson, 1983).

Spitzer, Alan B., "The Ambiguous Heritage of the French Restoration: The Distant Consquences of the Revolution and the Daily Realities of the Empire," in Jaroslav Pelenski (ed.), *The American and European Revolutions, 1776–1848: Sociopolitical and Ideological Aspects* (Iowa City: University of Iowa Press, 1976) pp. 208–26.

Spring, David, "Earl Fitzwilliam and the Corn Laws," *American Historical Review*, 59 (1954) 287–304.

Spring, David, "The Role of the Aristocracy in the Late Nineteenth Century," *Victorian Studies*, 4 (1960) 55–64.

Spring, David, *The English Landed Estate in the Nineteenth Century: Its Administration* (Baltimore, MD: The Johns Hopkins University Press, 1963).

Spring, David, (ed.), *European Landed Elites in the Nineteenth Century* (Baltimore, MD: The Johns Hopkins University Press, 1977).

Spring, David, "An Outsider's View: Alexis de Tocqueville on Aristocratic Society and Politics in 19th-Century England," *Albion*, 12 (1980) 122–31.

Spring, David, "Land and Politics in Edwardian England," *Agricultural History*, 58 (1984) 17–42.

Spring, David and Eileen Spring, *The First Industrial Society: England in the Mid-19th Century* (New York: Macmillan, 1975).

Spring, David and Eileen Spring, "Social Mobility and the English Landed Elite," *Canadian Journal of History*, 21 (1986) 333–51.

Spring, David and Eileen Spring, "Debt and the English Aristocracy," *Canadian Journal of History*, 31 (1996) 377–94.

Spring, Eileen, "Landowners, Lawyers, and Land Law Reform in Nineteenth-Century England," *American Journal of Legal History*, 21 (1977) 40–59.

Spring, Eileen, *Law, Land, and Family: Aristocratic Inheritance in England, 1300–1800* (Chapel Hill, NC: University of North Carolina Press, 1993).

Spring, Eileen with rejoinder by W. D. Rubinstein, "Businessmen and Landowners Re-engaged," *Historical Research*, 72 (1999) 77–91.

Spring, Eileen and David Spring, "The English Landed Elite, 1540–1880," *Albion*, 17 (1985) 149–80 and 393–6.

Stadler, K. R., "Austria," in S. J. Woolf (ed.), *Fascism in Europe* (London: Methuen, 1981) pp. 93–115.

Starhemberg, Ernst Rüdiger, Prince, *Between Hitler and Mussolini* (London: Hodder and Stoughton, 1942).

Staves, Susan, *Married Women's Separate Property in England, 1660–1833* (Cambridge, MA: Harvard University Press, 1990).

Steiner, Zara S., *The Foreign Office and Foreign Policy, 1898–1914* (Cambridge: Cambridge University Press, 1969).

Stekl, Hannes, "Zwischen Machtverlust und Selbstbehauptung," in Hans-Ulrich Wehler (ed.), *Europäischer Adel 1750–1950* (Göttingen: Vandenhoeck & Ruprecht, 1990) pp. 144–65.

Stern, Fritz, "Prussia," in David Spring (ed.), *European Landed Elites in the Nineteenth Century* (Baltimore, MD: The Johns Hopkins University Press, 1977) pp. 45–67.

Sternberg, Countess Cecilia, *The Journey* (London: Collins, 1977).

Stevenson, John, *British Society, 1914–45* (London: Penguin, 1984).

Stilling, Niels Peter, *Danske Herregarde: Arkitektur, Historie og Landskab* (Copenhagen: Nyt Nordisk Forlag Arnold Busck, 1999).

Stimmer, Gernot, *Eliten in Österreich, 1848–1970*, 2 vols (Vienna: Böhlau Verlag, 1997).

Stjernquist, Nils, "The Swedish Bicameral System and Beyond," in H. W. Blom, W. P. Blockmans, and H. de Schepper (eds.), *Bicameralism: Tweekamerstelset Vroeger En Nu* (Gravenhage: SUK, 1992) pp. 423–38.

Stone, Lawrence and Jeanne C. Fawtier Stone, *An Open Elite? England 1540–1880* (Oxford: Oxford University Press, 1984).

Stoneman, Mark R., "Bürgerliche und Adelige Krieger," in Heinz Reif (ed.), *Adel und Bürgertum in Deutschland*, vol. II (Berlin: Akademie Verlag, 2001) pp. 25–63.

Storrs, Christopher and H. M. Scott, "The Military Revolution and the European Nobility, c. 1600–1800," *War in History*, 3 (1996) 1–41.

Struve, Walter, *Elites against Democracy* (Princeton, NJ: Princeton University Press, 1973).

Sturgess, R. W., *Aristocrat in Business: The Third Marquis of Londonderry as Coalowner and Portbuilder* (Durham: Durham County Local History Society, 1975).

Sutherland, Christine, *The Princess of Siberia* (London: Robin Clark, 1985).

Sutherland, Christine, *Enchantress: Marthe Bibesco and Her World* (New York: Farrar, Straus & Giroux, 1996).

Sutherland, Donald, "Land and Power in the West of France, 1750–1914," in Ralph Gibson and Martin Blinkorn, *Landownership and Power in Modern Europe* (London: HarperCollins, 1991) pp. 37–52.

Sutherland, D. M. G., *The French Revolution and Empire: The Quest for a Civic Order* (Oxford: Blackwell, 2003).

Swann, Julian, "The French Nobility, 1715–1789," in H. M. Scott (ed.), *The European Nobilities in the Seventeenth and Eighteenth Centuries*, 2 vols. (New York: Longman, 1995) I, pp. 142–73.

Sykes, Christopher Simon, *The Big House* (London: HarperCollins, 2004).

Szczepanski, Jerzy, "Zainteresowania Arystokracji Polskiej Angielska Technika," *Kwartalnik Historii Nauki I Techniki*, 38 (1993) 61–71.

Szelle, Béla, "Az Arisztokrácia Irodalompártolása az Önkényuralom Idoszakában," *Magyar Könyvszemle*, 114 (1998) 113–24.

Szulc, Tad, *Pope John Paul II, the Biography* (New York: Scribner, 1995).

Szwarc, Andrzej, "Ksiaze Imeretynski, Minister Goremykin I Ugodowcy Warszascy," *Prezglad Historyczny*, 80 (1989) 549–69.

Temime, Emile, "Les Pouvoirs des Familles Notables dans le Monde Méditerranéen Occidental," *Pensiero Politico*, 13 (1980) 103–9.

Tenno, Ann and Juhan Maiste, *Läbi Aegade: Manor Houses of Estonia* (Tallin: Ann Tenno, 1996).

Thaden, Edward C. (1984a), "Finland and the Baltic Provinces: Elite Roles and Social and Economic Conditions and Structures," *Journal of Baltic Studies*, 15 (1984) 216–27.

Thaden, Edward C. (1984b), *Russia's Western Borderlands, 1710–1870* (Princeton, NJ: Princeton University Press, 1984).

Thaden, Edward C., "Traditional Elites, Religion and Nation-Building in Finland: The Baltic Provinces and Lithuania, 1700–1914," in Michael Branch et al. (eds.), *Finland and Poland in the Russian Empire* (London: School of Slavonic and East European Studies, 1995) pp. 1–15.

Thane, Patricia, "Aristocracy and Middle Class in Victorian England: The Problem of 'Gentrification,'" in Adolf M. Birke and Lothar Kettenacker (eds.), *Bürgertum, Adel und Monarchie* (Munich: K. G. Saur, 1989) pp. 93–108.

Thirsk, Joan, "The European Debate on Customs of Inheritance, 1500–1700," in Jack Goody et al., *Family and Inheritance: Rural Society in Western Europe, 1200–1800* (Cambridge: Cambridge University Press, 1976) pp. 177–91.

Thomas, David, "The Social Origins of Marriage Partners of the British Peerage in the Eighteenth and Nineteenth Centuries," *Population Studies*, 26 (1972) 99–111.

Thomas, Hugh, *The Spanish Civil War*, 3rd ed. (London: Hamish Hamilton, 1986).

Thompson, E. P., *The Poverty of Theory and Other Essays* (London: Merlin Press, 1978).

Thompson, F. M. L., *English Landed Society in the Nineteenth Century* (London: Routledge & Kegan Paul, 1969).

Thompson, F. M. L., "Britain," in David Spring (ed.), *European Landed Elites in the Nineteenth Century* (Baltimore, MD: The Johns Hopkins University Press, 1977) pp. 22–44.

Thompson, F. M. L., "English Landed Society in the Nineteenth Century," in Pat Thane, Geoffrey Crossick, and Roderick Floud (eds.), *The Power of the Past* (Cambridge: Cambridge University Press, 1984) pp. 195–214.

Thompson, F. M. L., *The Rise of Respectable Society: A Social History of Victorian Britain, 1830–1900* (London: Fontana, 1988).

Thompson, F. M. L., "Aristocracy, Gentry, and the Middle Classes in Britain, 1750–1850," in Adolf M. Birke and Lothar Kettenacker (eds.), *Bürgertum, Adel und Monarchie* (Munich: K. G. Saur, 1989) pp. 15–35.

Thompson, F. M. L., "English Landed Society in the Twentieth Century: I Property: Collapse and Survival," *Transactions of the Royal Historical Society*, 40 (1990) 1–24.

Thompson, F. M. L., "Moving Frontiers and the Fortunes of the Arsitocratic Town House 1830–1930," *London Journal*, 20 (1995) 67–78.

Thompson, F. M. L., *Gentrification and the Enterprise Culture: Britain 1780–1980* (Oxford: Oxford University Press, 2001).

Thompson, I. A. A., "The Nobility in Spain, 1600–1800," in H. M. Scott (ed.), *The European Nobilities in the Seventeenth and Eighteenth Centuries*, 2 vols. (New York: Longman, 1995) I, pp. 174–236.

Thorson, Playford V., "Free Enterprise Defense in Sweden: The Pansar Boat Collection of 1912," *North Dakota Quarterly*, 36 (1968) 42–9.

Thursfield, Patrick, "The Great Hungarian Novel," *Contemporary Review*, 267 (July 1995) 44–6.

Tillyard, Stella, *Aristocrats: Caroline, Emily, Louisa, and Sarah Lennox, 1740–1832* (New York: The Noonday Press, 1995).

Tilton, Timothy A., "The Social Origins of Liberal Democracy: The Swedish Case," *American Political Science Review*, 68 (1974) 561–71.

Tocqueville, Alexis de, *Recollections* (New York: Meridian Books, 1959).

Tolstoy, Leo, *Anna Karenina* (New York: Penguin, 2002).

Tomasevich, Jozo, *Peasants, Politics, and Economic Change in Yugoslavia* (London: Oxford University Press, 1955).

Toumanoff, Cyrille, *Catalogue de la Noblesse Titrée l'Empire de Russie* (Rome: 1982).

Tovrov, Jessica, *The Russian Noble Family: Structure and Change* (New York: Garland Publishing, 1987).

Trevor-Roper, H. R., "The Phenomenon of Fascism," in S. J. Woolf (ed.), *Fascism in Europe* (London: Methuen, 1981) pp. 19–38.

Trumpa, V., "The 1863 Revolt in Lithuania," *Lituanus*, 9 (1963) 115–26.

Tudesq, André-Jean, *Les Grands Notables en France, 1840–1849: Etude Historique d'une Psychologie Sociale*, 2 vols. (Paris: Presses Universitaires de France, 1964).

Tudesq, André-Jean, "Les Survivances de l'Ancien Régime: la Noblesse dans la Société Française de la Première du XIXe Siècle," in D. Roche and C. E. Labrosse (eds.), *Ordres et Classes* (Paris: Mouton Editeur, 1973) pp. 199–214.

Tudesq, André-Jean, "L'Élargissement de la Noblesse en France dans la Première Moitié du XIXe Siècle," in *Les Noblesses Européennes au XIXe Siècle, Collection deL'École Française de Rome 107* (Milan and Rome: Università di Milano and École Française de Rome, Rome, 1988) pp. 121–35.

Turgenev, Ivan S., *Fathers and Sons* (London: J. M. Dent, 1921).

Upton, A. F., "The Swedish Nobility, 1600–1772," in H. M. Scott (ed.), *The European Nobilities in the Seventeenth and Eighteenth Centuries*, 2 vols. (New York: Longman, 1995) II, pp. 11–40.

Ustinov, Peter, *House of Regrets* (London: Jonathan Cape, 1943).

Valebrokk, Eva, Geir Thomas Risasen, and Bo-Aje Mellin, *Norske Slott: Herregarder og Gods* (Oslo: Andrese & Butenschon, 1997).

Vascik, George, "Agrarian Conservatism in Wilhelmine Germany," in Larry Eugene Jones and James Retallack, (eds.), *Between Reform, Reaction, and Resistance* (Oxford: Berg, 1993) pp. 229–60.

Vassili, Count Paul [Princess Catherine Radziwill], *France from Behind the Veil: Fifty Years of Social and Political Life* (London: Cassell, 1914).

Vassiltchikov, Princess Marie, *Berlin Diaries, 1940–1945* (New York: Alfred Knopf, 1985).

Verdery, Katherine, *Transylvanian Villagers* (Berkeley, CA: University of California Press, 1983).

Verney, Douglas V., *Parliamentary Reform in Sweden, 1866–1921* (Oxford: Oxford University Press, 1957).

Vicary, Amanda, *The Gentleman's Daughter* (New Haven, CT: Yale University Press, 1998).

Villani, Pascuale, "Le Royaume de Naples Pendant la Domination Française (1806–1815)," *Annales Historiques de la Révolution Française*, 44 (1972) 66–81.

Vocelka, Karl, "Adel und Politik in der Habsburgermonarchie der Zweiten Hälfte des 19. Jahrhunderts," in *Les Noblesses Européennes au XIXe Siècle, Collection deL'École Française de Rome 107* (Milan and Rome: Università di Milano and École Française de Rome, 1988) pp. 541–9.

Von Laue, T. H., "Count Witte and the Russian Revolution of 1905," *American Slavic and East European Review*, 17 (1958) 25–46.

Walta, Göran, "Örnulf Tigerstedt och 'De Svarta'," *Historiska och Litteraturhistoriska Studier*, 69 (1994) 85–127.

Walther, Gerrit, "Adel und Antike: zur Politischen Bedeutung Gelehrter Kultur tur für die Führungselite der Frühen Neuzeit," *Historische Zeitschrift*, 266 (1998) 359–85.

Wank, Solomon, "Political Versus Military Thinking in Austria-Hungary, 1908–1912," *Peace and Change*, 7 (1981) 1–15.

Wank, Solomon (1992a) "Aristocrats and Nationalism in Bohemia, 1861–1899," *History of European Ideas*, 15 (1992) 589–96.

Wank, Solomon (1992b) "Aristocrats and Politics in Austria, 1867–1914," *East European Quarterly*, 26 (1992) 133–48.

Wank, Solomon, "Some Reflections on Aristocrats and Nationalism in Bohemia, 1861–1899," *Canadian Review of Studies in Nationalism*, 20 (1993) 21–33.

Ward, J. T., and R. G. Wilson (eds.), *Land and Industry: The Landed Estate and the Industrial Revolution* (Newton Abbot: David and Charles, 1971).

Warner, G., "France," in S. J. Woolf (ed.), *Fascism in Europe* (London: Methuen, 1981) pp. 307–28.

Warren, Donald, *The Red Kingdom of Saxony* (The Hague: Martinus Nijhoff, 1964).

Wasson, Ellis Archer, "The Third Earl Spencer and Agriculture, 1818–1845," *Agricultural History Review*, 26 (1978) 89–99.

Wasson, Ellis Archer, *Whig Renaissance: Lord Althorp and the Whig Party, 1782–1845* (New York: Garland Press, 1987).

Wasson, Ellis Archer, *Born to Rule: British Political Elites* (Stroud: Sutton, 2000).

Wasson, Ellis Archer, "The Whigs and the Press, 1800–1850," *Parliamentary History*, 25 (2005) 68–87.

Wasson, Ellis Archer, "Irish Country Houses: A Survey," unpublished research paper, 2006, copy available on request.

Waterfield, Giles, "The Town House as Gallery of Art," *London Journal*, 20 (1995) 47–66.

Waugh, Evelyn, *Sword of Honour* (London: Penguin Books, [1965] 2001).

Weber, Christoph, "Papsttum und Adel im 19. Jahrhundert," in *Les Noblesses Européennes au XIXe Siècle, Collection de L'École Française de Rome 107* (Milan and Rome: Università di Milano and École Française de Rome, Rome, 1988) pp. 607–57.

Wehler, Hans-Ulrich (ed.), *Europäischer Adel, 1750–1950* (Göttingen: Vandenhoeck & Ruprecht, 1990).

Weintraub, Wiktor, "The Noble as Hero and the Noble as a Villan in Polish Romantic Literature," in Ivo Banac and Paul Bushkovitch (eds.), *The Nobility in Russia and Eastern Europe* (New Haven, CT: Yale Concilium, 1983) pp. 47–63.

Weis, Eberhard, "Hardenberg und Montgelas: Versuch eines Vergleichs ihrer Persönlichkeiten und ihrer Politik," *Zeitschrift für Bayerische Landesgeschichte*, 61 (1998) 191–207.

Weitz, K. R., "Die Denkschrift des Niederrheinischen und Westfälischen Adels vom 26. Februar 1818," *Rheinische Vierteljahrsblätter*, 35 (1971) 201–73.

Wende, Peter, "Die Adelsdebatte der Paulskirche," in Adolf M. Birke and Lothar Kettenacker (eds.), *Bürgertum, Adel und Monarchie* (Munich: K. G. Saur, 1989) pp. 37–51.

West Rebecca, *Black Lamb, Grey Falcon: A Journey through Yugoslavia*, 2 vols. (New York: Viking Press, 1940–1).

Whalen, Robert Weldon, *Assassinating Hitler: Ethics and Resistance in Nazi Germany* (London: Associated University Presses, 1993).

Wheeler, Douglas L., *Republican Portugal: A Political History, 1910–1926* (Madison: University of Wisconsin Press, 1978).

Wheeler-Bennett, John W., *The Nemesis of Power: The German Army in Politics, 1918–1945* (New York: Viking, 1967).

Whelan, Heide W., *Adapting to Modernity: Family, Caste and Capitalism among the Baltic German Nobility* (Cologne: Böhlau Verlag, 1999).

Whitcomb, Edward A., "Napoleon's Prefects," *American Historical Review*, 79 (1974) 1089–118.

Whiteside, Andrew G., *The Socialism of Fools* (Berkeley, CA: University of California Press, 1975).

Wiener, Martin, *English Culture and the Decline of the Industrial Spirit, 1850–1980*, 2nd ed. (Cambridge: Cambridge University Press, 2004).

Wightman, Andy, *Who Owns Scotland* (Edinburgh: Canongate, 1996).

Windischgraetz, Prince Lajos, *My Adventures and Misadventures* (London: Barrie and Rockliff, 1965).

Winter, J. M., *The Great War and the British People* (London: Macmillan, 1986).

Wirth, Zdenek and Jaroslav Benda, *Burgen und Schlösser* (Prague: Artia, 1955).

Wiskemann, Elizabeth, *Italy since 1945* (London: Macmillan, 1971).

Witherell, Larry L., "Lord Salisbury's 'Watching Committee' and the Fall of Neville Chamberlain," *English Historical Review*, 116 (2001) 1134–66.

Witte, E., "Wijzigingen in de Belgische Elite in 1830," *Bijdragen en Mededelingen betreffended de Geschiedenis der Nederlanden*, 94 (1979) 226–52.

Wolin, Sheldon S., *Tocqueville Between Two Worlds* (Princeton, NJ: Princeton University Press, 2001).

Woods, Michael, "Discourses of Power and Rurality: Local Politics in Somerset in the 20th Century," *Political Geography*, 16 (1997) 453–78.

Woodward, Christopher, *In Ruins* (New York: Pantheon, 2001).

Woodward, E. L., and Rohan Butler, *Documents on British Foreign Policy, 1919–1939*, first series, vol. III (London: HMSO, 1949).

Worsthorne, Peregrine, *In Defence of Aristocracy* (London: HarperCollins, 2004).

Wrangel, Baron N., *From Serfdom to Bolshevism: The Memoirs of Baron N. Wrangel, 1847–1920* (London: Ernest Benn, 1927).

Yorck von Wartenburg, Countess Marion, *The Power of Solitude: My Life in the German Resistance* (Lincoln: University of Nebraska Press, 2000).

Youssoupoff, Prince Felix, *Lost Splendor* (New York: Helen Marx Books [1953], 2003).

Zamagni, Vera, "The Rich in a Late Industrialiser: The Case of Italy, 1800–1945," in W. D. Rubinstein (ed.), *Wealth and the Wealthy in the Modern World* (New York: St. Martin's Press, 1989) pp. 122–66.

Zanetti, D. E., "The Patriziato of Milan," *Social History*, 6 (1977) 745–60.

Zangerl, Carl H. E., "The Social Composition of the County Magistracy in England and Wales, 1831–1887," *Journal of British Studies*, 11 (1971) 113–25.

Zaniewicki, Witold, "De la Republique Nobiliaire au Regime Tsarist: la Disparition de la Petite Noblesse Polonaise, 1772–1868," *Cahiers d'Histoire*, 22 (1977) 71–5.

Zeldin, Theodore, "English Ideals in French Politics during the Nineteenth Century," *Historical Journal*, 2 (1959) 40–58.

Zeldin, Theodore, *France, 1848–1945*, 2 vols. (Oxford: Oxford University Press, 1973).

Zeldin, Theodore, "France," in David Spring (ed.), *European Landed Elites in the Nineteenth Century* (Baltimore, MD: The Johns Hopkins University Press, 1977) pp. 127–39.

Zelechow, Bernard, "The Opera: The Meeting of Popular and Elite Culture in the Nineteenth Century," *History of European Ideas*, 16 (1993) 261–6.

Zmora, Hillay, *Monarchy, Aristocracy and the State in Europe, 1300–1800* (London: Routledge, 2001).

INDEX